T0340153

Post Walrasian Macroeconomics

Macroeconomics is evolving in an almost dialectic fashion. The latest evolution is the development of a new synthesis that combines insights of new classical, new Keynesian and real business cycle traditions into a dynamic, stochastic general equilibrium (DSGE) model that serves as a foundation for thinking about macropolicy. That new synthesis has opened up the door to a new antithesis, which is being driven by advances in computing power and analytic techniques. This new synthesis is coalescing around developments in complexity theory, automated general to specific econometric modeling, agent-based models, and nonlinear and statistical dynamical models. This book thus provides the reader with an introduction to what might be called a Post Walrasian research program that is developing as the antithesis of the Walrasian DSGE synthesis. While both the Walrasian and Post Walrasian approaches assume rational agents, they differ in the environment in which they model the interaction of those agents. To make their models tractable the DSGE approach, which is the culmination of the Walrasian modeling tradition, assumes either that agents operate in an information-rich environment, or that there is an outside controller who processes all information. The Post Walrasian model, which this collection explores, assumes that agents operate in information-poor environments, without any outside controller.

David Colander has been the Christian A. Johnson Distinguished Professor of Economics at Middlebury College, Middlebury, Vermont since 1982. He previously taught at Columbia University, Vassar College, and the University of Miami. Professor Colander has authored, co-authored, or edited more than 35 books and 100 articles on a wide range of topics. His books have been, or are being, translated into a number of different languages, including Chinese, Bulgarian, Polish, Italian, and Spanish. He is a former President of both the Eastern Economic Association and History of Economics Society and is, or has been, on the editorial boards of the *Journal of the History of Economic Thought, Journal of Economic Methodology, Eastern Economic Journal, Journal of Economic Education, The Journal of Socioeconomics*, and *Journal of Economic Perspectives*. He has also been a consultant to Time-Life Films, the U.S. Congress, a Brookings Policy Fellow, and a Visiting Scholar at Nuffield College, Oxford. In 2001−02 he was the Kelly Professor of Distinguished Teaching at Princeton University.

Post Walrasian Macroeconomics

Beyond the Dynamic Stochastic General Equilibrium Model

Edited by

DAVID COLANDER

Middlebury College

CAMBRIDGE
UNIVERSITY PRESS

CAMBRIDGE UNIVERSITY PRESS
Cambridge, New York, Melbourne, Madrid, Cape Town, Singapore,
São Paulo, Delhi, Dubai, Tokyo

Cambridge University Press
32 Avenue of the Americas, New York, NY 10013-2473, USA

www.cambridge.org
Information on this title: www.cambridge.org/9780521865487

First published 2006

A catalog record for this publication is available from the British Library

Library of Congress Cataloging in Publication data

Post Walrasian macroeconomics: beyond the dynamic stochastic general
equilibrium model/edited by David Colander.
p. cm.
Includes bibliographical references and index.
ISBN-13: 978-0-521-86548-7 (hardback)
ISBN-10: 0-521-86548-4 (hardback)
ISBN-13: 978-0-521-68420-0 (pbk.)
ISBN-10: 0-521-68420-X (pbk.)
1. Macroeconomics–Mathematical models. 2. Equilibrium (Economics). I.
Colander, David C. II. Title.
HD172.5.P67 2006
335.901′5195–dc22   2006011568

ISBN 978-0-521-86548-7 Hardback
ISBN 978-0-521-68420-0 Paperback

Transferred to digital printing 2009

Contents

List of Contributors

Masanao Aoki has taught at UCLA, UC Berkeley, University of Illinois, Osaka University, Tokyo Institute of Technology, and the University of Cambridge. He is a past President of the Society for Economic Dynamics and Control, Fellow of the Econometric Society (inactive), and a Fellow of the IEEE Control Systems Society (inactive). He has served as editor and associate editor of a number of journals, such as the *International Economic Review* and the *Journal of Economic Dynamics and Control*. He is the author or editor of a dozen books, including *Modeling Aggregate Behavior and Fluctuations in Economics* for which he received the 2003 Nihon Keizai Shinbun Center for Japanese Economic Research Prize.

Rob Axtell is a Senior Fellow in Economic Studies at the Brookings Institution. He is co-founder of the Center on Social and Economic Dynamics there, a research center dedicated to promulgating agent-based computational modeling techniques across the social sciences. He is also an External Faculty Member of the Santa Fe Institute. He is the co-author of *Growing Artificial Societies: Social Science from the Bottom Up* with J. M. Epstein. His research has been published in leading general science journals (e.g. *Science, Proceedings of the National Academy of Sciences*) and disciplinary journals. His new book, *Artificial Economies of Adaptive Agents*, will appear soon.

Robert L. Basmann studied agricultural economics and econometric statistics at Iowa State University. The focus of his graduate research was on (1) filling some gaps in the neoclassical demand theory by incorporating budget constraint prices, income, random disturbances, and other factors as preference-changers of indifference maps and (2) finite-sample properties of distributions of new estimators and test statistics for simultaneous equations models. He is well known for his work in developing the two-stage least squares technique. He has published many articles and books on statistical problems, often inspired by former students' interests in special applications.

William A. Branch is an Assistant Professor at the University of California, Irvine. He is the author of many articles on heterogeneous expectations and adaptive learning in macroeconomics. Recent publications document evolving distributions of heterogeneity in survey data on inflation expectations. Contributions to the literature on Post Walrasian Macroeconomics include deriving heterogeneous expectations as an equilibrium outcome, stochastic volatility in macroeconomic models with misspecified beliefs, and bounded rationality explanations for the Great Moderation. His current research interests are the implications of heterogeneous expectations for monetary policy in fully specified business cycle models.

William A. "Buz" Brock is Vilas Research Professor, Department of Economics, University of Wisconsin, Madison. He is a Guggenheim Fellow (1987), as well as a Fellow of the Econometric Society, American Academy of Arts and Science (since 1992), National Academy of Sciences (USA) (since 1998), and Distinguished Fellow, American Economics Association (2004). He is known for his work on dynamical systems, time series analysis, political economy, macroeconomics, finance, and ecological economics.

David Colander is the Christian A. Johnson Distinguished Professor of Economics at Middlebury College. In 2001–02, he was the Kelly Professor of Distinguished Teaching at Princeton University. He has authored, co-authored, or edited over 35 books and 100 articles on a wide range of topics. He has been the President of both the Eastern Economic Association and the History of Economic Thought Society and is, or has been, on the editorial boards of numerous journals, including *Journal of Economic Perspectives* and the *Journal of Economic Education*, and *Journal of the History of Economic Thought*.

Russell Cooper is currently the Fred Hofheinz Regents Professor of Economics at the University of Texas, a position he has held since 2003. He previously taught at Yale, the University of Iowa and Boston University. He is an NBER Faculty Research Associate and a Fellow of the Econometric Society. He is best known for his work on coordination issues in macroeconomics.

Steven N. Durlauf is Kenneth Arrow Professor of Economics at the University of Wisconsin at Madison. A Fellow of the Econometric Society,

Durlauf received his Ph.D. from Yale in 1986. He is a Research Associate of the National Bureau of Economic Research, co-editor of the *Journal of Applied Economics*, and editor of the forthcoming edition of the *Palgrave Dictionary of Economics*. Durlauf's research areas include macroeconomics, econometrics, and income inequality.

Roger Farmer is a Professor at the University of California at Los Angeles. He has previously held positions at the University of Toronto, the University of Pennsylvania, the European University Institute, Cambridge University, and the Innocenzo Gaspirini Institute in Milan. He is a consultant for the European Central Bank, and is a Fellow of the Econometric Society, a Research Fellow of the Center for Economic Policy Research, and a Fellow Commoner of Churchill College, Cambridge. He is an associate editor of *Macroeconomic Dynamics*, the *Journal of Public Economic Theory*, and the *Economic Bulletin* and co-editor of the *International Journal of Economic Theory*.

Kevin D. Hoover is a Professor of Economics and Philosophy at Duke University. Previously, he was the Professor and Chair of Economics at the University of California, Davis. He is a past President of the History of Economics Society and past Chairman of the International Network for Economic Method, and was an editor of the *Journal of Economic Methodology* for ten years. In addition to numerous articles in macroeconomics, monetary economics, economic methodology, and the philosophy of science, he has edited or written several books, including *Causality in Macroeconomics* and *The Methodology of Empirical Macroeconomics*.

Peter Howitt is a Professor of Economics and the Lyn Crost Professor of Social Sciences at Brown University. He was on the faculty of the University of Western Ontario from 1972 to 1996 and the Ohio State University from 1996 to 2000. Most of his research has been in the area of macroeconomics and monetary economics. He is one of the creators of the modern "Schumpeterian" approach to the theory of economic growth. He has been active in the search for new foundations to macroeconomics and monetary theory, and has written extensively on the subject of Canadian monetary policy.

Søren Johansen is a Professor of Statistics at the University of Copenhagen and is best known in economics for his work on cointegration. He has been on numerous editorial boards, including the *Scandinavian Journal of Statistics, Econometric Theory*, and *Econometrica*. He is a Fellow of the

Institute of Mathematical Statistics, the International Statistical Institute, and the Econometric Society. In 1997, he received an award from Dir. Ib Henriksens Fund for outstanding research; in 1993–06, he was recognized as the most cited European economist, and in 1990–2000, was the most cited researcher in economic journals in the world.

Katarina Juselius is a Professor at the University of Copenhagen and was appointed the Chair of econometrics in 1996. She has published extensively on the methodology of cointegrated VAR models with applications to monetary transmission mechanism, policy control rules, price linkages, and wage, price, and unemployment dynamics. Her forthcoming book *The Cointegrated VAR Model: Methodology and Applications* by Oxford University Press explores these issues in depth. She is on the editorial boards of several journals, was a member of the Danish SSR, and is presently a member of the EUROCORES committee at the European Science Foundation.

Alan Kirman studied at Oxford and did his Ph.D. on applying non-cooperative game theory to international trade at Princeton with Harold Kuhn. Learning that this had no future, he moved into the area of general equilibrium theory. However, he then became interested in the relation between micro and macroeconomics and, in particular, how actual markets work. He has held posts at Johns Hopkins, Louvain, Brussels, Warwick, EUI Florence, and Aix-Marseille where he founded a research group, the GREQAM. He is a Fellow of the Econometric Society, was awarded the Humboldt Prize, elected to the Institute Universitaire de France, and is a member of the Institute for Advanced Study at Princeton.

Blake LaBaron is the Abram L. and Thelma Sachar Chair of International Economics at the International Business School, Brandeis University. He is a Research Associate at the National Bureau of Economic Research, and was a Sloan Fellow. LeBaron also served as the Director of the Economics Program at The Santa Fe Institute in 1993. LeBaron's research focuses on the nonlinear behavior of financial and macroeconomic time series, and he has been influential both in the statistical detection of nonlinearities and in describing their qualitative behavior in many series. LeBaron's current interests are in understanding the quantitative dynamics of interacting systems of adaptive agents and how these systems replicate observed real world phenomena.

Axel Leijonhufvud is a Professor of the Monetary Theory and Policy at the University of Trento, Italy. Previously, he taught at the University of

California at Los Angeles and was a Fellow at the Institute of Advanced Studies in Princeton. His best-known work is *On Keynesian Economics and the Economics of Keynes: A Study in Monetary Economics* (Oxford, 1968). The approach to macroeconomics discussed in that book was pursued further in *Information and Coordination* (Oxford, 1981), in *High Inflations* (coauthored with Daniel Heymann, Oxford, 1995) and in *Macroeconomic Instability and Coordination* (Elgar, 2000). He is listed in the *100 Great Economists Since Keynes* (M. Blaug, editor), in the *International Who's Who, Who's Who in America,* etc.

Peter H. Matthews is an Associate Professor and current Chair of the Department of Economics at Middlebury College in Vermont. His recent research interests include the evolution and enforcement of social norms and their implications for economics.

Perry Mehrling is a Professor of Economics at Barnard College, Columbia University, where he has taught since 1987. His research concerns the monetary and financial side of macroeconomics, a broad subject that he approaches from a variety of methodological angles. His best-known work to date has taken an historical approach to the field, describing the twentieth century American monetary economics through a series of biographical sketches of important figures such as Allyn Young, Alvin Hansen, Edward Shaw, and most recently, Fischer Black. His current work focuses more on the theoretical foundations of monetary economics with special attention to the role of the monetary authority in financially developed economies.

Leigh Tesfatsion is currently a Professor of Economics and Mathematics at Iowa State University. She specializes in Agent-based Computational Economics (ACE), the computational study of economic processes modeled as dynamic systems of interacting agents, with a particular focus on restructured electricity and labor markets. She is the coeditor of the *Handbook of Computational Economics, Volume 2* and is also an associate editor for the *Journal of Economic, Dynamics and Control,* the *Journal of Economic Interaction and Coordination,* the *Journal of Public Economic Theory,* and *Applied Mathematics and Computation.*

Foreword

In the past those who had been brought up in the Walrasian General Equilibrium tradition considered the field of Macroeconomics as essentially corresponding to the problem of aggregation. What meaningful relationships, they asked, among aggregate variables could be established starting from a set of independent utility maximizing individuals. This has not always been the case. Many earlier authors were content to specify the relations among aggregate variables and to test them without having recourse to models of individual behavior. It was nevertheless common practice to invoke individual decisions as a way of justifying the assumptions about, for example, the signs of the derivatives of the functions involved. This explains the famous remark that "70% of Keynes' *General Theory* is microeconomics." What is referred to as Walrasian macroeconomics (whether this is appropriate or not as an appellation can be judged by looking at Donald Walker's (2005) "Walrasian Economics") may be thought of as taking individual utility or profit maximizing behavior and translating it to the aggregate level. Generally, to avoid the aggregation problem, the aggregate data is treated as if it were the result of one individual's decisions. This, as is well known, is not legitimate from a theoretical point of view. Indeed, in the DSGE (Dynamic Stochastic General Equilibrium) synthesis the problem is not solved, just treated as if it were solved.

We continue to treat economic aggregates as though they correspond to economic individuals. It is this simple observation that makes the structure of the sophisticated models that economists build, unacceptable. All of the authors of the papers in this book agree with that observation, and in their papers they attempt to put their fingers on various weaknesses of standard macroeconomic models, to explain how these weaknesses arose, and to offer ways around them.

The attempt is heroic, and is only in the beginning stages. So a key question posed throughout the book is: What are the basic ingredients that we require from an alternative view? Given that this question is central, in this foreword I will suggest those themes that I believe should be included. I would include four main themes. First, we would like to model the economy as a system in which there is a *direct interaction* among individuals. We would like to specify agents who, in a sense, have local as opposed to global knowledge. It may well be the case that they have a limited, even wrong, view of the world. Second, we should require that agents behave in a "reasonable" but not "optimal" way; for example they may use simple rules and they should not act against their own interests. Moreover, these reasonable agents should evolve in the sense that they learn from previous experience. Third, the system should function over time but without necessarily converging to any particular state. It would be good to have a different notion of equilibrium from the standard one, a notion that corresponds to an economy that is in continual movement. Finally, whatever model we develop should have some testable conclusions; we should be able to imagine some empirical evidence that would lead us to refute our model.

Reading through the various contributions to this volume suggests that we have made progress in advancing towards an economic theory that incorporates the considerations I have just outlined. While we are far from general agreement on a particular paradigm, there are many positive indicators as to general progress.

THE ROLE OF INFORMATION

Throughout this book we find references to the importance of information: who has it, and how it is processed by individuals and the system. In his introduction David Colander argues that this is key in understanding where Post Walrasian economics differs from its Walrasian counterpart. While I agree that information is central, I do not see the issue in quite the same way that he does. He characterizes Walrasian individuals, as is frequently done in the literature, as agents who possess a great deal of information, in effect all the information that there is in the economy, and who also have remarkable capacities to process it. Given that characterization he contrasts these Walrasian individuals with Post Walrasian individuals. In his Post Walrasian economics, these Walrasian omniscient agents are replaced by Post Walrasian agents who have more limited calculating power and more limited and local information.

The problem with this view, as I see it, is that in the formal Walrasian General Equilibrium, setting the amount of information that individuals have to treat is negligible. All that they need to know is the current vector of prices and they have to announce their excess demand vector which is then processed centrally. It is the extraordinary informational parsimony of the Walrasian system, as shown by the results of Jim Jordan (1982), that is so striking. From the Jordan perspective, a key to the internal breakdown of the Arrow-Debreu theory in the face of the Sonnenschein Mantel Debreu theorems is the information problem, but it is a different informational problem than Colander poses.

Suppose that we take the pure Debreu-like position and say that all that we seek is a set of prices that will clear the markets. The individuals have to know nothing about how these prices were generated or what mechanism is behind this. Despite their lack of information we can say that, given the assumptions, "if these prices were announced then the economy would be in equilibrium." We can say the same thing about the model extended to one with uncertainty. If all the agents had the same and appropriate view of the future distribution of prices, then this would coincide with the actual distribution of prices and we would be in a "rational expectations" equilibrium. Thus we need to attribute no calculating power to our agents and we can simply argue that should the economy, by some chance, wind up in this situation it would be in equilibrium. We do not explain why agents should have these beliefs nor do we say anything about their understanding of the economy. Of course, that assumes that a mechanism exists to generate those prices — a mechanism that Leijonhufvud named the Walrasian auctioneer. Assuming the Walrasian auctioneer, little information is needed by individual agents; the information has all been processed for them.

There seems to be a contradiction here but I believe that it has a rather simple explanation that can be explained by different views of what the Walrasian system is. Colander's characterization of Walrasian economics sees individuals interacting in an uncontrolled system — they must arrive at equilibrium through bargaining with others on their own. This is the sort of view that was expressed by Friedman when he defined the natural rate of unemployment as "the level that would be ground out by the Walrasian system of general equilibrium equations, provided there is imbedded in them the actual structural characteristics of the labor and commodity markets, including market imperfections, stochastic variability in demands and supplies, the cost of gathering information about job vacancies and labor availabilities, the costs of mobility and so on." (Friedman 1968, p. 8)

Jordan's view of the Walrasian system is more abstract and precise. It assumes a central processor of information, which does the calculations, leaving the agents simply to react to the prices they face. For Colander the Walrasian agents incorporate all the processing capabilities required of the system — each is a central processor in their own right. From the Jordan perspective, there is a central processor who does all the work for them.

The problem with the informal Walrasian tradition is that it skips over the discussion of how, precisely, prices are arrived at, or simply assumes "price taking" behavior without answering the question of what "price taking" can mean if all the agents are doing the information processing themselves.

The formal Walrasian model, as captured by Arrow-Debreu does not have the problem. It is an equilibrium model, and does not pretend to be otherwise. That is, there is a price vector which all the agents face at any one time. One could think of some sort of computer that takes in the bids and offers for goods and does the calculations necessary to find an equilibrium price vector. This is what happens at the opening of the Paris Bourse today. The informal view of the Walrasian market, which Colander is referring to, involves agents interacting freely with each other and finding prices through bargaining. While this is surely what the early followers of Walras and Walras himself would have liked, my impression is that almost all of the formal Walrasian literature certainly, since Arrow-Debreu, works within the Jordan framework. The central goal of work within this formal Walrasian framework is to find a set of prices for which aggregate excess demand is zero for all goods. Yet, demand is not even defined unless prices are given. Thus within the strict Arrow-Debreu framework we have to assume that someone other than the agent is setting the prices. This is neither realistic nor philosophically satisfactory but is, I believe, why the Walrasian literature has retained what we can call the Jordan perspective.[1]

Since the Jordan perspective accepts the idea of some sort of central price setting mechanism all we look for in the models is what the system needs, in terms of information, to function at equilibrium. The Jordan results I have just mentioned provide an answer: if you want to have the economy functioning in a Pareto efficient state, then you cannot do better than the Walrasian system. Unfortunately applying the result to the real world

---

[1] There have, of course been sporadic attempts by distinguished general equilibrium theorists to incorporate price setting into the Walrasian model, see e.g. Negishi (1961, 1962), Novshek and Sonnenschein (1978), Mas-Colell (1982) and Dierker and Grodal (1986). However this has remained marginal.

situations doesn't get us very far. To see this, suppose that you ask the question: how much information would this system require to move from out of equilibrium to equilibrium, or to move from an inefficient state to an efficient state? To find an adjustment system that would do this for the Walrasian system would, as Saari and Simon (1978) showed, take an infinite amount of information. This is terribly destructive to any argument for a Walrasian system; it says that I cannot guarantee the convergence of a price adjustment mechanism given that my agents have the same knowledge that they have in the Arrow-Debreu world, even if I maintain the fiction of a centralized market-clearing system. We do not even have to worry about the introduction of more complicated informational systems to get into trouble. This is the mirror image of the information rich versus information poor trade-off. The formal Walrasian world is information poor — much too poor to function away from equilibrium.

So, despite their seeming differences, both perspectives lead to the same place in terms of the need for change, and in the direction of future research. They both direct researchers toward constructing a more realistic model of how information is processed by individuals and how they manage to coordinate their different wants.

MODEL UNCERTAINTY

A crucial problem, when we move to a world where the individuals have limited knowledge and calculating capacities, concerns what information these agents do have. Brock and Durlauf's contribution points out that significant difficulties may arise if agents do not have the correct model of their environment. This may lead agents to behave "incorrectly." However, as Brock and Durlauf indicate, behaving incorrectly may actually be advantageous in certain circumstances. If their forecasting rules are not those that are optimal for the true model it may be the case that their behavior will be stabilizing. And, if they use the appropriate rule, their resultant behavior may tend to destabilize the economy. This insight is related to earlier work by Brock and Hommes (1997) where agents use good forecasting rules, but, as the economy settles to a steady state, less-good but less-costly rules do just as well; however, when the agents learn to adopt these rules, the economy becomes less stable and the better rule comes back on its own. This switching among rules leads to complicated dynamics. The important ideas that their work captures are that the learning may have a strong impact on the dynamics of the economy, and that macromodels must incorporate that learning.

There is however, another aspect of this problem. Specifically, agents may believe in the "wrong model" but, by behaving accordingly, what they observe may confirm their beliefs. This was the message of the "sunspots" literature (Cass and Shell [1983]). Woodford (1990) compounded this problem by showing that agents might rationally learn their way to these wrong, but self fulfilling, beliefs. (In Kirman [1983a], I analyzed a very simple duopoly model where the two agents believed that they were monopolists and I showed the same sort of result. A reasonable learning process would lead them to a view of the world that was wrong, but which was perfectly consistent with what they observed.) The basic message of the work is that if we have agents who are doing their best to learn about what is going on, but who have a view of the world that is incorrect, we have no guarantee that they will converge to the "truth."

Such processes might well correspond to what is going on in many economic situations. Agents have a view of the world and they are doing the best that they can given that view. It is only if something exogenous disturbs this comfortable situation that they will reflect on the situation. This is simply because the space over which they are learning is not big enough to contain alternative models. This recalls work by Kalai and Lerner (1993) who showed that, if people are to converge, through learning, on an equilibrium, their initial views of the world have to have something in common. (The condition they use is technical, and essentially means that players cannot assign zero probabilities to any of the outcomes of the game which are actually possible.) This brings up a crucial problem when dealing with heterogeneous agents who have, in particular, differing beliefs about the world in which they function. If agents have a totally false idea of reality there is little hope for convergence to an equilibrium of the "true" model.

In the context of this book, the above propositions suggest that people living in a high dimensional world, but who only have a low dimensional view of it, may never learn about the other dimensions. (This is not exactly what has been argued by Brock and Durlauf but is closely related to the questions that they raise.) Indeed, in this I am reiterating many of the points made by Branch (Chapter 7 in this volume). As he shows, heterogeneity of expectations can arise in a misspecified equilibrium situation. Such results are reassuring for those who have been puzzled by the persistent empirical evidence for such heterogeneity of expectations. Perhaps the most important idea here is that we should not regard learning as a way of justifying the static or steady state equilibrium that we are interested in, but we should accept that the learning process itself may lead the economy to have interesting dynamics which do not converge to an equilibrium in the standard sense.[2]

SOCIAL AND ECONOMIC INTERACTION AND NOTIONS OF EQUILIBRIUM

It has been observed by many people that direct interaction among economic agents can modify aggregate behavior. This is something that is largely absent from Walrasian models, and Brock and Durlauf's other contribution to this book gives a nice account of such issues. A long time ago Koopmans said that it would not matter if people's preferences and choices changed at random so long as there were many of them and the individual changes were sufficiently independent. Föllmer (1974) was the first to provide a formal analysis of this insight. What he showed was that equilibrium prices would not be modified even if individuals' preferences were affected by their neighbors' *provided that the influence was not too strong.* The policy problem is to determine what is "too strong" and when we are likely to be in such situations. Finding answers to these questions is important because once local interaction has a significant influence on the behavior of economic agents, all sorts of aggregate effects can appear.

The insight about aggregate effects of interactive agent behavior was the basis of Schelling's famous segregation model. LeBaron's contribution to this volume captures some of the insights of models of financial markets in which individuals change their forecasts as a result of the opinions of their neighbors or, as a result of their own experience. (See e.g. Kirman [1991], Lux and Marchesi [1999], and Föllmer, Horst, and Kirman [2005].) These models demonstrate that the population of traders will likely switch from forecasting in one way to another and that these switches will be reinforced by the feedback into prices. As a result, as the population of traders changes from being dominated by one type of forecast, based on fundamentals for example, to another type, based perhaps on extrapolation, bubbles and crashes will occur.

Since there is no equilibrium in the standard sense, the question then is: can we find some sort of equilibrium notion, or do we have to content ourselves with saying that "anything can happen." In Föllmer, Horst, and Kirman (2005) we suggest such an alternative notion. Although prices are

---

[2] My impression is that misspecified equilibria lie behind much of the fascinating work of Evans and Honkopohja (2001) and all the authors that they refer to.

constantly changing and never settle to any steady state, we can show that the time averages of prices will converge, that the process is ergodic, and that a unique limit price distribution will exist. Thus, despite complicated dynamics, there is some structure in the evolution of prices such that, though they never settle down, it is an appropriate concept of equilibrium. Why is this interesting? Because I think this gives us an idea of equilibrium which is not Walrasian in the usual sense, but which is specifiable, and which is consistent with the empirical evidence because it also allows us to explain a number of the stylized facts in financial time series such as "fat tails" and "long memory."

CONCLUSION

The work in this volume is on the right path, and should give young researchers many indicators as to where they should go. How could one not be persuaded by Leigh Tesfatsion, Rob Axtell, and Blake LeBaron's arguments for more agent-based modeling; such work is likely to become more and more important over time. In terms of empirical work, Søren Johansen and Katarina Juselius show that we can do much better than we currently are doing in extracting information from data, and that some of the tests of DSGE models are more problematic than is generally believed. They show us how we can put ourselves in a position to reject certain hypotheses or conclusions from the theory, a result that, as I said at the outset, is of fundamental importance.

The book also has insights in terms of policy. Peter Howitt joins me in comparing human economic agents to ants. This analogy does not go down well in all circles but, as he says, we can learn a lot from the metaphor. Dynamics are important, and assuming away the possibilities of internally generated bubbles in one's models, as is done by most DSGE models, will give us little insight into how to deal with such bubbles should they actually occur.

This book helps open the door to the macroeconomics of the future, even though it would be too optimistic to say that we are right on the threshold of a new and complete macroeconomic paradigm. It sketches out the outline of a paradigm that is beginning to take form, showing that many of the elements are there. The work in this volume puts the emphasis on the right questions. But there are so many possible paths that we find ourselves in the position that a well-known professor of medicine explained in his first lecture which my father attended as a medical student, "Ladies and Gentlemen," said the professor. "In twenty years time you will come to realise that half of what I will teach you will turn out to be wrong! Unfortunately I cannot tell you now which half it will be."

Alan Kirman
Institute for Advanced Study, Princeton
GREQAM, EHESS and Université d'Aix-Marseille lll

Introduction

David Colander

The field of macroeconomics can be divided loosely into two branches, a theoretical branch, which sets out the vision of how macroeconomic problems may come about and how they might best be dealt with, and an applied branch, which talks about actual policy — questions such as: Should one use monetary policy to stimulate output? Should one use fiscal policy to offset recessions? And: Should the interest rate or the money supply be used as a measure of monetary tightness? The two branches are of course related with theoretical work guiding policy, and experience in policy guiding theoretical work. But the relation is loose and indirect.

Over the last 30 years, the two branches of macro have become further and further divided as the theoretical macromodels have become more complicated and as our understanding of the statistical problems of fitting the models to the empirical evidence has improved. Today, almost all economists agree that the simple models of yesterday — both theoretical IS/LM type models and the structural macroeconometric models that accompanied them — were far from adequate as theoretical models or as a guide to policy. In response, modern macrotheory has become a highly technical theoretical and statistically sophisticated field of study in which microfoundations of macrotheory play a central role.[1]

Because of the technical difficulty of the tools needed to study macroeconomic theory grounded in microfoundations, the underlying vision of macrotheorists is often given short shrift in both the theoretical debates and in the training of students. Instead of talking about vision researchers focus on resolving technical issues, and teachers focus on

---

[1] Another branch of macroeconomics has moved away from these short-run issues and has concentrated on growth theory. This book does not deal with these broader growth theory issues. It concentrates on shorter run coordination issues that have traditionally been the focus of macrotheory since the 1930s.

providing students with the tools for resolving technical debates. The result is that, today, when graduate students study macroeconomics, they are given little sense of the history of macroeconomic debates, of how macropolicy works, or of the vision behind the model. They are left on their own to figure out such issues.[2]

ALTERNATIVE MACROECONOMIC RESEARCH PROGRAMS

Since the vision behind the research is central to an understanding of the nature of the macroeconomic debate of which this volume is part, it is probably best to begin with a short summary of what I see as the dominant macroresearch program, which I will call a Walrasian research program, and to contrast it with an alternative research program, which I will call a Post Walrasian research program.[3] Both these research programs have their foundations in a broad economic vision, a vision of the economy in which markets coordinate agent's actions through an invisible hand. Where they differ is, in their sense of what type of theoretical simplifications can shed light on macropolicy issues. Different simplifications lead to different research programs.

I find it helpful to begin distinguishing the two research programs by the assumptions they are willing to make about the information processing capabilities of agents and the information set available to those agents. Walrasians assume high-level information processing capabilities and a rich information set; Post Walrasians assume low-level information processing capabilities and a poor information set.[4]

---

[2] Just how much they are left on their own was made clear when I interviewed graduate students at top schools (Colander 2005). Consistently I was told by graduate students that at top universities monetary and fiscal policy were not discussed in their macro class, and that they had little idea of what the underlying vision was.

[3] I will discuss the choice of the Walrasian–Post Walrasian classification below.

[4] As Alan Kirman points out in his foreword, in formal general equilibrium theory, researchers assume the existence of a central information processor who has all the information he needs to achieve equilibrium. Macro thinking and theorizing has not closely followed formal general equilibrium theory; instead, it developed an informal Walrasian microfoundation that pictured individuals optimizing in an environment experiencing stochastic shocks of various types. That led to notions of search equilibria, "natural rates" of unemployment and "rational expectations equilibria" that did not fit in a formal general equilibrium where there was a central information processor with full information. It is these notions that I am terming as the Walrasian tradition in macro. It is this tradition that resolved the modeling problems presented by information processing by assuming a single representative agent, thereby avoiding all heterogeneous agent coordination issues that are a central concern to the contributors of this book.

Thus, Walrasians ask the question:

How does the market coordinate agents with high-level information processing capabilities operating in information-rich environments?

Post Walrasians ask the question:

How does the market coordinate agents with low-level information processing capabilities operating in information-poor environments?

The above distinctions are too stark. There is a continuum of processing capabilities and information sets that one can assume, and thus the Walrasian and Post Walrasian research programs blend together. All macroeconomists recognize that systems are complex and that ultimately agents have limited processing capabilities and operate in less-than-full information environments. But the aggregate analysis of such systems is far beyond our current technical analytic capabilities, and it is not clear that the partial analysis that we are currently able to do, which deals seriously with Post Walrasian concerns, yields relevant insights. So the choice is a Walrasian modeling approach that arrives at fairly clear conclusions for a system that is far from the system we want to describe, or a Post Walrasian modeling approach that arrives at ambiguous conclusions for a system that is closer to what we want to describe.

In the 1980s, most cutting-edge macrotheorists chose the Walrasian path, and economists who insisted on asking the Post Walrasian question were outside the mainstream. But, because of technological advances in analytic and computing technology, and the sense that, because of the recent research, we have a better grasp of the Walrasian question, more and more macroresearchers are turning to the Post Walrasian question. This volume is an introduction to that work.

When we think about the work presented in this volume, it should be clear that the Walrasian/Post Walrasian classification is not black and white, and that researchers can be working on both research programs simultaneously. For example, Michael Woodford, who has been instrumental in developing the Walrasian research program, did early work on the Post Walrasian research program (Woodford [1990], Woodford and Farmer [1997]). In fact, many of the Post Walrasian researchers are the students of key Walrasian researchers, and have been encouraged in their work by their Walrasian predecessors. Thus, the Walrasian/Post Walrasian distinction is a distinction about the nature of the research, not about researchers. With those qualifications, let me now discuss the research agendas of the two groups.

The Walrasian Question and the DSGE Synthesis

The dominant strand of research being done in macroeconomic theory today is designed to shed light on the Walrasian question. It is a question that a branch of applied mathematics, optimal control theory, is especially useful in answering, and researchers working in this tradition come into their work with a significant knowledge of dynamic stochastic optimal control theory. For that reason, work in this tradition has recently acquired the name the *dynamic stochastic general equilibrium (DSGE) synthesis*.

In the DSGE research program, general equilibrium theory is conceived of as solving a set of interdependent equations describing globally rational agent intertemporal optimization.[5] The general solution to this set of equations serves as a theoretical foundation for our understanding of macroeconomic coordination issues. I call it Walrasian because this research program is usually associated with Walras, who in *Elements of Pure Economics* attempted to provide a mathematical structure of how the aggregate economy would operate when conceived of as a set of interdependent equations capturing the actions of rational optimizing agents.[6]

The initial work on this Walrasian question began with a study of how globally rational agents with perfect information and foresight would operate because that was felt to be the easiest problem, and because it was felt that the solution to that problem would provide important insight into situations where there is less than perfect information. This meant that the Walrasian research agenda has been to study the coordination of an economy in which globally rational agents are optimizing in information-rich environments. Even when we limit the problem in this way, it is still necessary to make numerous simplifying assumptions to make the problem tractable. This includes eliminating all aspects of the problem that would lead to multiple solutions so that the model yields a unique, or at least a small number of, solutions.[7]

---

[5] Developing this vision proved very fruitful in finance, and in some ways the Walrasian research program in macro can be seen as an attempt to extend the work done in finance to macroeconomics.

[6] Whether this was Walras' vision is debatable. It follows from Jaffe's translation of Walras' 5th edition, but Walker (1983) argues that earlier editions provide a quite different vision, and that they are the better source of the Walrasian vision. He calls the work that has been done in this tradition neoWalrasian rather than Walrasian.

[7] Schumpeter stated that the existence of a unique solution was absolutely necessary for economics.

To achieve a unique solution, one must significantly limit the allowable interactions of heterogeneous agents in the model, which has generally been done by focusing on models that include a single representative agent. One must also restrict the analysis to models with linear dynamics, a restriction that assumes *away* a whole host of potential policy problems. Unfortunately, these assumptions are crucial to drawing policy implications from the Walrasian model, and are what allow Walrasian macroeconomists to make concepts such as the natural rate of unemployment and the natural rate of interest operational.

Since the assumptions are so important for drawing policy implications from the model, Walrasian researchers agree that there are substantial addenda that need to be made to the theoretical models before results can be drawn for policy. Thus, there is an active Walrasian research program focusing on modifying the assumptions that have been made to make the model tractable. However, until those expanded models come to fundamentally different conclusions from the standard model, most Walrasians believe, either explicitly or implicitly, that the perfect information model (with the necessary assumptions to make it tractable) serves as an intuitive guide for considering policy.

The dynamic stochastic general equilibrium (DSGE) synthesis is the newest, and in many ways the culmination of the developments in the Walrasian tradition. Essentially, it moves beyond perfect information by adding stochastic risk, describable by probability distributions, to the general equilibrium optimization problem over time. The DSGE synthesis sees the macroeconomic problem as a gigantic dynamic stochastic general equilibrium optimal control problem, and looks at the full optimization of individuals and firms, arriving at a solution by using rational expectations and model consistency assumptions. While the direct origins of the DSGE synthesis are in the real business cycle literature that evolved from the New Classical work, it is called a synthesis because much of the recent work within this New Classical tradition has included assumptions of nominal and institutional rigidities, work that has often been classified as New Keynesian. So the DSGE synthesis is the merging of the New Keynesian and New Classical traditions into a single approach. DSGE models consider agents who dynamically maximize their intertemporal objectives subject to budget and resource constraints within a variety of general equilibrium institutional settings that may include institutional and nominal rigidities. The most developed of this work can be seen in Woodford's recent book (2003), which spells out a variety of models and teases out policy implications from those models.[8]

In terms of policy, the DSGE synthesis models suggest much more caution about the use of discretionary monetary or fiscal policy than did the neoclassical/NeoKeynesian synthesis models. The reason is that in an intertemporal equilibrium, the effects of most expected demand-based policy wash out as individuals adjust their actions to take expected policy into account. Walrasian agents are forward looking, and act on expectations of policy; they are not passive responders to policy action by government, as they were in IS–LM models. The most well-known DSGE policy prescription, which Woodford has strongly advocated, is the need for inflation targeting, in which the central bank announces an inflation target. This inflation targeting allows agents to base their dynamic optimization on a firmer foundation, which means that inflation targeting helps coordinate individual decisions. Work within the DSGE Walrasian approach is concentrating on checking robustness of the policy conclusions derived from the standard model when the models are expanded to include nominal and institutional rigidities.

With sufficient nominal price rigidities, some discretionary demand-based policy may be warranted, but that is only a slight adjustment to the general Walrasian policy view that aggregate demand-based policies will be ineffective in the long run. What this means is that much of the policy action is in expected policy, not in the actual policy; policy is considered in a broader context of policy regimes rather than in terms of specific policies to be followed in specific instances. Thus, modern DSGE macropolicy discussion focuses on credibility, credible rules, and optimal dynamic feedback rules.[9]

---

[8] Woodford's book is a tour de force that, according to one reviewer, is likely to become a "bible for central bank economists who regard themselves as having a public charge to design and implement stabilization policy as best they can." (Green, 2005, p. 121)

[9] Numerous other policy suggestions follow from the analysis but these have not been taken up generally. For example, in the *Handbook of Macroeconomics* (1999) edited by Taylor and Woodford, Chari and Kehoe suggest four substantive lessons for policymaking from the DSGE model without nominal rigidities: (1) Capital income taxes should be high initially and then roughly zero; (2) tax rates on labor and consumption should be roughly constant; (3) state-contingent taxes on assets should be used to provide insurance against adverse shocks; and (4) monetary policy should be conducted so as to keep nominal interest rates close to zero (Chari and Kehoe, 1999, p. 1673).

The type of policy discussion that is taking place can be seen in a recent paper by Schmitt-Grohé and Uribe (2005). In it they argue that the policy advice of "smooth distortionary income tax rates and highly volatile and unpredictable inflation rates" that follows from the model with no nominal rigidities is significantly modified if one has nominal rigidities.

Modern empirical work in the Walrasian macrotradition has given up trying to directly forecast with the theoretical models, and has concentrated more on showing general consistency of the model with filtered empirical evidence by calibrating the models with out-of-sample data. Success is interpreted to be when the data being generated by the model cannot be differentiated from real world data.

VAR analysis, not calibration, is generally used by Walrasians for forecasting and policy work. In terms of forecasting there has been no clear-cut empirical winner or loser in the formal empirical analysis, although restricted VAR forecasting comes out relatively well (Robertson and Tallman [1999]). The empirical forecasting debate is on the nature of restrictions one uses, and how those restrictions relate to theory. There is some work (Diebold [1998], Ingram and Whiteman [1994], Del Negro and Schorfheide, forthcoming) attempting to combine the DSGE insights with vector autoregression models, using the DSGE model as a Bayesian prior. In this work, the DSGE model is used to help guide the selection of variables within the VAR.

THE POST WALRASIAN QUESTION

From a Post Walrasian perspective, there is nothing wrong with the logic of the DSGE work, but there are serious questions about its relevance. At issue are the strong assumptions necessary to arrive at tractable models, assumptions that do not fit anyone's intuition about how the economy is likely to function. Thus while Post Walrasians see the development of the DSGE synthesis as an important stepping stone, they believe that it is, at best, a first step, and they have serious concerns about using that model to guide macropolicy considerations. Their work does not focus on looking at robustness relative to nominal and institutional rigidities, as the Walrasian work does, but instead considers the robustness relative to information processing capabilities of agents and the information set available to agents.

What motivates Post Walrasian work is a concern whether the policy results drawn from the DSGE synthesis will carry through once more realistic assumptions about these information-coordination issues are integrated into the model. The difference in views is captured by the well-known "economist searching for car keys under a streetlight" joke.[10]

The Post Walrasian/Walrasian debate is not limited to macroeconomics. The appropriate degree of rationality and information to assume available

---

[10] Of course, that joke also captures the difficulties with the Post Walrasian approach; Post Walrasians are searching for the keys in the dark.

to agents has long separated economists. Alfred Marshall, for example, shied away from general equilibrium analysis and concentrated on partial equilibrium analysis precisely because he felt that individuals did not have the capability of processing the large degree of information necessary to assume that the results of general equilibrium models were applicable. Modern behavioral economics is another manifestation of this issue: it suggests that the foundations of economic models must be empirically founded in individual's actions, not in an assumed global rational logic.[11]

While all economists accept that individuals are purposeful, and that markets coordinate aggregate activity, the debate is still open about how that takes place, and the Post Walrasian perspective sees the coordination problem as far more complicated than does the Walrasian perspective. From a Post Walrasian perspective, before one can draw policy implications from the model, those complications must be dealt with. The reason is that the interactions among agents in the macroeconomy are so complex, so intuitively likely to influence the aggregate results, that it seems beyond believability that the relevant aspects of such systems could be captured by a solvable system of simultaneous equations with a unique equilibrium that does not take those interactions into account.

The complexity that Post Walrasians see characterizing the macro-economy presents a very serious problem for formal modeling because the lack of a unique equilibrium feeds back on the specification of the rationality of agents. With many potential equilibria, the specifications of agent rationality no longer can rely on agents fully understanding the underlying system unless they have a metamodel (models of models) to choose among equilibria. It is even unclear whether the underlying system can be fully specified. The best one can hope for is for agents to exhibit *metamodel consistent expectations*, and, even if one can specify precisely how selections can be made among alternative models, there is little presumption of expectational stability in metamodels since it is easy to conceive of metamodels that have sudden large shifts in expectations, as expectations shift from one model to another. This raises serious policy questions since such shifts can fundamentally alter policy prescriptions.[12]

---

[11] While agent actions may not be globally rational, they will likely be locally rational, if one can back out the actual decision process within the local environment. So the debate is not about rationality, but about the nature of rationality to use, and how to discover that rationality.

[12] At most, there are basins of attractions and any meaningful theory must deal with the questions: which basin of attraction will the economy gravitate toward, and how stable are the various basins?

In short, the Post Walrasian concern with the DSGE synthesis is that the complexity of interactions that characterizes complex systems is central to macropolicy problems, but is assumed away in DSGE models. It is for that reason that the Post Walrasian approach is associated with the complexity work that was done at Santa Fe and at various universities around the world. It may even be that the system of equations describing the agent interactions is currently unsolvable either because that system of equations with realistic interactions is analytically intractable or incomputable either because the dimensions of the interactions involve higher order inter-relationships than we are capable of solving, or because of the sheer number of equations necessary to deal with the expectational heterogeneity.[13]

Taking complexity seriously presents a major challenge to any rational expectations of the macromodel. If we cannot assume that economists understand the economy, we cannot assume that the agents understand the economy. Thus, what we mean by agent rationality is called into question, and the foundations of agent behavior must be found in behavioral study, not in logic. This means that, from a Post Walrasian perspective, before we have an adequate model of the macroeconomy, we must deal specifically with model uncertainty by agents and by economists.

Notice that the difference between the Walrasian and Post Walrasian research programs concerns acceptable simplifications in modeling processes; the two approaches are not asking fundamentally different questions. A Post Walrasian would agree that simplifications must be made if the system is to be solvable. But they argue that the Walrasian simplifications violate Einstein's "more so" criterion because, by eliminating central elements of agent interactions, Walrasians make macrotheory more simple than it can be. Two standard Walrasian simplifications that Post Walrasians find objectionable are the representative agent assumption and agent rationality assumptions. The first is problematic because Post Walrasians see interactions of agents as significantly influencing the macroeconomy. The second is problematic because agent behavior in high-level uncertain systems is likely to be fundamentally different than in stochastically certain systems. For a Post Walrasian, information and institutions cannot be addenda because they are central to the core theory.

THE DIFFERENT QUESTIONS POSED

The different visions lead Walrasians and Post Walrasians to ask different questions about what is happening in the macroeconomy in their

---

[13] Alan Kirman has nicely captured these issues (Kirman, 1992).

research programs. Walrasians are searching for reasons for fluctuations; their underlying model is one of global equilibrium and stability in the absence of rigidities. Fluctuations come from exogenous supply shocks, which are not perfectly dampened because of nominal and institutional rigidities. That's why the research focuses on the implications of those rigidities. Thus the Walrasian question is: why are there fluctuations in the economy? Post Walrasians' underlying conception of the competitive macroeconomy is of a system with strong tendencies toward chaotic behavior, which is kept under control by institutions. For that reason the Post Walrasian question is the opposite of the Walrasian question. The Post Walrasian question is: why is there as much stability in the economy as there is? From a Post Walrasian perspective, what is unusual about the macroeconomy is not that it exhibits instability; it is that it is not in total chaos. Post Walrasians hypothesize that institutions place limits on chaos, which means that the modeling of microfoundations of the macroeconomy must take that institutional richness into account because those institutions impose stability on an otherwise chaotic system. Thus, whereas the Walrasian DSGE model sees institutional and nominal rigidities as slowing the movement to equilibrium, the Post Walrasian model sees institutions and nominal rigidities as central to how the macroeconomy maintains its stability.

THE DIFFERENT TOOLS AND MODELS USED

The different questions asked by the two research programs lead to differences in the tools. As I stated above, the DSGE model is structured around the stochastic dynamic optimal control theory generally assuming linear dynamics and unique equilibria. Post Walrasian analytic theory also uses stochastic dynamic control theory. However, because Post Walrasian researchers are attempting to deal with far more complicated systems (because they are not willing to make the Walrasian assumptions necessary to make the systems less complicated), their models tend to be much more complicated, and generally do not yield clear-cut analytic solutions. Post Walrasian models shed light on, but do not solve, the problem.[14]

Post Walrasians agree that a reasonable assumption of any model is *agent-modeler consistency:* the requirement that the agents in the model

---

[14] Thinking in reference to the streetlight joke mentioned above, the Post Walrasians' use of models is the equivalent of rubbing two sticks together in the hope that one can create a spark that might provide some guidance.

have the same information as do the economists modeling the economy. The Walrasian DSGE model achieves this *agent-modeler consistency* by assuming that economists know the right model and hence the agents know the right model. Rational expectations is *agent-modeler consistent* in this case. DSGE modelers then use the insights from that model to provide guidance for situations when the agents do not know the right model.

The Post Walrasians achieve consistency by assuming that neither economists nor agents know the right model, and that a right model may well not exist. This assumption changes the analysis fundamentally because it eliminates rational expectations as the close of the model. Before one can specify agents' expectations, one must now have an analysis of model selection and learning; there is no fixed point to fall back upon to determine rationality. Instead, one must look to how people act to determine what is rational. Behavioral economics, not utility theory, forms the microfoundation of Post Walrasian economics, and it is an empirical, not a deductive, foundation.

Because Post Walrasians don't see first-principle analytic models as shedding much light on the problem, they are much more likely to be open to whatever evidence is available. This leads to a second difference between them and Walrasians. Post Walrasians tend to be much more open to case studies, surveys, and institutional research. For example, Post Walrasians see research done by Blinder et al. (1998) and Bewley (1999) as important to understanding price and wage rigidities, and they try to build such insights into their models; Walrasians tend to disregard it.

Another difference is in what Post Walrasians consider a useful model. Because of the need to deal with heterogeneous agents, Post Walrasian models tend to focus on more complicated models involving statistical equilibria in which agent level equilibrium cannot be specified. Because their models often cannot be solved analytically, they also rely more on simulations to provide insight into the models.[15]

The difficulty of analytically solving models with assumptions that Post Walrasians find appropriate leads Post Walrasians to be open to a quite different approach to studying the macroeconomy: agent-based computational economics (ACE) modeling. ACE models do not rely upon specification of the analytic structure of the model. Instead, agent-based modelers endow heterogeneous virtual agents with local optimizing strategic rules and allow them to compete in a virtual economy — seeing

---

[15] With software programs such as Mathematica, much more complicated analytic problems can be solved in much less time than previously.

both — what strategies win out and how the strategies interact. The resulting model, called an agent-based model, helps the researcher specify which characteristics are sustainable, and what the nature of an aggregate system would be when populated by such agents. In agent-based modeling, agent learning is not tacked onto the model but is inherent in it. Different learning rules and specifications of rationality compete, and the model provides insight into which strategies are viable and how they interact. Agent-based modeling also allows the researcher to study the dynamics of the model, with no external equilibrium condition imposed, and to pretest the effectiveness of various policies in the virtual economy that has been set up.[16]

At present, agent-based modeling is still in its infancy, but it offers hope of an alternative to finding analytic solutions of complex systems. This development moves parallel with another element into macro, behavioral economics. In behavioral economics one studies how real-world agents behave. Agent-based models are closely tied to behavioral economics because they use the characteristics, which behavioral economists find characterize individuals, to create the strategic interaction rules with which they endow their virtual agents.[17]

A final difference in the tools used by Walrasians and Post Walrasians concerns macroeconometrics. For applied macropolicy work, Post Walrasians are much more likely to use data-driven empirical methods with less reliance on theory than is demonstrated in Walrasian applied macropolicy work. In some ways, this parallels a change in Walrasian macro, which also has moved to structural VAR models when actually doing forecasts and applied policy. But there is a major difference between the two. Since Post Walrasians see theory as far less definitive, they rely more heavily on pulling out information from the data with cointegrated VARs, looking to the data to chose among alternative theories, whereas

---

[16] Agent-based modeling simulation is fundamentally different than equation simulation described above, because in agent-based modeling one is not using simulation to solve equations but is instead simulating the system. One is not looking for any analytic solution.

[17] While drawing constructive results from agent-based models might be a long way away, these models do offer an important test of theories — what might be called "an agent-based empirical model consistency" test. The test is that one should be able to develop an agent-based model corresponding to an analytic model, with some specification of agents, that calibrates reasonably well with the data. If an analytic model cannot meet this test, then the results one gets from such an analytic model are highly suspect. This destructive aspect of agent-based models is important because the standard DSGE representative agent models do not, and I suspect cannot, meet this test.

Walrasians tend to start with the presumption that the DSGE model is the correct one, and look to the data for confirmation of that model.

The difference between the Walrasian and Post Walrasian approaches is in the assumed priors. Walrasian economics uses DSGE priors; Post Walrasian work uses a "general to specific" approach, in which theories are chosen simultaneously with analyzing the data; econometric analysis is used to choose among assumptions and alternative theories, not to test a theory. This requires a looser theoretical, but more highly disciplined statistical, approach than characterizes the Walrasian approach.[18]

In many ways the Post Walrasian approach is a return to the Classical Marshallian approach to macropolicy updated to take account of new statistical and computational developments. Classical economists had no formal theory; they approached policy using an informal theory to loosely organize their thoughts. Walras's approach was different: for Walras the system of interdependent equations was the centerpiece of his analysis of the aggregate economy.

Marshall carried through that Classical approach in his methodology, and the difference between the two visions' uses of theory can be seen by contrasting Marshall's approach to general equilibrium with Walras' approach.[19] For Marshall, general equilibrium of this type was a one-page footnote (footnote 21 in *Principles*), worth keeping in the back of his mind, but not worth developing seriously in a theoretical sense or in an applied policy sense.[20]

The differences in theoretical approaches carry over into policy lessons drawn from theory. Walrasian policy insights tend to follow from theory based upon the strong assumptions that they argue are necessary to draw policy implications from the theory. Post Walrasians are far less certain about those theoretically-based policy insights. In the Post Walrasian approach, policy is driven primarily by empirical evidence, with theory

[18] The approach I believe it will follow is similar to Marshall's "one thing at a time" approach in which common sense is merged with theoretical insights and both are continually being judged in relation to the empirical evidence.

[19] Marshall's methodological approach was grounded in a broader Classical approach relating economics and policy. That approach began disappearing in the economics profession in the 1930s and became almost forgotten by the 1970s, as Walrasian methodology, which more closely related theory and policy, spread. This Walrasian methodology required one to ground all policy advice theoretically, which led Walrasians to develop tractable models. Macro actually followed micro in moving to this Walrasian mythology, and only adopted it fully with the success of the new Classical revolution.

[20] For Marshall the theoretical domain of macroeconomics was to be found in the more complicated mathematics of thermodynamics which he did not have the mathematical ability to deal with, so he did not deal with it.

serving as an aid in interpreting the empirical evidence. Post Walrasian policy prescriptions are much more tentative than Walrasian policy prescriptions: here is what's worked in the past; maybe it will work in the future. Policy insights are derived more from educated common sense, to which theoretical insights contribute but do not determine.

IS THE TIME RIPE FOR A POST WALRASIAN MACRO?

If economists have always shied away from developing a Post Walrasian macrotheory in the past because of its overwhelming difficulties, why do I see the Post Walrasian research program as having a chance today? There are three reasons why. The first is the recent developments that have occurred in macro. The New DSGE Synthesis makes clear the strong assumptions necessary to come to any conclusion by the Walrasian modeling path — assumptions that the neoclassical/Keynesian synthesis hid. Thus, the New Synthesis makes transparent the difficulty of pulling out policy advice from the theory in a way that the neoclassical/neoKeynesian synthesis did not.

A second reason is that today macroeconomic theory is consciously scientific in ways that it previously was not. It is directly concerned with bringing theory to data, and the technical tools to do so have advanced sufficiently to where it is a realistic goal to attack the more complicated problem. Although the macroeconomic tradition out of which the DSGE synthesis developed saw itself as scientific and choice-theoretic oriented, it did not have the empirical tools to choose among alternative hypotheses. Because those tools were lacking, explanations of observations not grounded in choice-theoretic models were disregarded. Thus, when James Duesenbury suggested the relative income hypothesis to explain the difference in the slopes of the short-run and long-run consumption functions, it was disregarded as macroeconomists focused on the choice-theoretic explanations: Modigliani's life-cycle savings and Friedman's permanent income hypothesis. As empirical tools have improved, there is a push to choose whatever explanation best fits the data.

A third reason is that the techniques available to researchers have changed, and analytic questions that have been "too hard" are becoming feasible. Up until recently, the profession simply has not had any tools that could deal with the complexity of models in which heterogeneous agents have varying expectations, or to hope to deal analytically with institutions and sociological explanations. At the same time that analytic mathematical and statistical tools were developing, computing power has also developed, allowing researchers to use simulations to gain insight into solutions of complicated systems of equations that previously were intractable. The developments in computing power also open the way to agent-based modeling discussed above. That same advance in computing power makes us much more able to bring the data to the theory, using data to choose among alternative theories. These developments allow researchers to quickly analyze large data sets and pull out information from the data that previously was impossible to discern.

It is these developments that make a Post Walrasian macro feasible today, and it is these developments that this book discusses. I am quite hopeful about these developments because of the way I understand how ideas work their way through the profession.

IS POST WALRASIAN THE CORRECT NAME FOR THE NEW DEVELOPMENTS IN MACRO?

I have called this new work Post Walrasian because I find that the name is useful in helping students distinguish the work I am describing from the Walrasian DSGE alternative. I like it, in part, because it is both inclusive and distinguishing. It captures its connection to the Walrasian DSGE work, but also its difference.

Another aspect of the Post Walrasian distinction that I like is that it supersedes the earlier Keynesian/Classical classifications. I have come to believe that, as a description of what is currently happening in macro, these earlier classifications obscure more than they illuminate. The reason is that the modern debates cross classical/Keynesian/monetarist lines. To understand the modern macro debate one must look at the differences from a quite different perspective, a perspective that the Walrasian/Post Walrasian classification at least partly captures.[21]

Specialists will easily see problems and limitations with the classification, and I would agree with many of them. But classifications are not for specialists; they are for students and nonspecialists, and what one hopes is that the classification provides students and nonspecialists with an entrée

---

[21] Besides me, both Joseph Stiglitz (1993), and Sam Bowles and Herb Gintis (1993) have used the Post Walrasian term although they use it somewhat differently than I do. I suspect many more people have as well. In earlier writing (Colander, 1998), I argued against the new, Post, "neo" prefixes as being inappropriate. But that was when I was thinking of classification systems as being more permanent. Once one sees classification systems as fleeting introductions into changing debates, these prefixes serve the useful purpose of bringing the distinction one is trying to make to mind.

to debates that would otherwise be unintelligible. The current tendency of graduate macro texts to avoid classifications has made macroeconomics seem more unified than it actually is. Thus, I believe that classifications are both useful and necessary, as long as they are seen as temporary and presented as simply an entrée into broader debates, and as having innumerable problems that one will discover as one gets more deeply into the subject.[22]

THE ROLE OF THIS VOLUME

The chapters in this volume are a follow-up of the previous book I edited on Post Walrasian macroeconomics (Colander, ed., 1996). That previous book took on the easy task — outlining the problems with the Walrasian agenda. This book takes up the much harder question: specifying a positive program that constitutes a Post Walrasian macro research agenda. It introduces the reader to the areas that researchers who accept, or at least are willing to consider this broader Post Walrasian vision, are working on. The book is divided into five parts.

Part One, "Where Are We in Macro and How We Got There?" sets the stage for the later, more technical, chapters. The chapters in this part explore the history of macro and develop the ideas that are discussed in the volume in a more general way. The first chapter, "Episodes in a Century of Macroeconomics," by Axel Leijonhufvud, looks at the history of macro, arguing that the modern DSGE approach is a fairly recent development and that the Post Walrasian approach has numerous historical connections. The second chapter, "Post Walrasian Macroeconomics: some Historic Links" by David Colander, takes a shorter range focus, considering more recent history, and argues that the Post Walrasian ideas were central to the

---

[22] Another possible name that some have suggested for the work that I am characterizing as Post Walrasian would be Marshallian, rather than Post Walrasian. Arguments for calling it Marshallian are that the classification Post Walrasian is ambiguous, and not descriptive enough, and that there have been too many "Posts" (and with the overuse of the term post modern, this is a good point). Supporters of the Marshallian classification argue that, if the roots of the approach can be traced to Marshall, why not call the approach Marshallian? I have shied away from the Marshallian terminology for a number of reasons. The first is that I don't see the roots of this approach in Marshall; rather I see them going back further to a broader Classical tradition. Second, few nonhistorians of thought today are familiar with Marshall, and therefore the Marshallian terminology would not be helpful to them. Third, those economists who are familiar with Marshall tend to associate him with an anti-mathematical and anti-statistical approach to economics, and Post Walrasian work is both highly mathematical and highly technical statistically. Thus I believe that the Marshallian classification would mislead them.

classical economics world view and they continued to be considered by economists even as macroeconomics evolved into its modern form. But because the techniques were not sufficiently developed, until recently, this work could not meet the institutional requirements for survival.

The third chapter, "The Problem of Time in the DSGE Model and the Post Walrasian Alternative" by Perry Mehrling, develops an argument similar to Leijonhufvud's, but argues that it is best to see the Post Walrasian alternative as a blending of the Classical approach, in which the past determines the present, with the modern DSGE approach, in which the future determines the present. The Post Walrasian research program integrates these two and sees the present, influenced by both the past and the future, determining the present. The fourth chapter, "Who is Post Walrasian Man?" by Peter Matthews, contrasts the characterization of agents in a Walrasian setting with agents in a Post Walrasian setting, arguing that the Post Walrasian economist's "purposeful action" can be specified in experimental, empirical, and evolutionary game theoretical work. Thus, it places Post Walrasian microfoundations in the behavioralist, expectational, and evolutionary game theory camps.

Part Two, "Edging Away from the DSGE Model," explores work that is closest to the Walrasian dynamic stochastic general equilibrium approach.[23] These chapters demonstrate that it is not a different specification of the macro problem that separates Walrasian and Post Walrasian researchers but, rather, the willingness of Post Walrasians to accept less precise results, and to use nonlinear dynamics, computational modeling techniques, or whatever tools are available, in order to incorporate more heterogeneity among agents in their models. The chapters in this part show how model uncertainty, agent learning, and statistical equilibria models can integrate agent heterogeneity into macromodels.

The first two chapters are by Buz Brock and Steven Durlauf. Their first chapter, "Social Interactions and Macroeconomics," surveys the "good faith attempts to introduce substantive sociological factors into economic modeling" as they relate to aggregate or macroeconomic phenomena. They develop the general structure of social interactions models and the concept of social multipliers, which increases the level of complementarities in the system. They explore the econometric issues that social phenomena create and relate the work to the macroeconomic growth literature, concluding with the observation that, while the social interactions literature is young, as

---

[23] The primary difference with that work is that it is a bit more adventurous in its Walrasian counterpart, but it could have appeared in the recent Phelps volume (Aghion et al., 2003) as well as here.

is the model uncertainty work, the expected payoff from this research warrants its undertaking. The second Brock–Durlauf chapter, "Macroeconomics and Model Uncertainty," considers a similar issue to that considered by Branch – the problem of model uncertainty and how "ignorance of individuals and policy makers about the true structure of the economy should and does affect their respective behavior."[24] They argue that this work is developing in parallel with empirical work in the field and that it offers a large potential for future research. The third chapter, by Bill Branch, "Restricted Perceptions: Equilibrium and Learning in Macroeconomics," considers the problem of expectations and learning, and is representative of the burgeoning literature exploring alternatives to rational expectations. It advocates an approach that closes the macro model by an equilibrium requirement between optimally misspecified beliefs and the stochastic generating process for the economy, calling such an equilibrium a "restricted perceptions equilibrium." Branch argues that restricted perceptions equilibrium models can help explain the loss of potency of oil price shocks in the 1990s.

The final chapter, "Not More So: some Concepts Outside the DSGE Framework" by Masanao Aoki, approaches the problem from another perspective, introducing an entirely different set of mathematical models that can describe macroeconomic equilibria. He argues that many of the DSGE models are too simple to capture the phenomena that they want to capture, and assume away characteristics of the economy that are likely to be important in understanding what is going on and designing policy to deal with it. He argues that models should be as simple as possible, but not more so. He points out that a variety of models and concepts have developed outside of economics to deal with situations where there are enormous amounts of agent interactions, and macro statistical equilibrium in the face of enormous micro level disturbances. In the chapter, he goes through a brief discussion of one of these – random cluster analysis – based on probabilistic combinatorial analysis, and relates it to a model of the Japanese slump, pointing out that it provides a different view of the problem and the solution than did the standard models. He then briefly discusses the problem of multiple equilibria and the tool of ultrametrics. The chapter demonstrates the degree of technicality that must be introduced to even start to deal analytically with the Post Walrasian concerns about agent interaction, as they relate to the aggregate economy.

---

[24] This is an approach they have pioneered in their analysis of Bayesian model selection (Brock, Durlauf, and West, 2003).

Part Three, "Leaping Away from the DSGE Model," considers a quite different approach to undertaking and conceptualizing the macroeconomy. It outlines a computational agent-based modeling research program and its implications for macro. This research program follows quite a different path than the analytic approaches discussed in Part Two. Instead of trying to solve problems analytically, this research program attacks them computationally. That is, it attempts to simulate macro results by creating a virtual economy that mimics the results of the macroeconomy, and which eventually can be used to study complex systems through simulation, not through analytic solutions.

The first chapter, "Agent-based Computational Modeling and Macroeconomics" by Leigh Tesfatsion, discusses the objectives of agent-based computational economics (ACE) modeling and how it differs from simulations used to solve equations and other analytic approaches. She explains that the defining characteristic of ACE modeling is "the constructive grounding in the interactions of autonomous agents," arguing that ACE models allow an alternative entrée to the array of complications that Post Walrasian economics argue must be taken seriously. The next chapter, "Multi-Agent Systems Macro: A Prospectus" by Rob Axtell, takes a more visionary approach and sketches "the kind of agent-based models that might emerge from a computational reformulation of the microfoundations' work." While he admits that we are a long way from the promised land, he argues that, with expected future gains in computational technology, someday we may arrive.

The final chapter, "Agent-based Financial Markets: Matching Stylized Facts with Style" by Blake LeBaron, is an example of how agent-based models are used in studying macroissues. It considers agent-based financial models of financial markets and finds that such models can replicate aspects of the empirical data such as volatility, excess kurtosis, and conditional heteroscedasticity that are impossible to replicate by single representative-agent models. LeBaron's chapter also provides a transition to the next section by showing a central characteristic of Post Walrasian work — that ultimately it is not the logic of the model that determines its success but its ability to fit out-of-sample data.

The chapters in the first two parts dealt with abstract theoretical issues, but they advance no claims that they could provide a solid foundation for policy. All those models were highly complex and tentative, and have questionable implications for policy. This raises the question: how does one undertake macroeconomic policy when all one has are such highly complex and tentative models? The previous two parts of the book deal with that question. Part Four, "Letting the Data Guide Theory," shows the way in which we can proceed econometrically without a firm theoretical anchor.

The first chapter, "The Past as the Future: the Marshallian Approach to Post-Walrasian Econometrics" by Kevin Hoover, provides a broad overview of the theoretical problems with current macroeconometric practices. He explains how the Cowles Commission approach led to the Sims critique and the Lucas critique, which in turn led to the current practice of using structural VARs and calibration. He then discusses the problems with these approaches and briefly introduces a European or "Old World" approach to macroeconometrics. This approach uses a cointegrated "general-to-specific" approach to empirical macro modeling that combines data analysis with identification problems in a quite different way than does Walrasian macroeconometrics.[25] He argues that this approach should be seen as a continuation of a Marshallian methodology, and in that sense, Post Walrasian means giving up what he considers the Walrasian assumption "that to know anything one must know everything," and replace it with the Marshallian attitude "to know anything, you have to dig."

The second chapter, "Old World Econometrics and New World Theory" by Roger Farmer, shows a serious concern about current practices in macroeconometrics and distinguishes two distinct approaches to macro-econometrics. It points out that, in practice, the difference between the two approaches concerns the filtering of data. The calibration method favored by U.S. macroeconometricians "insists on passing data through a two-sided filter," which, he argues, loses information. Yet, he also argues that there is a need to take expectations as forward looking, and therefore describes his agenda as combining "the general-to-specific methodology favored by European econometricians with parsimonious theory-driven rational expectations models." The chapter summarizes the progress he has made in that approach.

The third chapter, "Four Entrenched Notions Post Walrasians Should Avoid" by Robert Basmann, considers the history of what became known as the Cowles Commission approach and argues that there was an alternative Cowles Commission approach that was much more consistent with the approach advocated by Hoover. It was very similar to what I am currently describing as the Post Walrasian macroeconometric approach and was an approach that consciously concentrated on bringing the theory

---

[25] It is called European because it has been advocated and developed by macro-econometricians at LSE and Copenhagen, and tends to be used much more in Europe than in the United States. Farmer calls it "Old World," where "Old World" refers to Europe (Woodford and Farmer, 1997).

to the data. It was an approach that used econometrics as a way of choosing among theories, not as a way of testing theories.

The fourth chapter, "Confronting the Economic Model with the Data" by Søren Johansen, demonstrates the specifics of the complaints made by Post Walrasians about the way in which the DSGE model is related to the data. It looks at a specific example in which a DSGE model is modified into a statistical model so that the likelihood function can be calculated using the Kalman filter. Johansen discusses how easy it is to make mistakes if, when doing this, the researcher does not continually check to see if the chosen model fits the data at hand. In this instance, he finds that in the DSGE work he considers, the assumptions for use of the likelihood function are not fulfilled, and therefore its results are at best unreliable, and most likely meaningless. He concludes by pointing out that "even if the likelihood tests are satisfied, the asymptotic results may not be enough to conduct inference."

The last chapter, "Extracting Information from the Data: A European View on Empirical Macro" by Katarina Juselius and Søren Johansen, demonstrates the alternative cointegrated general-to-specific approach to data and macroeconometrics that is more consistent with a Post Walrasian view of the world. They use this method to arrive at a number of testable hypotheses for Danish data, and demonstrate how the cointegrated VAR approach can do a much better job of accounting for feedback and interaction effects than can the alternatives.

Part Five, "Policy Implications," specifically considers Post Walrasian policy. It is shorter than the other parts because it is the least formally developed of the research agendas. It relies upon empirical work and data analysis combined with a broad sense of theoretical considerations much more than it uses formal models. Post Walrasian macropolicy has no grand conclusions; it is institution and context specific, and takes seriously Brainard's Law, which states that if you don't know what you are doing, for God's sake do it carefully. The first chapter, "Economic Policy in the Presence of Coordination Problems" by Russ Cooper, specifies government macro policy as a coordination failure problem designed to direct the economy to a preferable equilibrium in a multiple-equilibrium world. Cooper argues that while the existence of a multiplicity of equilibria creates problems for government policy, there is also a possibility that government policy interventions may actually help identification of the presence of complementarities.

The final chapter, "Monetary Policy and the Limitations of Economic Knowledge" by Peter Howitt, develops the Post Walrasian lack-of-information theme in relation to a variety of issues in monetary policy, including the central DSGE policy result – inflation targeting. He discusses seven specific lessons that he believes one can learn by thinking about the economy as a complex system that individuals cannot fully understand. He argues that one of our primary goals as monetary theorists should be to find out what kinds of monetary policies promote systemic stability, and he sees inflation targeting as one possible way of doing this.[26] But whatever the actual policy conclusions, he argues that we must "develop objective models that are capable of being confronted with real world data."

CONCLUSION

It should be clear from the above discussion that the Post Walrasian research program is broad reaching and incorporates many different tools and approaches. But there is a connecting theme to Post Walrasian work, and that connecting theme is that economic reality is far more complex than the economic reality being described by the alternative Walrasian approaches. Consequently, if we are to provide appropriate guidance in dealing with that economic reality, we must take that complexity seriously. What makes it possible to do so is technological change, both in analytics and computers, and the work being described here as Post Walrasian is simply a continuation of the Walrasian work with these new tools. These new tools mean that the Post Walrasian approach (1) takes more seriously the problem of multiple equilibria and equilibrium selection mechanisms; (2) takes model uncertainty much more into account; (3) takes seriously the problem of agent heterogeneity and interdependence; (4) takes the problem of agent learning much more seriously; (5) is more driven by empirical regularities than theory in guiding its policies; (6) is more likely to use general-to-specific cointegrated VAR statistical analysis loosely limited by a broad sense of theory rather than to use theory limited by empirical observations; and (7) is far less certain about policy, seeing policy as a way of helping coordinate agents by giving them a focal point.

In my view, Post Walrasian work is a natural evolution in macro-economics thinking. Now that we've dealt with the easy puzzle, let's start dealing with the much more difficult puzzle. Unlike its dissident predecessors, who did not have any "scientific" way of dealing with these

---

[26] Thus, ironically, Post Walrasian thinking can come to a similar conclusion as does Walrasian thinking, but it comes to that conclusion for quite different reasons.

more difficult puzzles, macroeconomists today have methods to approach these puzzles. Nonlinear modeling, behavioral economics, evolutionary game theory, agent-based modeling, and general-to-specific econometrics are all cutting-edge developments that eventually will reshape economics. There are hundreds of dissertations waiting to be written incorporating these new techniques, and it is the development of these new techniques that lead to my optimism that the time for Post Walrasian macro has finally arrived.

PART I

WHERE WE ARE IN MACRO AND
HOW WE GOT THERE

1

Episodes in a Century of Macroeconomics

Axel Leijonhufvud

In this chapter, I give an alternative view to those of Blanchard (2000a) and Woodford (1999) of the history of macroeconomics over the century just past. One cannot attempt to tell the whole story in the space of a chapter. So my account will be episodic. I like to think of the history of thought as a decision tree with the current generation of economists occupying the highest twigs, not all of which will grow into sturdy branches bearing ample fruit. Down below in the tree are a number of more or less important forks, where our predecessors have decided to go one way rather than another. My intention is to revisit some of those forks, to try to understand how people saw the issues at the time and why the majority chose the path that they took, and then ask how the choices made look in hindsight. If we want to learn from the history of thought, I believe, this is the way we have to go about it.

WICKSELL AND FISHER

One hundred years ago, economists had some quantitative information on money, interest and prices, and on very little else. So the story begins with monetary theory and the two great names of Irving Fisher and Knut Wicksell. Fisher and Wicksell shared a passionate concern for distributive justice that is no longer in much evidence among macroeconomists. Their shared conviction that changes in the price level had arbitrary and unfair distributive effects motivated their work on monetary theory. The objective was to learn how the price level could be stabilized.[1]

---

[1] In Fisher's later years, of course, his attention shifted to the question of how to offset the distributive consequences of price level changes through his *compensated dollar* scheme.

Beyond these commonalities, however, the differences between the two are stark. Fisher's quantity theory was basically one of *outside* money, *exogenously* determined. Wicksell's (1898) model of the "pure credit economy" was one with only *inside* money, *endogenously* determined. For several decades, Wicksell's heritage, through the Austrian, Swedish, and Cambridge schools, had by far the stronger influence on theoretical work,[2] although throughout the 1920s, Fisher in the United States and Gustav Cassel in Europe had more say in matters of monetary policy.

The Wicksell connection got lost in the Neoclassical Synthesis confusion from the 1950s onwards, whereas essentially Fisherian ideas experienced a great renaissance in the monetarism of Milton Friedman, Karl Brunner, and Allan Meltzer. I will return to that later.

Wicksell will make a comeback.[3] For the last 30 years or so, monetary economists have been almost exclusively preoccupied with outside money inflations driven by government deficits. The thrust of Wicksell's theory, of course, was that in systems where the gearing between outside money and inside credit is not very tight, the private sector can cause trouble all by itself. The number of bubbles that have burst in recent years around the world — and those still building — should bring him back to mind. Meanwhile, the erosion of effective reserve requirements and of government monopolies of currency production is making the gearing of inside to outside money steadily less reliable (Leijonhufvud 1997).

CAPITAL THEORY

In passing, let us note that Fisher and Wicksell also mark another fork in the doctrine historical decision tree. Wicksell was a proponent of Böhm–Bawerkian capital theory. Despite the persistent attempts by American Austrians to keep it alive, this tradition in capital theory has been all but completely eclipsed in the current vogue for intertemporal general equilibrium theory — the bloodlines of which go straight back to Irving Fisher.[4]

---

[2] Cf. Leijonhufvud (1981)

[3] Michael Woodford's recent book (2003) makes this less of a bold prediction than only a year or two ago.

[4] The revival of Fisher's interest theory is to be very largely credited to Jack Hirshleifer (1958, 1970).

Fisher did not have a capital theory in a proper sense (and neither does IGE theory), but he showed how a theory of intertemporal prices could be built on choice-theoretical foundations, assuming smooth convexity of production sets in all dimensions. The reason that Austrian capital theory has not managed to survive in the latter half of the twentieth century, I surmise, is that nonconvexity is absolutely central to it. It is in essence, a translation of Smithian division of labor theory into a sequential temporal context and the *productivity of increased roundaboutness* is Smithian increasing returns in a somewhat new dress. And increasing returns will not fit in Fisherian IGE theory.

THE METAMORPHOSIS OF
NEOCLASSICISM

Before proceeding with macro issues, we need to pay some attention to microfoundations because the evolution of macroeconomics in the second half of the twentieth century, as I see it, has to a large extent been driven by a metamorphosis of our understanding of what might constitute appropriate such foundations. This metamorphosis of common understanding has almost escaped notice, not only because it has been slow and gradual but also because it has taken place at a conceptual level below formalized economic theory.

Optimality at individual and competitive equilibrium at aggregate levels are the hallmarks of what we mean by neoclassical theory today. But the meanings attached to *"optimality"* or *"maximization,"* to *"equilibrium"* and to *"competition"* are context dependent and the conceptual context is today utterly different from what it was 100 years ago. Neoclassical theory, as is true of so many things, *ain't what it used to be.*

In the early decades of the twentieth century, all economists distinguished between *statics* and *dynamics*. By "dynamics," they did *not* mean *intertemporal* choices or equilibria but instead the adaptive *processes* that were thought to converge on the states analyzed in *static* theory. The early neoclassicals conceived of both *optima* and *equilibria* as point attractors of individual and collective adaptive processes, respectively. Statics referred to the parts of theory that could be formalized — more or less. In contrast, individual adaptive learning and market equilibrating processes were loosely sketched at best. Not much of

substance was known about them and, in any case, next to
nothing was known about a mathematics suitable to formalize them.
Nonetheless, it is a grave mistake to identify the original neoclassical theories with just the static models. One should recognize
instead the technical limitations that prevented generations of
theorists from even attempting to formalize the dynamics underlying
the propositions of static theory. In so saying, however, I do not intend
to suggest that modern neoclassical theory differs from the older
theory mainly in having overcome these technical difficulties. It is more
accurate to say that very little has been done to address the unfinished
business of the older neoclassical theory. By and large, it remains
unfinished.

The conceptual issues that divide old and modern neoclassical theory
are both numerous and important. The transformation of how we have
come to understand neoclassical theory began, as I see it, when instead of
interpreting various optimality conditions as characterizing the attractor
of some loosely described adaptive process, we began to think of
*constrained optimization as the way in which economic subjects make
decisions* (Leijonhufvud, 2004b). If observed behavior is to be interpreted
as reflecting optimal choices, one is forced to assume that economic
agents know their opportunity sets in all potentially relevant dimensions.
If this is true for all, the system must be in equilibrium always.
Generalizing to intertemporal choice and choice under uncertainty – and
the consequent equilibria – comes easy. The end point of this evolution
has agents calculate optima over infinite dimensional spaces and
coordinating their choices perfectly – with or without the help of
markets. The train of logic departs from a picture that economists of a
hundred years ago would recognize as familiar – Robinson Crusoe
allocating effort between fish and bananas, say – but barrels along at
uncomfortable speed, picking up loads of subscripts on the way, into a
fantasy land where the assumptions made about what people are able to
know, to forecast and to calculate would leave them utterly bewildered
and incredulous.

Rather than belabor this metamorphosis of neoclassical
economics further, let me simply reproduce a table that I have used on
a couple of previous occasions (e.g. Leijonhufvud, 1999). Here I use
"Classical" for the older neoclassical tradition in order to stress its
link to the *magnificent dynamics* (Baumol, 1951) of the British Classical
School.

	Classical	Modern
Objective of theory	Laws of motion of the system	Principles of efficient allocation
Individual motivation	Maximize utility or profit (intent)	Maximize utility or profit (performance)
Individual behavior	Adaptive, "Procedural rationality" (often gradient climbing)	Optimizing choice, "Substantive rationality"
Behavior and Time	Backward-looking causal	Forward-looking teleological
Cognitive competence	Capable of learning, well-adapted "locally"	"Unbounded"
Role of institutions	Essential in guiding behavior; making behavior of others predictable	Problematic: Why use money? Why do firms exist?
Equilibrium concept	Constancy of observed behavior (point attractor)	Mutual consistency of plans

MARSHALL'S AGENTS

I like to use Marshall as my main illustration of the points just made. He fits here because Marshall plus Wicksell will bring me to Keynes.

Book V of Marshall's *Principles* is usually regarded as the core of his contribution. That is debatable but what is not debatable is that it survived the longest. Yet, I believe it is most often misunderstood as a seriously flawed version of "Modern" theory. It is more accurately understood as an early attempt at what we today label *agent-based economics*. Recall that Marshall worked with individual demand-price and supply-price schedules. (This is why he drew his diagrams with quantity on the horizontal axis, etc.) From this, it is obvious that he did not build from choice-theoretical optimization. Instead, the demand-price and supply-price schedules give rise to simple decision-rules that I like to refer to as "Marshall's Laws of Motion."

> For consumers: if demand-price exceeds market price, increase consumption; in the opposite case, cut back.
>
> For producers: if supply-price exceeds the price realized, reduce output; in the opposite case, expand.[5]

---

[5] And for the capitalist: if the rate of profit exceeds the normal, add to capacity, etc. But I will confine the discussion here to the short run.

And we should imagine a similar rule for price-setters:

> For middlemen: if inventory turnover slows down, reduce prices to both the customers and suppliers; in the opposite case, raise them.

Please note for future reference that, if all this is going on at once, God only knows what kind of messy nonlinear dynamics would result. Marshall tamed the dynamics by assuming a strong ranking of adjustment speeds that gave him a tidy ordering of market day, short-run and long-run equilibria. These equilibria, of course, have no counterparts in choice-theoretically based modern constructions.

For now, the point is this: up through the 1920s, virtually all economists were convinced that *as long as everyone obeyed Marshall's Laws of Motion, it was a foregone conclusion that an economic system would go to a full employment attractor.* The intellectual situation was, in this important respect, the same as the one we have returned to in the last couple of decades, namely, the general belief that only "rigidities" or "inflexibilities" of some sort can explain departures from general equilibrium.

Keynes began to doubt this presumption already while writing the *Treatise on Money* and became increasingly convinced that it had to be wrong as the Great Depression deepened.

KEYNES

Wicksell had been critical, scornful even, of the attempts by others to use his "cumulative process" in the explanation of business cycles. His reason, I would infer, was that the "neutral equilibrium" of the price level could hardly apply to real magnitudes.[6] It had to be a purely nominal phenomenon.

In the *Treatise*, Keynes used Wicksell's natural vs. market rate concepts. He traced the problems of Britain in the late 1920s to a market rate in excess of natural rate. As in Wicksell, this leads to a cumulative deflation. Like everyone else, then and now, he noted that wages are sticky so that deflationary pressure is apt to produce unemployment. But this is a common sense appendage and not a part of his model which can only handle full employment.

---

[6] Recall that he used a cylinder resting on a plane as his illustration of "neutral equilibrium." Displaced, it would have no tendency to return to its prior equilibrium.

However, in a rather odd passage, known as the "banana parable" (Barens 1989), he toys with the (not very convincing) idea that real saving exceeding real investment might produce a cumulative process ending in total collapse of output. Subsequently, and eventually with some help from Richard Kahn, he worked out how the multiplier process would converge and not implode. It would converge on a state of less than full employment.

Could this state be an equilibrium?[7] Keynes knew that if the economy stayed (somehow) at full employment, accumulating pressure on the market rate would eventually have to bring it into line with the natural rate. He also knew that if the two rates were equal, so that investment equaled saving out of full employment income, wage flexibility would guarantee the achievement of full employment. But if the intertemporal and the labor market coordination failures occurred together, general obedience to Marshall's Laws of Motion did not seem to guarantee convergence to the full employment equilibrium. The sequence of events is important: (1) declining prospective returns make investment fall below full employment saving; (2) liquidity preference prevents the interest rate from falling enough to close the gap;[8] (3) real output and income fall until saving equals investment. At this point, the real interest rate is too high, but the excess demand for "bonds" is zero, so there is no market pressure for it to change. At the same time, wages are roughly what they should be in general equilibrium — neither labor's productivity, nor the outside money stock has declined — but unemployment is putting downward pressure on wages. The price that is "wrong" does not change, whereas the price that is "right" tends away from that level. So Keynes concludes that wage stickiness is actually good for you in this situation since a high degree of flexibility would set in motion a Wicksellian deflation that might wreck the financial system without restoring full employment.

It is finding this instability of the full employment state that motivates and justifies Keynes's claim to a more *general theory*. The adaptive dynamics of his theory are more general than his predecessors. And it

---

[7] Equilibrium *nota bene* in a Marshallian, obviously not Walrasian, sense.

[8] In the *Treatise*, Keynes had a nice analysis of liquidity preference showing how the decline in expected return to capital causes ripples of substitutions all along the term structure. At the shortest end, the banks do not find returns attractive enough to relend all the funds that flow back in repayment of loans as production declines. Thus the process shows an induced decline in the stock of *inside* money, the counterpart of which is an increased demand for *outside* money as the banks act to bolster their own liquidity positions. (Note that here, there is a very good reason to prefer the term "liquidity preference" to the ambiguous "demand for money.") If Keynes had retained this analysis in the *General Theory*, we would have been saved quite a bit of later confusion!

makes it possible to understand mass unemployment as resulting from causes other than rigidities or waves of contagious laziness.

Why doesn't the system "automatically" straighten itself out? Because, Keynes maintained, saving is not an effective demand for future consumer goods and the offer of unemployed labor to work is not an effective demand for present consumer goods.[9] *Effective* excess demands summed across all markets do not necessarily sum to zero. In this sense, therefore, Say's Law does not hold: *Supply cannot be counted on to create its own demand.* So, from the rejection of Say's Law, stems the original rationale for stabilization policy, understood as aggregate demand management.

But Keynes did not get everything right and besides he was not generally well-understood. But before taking note of some of the confusions and their consequences for later developments, we had better stand back and take stock a bit.

HOW ECONOMISTS UNDERSTAND THE WORLD THEN AND NOW

At about mid century, the experience of the Great Depression and the intellectual influence of Keynes (and others) had combined to instill in most economists a worldview[10] which saw the private sector as unstable, riddled with market failures, and prone to fluctuations amplified by multiplier and accelerator effects. But most economists also believed that a benevolent, competent, and solvent government, dependable in its democratic role as the honest agent of the electorate, could stabilize the economy and ameliorate most market failures.

Fifty years later, mainstream economists believe that the economy maintains itself on an intertemporal equilibrium path. As long as they are not disturbed by stupid policies, markets will take care of all coordination problems. The coordinated timepath may be somewhat less than ideal. If labor market "inflexibilities" are tolerated, the natural rate of

---

[9] An "effective demand failure" occurs when some category of transactions assumed to be feasible in general equilibrium models cannot be carried through. In addition to the two types of such failures prominent in the *General Theory*, a third type of effective demand failure may occur when, in a financial system loaded down with bad loans, the promise of revenues from future output cannot be used to exert effective demand for the present resources required to produce that future output. The traditional Keynesian deficit-spending policy was designed to relieve the liquidity-constraints on households. Japanese experience in the 1990s would seem to indicate that this is not the right policy in the case of an effective demand failure of this third type.

[10] Here I am paraphrasing my paper in the Fitoussi Festschrift (Leijonhufvud, 2004a).

unemployment may be quite high. And governments are seen as prone to excessive deficits and inflationary finance, as constitutionally time-inconsistent, and as addicted to playing the unstable Phillips-curve for no good reason and to no good effect. Macropolicy no longer means the active management of aggregate demand, but rather the political art of finding ways to constrain governments.

The main task for the history of the economic thought of the second half of the twentieth century must surely be to explain this 180-degree turn in the worldview of the representative economist. That will not be accomplished here. In particular, it is not possible to do justice to the macro-econometric work which has given us a far better and richer quantitative picture of the complex system under study. But some of the conceptual elements in this radical transformation can be readily identified.

ON KEYNES'S PROBLEMS AND
PROBLEMS WITH KEYNES

To begin with, let us consider the flaws in the Economics of Keynes and subsequently in what became Keynesian Economics.

First, one should perhaps mention some beliefs that Keynes held that present-day economists (at least in the *first world*) have little reason to share. Among them (1) the belief inherited from Ricardo, Marx, and Marshall that the accumulation of capital would sooner or later depress the marginal efficiency of capital to near zero.[11] Also (2) the conviction that the modern economy has a chronic tendency to save more than could be profitably invested.[12] Furthermore (3) the view that workers live more or less hand-to-mouth, so that consumption is simply a function of current income. This last proposition may have had some verisimilitude in the early part of the twentieth century which, obviously, it has since lost. The second and the third together may, I think, explain why the *General Theory* fails to emphasize sufficiently the financial crash as the key factor in the Depression.[13]

---

[11] This is the proposition that Allan Meltzer in his book on Keynes (1988) saw as central to Keynes's theory.

[12] For the last couple of decades American economists have had little reason to worry about too much household saving. Keynes, one may surmise, might have attributed the low rate of U.S. unemployment in the 1990s to the great decline in the American saving rate rather than to labor market flexibility.

[13] In various papers written between the *Treatise* and the *General Theory*, Keynes was both clear and forceful on the role of financial factors in the depression. Hyman Minsky developed these elements in Keynes's thought much further (e.g., Minsky [1975]).

All that said, Keynes had one thing right that is most often missing from modern macro. He knew that macroeconomic catastrophies still happen and that, when they do, they threaten the social order.

What is more interesting than Keynes's outdated beliefs are the technical difficulties that he faced. Recall that combining Marshall's Laws of Motion for price and output in an isolated market results in a nonlinear process. Marshall "tamed" it by assuming that one could take output as "constant" while price adjusted. The justification for this was tenuous at best by the 1930s.[14] Consider then, a system of multiple and interdependent such markets with varying lag structures, etc. A complex, multi-dimensional, nonlinear nightmare! Is it likely that one might find a sensible and useful *static* model for such a multi-market Marshallian dynamic system? This would require finding a partition of the endogenous variables such that when the slow-moving variables of the one set are "frozen," the others can reasonably be assumed to converge rapidly to a point-attractor. Furthermore, this partition should be reasonably stable so that it would not have to be changed each time the question posed to the model is changed. It is not obvious that the real world would always oblige the economist by conforming to these requirements.

Moreover, this was not the only technical difficulty. Keynes's explanation of "involuntary unemployment" involved, as we have seen, prices diverging from their general equilibrium values in a particular way. To explain why the system did not tend strongly towards the full employment state, Keynes did not only have to model the structure of relative prices but needed also to keep track of the flow-of-funds through the system since workers (at least) were liquidity constrained.[15] Keynes thought he eventually had a static ("equilibrium") model that would satisfy these requirements.[16] And IS–LM seemed to him at first and to countless others later, a fully adequate formal representation of the theory.[17]

---

[14] John Hicks (1965, Chapter 5; 1989, Chapter 3) used to note that this might have been a plausible ranking when Marshall first began working in economics but that it will not fit the later "fix-price" markets for branded commodities.

[15] The "hydraulic" element of Keynesian economics to use Coddington's term.

[16] Hicks who had wrestled with this kind of problem along the lines learned from Erik Lindahl was impressed as evidenced by his original review of the *General Theory* (Hicks, 1936).

[17] Hicks who was, of course, one of the co-inventors of IS–LM came to conclude many, many years later that the model was deeply flawed because the "partitioning" did not make sense. The length of the "periods" relevant to the equilibration of IS and of LM could not be the same, even approximately (see Hicks, 1983).

But all was not well. Keynes got himself into a real muddle over the theory of interest. Reasoning that since saving and investment determined real income (and therefore not the rate of interest), liquidity preference and the money stock must determine the interest rate (and not the price level), he on the one hand provided a spurious rationale for the pernicious doctrine of saving as an anti-social activity and, on the other, severed any understandable relationship to the quantity theory. It is worth noting, however, that the manner in which he arrived at the liquidity preference (LP) theory of interest determination while rejecting the loanable funds (LF) theory shows beyond any doubt that he was thinking *not* in terms of a simultaneous equation model, but in terms of adaptive dynamics.

The current generation of economists have been taught to think of Keynes simply as an incompetent. However, anyone who has worked with agent-based models will appreciate the near-impossibility of making headway with Keynes's problem with the tools he had at hand. Not many people understood his theory in these terms, however. No one could make sense of the Liquidity Preference vs. Loanable Funds issue in a simultaneous equation context, for example. Yet, the LP theory ruled for decades, made most explicit in the so-called "Paradox of Thrift" which was treated as an important Keynesian doctrine for students to know in the 1950s only to gradually fade out in successive editions of Samuelson's textbook until it was no longer made explicit but, like the grin of the Cheshire Cat, still lurked within the simple Keynesian cross.

In the IS–LM-based Keynesian literature, one does not find many inklings of the adaptive dynamics behind the explicit statics. The model could not be used to explain why Keynes rejected Say's Law, or what role effective demand failures played in the theory, or what Keynes himself meant by "involuntary unemployment." But despite all that IS–LM did have important "Keynesian" properties. In particular, it lent itself to all sorts of exercises showing how aggregate demand management might be good for you. It did so because, although often referred to as an "aggregative general equilibrium" model, it wasn't. It did not obey Say's Law but permitted all manner of violations of it.

LOSING TRACK

The "Neoclassical Synthesis" was so named by Paul Samuelson. But many people had a hand in it, all converging on the same conclusion, namely, that Keynesian unemployment was simply a consequence of money wages being too high relative to nominal aggregate demand and that its persistence was due to downward wage rigidity. Of all the IS–LM exercises by various writers, Modigliani's famous paper (1944) shows the logical progression to an illogical conclusion most clearly. He first provided the static equations for a "classical" model with (of course) a full employment solution. Next, he added first the restriction $w > w^*$, letting the labor market clearing condition go, and thus obtained his basic case of unemployment. Next, starting again from the "classical" reference case, he considered the restriction $r > r^*$, and once more let the necessary violation of the classical equilibrium fall on the labor market. This case, which he termed "Keynes' special case," he identified with the Liquidity Trap and not with the old Wicksellian theme. So, nobody much mourned it, when Patinkin (1948) demonstrated that a sufficiently strong Pigou-effect should dispose of the Trap case. Modigliani (1963) later concurred. Such was the undeniable logic of IS–LM comparative statics.[18] So Keynesianism was left with the ages-old rigid wages case.

With this conclusion, Keynes's intertemporal coordination problem basically disappeared from view and so did the relative price structure of the original theory.[19] Keynesian economics then evolved into a curious hybrid form. The Modigliani-Brumberg-Ando consumption function, Jorgensen's investment function, Tobin's and Markowitz's portfolio theory, were all built according to approved neoclassical recipes but were then inserted into an IS–LM structure that lacked the budget constraints of GE models and therefore remained free of the shackles of Say's Law. At the policy-level, the focus was altogether on the relationship between nominal aggregate demand and the money wage rate, best exemplified by the simple calculations of the high employment surplus and the multiplier at the core of Arthur Okun's work at the Council of Economic Advisors (Okun, 1983). This was the context in which the assumption of a stable Phillips curve was so very convenient. The large econometric models of Brookings or FRB-MIT with their hundreds of equations and identities were basically little more than disaggregated versions of the Keynesian cross.

---

[18] One has to remember that IS–LM was considered "mathematical economics" at that time.

[19] Eventually leading to textbooks complementing IS–LM with an aggregate supply function! As Barens (1997), Colander (1995), and others have pointed out, supply or supply-price functions are of course already subsumed in the IS reduced form.

THE MONETARIST CHALLENGE

It was this brand of Keynesianism that had to contend with the Monetarism of Friedman, Brunner, and Meltzer. In teaching, I've found it convenient to divide the Monetarist controversy into five rounds (cheating a bit on the actual chronology):

Round I: The exchange between Friedman-Meiselman (1963) and Ando-Modigliani (and others) (1965) on the issue of the "relative stability" of Velocity and the Multiplier. The Friedman-Meiselman paper was received with much irritation by Keynesians because of its simplistic Econ 1 structure. But it was in fact a clever polemical thrust against applied Keynesianism of the Okun variety. Round I was significant mainly because Ando and Modigliani were unable to "win" but could achieve only a "draw" in the statistical context. This helped make Quantity Theory reasoning respectable again.

Round II: The St. Louis Fed paper on the relative effectiveness of monetary and fiscal policy. The Andersen-Jordan regressions (1968) strongly supported the efficacy of money stock policy. Their results were less than conclusive with respect to fiscal policy, but it took some time before this was realized.

Round III: The main Keynesian argument against Monetarism had been that empirical evidence on the interest elasticities of IS and LM ran strongly against the presumption of stable monetary velocity and strong effectiveness of money stock policy. When Friedman presented his "theory of nominal income" in IS–LM terms (Friedman, 1970, 1971), Tobin and others thought the battle finally won (Tobin, 1974). In response, Friedman modified his and Anna Schwartz's earlier account (1963) of monetary transmission. In place of the conventional focus on transmission via real interest rates, he now stressed the response of nominal income expectations to monetary policy action. Deep flaws in mainstream IS–LM now began to become apparent. The IS–LM curves were not independent of each other but linked through nominal expectations. The standard IS–LM comparative statics — shifting one of the curves, keeping the other fixed — were not valid in this case. Everything hinged on how fast expectations adapted to a nominal shock.

Round IV: Friedman also had to deal with a stylized fact that ever since Thomas Tooke had always been raised against monetary impulse hypotheses of the business cycle, namely, the so-called Gibson's

Paradox. Tooke's (and later, Gibson's) point was that interest rates and the price level tend to be positively correlated over the cycle whereas money supply impulses should cause them to be inversely correlated. Friedman's defense on this issue was based on a "dynamic" version of the quantity theory,[20] which meant simply the quantity equation in first differences – proportional rates of change of money, prices, and real output instead of their levels – supplemented by the Fisher equation. Again, adaptive expectations were the crux. As people caught on to the inflationary effects of a rise in the growth rate of money, inflation expectations would raise the nominal interest rate above the more or less constant real rate. Hence the theory thus reformulated was consistent with Gibson's paradox.

Round V: Rounds III and IV showed Friedman playing skillful defense against Keynesian criticisms. But the reformulated Monetarist model also proved an ideal weapon of attack on the Keynesian reliance on the stability of the Phillips curve. His 1967 Presidential Address (Friedman, 1968) became a pivotal contribution. Hailed by many as the most important paper in the second half of the century, the theory advanced in it had two main components that need to be considered separately.

The first component is, again, the role of inflation expectations returning here as the source of the instability of the Phillips locus. If money is neutral and if expectations adapt to (or anticipate) inflation, then higher growth rates of money should shift the locus upwards. So it should be "unstable" in relation to variations in the growth rate of *outside* (neutral) money. Friedman's theory gained immense prestige when the inflation of the 1970s verified its predictions that higher inflation would raise nominal interest rates and prove the Phillips curve to be unstable.

In retrospect, the American inflation decade has come to seem an exceptional episode. The Phillips curve seemed "stable" (although the criteria are less than clear) before and has regained an appearance of stability as the memory of the inflation has faded. Similarly, the idea that an expansionary monetary policy would raise (nominal) interest rates was a commonplace[21] in the late 1970s and early 1980s, but by the 1990s the old central bank verities had returned – easy monetary policy meant lower, not higher, interest rates. The Monetarist theory that won out over

---

[20] The "dynamic quantity theory" was fully worked out by Michael Darby and William E. Gibson (see Darby's [1976] textbook).

[21] And remained, of course a commonplace in Latin America, for example.

Keynesianism in the early 1970s, and the basic properties of which were brought into sharper focus in the Monetarist Rational Expectations model of the ensuing decade, runs into empirical trouble when applied to data before or after its heyday.

The major Monetarists never considered the distinction between inside and outside money to be important. Friedman dealt with M_2 in effect "as if" it was outside money, and the "money supply" in Lucas's work is also treated in this way. With the signal exception of James Tobin, the Keynesians usually ignored the distinction as well.[22] My tentative inference is that the "great American inflation" of the 1970s was a Fisherian outside money inflation and that the rest of the twentieth century has been largely Wicksellian. In Real Business cycle theory, of course, money stock variations over the cycle also have to be interpreted as endogenous movements in inside money.

NAIRU

The second component of Friedman's famous paper was, of course, the "natural rate of unemployment." Friedman defined the concept but Edmund Phelps (1967, 1968) earned the priority for providing a micro-founded model with the natural rate property. The two components – endogenous inflation expectations and NAIRU – were closely intertwined in Friedman's account of the instability of the price level on either side of the natural rate. But, although endogenous inflation expectations are necessary to produce the vertical long-run Phillips curve, the natural rate is not necessary in order to explain how inflationary expectations make the Phillips curve unstable.

The general acceptance of the NAIRU postulate is to my mind one of the most curious episodes in the whole muddled history of macroeconomics. One has little difficulty accepting the argument that a policy of attempting to maintain overfull employment by engineering an outside money inflation would produce the kind of instability postulated by Friedman. But surely this is not inconsistent with the possibility that the "stable" (sic!?) historical scatter of observations might have been produced by some real business cycle mechanism together with a monetary policy allowing accommodating endogenous variations in inside money.

---

[22] Cf. esp. Tobin (1963). Years ago, I once asked Jim Tobin why he had not pressed this issue more insistently in his long-running battles with Monetarism. He answered to the effect that "if you have said your piece once and people won't listen, there is no point repeating yourself." The present chapter, I am afraid, violates that precept from beginning to end.

The absence of any effective Keynesian opposition is particularly striking and can only be understood as a result of the Neoclassical Synthesis. Keynesians who accepted the Synthesis were themselves convinced that only wage rigidity stood in the way of full employment. The saving-investment problem had been forgotten. The easy objection to the NAIRU doctrine would have been that wage flexibility alone would not get you full employment unless real saving equaled real investment at full employment output. If intertemporal coordination were to be assured, as Keynes knew, wage flexibility would do the trick. The characteristic Keynesian instability of full employment is then precluded.

The natural rate of unemployment doctrine reinstates Say's Law. Supply once again creates its own demand. All that is needed for full coordination is that everyone obey Marshall's Laws of Motion — adaptation in response to excess demands and supplies in the various markets will make the system home in on the fully coordinated state. Just wait for some frictions to be overcome and general equilibrium will arrive.

Because Keynes's theory had not been very well understood, it took time for the profession to realize that Say's Law was again in force. The logical consequences became clear only gradually as general equilibrium models became the standard in macroeconomics. The budget constraints of GE models will not allow effective demand failures and, consequently, can provide no tenable rationale for aggregate demand policies. IS—LM was still taught to uncountable thousands of undergraduates and one hears whispers that here and there policy-makers might still use it. In IS—LM you may still hew to (Alvin) Hansen's Law, as Robert Clower used to call it, namely, that "demand calls forth its own supply." But where Say's Law is in force, macropolicy can only be the supply-side policy.

The Rational Expectations revolution let loose a new wave of technical innovation in macroeconomics, but the natural rate doctrine, in my opinion, has been the real watershed separating the verities of modern from those of the older, Keynesian macroeconomics. It does not require a lot of rationality but "only" (the never proven) stability of general equilibrium. And that postulate takes us basically all the way from the economists' worldview of 50 years ago to that of today.

COMPLETING THE METAMORPHOSIS: RATIONAL EXPECTATIONS

From its inception the rational expectations development has been widely thought of as a "revolution." Undeniably there has been a revolution, taking us from one worldview to a completely different one. But the revolution stemmed mainly from the Phelps-Friedman natural rate of unemployment and its implicit reassertion of the stability of full employment equilibrium. Rational expectations played an important role in ferreting out the "New Classical" implications, particularly the various policy ineffectiveness or irrelevance propositions (e.g. Sargent and Wallace, 1975).

If Friedman's Presidential Address was the most important macroeconomics paper in the last 50 years, Lucas' "Expectations and the Neutrality of Money" (1972a) must surely be rated a close second. However, as a theory of what causes business fluctuations or a theory of how monetary policy works, it is seen in retrospect largely as a failure. The eclipse of Lucasian Monetarism, moreover, has brought with it also that of the Monetarism of Friedman and Brunner and Meltzer — although the latter never accepted the idea that only "unanticipated" money matters. Yet, as a model of how to model, Lucas (1972a) retains enormous influence, amplified of course by subsequent contributions of Lucas himself, Sargent, Prescott, and others.

From the perspective taken in this chapter, rational expectations figures mainly as a bridge from macroeconomics to the intertemporal generalization of neoclassical *statics* of Arrow and Debreu. The intertemporal version of the Walrasian general equilibrium model represents the logical culmination of the metamorphosis of neoclassical theory that had been underway for decades. Walras had already found that his mode of construction precluded any kind of *adaptive market process*. His various *tâtonnements* were purely virtual thought experiments, not representations of possible interaction processes. The temporary equilibrium method of Lindahl and Hicks, and later of Grandmont, had been an attempt to compromise so as to retain a vestige of learning and adaptation in a structure where each period was a Walrasian equilibrium but where the intertemporal trajectory of the system was not an equilibrium time-path.[23] In intertemporal general equilibrium constructions, the information required for each individual optimization includes the equilibrium prices for all future (contingent) markets. Hence *everyone's choices have to be reconciled before anyone's choice can be made*. Rational expectations is a clever way of proceeding as if this has somehow been accomplished.

---

[23] Lucas's signal extraction model also had a temporary market clearing state which, however, would revert to a full equilibrium as soon as the true value of the money supply was known. With the decline of interest in "unanticipated money," this vestige of the temporary equilibrium method seems pretty much to have disappeared from the New Classical view.

But the problem then becomes how these expectations are learned and what are the properties of the system that provides the environment in which this learning takes place.

In recent years, learning has become a priority topic in macroeconomics (Sargent, 1991; Evans and Honkapojha, 2001) although motivated, perhaps, more by the problem of multiple IGE equilibria, than by the stability issue. About 35 years ago, Arrow and Hahn (1971, Chapters 13 and 14) sized up the state of knowledge on the stability of general equilibrium. The main claim they made for their survey was that it was valuable to know *how very little* can be asserted about the stability of economies with production and without recontracting. So far, I believe,[24] the new macroliterature on learning has not provided grounds for a more positive assessment — it tends to believe that agents learn the properties of an underlying system that can be presumed to be stable.

A POST WALRASIAN MACROECONOMICS?

A small minority of macroeconomists, to which I belong, regards intertemporal general equilibrium theory as an intellectual trap from which there is no escape if we continue to obey the "Walrasian code" (Howitt, 1996). For those who would contemplate escape from this modern neoclassicism, the question becomes: what direction to take? On that question, however, one cannot expect unanimity even within that minority.

My own predilection is to return to the unfinished business of the original neoclassical economics. Marshall has been unfairly treated for several decades now by people who did not understand what he was trying to do and thought him no more than a muddled version of Walras. But today, he would make a better patron saint than Walras. I have tried to make clear above how utterly impossible as a research program — impossible in macroeconomics at any rate — this neoclassical economics was 100 years ago, or 70 years ago, or for that matter 50, 40, 30, or perhaps, even 20 years ago. Complex dynamical systems full of nonlinearities and sundry time-lags have been completely beyond the state of the arts until rather recently. Of course, formidable challenges still remain. But mathematicians and systems scientists today know a lot more about partial differential equations than, in Marshall's time, did Poincaré. And market

---

[24] The qualifier is unfortunately necessary. I have sampled this literature but am far from having surveyed it.

experiments and agent-based simulations make it possible to investigate problems that Marshall and Keynes could only "talk" about.

For myself, I hope to be around long enough to see agent-based simulations on small macrosystems that will give us a better basis for judging how seriously to take the instability issues raised by Keynes — and, conversely, how seriously we should take general equilibrium theory.

A SMALL POSTSCRIPT

Could it have gone otherwise? That is of course a rather futile question but may be worth some reflection nonetheless.

Rational reconstructions of scientific or other intellectual developments tend to lend them an air of inevitability in a way that is rather similar to how economists' theories of rational behavior make that behavior inevitable. The history of macroeconomics does not lack for developmental sequences of the sort where a question, once raised, is eventually seen to have only one answer, which in turn raises a new question which is in time seen also to have a definite answer within some given frame of reference. From a certain point, the metamorphosis of neoclassical economics, as I have called it, was a logical progression of this sort, although it took decades before the full implications were realized. Much of the Monetarist Controversy seems to me also to partake of this logical inevitability.

But these logical chains are only part of the story. The questions from which they start may sometimes stem from a misunderstanding or be posed in such a manner as to give rise to misunderstandings, but this is clear — if it is ever clear — only in retrospect and then usually as a result of a shift in the frame of reference. At this metalevel, the contention is not just a "simple" matter of logic or of empirical evidence. In the twentieth century story of macroeconomics, Keynes, Hicks, Samuelson, Friedman, and Lucas are all examples of men who by force of personal intellect have had a profound influence on the course that economics has taken. If in retrospect we are critical of some of the twists and turns of that course, we have to recognize that their influence has been so great in large part due to the lack of countervailing intellectual force on the opposing side.

2

Post Walrasian Macroeconomics:
some Historic Links

David Colander

In many ways the developments in the last 50 years in macro — Keynesian economics, the IS—LM model, and the New Classical Revolution — were deviations from Classical thought that took seriously the complexity of the macroeconomy, and did not see the macroeconomy as controllable. The Post Walrasian work discussed in this volume is beginning to take that complexity seriously, and is beginning to struggle with developing a theoretical foundation for a complex-system view of the macroeconomy. This chapter discusses aspects of the history of macroeconomics, providing some historical links for Post Walrasian work, and explores why that earlier work did not succeed.

I begin with a brief review of Classical macroeconomics and I discuss the Neoclassical—NeoKeynesian synthesis, the New Classical Revolution, and the DSGE synthesis, and then I conclude with a brief discussion of why Post Walrasian work is more closely tied to Classical economics than is the DSGE synthesis.

CLASSICAL MACROECONOMICS

The consideration of macro issues has been around since the beginning of economics, but the actual corpus of work fitting into a course entitled macroeconomics began only in the 1950s, reflecting an evolution of thinking in macro that was closely tied to the Keynesian revolution. Before the Keynesian revolution, a formal macroeconomic theory was considered too complicated to deal with; it pushed the chain of reasoning beyond what the empirical evidence or the analytic structure could support. For Classical economists, macroeconomic issues were beyond formal science and had to be dealt with by what might be called "informal science" — loose general laws that served to guide thinking about macro issues.[1]

One such law was the quantity theory, which was a loose summary of insights about the way in which real and nominal forces interacted. The quantity theory was not a formal theory in the way we think of a theory today, but instead it was a rough reference point. It was generally accepted because it embodied understanding that cleared up earlier confusions that had permeated discussions of macroissues, specifically, the failure to draw a distinction between a price level and a relative price, and to distinguish between real and nominal, index-dependent, issues.

Debates about the application of the quantity theory to real world policy, such as the debate between the banking school and the currency school, or between the bullionists and the anti-bullionists, occurred periodically.[2] These debates concerned how much institutional structure to fit into the quantity theory analysis when drawing out policy conclusions. Because the quantity theory was only a loose guide, economists on both sides of these debates accepted the general insights it embodied, but they differed in the way they saw institutional structure slowing the adjustment process and complicating the real-world macroequilibration process. Almost all the macropolicy debates that we are currently having in the early 2000s can be seen in these earlier debates, where they were often discussed with amazing sophistication.

A second guiding vision of Classical macroeconomics was Say's Law, which was another loose summary of insights rather than a formal theory. It concerned the way in which markets were connected, and, like the quantity theory, was designed to avoid the logical mistakes that earlier writers had made in thinking about the aggregate economy. Say's Law stated that the simple arguments that increased aggregate production would automatically lead to gluts were incorrect. Like the quantity theory, Say's Law was subject to many different interpretations, and was primarily a statement meant to avoid logical fallacies, such as that if aggregate production was increased, unemployment would necessarily result because

---

[1] Classical economists were interested in growth and development, for example, Adam Smith's book considered the forces that led to the wealth of nations. Later New Classical economists have also returned to a consideration of growth as a central element of macro. For space considerations, the focus of this chapter will be on macroeconomic thought relating to inflation and output fluctuations.

[2] In his chapter Axel Leijonhufvud discusses Wicksell and Fisher who were writing at the time that Classical economics was evolving into neoclassical economics. I see both of them fitting into the broader quantity theory tradition, with Fisher a continuation of the currency school, and Wicksell, a continuation of the banking school.

there would be a shortage of demand. It did not say that there could be no aggregate unemployment or temporary deficiency of aggregate demand.[3]

The Great Depression brought about a resurgence of theoretical interest in macro issues. In their recent books, David Laidler (1999) and Perry Mehrling (1997) discuss the richness and diversity of this theoretical work. One branch of this work, undertaken by economists such as Dennis Robertson, was exploring how far one could extend the microeconomic chain of reasoning into macro issues. His work saw the macroeconomic problem as a dynamic coordination problem within a loose microeconomic framework. Robertson (1915, 1926) developed an analysis of a sequence economy in which what happened in one sector affected another sector, which in turn affected another sector.

To say that this work was taking place is not to say that it was generally understood or accepted by the economists at the time. The reality was that almost all of it was difficult going for the period's average economist, as cutting-edge work generally is, and few economists could follow it.[4] This work never had much influence on mainstream economic thinking, and is not discussed in recent standard histories of macro (Blanchard, 2000a; Woodford, 1999). However, it is important to note its existence because it demonstrates that cutting-edge economists of the day were fully aware that the quantity theory and Say's Law were quite compatible with business cycles, unemployment, and serious coordination problems, and that even with their acceptance of these laws, they believed that such coordination problems could develop and could possibly require government action. For them, however, discussion of such policy issues belonged in the art of economics, not in economic theory, because the issues were too complicated for formal theoretical analysis, and the policy issues of macro involved much more than economic theory. While macroeconomic specialists were working on expanding previous insights to include a better analysis of coordination failures that might lead to such problems in the models, they did not know how to capture these problems in simple,

---

[3] See for instance Per Jonson (1995), who cites the following quotation from Say: "In the first place my attention is fixed by the inquiry, so important to the present interests of society: What is the cause of the general glut of all the markets in the world, to which merchandise is incessantly carried to be sold at a loss? What is the reason that in the interior of every state, notwithstanding a desire of action adapted to all the developments of industry, there exists universally a difficulty of finding lucrative employments? And when the cause of this chronic disease is found, by what means is it to be remedied? On these questions depend the tranquility and happiness of nations" (Say, 1821, p. 2).

[4] It might be seen as similar to work today being done on the implications of nonlinear dynamics for macropolicy.

meaningful analytic models that could be related to the data, given the data and empirical technology that existed at the time.[5]

J. M. Keynes was part of this cutting-edge group of British Classical economists, and in 1930 he wrote a two-volume treatise on money (Keynes, 1930) that considered how fluctuations could be explained within a quantity theory framework. However, soon after writing that book, Keynes became convinced that the quantity theory and Say's Law were diverting attention away from certain dynamic coordination insights, such as Kahn's multiplier model; or the saving/investment disequilibria model being explored by Wicksell (1901), which suggested that, under certain circumstances, differences between savings and investment could lead to systemic breakdown. These dynamic coordination insights did not integrate well into the vision of macro that was inherent in these loose general "laws."[6]

Given this conviction, Keynes turned his attention to writing *The General Theory* that deemphasized the quantity theory, Say's Law, and the general long-run insights contained in them. In their place, he worked on developing an analysis that focused primarily on the short-run coordination problems that could exist in a macroeconomy. But instead of analyzing the dynamics of a disequilibrium sequence economy, as Robertson and others were trying to do, he eliminated all dynamics from the basic model. In their place, he presented a comparative static framework that looked only at the short-run equilibrium that would be arrived at given a set of simple behavioral assumptions that were not grounded in formal microeconomic reasoning, but instead were grounded in general observations and proclivities. Hence the name, macroeconomics. The analysis following from those behavioral assumptions became known as the multiplier analysis, and early considerations of Keynes made that multiplier process central to the Keynesian message.[7]

---

[5] Given the highly limited macrodata, and the limited analytic models available to them, this is not surprising. Marshall, for example, writes that general equilibrium issues likely lay in the domain of thermodynamics, a field of study that was just emerging (Marshall, 1890). In terms of empirical work, this is long before computers or even advanced mechanical calculating machines, and at the time the ability to statistically analyze data was largely undeveloped.

[6] How many of his ideas came from others and how many came from his own thinking is beyond the scope of this chapter. See Lerner (1940). Also, see Colander and Landreth (1996) for a discussion of these issues.

[7] Since formal macromodels did not exist at the time, Keynes's approach should not be seen as a "cop out," but simply as an alternative loose summary of insights to those in the quantity theory and Say's Law.

THE KEYNESIAN REVOLUTION

Although Keynes had great hopes for his book, it was not especially well-received by older economists, especially those who had specialized in macro issues. In reviews it was pointed out that Keynes's analysis was ambiguous on many issues, and was difficult to comprehend. Moreover, for many cutting-edge macroeconomists, Keynes's analysis was too simple, and made too many simplifying assumptions. Keynes had not unraveled the Gordian Knot that tied the intertemporal sequencing problems of the macroeconomy together, but had instead cut it, by simply not dealing with dynamic issues that cutting-edge Classical theorists were struggling with.

Still, because of Keynes's stature, and his expository brilliance, the book attracted much attention. It was seen as an interesting, but flawed, attempt to deal with the problems facing the economy. In normal circumstances the book would likely have been well-received at first, and then moved to its place on library shelves, where it would be looked at, and referred to, with decreasing frequency. But these were not normal circumstances. Instead, through a confluence of events the book led to a revolution that significantly influenced the economics profession and the practice of macroeconomics for half a century.

With the benefit of historical hindsight we can now say that the Keynesian revolution was far less a revolution than it first seemed, and that it is better called the Keynesian episode. The reason is that the models and modeling processes associated with the Keynesian revolution did not last. By the 1990s, the economics profession had, to a large degree, abandoned those Keynesian models and the Keynesian label.

To understand why the Keynesian revolution was abandoned, we must consider what the Keynesian revolution was. In my view, it was not a single directed revolution at all, but instead a multifaceted set of developments in theory, pedagogy, policy, and empirical work, each of which was part of an ongoing evolution in economics that was occurring independent of Keynesian economics and which would have influenced economic thinking, whether or not these developments had been placed under the Keynesian name.[8] These developments reflected the changing technology and changing institutions of the time, and often worked

---

[8] Why all these disparate developments came under the Keynesian moniker is a difficult question in social thought, and one that I will not deal with here. I point it out here because in order to understand the history of macro one must recognize these disparate elements of the Keynesian revolution and that many of these developments worked at cross purposes.

at cross-purposes.[9] Because of its multifaceted nature it is best to think of the Keynesian revolution not as a revolution of like-minded individuals with common goals and views, but to think of it as a collection of developments all of which were classified under a broad umbrella term called "Keynesian."

The first of these developments involved theory. In the 1930s, there was the movement from a Marshallian to a Walrasian methodological approach, or alternatively from partial equilibrium thinking in which models were engineering tools meant to shed light on particular policy issues, to general equilibrium thinking in which models were meant to show how the economy operated. Put another way, Marshall's "one thing at a time" approach, which characterized Robertson's work as well, was giving way to the joint consideration of many markets and formal specifications of aggregate equilibrium. Consistent with this change, formal analytic models of multiple markets were replacing the broad general laws and armchair theorizing manifested in earlier economics. Hicks's *Value and Capital* (1939) and Samuelson's *Foundations* (1947) both developed the analytic foundations of multiple market equilibrium, and an increasing number of economists were beginning to think in terms of a general equilibrium relationship of markets. This meant that the loose general laws that had previously described the aggregate economy were no longer acceptable, and would have to be replaced.

Although Keynes followed Marshall on method, his models quickly became tied in with general equilibrium. As Young (1987) described, in a seminar in 1937 three economists, John Hicks, Roy Harrod, and James Meade, took on the task of explaining what the Keynesian revolution was all about, and how it related to Classical economics. All came up with a variation of the IS—LM model that integrated the monetary sector and the real sector in a general equilibrium model, and distinguished Keynesian and Classical views within that model. This general equilibrium modeling approach was quite incompatible with Marshall, but it was a boon to researchers. There were numerous models that needed to be developed, which meant large numbers of articles and dissertations exploring issues such as money neutrality, Pigou effects, multipliers, and alternative specifications of IS and LM curves flowed from this merging of Keynes's ideas and general equilibrium. The work became more and more explicitly

---

[9] It is precisely because the Keynesian revolution involves so many different elements, that there was always, and still is, enormous ambiguity about what precisely Keynesian economics was.

general equilibrium and by the 1960s, Patinkin's *Money, Interest and Prices: an Integration of Monetary and Value Theory* (1956), which tied Keynesian economics and Walrasian economics together in a general equilibrium model based on individual optimization, served as the foundation for cutting-edge macroeconomic theoretical thinking.

A second of these developments was the blossoming of statistical work in the 1940s. A new field of econometrics was developing that allowed economists to relate their models to the data in previously impossible ways. Economists had visions of developing models that could be used to actually control fluctuations in the economy. Keynes was not enthusiastic about this empirical work. In fact, as evidenced by his review of Tinbergen's work (Tinbergen, 1939), Keynes (1939) was highly suspicious of econometrics. However, the Keynesian macromodel soon became closely tied with econometric models as economists such as Jan Tinbergen, Ragnar Frisch, and Lawrence Klein found the developing Keynesian model useful in constructing their econometric macroanalysis. The combination of these two developments into Keynesian economics pushed the Keynesian revolution forward. The combination made Keynesian macroeconomics avant-garde, and gave it a scientific aura that it otherwise would not have had. It also increased its attractiveness to students enormously, providing both theoretical and empirical dissertations and articles to write.

A third development that was occurring was a change in the pedagogy of economics to accompany the changing method. Models were becoming central to the teaching of economics, and, whereas in the 1930s economics textbooks were broad treatises of reasonable insights about economic events, by the 1960s such books no longer fit the new methods that were becoming standard in economics. The change began in the 1940s. In the United States, for example, Laurie Tarshis (Tarshis, 1947) wrote the first U.S. "Keynesian" text, but it was written in the older literary tradition, and it soon came under explicit attack by anti-Keynesians, such as members of the Veritas Society. It was quickly replaced by Paul Samuelson's text (1948), which was more scientific, and more structured around simple formal models.

Samuelson's text became the prototype for modern economics texts. It created a separate macroeconomics, which led to the separation of the principles course into two courses: microeconomics and macroeconomics. It also introduced students to a macroeconomic framework centered on the AE/AP model and the IS–LM model, a model that was further developed and used in upper-level courses. These models served the purpose of introducing students to Keynesian ideas, but they also helped define the nature of Keynesian ideas, providing a framework for macro that in many ways was significantly different than the framework that can be found in Keynes's *General Theory*.

A fourth development that was occurring during this period was a changing view about policy and the ability of government to control the economy. Before the Depression, laissez-faire had strong support among economists, not as an implication of theory, but as a precept in the art of economics that combined broader insights from philosophy and political study with economic insights. The Depression challenged that view and led to discussions of the need for planning, more government control, and greater government involvement in the economy. Then came World War II, and Western governments were seen as having saved our economic and political system. The end result was that, after the war, governments in general had a much better reputation in policy, while the market and laissez-faire had a much worse reputation.

Economists were not immune to these views and, quite separately from Keynesian economics, they were exploring an expansion of government policies. Thus we had Henry Simon's *Positive Program of Laissez Faire*, and numerous calls from economists such as A. C. Pigou and Frank Knight for both monetary and fiscal policy to pull the economy out of the Depression. Initially these discussions were framed in the loose quantity theory—Say's Law framework of the earlier debates, but with the development of Keynesian models, and the Classical and Keynesian monikers, the policy discussion quickly changed from a discussion in which everyone started from the same quantity theory—Say's Law framework and talked about nuances of institutions, into a discussion in which there were specific differences among economists based on the assumptions of their models. The nature of the policy differences, which were seen as separating Keynesians and Classicals, evolved over time.

THE NEOCLASSICAL/NEOKEYNESIAN SYNTHESIS

Because the models were closely tied to policy, the evolving theoretical fights mirrored the policy fights. Initially, in the 1950s, the Keynesian policy position was that fiscal policy was effective and monetary policy was ineffective. The multiplier models used by Keynesians then emphasized the effectiveness of fiscal policy. Keynesian econometric work estimated consumer expenditure functions, and there were actual attempts to measure sizes of various multipliers. Students were taught that Keynesians and Classicals differed in their views on budget deficits and fiscal policy.

Keynesians favored fiscal policy governed by functional finance rules; Classicals favored laissez-faire policy and a fiscal policy governed by sound finance (balance the budget except under extreme conditions).

The fiscal policy debate associated with the beginning of the Keynesian revolution didn't last long since neither side accepted the position it was given in that early resolution. The debate quickly moved to a second-generation debate in which Keynesians no longer advocated fiscal policy only, but instead advocated a combination of monetary and fiscal policy. As this happened, the central pedagogical model switched from the multiplier model to the IS–LM model. Keynesians who advocated using that IS–LM model were often called neoKeynesians to differentiate them from the earlier Keynesians who emphasized animal spirits, uncertainty, and the multiplier rather than a full model that included multiple sectors.

This shift in the Keynesian position was matched by a shift in the Classical position, which was given various names depending on what particular Classical view was being emphasized. Those Classicals who accepted the IS–LM model were generally called neoclassicals, and initially these neoclassicals were differentiated from monetarists, who objected to IS–LM and preferred to stay with the Classical quantity theory approach. These fine distinctions were soon lost, however, as it became evident that the debate was going to be conducted in the IS–LM framework. At that point, the terms monetarist, Classical, or neoclassical were used interchangeably, and the debate came to be known as the neoclassical/ NeoKeynesian debate. The point man for the neoclassicals, who were also known as monetarists, was Milton Friedman; the point man for the NeoKeynesians was James Tobin.

In this debate, both sides held that money matters, and that monetary policy could significantly influence the economy. Monetarists, however, saw the workings of monetary policy as a black box. It was powerful, but it worked with a long and variable lag, so it could not be relied upon as a control policy. NeoKeynesians had a different view; they saw monetary policy as an effective short-run policy tool with modelable transmission mechanisms. Their views on fiscal policy also differed. Monetarists saw fiscal policy as working only with monetary support. Without that support, much of the expansionary effect of fiscal policy would be crowded out. NeoKeynesians saw fiscal policy as an independent tool.

Debates on these issues raged through the 1960s, and were summarized for students in an IS–LM framework. That IS–LM framework allowed both sides to be right; they were simply debating about the shape of the LM curve. Classicals were presented as seeing the LM curve as vertical;

Keynesians were presented as seeing the LM curve as horizontal. The upward-sloping LM curve was a synthesis position that merged the two views. The 1960s were the heyday of the IS–LM synthesis. The IS–LM model was seen as a useful introduction for students to structural econometric models, which were the focus of much of macroeconomists' work.

That IS–LM synthesis reflected the interests of the two sides in the debate. In this debate the long run was not at issue; and while there was much back-and-forth about the short-run policy, both sides accepted that in the long run, the economy would gravitate back toward full employment. Both sides also accepted that excess monetary expansion would be reflected in inflation, not increased output. Thus, the distinction between Keynesians and Classicals that was built into the models was that, technically, in the short run, Keynesians believed that nominal wages were fixed, while the Classicals believed that they were not fixed. Since it was obvious that in the short run wages were, at least to some degree, fixed, the Keynesians essentially owned the short run, and because it was also obvious that wages became unfixed in the long run, the long run was essentially owned by the Classicals.

Most NeoKeynesians in the debate saw the role of macrotheory in a different way than did Classical/monetarist economists, although that role was never made clear. NeoKeynesians saw theory as a rough and ready tool for guiding policy models. Their interest was policy, with theory serving as a guide for policy. Thus, they were quite happy to accept a synthesis that led to what they considered appropriate policy results — that monetary and fiscal policy could be used to guide the economy — even if it meant fudging a bit on precisely what monetary and fiscal policy would work. If assuming fixed wages would get you there, then NeoKeynesians would accept fixed wages, since fixed wages was a reasonable short-run assumption, and policy took place in the short run.

Monetarists also were reasonably satisfied with their position in the synthesis. After all, they had always believed that although monetary policy was effective, the point was that it had a long and variable lag.[10] The transmission mechanisms were far too complicated to model any short-run

---

[10] As I discussed above Classicals had always been willing to accept that the economy could experience short-run problems, and that, in the short run, monetary and fiscal policy might be theoretically useful in pulling the economy out of a depression, although they were extremely hesitant to support such policies for political and noneconomic reasons, and hence tended to support laissez-faire. But that support was what J. N. Keynes called a precept, and was largely based on noneconomic reasoning, rather than on economic theory.

David Colander

effect. Monetarists saw short-run structural theory as close to useless. Their approach to the theory was similar to the Classical approach discussed earlier: a theory was a general statement of the way the economy worked in the long run that focused on general tendencies, not precise structural models.[11] The monetarist basic position — that in the long run, with wage and price flexibility, the economy would return to a long run equilibrium position — was the position they most cared about. Because their position in the synthesis gave them the long run, they, too, were satisfied, even though the synthesis did not adequately capture their view of the short run.

In short, the synthesis satisfied both sides of the debate in terms of their primary interest, even though it was, in a larger sense, satisfying to neither side. NeoKeynesians were given short-run policy and neoclassicals were given long-run theory. The synthesis simply pushed aside other issues rather than resolving them. So the model that evolved was light on formal theory and heavy on policy usefulness. This presented another twist to the Keynesian revolution since, as I discussed above, these policy differences had little connection to Keynes's policy views in the *General Theory*. Keynes's only specific discussion of policy in the *General Theory* concerned government control of investment. Fiscal policy was not mentioned.[12]

I raise these issues not to disparage the developments, nor to say that what emerged as "Keynesian economics" was wrong; I raise them only in order to point out that the Keynesian economics that emerged in the 1950s and 1960s had only tangential connection to Keynes's initial vision; it reflected many more developments than those that can be found in Keynes's writings.[13] The Keynesian revolution was very much a revolution that followed the path of least resistance. It combined various developments that were occurring in the profession in a way that would insure its short-run existence. It was continually metamorphosizing itself into something other than it had been. If there were an opening for monetary

---

[11] There was a parallel debate during this period about the advantages of full econometric structural models that many NeoKeynesians favored, compared to the reduced form models based on the quantity theory, which many monetarists favored.

[12] In fact, Keynes often opposed deficit spending, and when Abba Lerner argued the "Keynesian position" at a Federal Reserve Seminar, he was rebuked by Keynes for not knowing what he was talking about. I recount this episode in Colander (1984). I should say that Keynes later recanted some of his rebuke, but carefully differentiated his public position on deficits from Lerner's.

[13] Much has been written about what Keynes really meant; I do not deal with that question here, and I suspect that, it has no answer; because of his health, and his focus on post-war policy issues, Keynes quickly pulled out of the major debates on Keynesian economics.

and fiscal policy, those policies would become Keynesian. If articles required econometric work, the Keynesian revolution embraced econometrics. If there were an opening for a simple pedagogical model, the Keynesian revolution would embrace a simple pedagogical model. If a workable synthesis between Keynesian and Classical economics required basing the synthesis on fixed wages as the fundamental problem with a macroeconomy, then fixed wages would be the foundation of the Keynesian position, rather than the nonergodic uncertainty that some people believed was its foundation. Again, I am not criticizing here, I am simply describing the nature of the situation. Were it not for that metamorphosizing tendency, the Keynesian revolution would have been unlikely to be the success it in fact was.

Whatever their origins, the combination of Keynesian ideas, the analytic structure of a Walrasian type general equilibrium model, the developing empirical work, and the "Keynesian" multiplier and IS—LM pedagogical models made up an explosive combination, creating a fertile ground for a "revolution." It offered teachers models to teach, researchers research to do, and empirically minded economists enormous opportunities to apply newly developed statistical techniques. But the combination also presented a problem. Because the models were so closely tied to policy issues, in many ways the science of macro did not progress during this time period. Somehow, Keynesian economists always seemed to come up with models that showed that government intervention was good, and monetarists always seemed to come up with models that showed that government intervention was bad. This left some observers with the sense that many of the real issues that differentiated the various positions were going unstated because those real issues were based on reasoning that was too complicated to capture in the analytic models available to researchers at the time, and the empirical tests of the data were too weak to answer the questions being asked. Specifically, the models that developed avoided many of the dynamic issues such as potential nonlinearities or multiple equilibria — these issues were simply not part of the debate. Only very simple dynamics were developed, such as the Harrod/Domar model, or the Solow growth model, and these were not integrated with the short-run model; they were generally developed separately from that short-run analysis.

Dissent

Actually, the convergence of the debate about macroeconomics into this two-part Keynesian/Monetarist debate and synthesis is an enormous simplification, hiding a much more complicated reality. When one looks closely at the literature of the period, one can find innumerable divisions within each of the two sides. Economists have identified at least ten different types of monetarist (Auerbach, 1982) and four different types of Keynesians. Each of these subgroups differed on varying dimensions – on the underlying conception of the economy, on policy, on assumptions, and on methods to interpret evidence. Depending on the dimensional cut one took, the divisions would come out quite differently. But the textbooks had to take a cut and in the 1960s the one textbooks made, and the one students learned, was the Keynesian/Monetarist cut.

Some of the monetarists' concern can be seen in the debate between Friedman and Tobin. Friedman strongly resisted translating his ideas into IS–LM, but ultimately he was forced to do, or risk being excluded from the mainstream debate. Soon, in textbooks, the multiple "monetarist" positions disappeared, and monetarism was presented as a belief that the LM curve was perfectly vertical.[14] Monetarists also opposed the structural econometric models and preferred using reduced form quantity theory models. These objections of monetarists are hardly mentioned in the recent histories, but in many ways what is sometimes called the monetarist counterrevolution was not that at all, but simply an integration of some monetarists' ideas into the synthesis model without really dealing with the major problems that many monetarists had with the synthesis. The "neo" synthesis was as unfair to monetarists as it was to dissenting Keynesians. Objections to the synthesis went beyond monetarists; there were also Austrian economists who strongly objected to the formalization of Keynesian models and the econometric developments that were giving it empirical content. For Austrians, the issues involved in the macrodebates had their basis in differences in ethics and philosophy.

Just as many Classical economists felt uncomfortable with the IS–LM synthesis, so too did many Keynesians. These include Fundamentalist Keynesians, Post Keynesians (with and without hyphens), and coordination Keynesians. These dissenting Keynesians saw the synthesis as missing the central elements of Keynes's views. Fundamentalist Keynesians, such as Alan Coddington (1976), felt the IS–LM model had lost the uncertainty that they saw as central to understanding Keynes. Post Keynesians, such as Paul Davidson or Hyman Minsky, emphasized Keynes's focus on the integration of the monetary and real sectors in an uncertain environment as

---

[14] Friedman (1972, p. 913) remarks, "The main issue between us clearly is not and never has been whether the LM curve is vertical or has a positive slope."

being central to Keynes's views. Fundamentalist Keynesians and Post Keynesians both felt that the IS–LM synthesis had completely lost Keynes's central message about the complexity of the economy and the uncertainty that the complexity created for individual agents operating within the economy. Finally, coordination Keynesians, such as Robert Clower and Axel Leijonhufvud, similarly saw problems with the synthesis, and advocated seeing macroeconomics as a coordination problem that needed a much deeper analysis than anything that was captured by the IS–LM type reasoning.[15] For all these groups there was a major distinction between, as Axel Leijonhufvud put it, Keynesian economics (interpret the NeoKeynesian position in the neoclassical synthesis) and the economics of Keynes.

Why the Dissident Views Were Lost

The fuel of a revolutionary movement in an academic field is the articles and dissertations that it can generate. For a view to develop, it must offer institutional advancement for the holders of that view; it must have dissertations for students to write, articles for assistant professors to publish, and textbook expositions that can spread the seeds of the ideas to students.[16] The dissenters failed on almost all of these criteria. In terms of ideas about how the macroeconomy operated, which could be studied by a "scientific researcher" (as economists had come to view themselves), the dissenters had little to say other than that the macroeconomy was too complicated to model, and that therefore the "neo" models, which assumed away the complications, were simply not adding much insight into the issues.

Many of the dissenters retreated into the history of thought, arguing that what Keynes actually said was not what the NeoKeynesians were saying. Thus, the best-known work of the dissenters is tied with the historical study of Keynes, where they pointed out that Keynes was a Marshallian, and that much of the work in the Keynesian revolution had left the Marshallian fold.

Most of that dissenting work is almost forgotten today, left out of the standard histories of macro. But its existence is important to note. It suggests that there has always been a conscious opposition to the neoclassical/ NeoKeynesian synthesis, and that that opposition was not associated with

---

[15] Reflecting back on IS–LM, Hicks (1980) agreed with these concerns and said that were he to do it again, he would not use IS–LM to build a macromodel.

[16] I make this argument in Colander (2004).

any particular policy position, but was concerned with vision. It was simply an opposition to the "too simple" formalization of macroeconomics into models.

PRECURSORS OF THE NEW CLASSICAL REVOLUTION

While the dissenters who challenged the underlying IS–LM modeling approaches did not have much of an impact, other changes, which were modifying what mainstream macro was, were occurring within macro. One of these developments was the addition of intertemporal elements in the consumption function analysis, such as Friedman's permanent income hypothesis and Modigliani's life cycle hypothesis.[17] This work shifted the analytic foundations away from the simple comparative statics upon which the original Keynesian model was built and toward an analytic foundation based on intertemporal optimization.

Another development that caught on in the 1960s was the Phillips curve, which was an inverse empirical relationship between prices and unemployment.[18] While this relationship had no underlying theory, it was initially broadly consistent with the data, and it served as a useful method of integrating inflation into the policy discussions that could then focus on the tradeoff between inflation and unemployment. In the texts, Keynesians and Classicals were presented as favoring different positions on the Phillips curve. Keynesians favored a bit more inflation and lower unemployment, while Classicals favored a bit less inflation and a bit more unemployment.[19] Even though the Phillips curve was a dynamic relationship about price level changes, and did not formally integrate with the IS–LM model, it was added informally because of its policy usefulness.

Trying to find a theoretical foundation for the Phillips curve led to work on the microfoundations of macro. In this work researchers analyzed price dynamics in an attempt to develop a foundation for the tradeoff.

[17] These theories developed to explain the difference between times series and cross-sectional estimates of consumption functions. The theories did not fit the evidence any better than Duesenberry's ratchet hypothesis (Duesenberry, 1948), but because they were based on microeconomic reasoning, they generated significant theoretical and empirical research, while Duesenberry's hypothesis was soon forgotten.

[18] When Phillips (1958) first specified it, the relationship was between wages and unemployment, but the textbook specification of it evolved and generally it was presented as a relationship between prices and unemployment.

[19] The standard reference for the policy use of the Phillips curve is Solow and Samuelson (1961). There, they caution about using this tradeoff view over a longer period, pointing out that it might not be stable, but that caution was not adhered to in the texts.

Phelps's volume (1971) on microfoundations is the most well-known such attempt; it brought together a group of people working on search equilibria and information theory in an effort to provide a theoretical foundation for the Phillips curve. The approach microfoundations researchers followed was the following: they assumed that, given the informational constraints, agents would choose optimally, and while an agent might be unemployed, that unemployment was a result of their optimal search process. Macroproblems were rooted in individual decisions.

This work began a formalization of those intertemporal individual decisions, picturing all macroproblems from the perspective of an individual on an island, who would have information flows and would be making decisions about whether to move. Reservation wage and optimal choice algorithms became central.

The microfoundations work could provide a justification for an individual market Phillips curve based on price dynamics, but it could not provide a justification for the aggregate Phillips curve and hence for inflation without imposing some arbitrary informational or institutional restrictions on wage and price movements. Instead, this work came to the conclusion that, in the long run, with fully rational individuals and competitive markets, there should be no aggregate tradeoff between unemployment and inflation. This conclusion led to a change in macroeconomic pedagogy and macroeconomic policy analysis. Instead of focusing only on a short-run unemployment rate determined by the IS–LM model, as had been done earlier, the textbooks and policy considerations began to a focus on a long-run natural rate of unemployment.

This shift in focus changed the policy prescriptions in the texts. The earlier approach gave the impression that macropolicy could be used to choose among various unemployment rates; the new approach gave the impression that any policy would have, at best, a temporary effect on output and unemployment. This meant that the Phillips curve tradeoff was just a short-run, temporary, tradeoff, and that any effects that monetary policy had occurred because agents had faulty predictions of the effect of money or because there were temporary institutional restrictions, such as fixed nominal contracts, limiting individuals' actions.

The inflation in the early 1970s was interpreted as a confirmation of this microfoundations analysis, and by the mid 1970s, the natural rate of unemployment was part of both the textbook presentation and theoretical thinking in macro. The rise of the natural rate of unemployment concept formally relegated Keynesian economics to the short run and gave greater importance to the Classical analysis of the long run. The textbook story changed from one in which government could choose the unemployment rate it wanted, to one in which government monetary and fiscal policy could not permanently change the natural rate, and in which the best government could do was to influence short-run fluctuations.

As these developments were occurring, another development, extending Patinkin's work on placing the Keynesian model within a Walrasian general equilibrium framework, was also appearing. The goal of this work was to provide a firm theoretical foundation for the Keynesian conclusion that aggregate output in the economy would fluctuate because of miscoordinated decisions by agents. Researchers hoped to show how miscoordination could lead the economy to undesirable unemployment equilibrium. This work, by economists such as Robert Clower (1965), Robert Barro and Grossman (1971), and Edmond Malinvaud (1977), argued that one could look at the macroeconomic problem as a coordination problem within a quasi-Walrasian general equilibrium system with fixed prices.

Clower's dual decision hypothesis (Clower, 1965) provides a useful summary of the approach. He developed Don Patinkin's distinction between "notional" and "effective" demand. Notional (Walrasian) demand would exist if all markets were in equilibrium; "effective" (Keynesian) demand would exist if one market got in disequilibrium and that disequilibrium spread to other markets. Clower's argument was that individuals who are constrained in one market will have feedback effects on other markets, and that the economy will move to a short-run equilibrium that differs from the long-run equilibrium. Thus, in this view, which has sometimes been called the disequilibrium Keynesian position, Keynesian unemployment equilibrium is seen as an institutionally constrained Walrasian general equilibrium. Axel Leijonhufvud's work (1968) was quickly connected to Clower's, and Leijonhufvud's characterization of Keynes as having switched the quantity and price adjustment mechanisms was popular in the late 1960s and early 1970s. Leijonhufvud was interpreted as saying that the macroproblem could be seen as a speed-of-adjustment problem.

This coordination Keynesian work generated a large amount of discussion both as to its historical accuracy about what Keynes actually meant, and its usefulness as a way of understanding the macroeconomic problem. On the historical side, it was quickly pointed out that Keynes was a Marshallian, not a Walrasian (Yeager, 1973; Davidson, 1996) and thus it was unlikely that Keynes was thinking in terms of a formal IS–LM model. On the more substantial "usefulness" side, it was pointed out that there were no good reasons for assuming fixed wages or prices to begin with within the Walrasian system. There was an extended debate about the role of explicit and implicit contracts in the economy, and the reasons price adjustment to equilibrium might not take place. This work would be taken up later by economists, such as Greg Mankiw, under the New Keynesian designation.

While the disequilibrium approach remained an active area of research in Europe through the 1970s, in the United States by the mid 1970s it quickly dissolved as almost all the individuals originally involved in these movements rapidly moved away from the project, although in quite different directions. Barro and Grossman moved into what came to be known as the New Classical camp, and Clower and Leijonhufvud moved out of the mainstream and into a heterodoxy of dissident macroeconomists. In terms of the standard histories of macro they simply moved off the screen.

THE NEW CLASSICAL REVOLUTION

The next stage in the development of macroeconomics is generally called the New Classical Revolution, and its story has been nicely told in the recent histories of macroeconomics, so I will treat it only briefly. The New Classical revolution developed out of the microfoundations work, the intertemporal optimization work of Friedman and Modigliani, and the disequilibrium Keynesian work. It is generally associated with the work of Robert Lucas (1972) and Thomas Sargent (1976). On a research level, this New Classical work had all the institutional criteria for success and it quickly began undermining the Keynesian foundations of macro, both on the research and graduate teaching levels. In terms of theoretical macro, the model of the 1970s was ripe for change. The fixed price disequilibrium models were having a hard time explaining why the economy would move to an unemployment equilibrium, and not to an excess supply rationing equilibrium, or why the two types of market disequilibria did not offset each other and thus lead to a normal stochastic equilibrium that was essentially the natural rate.

The microfoundations partial equilibrium models about individual markets were especially fertile for researchers, allowing them to fit a variety of tractable models to the data. However, on the macrotheoretical and empirical level, the microfoundations general equilibrium models were intractable. Nonetheless, given the difficulty macroforecasting based on structural macromodels was having, the profession was open to alternatives. To be accepted, however, the New Classical research program had to offer a feasible alternative to the then standard structural macromodels. That alternative was found in the assumption of rational expectations.

Rational expectations was an idea that came from John Muth (1961) who was working on a project with Franco Modigliani and Herbert Simon, studying the dynamic price adjustment process. The goal of this research was to come up with a better explanation of price fluctuations than that found in lagged price-adjustment models such as the cobweb model. Both Simon and Modigliani were adding institutional details to the price-adjustment process to make it more realistic. Muth took the opposite approach with an idea that he called rational expectations. He assumed that process did not matter and argued that the only logical position for a researcher to take was to assume that the agents in the model had the same information as the modelers. If the modelers knew the equilibrium was where supply equaled demand, then the agents in the model should be assumed to know that too, since agents can simply hire the modelers to tell them where the equilibrium is.

Muth's idea did not generate significant interest in the micro context in which it was developed; it was felt that the institutional issues were too complicated to make it reasonable to assume that economists or agents know where the equilibrium is. However, in macro (where the institutional issues are much more complicated), the assumption found a home because it provided a method that could close the otherwise intractable macro-models. Because rational expectations provided a simple measure of closure to intertemporal general equilibrium models, it allowed formal intertemporal analysis to be expanded significantly. This allowed economists to place policy analysis in a dynamic optimal control framework. In doing so, it opened up a whole set of articles and dissertations for students to write, and led to a significant burst of research activity. By the 1980s, rational expectations was becoming commonplace, and by the 1990s, it was a standard assumption in macro, used by macroeconomists of all persuasions. Thus, it was the assumption of rational expectations that allowed the theoretical New Classical revolution to take place.

The essence of the New Classical theoretical criticism of the neoclassical–NeoKeynesian synthesis model was that it was inconsistent in its assumptions about rationality, and was not built on firm micro-foundations. It assumed current optimization but did not consider dynamic feedbacks that would occur in a model with full intertemporal optimization. Thus, while various elements of the "neo" synthesis, such as liquidity preference and consumption behavior, claimed to be built on microfoundations, other elements were not, and unless one had fully integrated the rationality assumption at all levels, the "neo" synthesis was an ad hoc model. New Classicals argued that if the "neo" synthesis model was truly built on microfoundations, one should be able to derive the same results from rigorous models based on firm microfoundations.

The assumption of rational expectations undermined the Keynesian position in the neoclassical—NeoKeynesian synthesis. Essentially, rational expectations implied that whatever was expected to happen in the long run should happen in the short run or, if it did not, it was because of restrictions on behavior that had some long-run purpose. This meant that the NeoKeynesian position in the "neo" synthesis, which was built on the short-run rigidities, was untenable unless somehow one could explain why those rigidities existed, and why they did not reflect a long-run need.

The New Classical attack also undermined the theoretical foundation of the empirical structural macromodels. Lucas's analysis of rational expectations showed how the assumption of rational expectations could undermine the analysis of policy in these models because the expectations of the policy could change the structure of the model. He argued that a correct model would have to be shown to be structurally invariant to the policy, and formally that was difficult to do. Lucas's theoretical attack undermined structural macromodels but did not offer a tractable alternative in terms of fully modeling the economy. To actually develop policy-invariant empirically testable models was impossible, so New Classicals set their goals lower. Instead of trying to forecast from theory, they simply tried to calibrate their theory to the models.

Calibration was of little use in forecasting but New Classicals took the position that when forecasting was necessary, it made most sense to rely upon vector autoregression to use the increasing computer power that was developing. Vector autoregression, proposed by Chris Sims (1980), was an attractive alternative to structural models. Sims argued that, given the intractability of full structural models, researchers should pull as much information as they could out of the data with as few structural restrictions on the data as possible. Vector autoregression allowed researchers to do that. This acceptance of vector autoregression tied New Classical work with a developing econometric method and strengthened their position. Keynesians were presented as supporting the failed large structural macromodels; New Classicals were presented as using more modern alternatives.

The New Classical work caught on with graduate students and young assistant professors in much the same way that the Keynesian revolution had caught on earlier. In the early 1970s, it was seen as a new radical approach; by the mid 1980s it was the way macroeconomics was done. Along with the change in the way macro was done, there was also a change in the way theoretical macroeconomists thought about macropolicy. The New Classical work left little room for discretionary fiscal or monetary policy. Consistent with this view about the ineffectiveness of monetary and fiscal policy, New Classical work evolved relatively quickly into real business cycle analysis, which saw all shocks as being caused by real shifts in aggregate supply – rather than by nominal shifts in aggregate demand. Within this real business cycle framework, there was no room for traditional macropolicy, other than to provide a framework within which markets could operate.

The Keynesian response to New Classical economics was mixed. Keynesians became divided into New Keynesians, who accepted the new methodological approach based upon rational expectations and general equilibrium models, and old (neo)Keynesians who rejected New Classical economic method as being unhelpful. These old Keynesians generally supported the continued use of IS–LM models and large-scale structural econometric models. By 1990, New Keynesian economics (Mankiw and Romer, 1990) won out as older Keynesians aged and left the profession. The two places where the old Keynesian approach remained were in the intermediate textbooks, which centered their presentation on the IS–LM model, and in policy analysis where IS–LM served as the "trained intuition of macro policy makers."

The development of New Keynesian economics was essentially the death of Keynesian economics, because there was little Keynesian, or even NeoKeynesian, left in it. As Greg Mankiw (1991), one of the leading New Keynesians, stated, New Keynesian economics could have been as easily called New Monetarist economics.[20] New Keynesian work became associated with partial equilibrium models that explained price rigidities, such as menu cost and implicit contract models. Thus, New Keynesian economics was soon interpreted as being New Classical economics with price rigidities. However, there was not a full integration of the two. Because of the difficulty of developing full general equilibrium models,

---

[20] This was not entirely true since there were many different strains in the New Keynesian literature (see Colander [1992]) and one of those strains, which emphasized the coordination problems that could develop (Cooper and John, 1988), had connections to the work of earlier dissident Keynesians. But the difference between New Keynesians and New Classicals that Mankiw and Romer emphasized was that New Keynesians accepted that real market imperfections were important in explaining macroeconomic fluctuations whereas the New Classicals did not.

most of the early New Keynesian models providing justifications for price rigidities were partial equilibrium models, and were never developed into full-fledged general equilibrium models with price rigidities.

THE NEW SYNTHESIS

The terms New Keynesian, New Classical, and even real business cycle analysis are seldom used any more; instead there is a growing consensus that a new synthesis has been reached (Woodford, 1999; Blanchard, 2000a). This new synthesis is called the dynamic stochastic general equilibrium (DSGE) synthesis and it is providing the structure of much modern theoretical macroeconomic research and macroeconomic thinking about policy. Essentially, the New Synthesis sees the macroeconomic problem as a gigantic dynamic general equilibrium optimal control problem, and looks at the full optimization of individuals and firms, arriving at a solution by using rational expectations and model consistency assumptions.

If one assumes that there are no nominal rigidities in the model, then one has a real business cycle approach, but that real business cycle approach has a hard time accounting empirically for the degree of fluctuations one sees in the economy. Therefore, there is a general acceptance that one needs to accept various types of nominal rigidities. This acceptance has merged New Keynesian and New Classical traditions into a single approach, which is what the New Synthesis is. DSGE models consider agents who dynamically maximize their intertemporal objectives subject to budget and resource constraints. Modelers take as given only tastes and technologies, which they call the deep parameters of the model, and argue that these will be policy invariant, thus avoiding the Lucas critique of the structural macroeconometric models.

In terms of policy, the New Synthesis models suggest much more caution about the use of discretionary monetary or fiscal policy than did the "neo" synthesis models. The reason is that in an intertemporal equilibrium the effects of most expected policy wash out as individuals adjust their actions to take expected policy into account. With sufficient price rigidities, some discretionary policy may be warranted, but that addendum is a slight adjustment to the general policy insight that aggregate demand-based policies will be ineffective. What this means is that much of the policy action is in expected policy, not in the actual policy; policy should be considered in a broader context of policy regimes rather than in terms of specific policies to be followed in specific instances. Thus, modern macropolicy analysis focuses on credibility, credible rules, and optimal dynamic feedback rules, and credible inflation targeting has become a key policy advocated by many macroeconomists on the basis of this New Synthesis model.

Modern empirical work in New Classical macro has given up trying to directly forecast with the theoretical models, and has concentrated more on showing general consistency of the model with the empirical evidence by calibrating the models with out-of-sample data. There is some work (Diebold, 1998; Ingram and Whiteman, 1994; Del Negro and Schorfheide, forthcoming) attempting to combine the DSGE insights with vector autoregression models, using the DSGE model as a Bayesian prior. Such work will, I believe, be a major research program in the coming years. At this point, in terms of forecasting there has been no clear-cut empirical winner or loser in the formal empirical analysis, although restricted VAR forecasting comes out relatively well (Robertson and Tallman, 1999). The empirical forecasting debate is on the nature of restrictions one uses, and how those restrictions relate to theory.

Two final points should be made about the New Synthesis and the New Classical/New Keynesian revolution. First, like the Keynesian revolution before it, the New Classical revolution should not be seen as a single revolution, but instead a collection of developments that come together under a single term. Thus it has a theoretical component that involves a change in the way macrotheorizing is done, and it has an econometric component that involves a change in the way econometrics is done. However, unlike the Keynesian revolution, as of 2004, it did not have a strong pedagogical component, at least at the undergraduate level, and the traditional way of teaching macro around IS–LM remained, although its use was different (Colander, 2004).

The second point is that this New Classical/New Keynesian revolution was both an attack on the neoclassical/NeoKeynesian synthesis and an extension of it, which explains the ambivalence of many of the dissidents about the new developments. The earlier "neo" synthesis had developed by following the path of least resistance, and had given up many of the ideas and concerns that dissidents had. Most of these dissidents did not accept that "neo" synthesis, and thus had no problem with agreeing with the New Classical criticisms of it. But accepting the New Classical arguments against the neoclassical synthesis did not mean that the dissidents agreed with the New Synthesis. Their problems with the New Synthesis were as major, if not more major, than were their problems with the earlier synthesis.

BEYOND THE NEW SYNTHESIS: POST WALRASIAN MACROECONOMICS

In many ways, the Post Walrasian research program is the same research program that Classical economists before Keynes were struggling with. The Keynesian revolution was a revolution to deal with the macropuzzle with the available tools. Keynes had a sense that the Classical assumption of a unique stationary state for an economy with true uncertainty was wrong, and he set out to propose an alternative, more general theory, that had multiple attractors, rather than a unique equilibrium. His revolution failed not because its vision was wrong, but because the tools were inadequate to the task at hand. Given the tools available, the Walrasian approach was forced to narrow the puzzle down to one that was manageable, or at least became manageable after 50 years of developments in analytic, computing, and statistical developments.

Now that the Walrasian question has been answered with the New Synthesis, the question we must now deal with is: how much insight does that New Synthesis provide to the broader question of how reasonable agents operate in information poor environments? The Post Walrasian work being described in this volume is the beginning of a formal attempt to deal with this question, and for that reason, one can see it as a return to the broader Classical question and the beginning of a true "New" Classical revolution.

3

The Problem of Time in the DSGE Model and the Post Walrasian Alternative

Perry Mehrling

The new DSGE synthesis in macroeconomics is nicely captured in Michael Woodford's *Interest and Prices* (2003), which pulls together many strands from an immense literature that has grown up over the last two decades. Woodford's book can be seen as the culmination of attempts to establish a new "neoclassical synthesis" that combines the best of the New Classical and Real Business Cycle literature that rose to prominence in the decade of the 1980s, with the best of the New Keynesian literature that rose up in reaction during the decade of the 1990s. Woodford is quite explicit about this. The Real Business Cycle model is, for him, the benchmark. It shows us how it is possible to understand output fluctuation as an equilibrium response to taste and technology shocks. But it can't explain everything we see, in particular VAR evidence that monetary impulses (both anticipated and unanticipated) have real effects (pp. 174–5). This evidence provides room for a New Keynesian elaboration of the RBC model to include sticky nominal prices and wages. The end result is a model that, because it is built from optimizing microfoundations, is immune to the Lucas (1976) critique of old-style Keynesian econometric models, but is nonetheless also able actually to fit (not just to calibrate) the data.

The point of reviving the neoclassical synthesis is not however primarily to influence academic economics. Rather, the central ambition of the book is to influence policy by providing a framework for policy analysis and discussion by practical central bankers. The subtitle makes this ambition explicit: "Foundations of a Theory of Monetary Policy." The whole point of reviving the neoclassical synthesis is to revive the role that economics once played as a policy science during the heyday of the original neoclassical synthesis. Now, instead of the Solow growth model as the benchmark we have the Real Business Cycle Model, and instead of the optimal response to an output gap at a moment in time we have optimal policy rules that take into account the effect of forward looking expectations. (Also, instead of fiscal policy, we have monetary policy, but that's another story.) It's all a lot more sophisticated than what used to be, but the family resemblance is impossible to miss for anyone who knew the parents.[1]

Since this synthesis is just now being digested by the profession, the question that any proposed Post Walrasian alternative must answer is: where does the Post Walrasian approach connect with that synthesis? In this chapter, I explore that question by distinguishing three views of the way time is treated in economic models: the classical, the Walrasian DSGE, and the Post Walrasian. While this is a slightly different take on the separation of Walrasian and Post Walrasian than Colander makes with his emphasis on information processing capabilities and available information sets, it is related. I emphasize that processing capability and information availability always fall short, not because of any human deficiency but rather because of the open-ended nature of the problem that real world agents face. The problem is time and unknowability of the future.

As Alan Greenspan has recently said, speaking about the problem of monetary management by the central bank, "despite extensive effort to capture and quantify what we perceive as the key macroeconomic relationships, our knowledge about many of the important linkages is far from complete and, in all likelihood, will always remain so." Our problem, he says, is not just probabilistic risk but also, more seriously, "Knightian uncertainty" in which the probabilities themselves are unknown. In the face of an unknown and unknowable future, Greenspan advocates what he calls a "risk-management approach to policy," an approach that explicitly recognizes the limits of our knowledge (Greenspan, 2004). What Post Walrasian economics does is to extend that same recognition to every other agent in the economy. We all face the problem of choosing appropriate behavior in the face of the unknown, and the aggregation of all our behaviors is the macroeconomics that we observe.

Classical Economics and Time

The classical economists who laid the foundations of our subject had a characteristic strategy for handling the uncertain future. They built their science by treating the present as determined by the past. The important thing about the past is that it has already happened. The past is a fact and

---

[1] I have developed these ideas in more detail in Mehrling (2006) from which the last two paragraphs are taken.

nothing we do today can change it. It is also a knowable fact, at least in principle, so we can hope in our economic theories to draw a deterministic link between known causes and observable effects. In pursuit of this hope, the classical economists sought to discover the laws of motion of the economic system.

Such laws, supposing they can be found, will generally leave some residual uncertainty about the motion of the system simply because of outside factors. But these factors are also presumably susceptible to explanation by deterministic laws which are not yet included in the analysis. Uncertainty about the future is, in this way of thinking, no different in principle from uncertainty about the present. It is just a matter of insufficiently detailed knowledge of the past and of the laws of motion linking that past to the future.

The one free variable in the classical system is human action, including collective human action. In Adam Smith's view, much of individual behavior is driven by innate human propensities, but reason offers each individual the opportunity to direct those propensities, and so to live a better life. The same reason also offers societies the opportunity to make their own history, not perhaps just as they might please, but also not as completely determined by the dead hand of the past. Economic theory, as a product of reason, has its purpose to provide direction for the application of reason, both individual and collective.

Because we don't know all the facts and laws of motion, we cannot know the precise effects of specific interventions, but that shouldn't stop us. We can, the classicals were confident, identify the most salient facts and laws and, having done so, employ our reason to improve on the results of simple animal instinct. We can each do this individually in our own lives, and the miraculous results of the market system are the consequence. And we can also do it collectively, by consciously removing any and all remaining obstacles to the full play of human reason. Reason says that we can do it, and so reason also says that we should do it.

This classical view of how to handle the problem of time persisted from Adam Smith throughout the nineteenth century, including the classic works of both Alfred Marshall (1890) and Leon Walras (1874). Marshall's famous epigram "*natura non facit saltum,*" nature does not make jumps, connects him firmly with the classical tradition in this regard. The continuity of the present with the past (and hence also the future with the present) was what made a scientific understanding of the present possible, and so provided traction for the reasoning powers of rational economic man.

The Twentieth Century

But the times they were achanging. What is rational to do today depends in part on what we expect to happen tomorrow, but attempts to expand the scope of economic reason to incorporate the future ran head on into what John Maynard Keynes famously called the "dark forces of time and ignorance which envelop our future" (Keynes 1936, p. 155). In the twentieth century view, uncertainty about the future was no longer something that science could hope eventually to penetrate. The salient fact about the world was no longer the continuity of the past and future, but rather the radical disjuncture between the two on account of the speed of change, not least the speed of technological change. The one thing the rational mind could know about the future is that it would in important ways be different from anything now imaginable, perhaps better but also perhaps worse.

Inevitably, the analytical problems posed by this new view of time emerged first in the world of finance, where the valuation of capital assets involves both assessment of future income flows and also appropriate discount factors for those flows. Keynes himself, having looked deeply into the matter of risk and uncertainty in his 1921 *Treatise on Probability*, emphasized the inherent limits of individual rationality in this regard, and placed his faith instead in the collective rationality embodied in various "semi-autonomous bodies within the State" (Keynes 1926). Keynes's answer to radical uncertainty was mechanisms of social control that he hoped could pick a path through the uncertain future, preserving the upside of expanded individual freedom while protecting against the downside of economic and social barbarism.

The post World War II development of the theory of monetary and fiscal policy can be viewed as the elaboration of two specific mechanisms of social control for this purpose. The famous Keynesian cross, that explained how the flow of current demand determines the flow of current output, set the pattern for how to do science in the face of an unknowable future. It was a theory that avoided the unknowable future by treating the present as determined by the present. "Animal spirits" that affect current expenditure are the free variables that, for individual agents, take the place of impossible rational analysis of the future. And fiscal and monetary policy are the free variables that, for the collectivity, select one future path among the many that are possible.[2]

---

[2] See Mehrling (1997) for the story of Alvin Hansen and the rise of American Keynesianism.

The Keynesian "present-determines-present" solution was however only temporary. Even if one agreed with Keynes that full extension of rational analysis to the future was impossible, surely one could ask for a better theory of individual choice than animal spirits! Further, the Keynesian project of rational collective policy choice seemed to require some specification of what is expected to happen in the future, if only because policy actions today actually have their impact in the future, notwithstanding the stylization of the Keynesian cross. For both projects, the work of the American Irving Fisher showed the way forward.

Here is Fisher's account of the "dark forces of time and ignorance" problem: "To attempt to formulate mathematically in any useful, complete manner the laws determining the rate of interest under the sway of chance would be like attempting to express completely the laws which determine the path of a projectile when affected by random gusts of wind. Such formulas would need to be either too general or too empirical to be of much value" (Fisher 1930, p. 316). Thinking about the problem in this way, Fisher decided that he could make the most progress toward a rational analysis of the future simply by assuming, as a first approximation, that the future is in fact completely known. Fisher's bold abstraction from the problem of uncertainty gave us what is arguably the first fully specified model of intertemporal general equilibrium, a model that is recognizably the direct ancestor of the DSGE models of today which extend Fisher's model of certainty to incorporate probabilistic risk.

Fisher summarized his worldview using the following diagram:[3]

	Present Capital		**Future Income**
Quantities	Capital-wealth	$\rightarrow$	Income-services
			$\downarrow$
Values	Capital-value	$\leftarrow$	Income-value

The arrow in the first row captures the classical view of time, in which the accumulation of capital-wealth from the past determines the flow of future income-services that people can enjoy. The arrow in the second row captures the twentieth century view of time, in which future income flows determine current capital valuations. The diagram captures perfectly the worldview of a man caught with one foot in the nineteenth century and

---

[3] Fisher (1907, p. 14). A similar diagram is presented in Fisher (1930, p. 15) using the terms "capital goods" and "flow of services" instead of capital-wealth and income-services. For a fuller treatment of the economics that Fisher developed to flesh out his world view, see Mehrling (2001).

the second in the twentieth. The past determines present physical quantities, but the future determines present capital values.

The third arrow, pointing down from the first row to the second, shows that Fisher kept most of his weight on the first foot. The simplifying assumption that the future is known pegs Fisher as ultimately a man of the nineteenth century. By abstracting from uncertainty he makes rational analysis of the future possible, but only by stripping that future of what the twentieth century would view as its most salient feature. As a consequence it was Keynes, not Fisher, who initially caught the spirit of the age. But, as I have suggested, it was Fisher, not Keynes, who served as the ancestor of the DSGE model that currently dominates macroeconomics. How did that happen?

What made possible the extension of Fisher's intertemporal general equilibrium to a world of uncertainty was the development within the subfield of finance of a theory of asset pricing in a world of risk. The key breakthrough was the Capital Asset Pricing Model (CAPM).[4] In this model, the quintessential form of capital is the equity share, which represents ownership of a risky future cash flow. Present value calculations have a long history in economics, but the advance of CAPM was to show how to price risk. The importance of CAPM came from the fact that, once you know how to price risk, you have a strategy for handling the "dark forces of time and ignorance" without any policy intervention by the state, simply by economizing on the willingness of people to bear risk. The theory says that first you want to eliminate as much of the unpriced risk as you can (by means of diversification), and then you want to shift the priced risk to those members of society who are best equipped or most willing to bear it.

Finance was first to crystallize a general equilibrium model of the twentieth century view that the future determines the present, but the wider significance of the new view was only felt as it found its way into economics. In macroeconomics, the most important consequences were the Rational Expectations revolution and then Real Business Cycles.[5] Just so, in modern DSGE models, present conditions are largely understood as the effect of an anticipated future. The physical capital stock of course is inherited from the past but the economic importance of that stock, as measured by its current valuation, all comes from the future.

The DSGE models thus offer a solution to the problem that both Keynes and Fisher thought was impossible; they offer a story about how rational

[4] For a fuller story of the rise of modern finance see Bernstein (1992) or Mehrling (2005).
[5] See Mehrling (2005, Chapter 8).

analysis can be extended to the unknown future. The consequence of that extension, we can now see clearly, is nothing less than an inversion of the classical strategy for handling the problem of time. One hundred years after Irving Fisher, we are now prepared fully to embrace the radical idea that the future, or rather our ideas about the future, determines the present. Like Irving Fisher, we have one foot in the past and one in the future, but unlike him most of our weight is on the future, not the past. In the modern view, it is expectations about future income that determine current capital value, and it is current capital value that determines the investments that get made and survive as current capital-wealth.

	Present Capital		**Future Income**
Quantities	Capital-wealth	$\rightarrow$	Income-services
	$\uparrow$		
Values	Capital-value	$\leftarrow$	Income-value

Inevitably, the extension of rational analysis to incorporate the future has had the effect of reducing the apparent scope for social control of the kind that Keynes (and Fisher too) thought would be necessary. Because markets provide sufficient scope for individual rationality to solve the problem of uncertainty, there is no problem for the collectivity to solve. This is the fundamental source of all of the New Classical policy-invariance results that have challenged the Keynesian world view. Just so, DSGE models with flexible prices have little room for macroeconomic policy intervention (Woodford 2003, Chapter 2).

Of course, sticky price versions of the DSGE model provide more scope. In Woodford's treatment, the emphasis is on the freedom of the central bank to set the nominal rate of interest which also, given price stickiness, sets the real rate of interest. Note well, however, that it is not the current rate of interest but rather the full policy rule, which rational agents project into the future, that produces the current effect. Even in a sticky price world, policy works mainly by affecting expectations about the future.

The Post Walrasian View

Post Walrasians take a different tack, emphasizing that the future is not a knowable fact, not even in principle, and not even in probabilistic terms. Theories of asset pricing that posit known probabilities abstract from this feature of the world, and so do the various versions of the DSGE model of the macroeconomy. As such, they offer nothing more than one possible story about one possible future. The important thing is that, to the extent that people believe this story, or any other story, they adjust their current behavior accordingly. In this sense, one of the most important lessons of the DSGE model is that economic theories themselves are the significant knowable facts in the modern world. Post Walrasians ask what happens in a world where a large number of people interact, each one behaving according to their own theory about the future.

The DSGE model that dominates standard macroeconomic discourse is of course one possible candidate story about one possible future, but it is clearly a very special case. Not only does it assume that everyone somehow converges on the same theory of the world, but the theory on which they are supposed to converge treats all uncertainty as merely exogenous risk with known probabilities. It is a theory that succeeds in taming the uncertain future merely by assuming that uncertainty is already tame. That's fine, of course, as an abstraction and a first step. The justification, fair enough, is that we must walk before we can run. But one major drawback, as we have seen, is the lack of room for a theory of economic policy, since in this special case individual rationality is enough to achieve social rationality and there is nothing much left for collective intervention to add.

Post Walrasian work represents an attempt to broaden out from the DSGE model in order to deal with the deeper uncertainty that the DSGE approach assumes away. In a world of uncertainty, rational choice no longer provides much analytical traction, so Post Walrasian work treats agents as dealing with information poor environments, and having limited information processing capabilities. Nevertheless, the general idea that behavior should be model-consistent remains attractive. Model consistency replaces rational expectations as the closure of Post Walrasian models.

The important thing is that Post Walrasian work seeks to model the *process* by which one among many possible futures is selected, rather than imposing constraints on the model that ensure only a single *equilibrium* outcome. In this regard, Post Walrasian work builds on the classical Marshallian concept of adaptive dynamics, but freed of the mathematical assumptions necessary to guarantee stability and convergence to a single equilibrium. The Swedish contemporaries of Keynes arguably had something like the Post Walrasian program in mind in their various attempts to model economic process, but the analytical difficulty of the problem defeated them.[6] As a consequence, what we got instead was Keynes, and

---

[6] Laidler (1999, pp. 57–59). The American institutionalists of the interwar period were similarly interested in modeling process, and were also similarly unsuccessful (Mehrling, 1997).

then Fisher (as I have recounted above). Post Walrasian work has, in this sense, been waiting in the wings for a century until the present moment when analytical technology has caught up to our analytical needs.

The payoff to be anticipated from such work is not only a richer picture of macroeconomic phenomena, but also a richer sense of the potential role for policy intervention to improve macroeconomic performance. Agents operating on their own, developing their own theories of the future to guide their present behaviors and interacting with each other through markets, will produce some macroeconomic outcome. But other macroeconomic outcomes will also be possible. Here there is a possible role for Keynes's "semi-autonomous bodies within the State," but also for economic institutions more generally, private as well as public. In the DSGE framework, a role for policy depends on some market imperfection, like sticky prices. In the broader Post Walrasian framework, a role for policy emerges naturally as a way of delimiting the range of possible futures.

The attraction of agent-based modeling is that it offers a way to do economic theory that takes uncertainty seriously while still retaining the analytical discipline of model-consistent behavior. Indeed model-consistent behavior is built in from the beginning in a model like LeBaron's (this volume, Chapter 11) since agents adapt their behavior in light of their experience. To date, the agent-based literature has focused on rather simple behavioral rules, like LeBaron's functions of past aggregate data. But there seems to be no reason in principle why higher order behavioral rules cannot also be investigated.

Agents could, for example, be endowed with some knowledge about the structure of the world in which they are living, and permitted to condition their behavior on certain deeper structural variables. The modeling of higher-order behavioral rules would, in effect, have the agents inside the model each formulating their own "model of the model," models that are subsequently adapted in the light of experience.[7] Behavior will thus always be model consistent even though agents never learn the "true" structure of their world.

The agent-based literature is full of examples that demonstrate how the aggregate behavior of the system changes when we add a new kind of agent. Here we can see a clear opening for development of a theory of economic policy. For example, the central bank could be considered as a new kind

---

[7] The phrase "model of the model" comes from Hyman Minsky, whose heterodox views on macroeconomics can in retrospect be seen as anticipating key features of the Post Walrasian program. See Mehrling (1999) for a fuller treatment.

of agent, operating perhaps with the very same information set as the most sophisticated agents in the model, but with different instruments and a different objective function. It seems unlikely that a world that includes such an agent will exhibit the same aggregate behavior as a world without such an agent. In other words, policy invariance is unlikely to be a robust feature of agent-based models, even when individual behaviors are all constrained to be model-consistent.

CONCLUSION

The Post Walrasian view builds on the tradition of Fisher and Keynes, both of whom recognized the problem of time as the significant challenge for further development of economics. In contrast to their classical forebears, Fisher and Keynes both recognized the degree of freedom offered by the open-ended future; when behavior depends on expectations about the future, volatility is the consequence. But both also held out hope that human reason, and the institutions that human reason would invent, could find ways to manage that volatility.

Following in the footsteps of Fisher and Keynes, modern economics has developed both modern finance and the DSGE model that now lies at the core of modern macroeconomics. These developments have gone a long distance toward grappling with the problem of time, but more work remains to be done. The Post Walrasian view envisions a world of even greater uncertainty than that embraced by modern finance and the DSGE model, and a world that is for that very reason amenable to a wider range of refinements and improvements than have yet to be considered. The volatility of capital values and incomes is just a fact, an inevitable consequence of shifting ideas about the future in a period of rapid technological change. The policy challenge remains to shift that volatility onto the shoulders of those most able and willing to bear it.

4

Who Is Post Walrasian Man?

Peter Hans Matthews

In his introduction to this volume, David Colander identifies *information* as the source of differences in the Walrasian and Post Walrasian app-roaches to macroeconomics. Walrasians, we are told, assume that econo-mic agents are superior "processors" who live in "information rich" environments, whereas Post Walrasians believe that agents must struggle to make sense of an information poor world. As a consequence, Colander advocates that the Walrasian "holy trinity" of *rationality, equilibrium,* and *greed* be replaced with *purposeful behavior, sustainability,* and *enlightened self-interest.*

But are these catchphrases little more than slogans? Kevin Hoover (this volume) is concerned that Colander's "beautiful words ... are a kind of free verse" and that "[even if we do not] know more about the economy from hewing to the structures of Walrasian economics ... there is something to be said for discipline." I want to argue that this concern is misplaced, that a commitment to the Post Walrasian enterprise is not a recipe for incoherence. Indeed, more than their Walrasian brethren, Post Walrasians have allowed experimental and other new sources of data to "discipline" their research, and are dedicated to the articulation of game theoretic and other theoretical models that rationalize this data. The conception of economic man embodied in Colander's "beautiful words," which shares some similarities with Samuel Bowles and Herbert Gintis' *homo reciprocans* (Bowles and Gintis, 2000) and with Alan Kirman's (1997) characterization of economic man as an *interactive* agent, is not an amorphous one. I will attempt to show that we have learned much about the character of "Post Walrasian one," the fraternal twin of *homo reci-procans* and the fourth cousin, seven times removed, of *homo economicus,* over the last decade or so. As it turns out, he too, is a purposeful actor, but one whose preferences and actions cannot be separated from the other actors and institutions around him and that, once this is taken into account, he is someone who is *amenable to rigorous economic analysis.*

Stepping back for a moment, however, it should be said that both old and new trinities presume that in some form or another, the "microfoundations project" is alive and well. If all that Post Walrasian macroeconomists aspired to was the detection of robust patterns in aggregate data – an impression that some discussions of related econometric methods should do more to correct – the character of Post Walrasian man would not matter much, in the same sense that a chemist does not need to know much about molecules to (re)discover Boyle's Law of Gases. This does not mean that Post Walrasians will share the neoclassical enthusiasm for representative agent models: the agent-based computational model of the labor market described in Giorgio Fagiolo, Giovanni Dosi, and Roberto Gabriele (2004), for example, in which the Beveridge, Okun, and wage curves are emergent properties, illustrates how broad, and ambitious, "bottom up economics" has become.[1] It is the dual premise of this chapter, however, that (a) recent theoretical and computer-based advances hold considerable promise, and (b) if there are microfoundations to be built, it is Post Walrasian man, not *homo economicus*, who will animate them.

So who, then, is Post Walrasian man? It is perhaps easier to start with who he is *not*, and no one has ever provided a more eloquent description than Thorstein Veblen, a Post Walrasian before his time. In "Why Is Economics Not An Evolutionary Science" (1898, p. 389), he wrote:

In all the received formulations of economic theory ... the human material with which the inquiry is concerned is conceived in hedonistic terms; that is to say, in terms of *a passive and substantially inert and immutably given human nature.* The psychological and anthropological preconceptions of the economists have been those which were accepted by the psychological and social sciences some generations ago. The hedonistic conception of man is that of a lightning calculator of pleasures and pains who oscillates like a homogeneous globule of desire of happiness under the impulse of stimuli that shift him about the area, but leave him intact. He has neither antecedent nor consequent. *He is an isolated definitive human datum, in stable equilibrium except for the buffets of the impinging forces that displace him in one direction or another.* Self-imposed in elemental space, he spins symmetrically about his own spiritual axis until the parallelogram of forces

---

[1] To some critics on both left and right, this will seem a distinction without a difference. To John Finch and Robert McMaster (2004), for example, the methodological individualism of Bowles and Gintis – and no doubt other Post Walrasians – is no less reductionist or ahistorical than their Walrasian counterparts. And the critics have a point: to paraphrase Gertude Stein, the laws of capitalist motion are the laws of capitalist motion are the laws of capitalist motion, with or without plausible microfoundations.

bears down upon him, whereupon he follows the line of the resultant. When the force of the impact is spent, he comes to rest, a self-contained globule of desire as before. Spiritually, the hedonistic man is not a prime mover. *He is not the seat of a process of living*, except in the sense that he is subject to a series of permutations enforce upon him by circumstances external and lien to him (emphasis added).

In contrast, Post Walrasian man is first and foremost not "an isolated human datum" but is instead someone who is *embedded* in various networks, whose *interactions* with other members of these networks, which both reflect and are reflected in the institutions that inform these interactions, mean that he can be neither "passive" nor "inert." The Post Walrasian vision is therefore consistent with the network or complex adaptive systems approach, which rejects "the idea that all individual economic agents are isolated from one another and ... only interact indirectly through the price system" (John Davis, 2005, p. 1).

Charles Manski (2000) distinguishes three broad categories of interaction, reflecting the channels through which an individual's actions affect one another. *Constraint interactions*, like the standard positive and negative externalities, are not especially Post Walrasian: neoclassical (and other) economists have considered their consequences — not least of which is their relationship to multiple equilibria in macroeconomics — for decades. This said, Post Walrasians do not discount constraint interactions, either.

Post Walrasians are also not alone in their insistence that learning, Manski's (2000) archetypal example of the *expectations interaction*, is an essential feature of economic life. In more provocative terms, the primitive in Post Walrasian models is often some sort of learning or adjustment mechanism, and not some static and a priori definition of equilibrium. Colander has this in mind, I believe, when he substitutes "sustainability" for "equilibrium." To mention one simple but provocative example, Kenneth Binmore, John Gale, and Larry Samuelson (1995) were able to rationalize observed behavior in ultimatum game experiments — offers are more fair, and unfair offers are rejected more often, than is consistent with subgame perfection — on the basis of a model in which the evolution of population shares associated with various pure strategies could be described in terms of the *replicator dynamic*. Although the dynamic had been familiar to biologists for decades (Peter Taylor and Leo Jonker, 1978), Binmore et al. showed that it was (also) consistent with simple forms of reinforcement-based learning.

It is the third sort of social interaction, *preference interaction*, that is most often identified with Post Walrasian accounts of economic man. As Manski (2000) reminds us, such interactions are a central feature of noncooperative games — each individual's preferences over the strategies available to him or her will depend on the strategies that others choose — but the Post Walrasian notion of "dependence" is even broader than this implies. To the extent that the preferences of Post Walrasian man are often *other-regarding*, or to the extent that he is sensitive to current norms and conventions — in short, to the extent that he is human — the map from material outcomes to psychological ones, and therefore "preferences," will be more complicated than some game theorists suppose. Indeed, if preference functions are defined over both outcomes and beliefs — the premise of *psychological games*, about which more below — the definition of preference interaction becomes more expansive still.

I still have not said much about the character of Post Walrasian man, however: if he is not Veblen's "homogenous globule of desire," then who is he? The first place we shall observe him "in action" is in the lab.

THE VIEW FROM THE LAB

There is a distinct Marshallian flavor to much of the Post Walrasian enterprise, and its portrait of economic man is, or ought to be, no exception.[2] For Post Walrasians, the question is not "How *might* agents endowed with narrow self-interest behave in an idealized price system in which there is no meaningful interaction?" but rather "What empirical regularities describe how individuals *do* behave in environments in which there is?" And while Jörgen Weibull's (2004, p. 1) claim that "moving from arm-chair theorizing to controlled lab experiments may be as important a step in the development of economic theory, as it once was for the natural sciences to move from Aristotelian scholastic speculation to modern empirical science" is more than a little overzealous, there is no doubt that our current understanding of Post Walrasian man owes much to the contributions of experimentalists and (other) behavioralists.

Consider the example of team production, often represented as a special case of the public goods problem, the quintessential "social dilemma." It is a robust feature of this game that under a wide range of experimental designs, including one shot and repeated stranger treatments, subjects are more *prosocial* than is consistent with standard interpretations of Nash equilibrium (John Ledyard, 1995). In short, workers in experimental labor

---

[2] If Veblen is the madwoman in the Post Walrasian attic, Alfred Marshall can be seen as the movement's popular, if "frumpy Victorian" grandfather (Bowles and Gintis 2000, p. 1411).

markets expend more effort, and free ride on the effort of others less often, than *homo economicus* would. Furthermore, in experiments that allow subjects to monitor and then punish one another, subjects both contribute and are prepared to sanction, at considerable cost to themselves, those who do not contribute their "fair share," behavior that seems at odds with subgame perfection, the relevant equilibrium refinement (Ernst Fehr and Simon Gächter, 2000). Jeff Carpenter (2002) has shown that this willingness to punish, however "irrational," even exhibits some Marshallian regularities, not least of which is a well-behaved demand curve: as the price of punishment rises, for example, experimental subjects spend less on punishment, controlling for the size of the "offense," and so on. Furthermore, those who are punished tend to alter their behavior.

Recent advances in neuroeconomics provide further support for this view. Ernst Fehr, Urs Fischbacher and Michael Kosfeld (2005), for example, review recent evidence from PET images that punishment of non-reciprocators in social dilemmas is associated with the activation of reward-related areas, and report on new results on the effects of oxytocin on prosocial behavior. On the other hand, such research also challenges, or rather qualifies, the Post Walrasian emphasis on information processing skills. As Fehr et al. (2005) observe, there are in fact, two distinct approaches to the "microfoundations of human sociality": in one, the evolution of *boundedly rational* strategies is featured (Larry Samuelson, 2005) while in the other, prosocial preferences are featured.

In the language of Bowles and Gintis (1998), an example of the preference-based approach, the evidence from experiments and artificial life simulations is that, at least in this context, Post Walrasian man is often *nice, punishing* but *forgiving*. He is nice, in the sense that he is cooperative in the earliest stages of economic relationships that reward cooperation, but punishing in the sense that, consistent with the existence of powerful norms, he will sanction antisocial behavior even at some cost to himself. He is also forgiving, however, because the desire to punish dissolves when antisocial behavior is abandoned. Furthermore, these preferences serve Post Walrasian man well: if a sufficient number of those he interacts with have similar preferences, he will even do better, *in material terms*, than *homo economicus*. In other words, one answer to the question that Robert Frank (1987) posed almost two decades ago − if *homo economicus* could choose his own utility function, would he want one with a conscience? − is that Post Walrasians believe that at least some actors have consciences, and are better off for them. Nor is this observation limited to public goods games: the simple tit-for-tat rule that won Robert Axelrod's (1984) much discussed prisoner's dilemma tournament is another example of nice, punishing but forgiving behavior.

Bowles and Gintis (2000) call the behavior observed in these experiments *strong reciprocity*, to distinguish it from either altruism or reciprocal altruism, the form of "enlightened self-interest" that sociobiologists often favor.[3] In addition, recent experimental evidence on "third party punishment" reveals that subjects will sometimes punish free riders both *within and across* groups (Carpenter and Matthews, 2005; Fehr and Simon Gächter, 2004). Consistent with the work of Jon Elster (1998) and others, the results in Carpenter and Matthews (2005) underscore the importance of *emotions* in Post Walrasian man: punishment *within* groups is attributed to "anger" but punishment *across* groups to "indignation." For macroeconomists, these results come as a mixed blessing: the relationship between compensation schemes and output per worker becomes more complicated than simple Walrasian models assume.

The preferences of Post Walrasian man can also be context- or process-specific, as the literature on *framing effects* reveals. Guzik (2004) shows, for example, that in three otherwise common pool resource experiments, there were small but significant differences in behavior when the experiment was framed as an exercise in natural resource use, workplace relations and a simple parlor game. The observation that differences in (even) verbal cues.

From a labor perspective, however, the most important variation in context is that from worker/worker to worker/firm interaction. (There are of course more fundamental strategic differences as well.) It should first be noted, therefore, that reciprocal behavior *is* sometimes manifest in worker/firm experiments. Fehr, Gächter, and Georg Kirchsteiger's (1996) much cited paper found, for example, that even with random matching and no effort enforcement mechanism, workers and firms "traded" more effort for higher wages, consistent with George Akerlof and Janet Yellen's (1990) gift exchange model. The norm that drives this behavior — "a fair day's work for a fair day's pay" — has important consequences for macroeconomists, not least of which is one explanation (Akerlof and Yellen, 1990) of *persistent* involuntary unemployment. The results of this and other similar experiments have also been used to rationalize Truman Bewley's (1999) findings that despite their real wage equivalence, workplace morale suffers more when nominal wages are cut than when the price level rises, a partial vindication of Keynes's much criticized views on wage determination.

---

[3] For this reason, Post Walrasians should interpret Colander's substitution of enlightened self-interest for greed with some care.

(One is tempted to speculate that this reflects Marshall's considerable influence — in particular, the interest in the "psychological propensities" of economic man — on Keynes.)

This does *not* mean, however, that the existence of "nice" preferences are the basis for a complete description of worker/firm interaction. Without obscuring the differences that separate self-identified Post Walrasians — at this point, the Post Walrasian tent is still a big one — it seems to me that without explanations for the conflict, opportunism, and power that sometimes characterize this interaction, the tent will soon start to sag.

Oliver Hart's (1995) argument that economic power exists when complete contracts are not feasible is an alternative point of departure, one that dovetails well with Colander's (2003a) judgment that Post Walrasian man operates in "information poor environments." It is a small step from here to Carl Shapiro and Joseph Stiglitz's (1984) characterization of equilibrium unemployment — or, for those who would prefer a more radical face, the existence of a reserve army — as a "worker discipline device" in a world where effort is difficult to monitor. Viewed from this perspective, Bowles and Gintis' (1993, 2000) interest in the existence of *short side power* in competitive (labor or credit) markets is an important contribution to the Post Walrasian literature.

Unlike the gift exchange paradigm, however, which has inspired dozens, if not hundreds, of experiments, the empirical literature on contested exchange is thin. Fehr, Kirchsteiger, and Arno Reidl (1996), which concludes that *all* of the core predictions of the Shapiro–Stiglitz model are observed in experimental labor markets, is the most notable exception.

These results also illustrate the considerable reach of experimental methods, a benefit that Post Walrasian macroeconomists should (continue to) exploit. As Armin Falk and Ernst Fehr (2003) observe in their "Why Labor Market Experiments?" it can be difficult, and sometimes impossible, to demonstrate the existence of the rents embodied in labor discipline models because of unobserved heterogeneities and (other) measurement difficulties. And while economists' newfound interest in survey data has produced some important insights, it is not clear how much light such data can shed on the "effort extraction problem." The observation that the human resources directors and others interviewed in Bewley (1999) professed to prefer "carrots" over "sticks," for example, is more difficult to interpret than first seems. Even if one abstracts from the problem of "survey bias" — What firm would admit, even to itself, that it threatens its workers? — the Shapiro–Stiglitz model predicts that *in equilibrium*, the threat of dismissal is never exercised. In more prosaic terms, it is difficult to reconcile such data with the fact that at this moment, there are hundreds, if not thousands, of cartoon strips featuring Catbert, the "evil HR Director" in Scott Adams' *Dilbert*, thumbtacked to office cubicles across America. Subject to legitimate concerns about external validation, about which more below, it seems a safe bet that over the next decade or two, a substantial number of the Marshallian regularities that describe the Post Walrasian worker will first be documented in the lab.

The focus to this point on labor-related experiments should not be construed to mean that Post Walrasians should limit their attention to these. And while it was almost inevitable that macroeconomists would be slower to embrace experimental methods than others, there is now considerable interest in them. The literature has become both broad and rich enough, in fact, that I shall do no more than mention a few contributions of particular interest to Post Walrasians, and urge interested readers to consult Colin Camerer and George Loewenstein's (2004) overview of the related literature in behavioral macroeconomics, and the references therein.

John Duffy and Eric O'N. Fisher (2004), for example, have found the first *direct* evidence of sunspot equilibria in the lab, an important result that is consistent with the Post Walrasian emphases on multiple equilibria and, somewhat less prominent, on extrinsic or nonfundamental uncertainty as a coordination mechanism. John Hey and Daniela di Cagno (1998), on the other hand, provide experimental support for Clower's dual-decision model. Neither experiment, however, tells us much new about the character of Post Walrasian man, unlike, for example, those of Eldar Shafir, Peter Diamond, and Amos Tversky (1998) or Fehr and Jean-Robert Tryan (2001), which suggests that Post Walrasian macroeconomists should not be as eager as their Walrasian brethren to renounce the "heresy" of money illusion: real and nominal frames, it seems, elicit different behaviors. There is also experimental evidence that Post Walrasian man creates "mental accounts" (Richard Thaler, 1991) to organize some kinds of economic information, is often loss averse (Amos Tversky and Daniel Kahneman, 1991) and discounts future outcomes at hyperbolic rates (Shane Frederick, George Loewenstein, and Ted O'Donoghue, 2002), with important consequences for intertemporal decisions.

THE VIEW FROM THE THEORIST'S OFFICE

As the previous section suggests, a complete characterization of Post Walrasian man will often draw on experimental data for empirical evidence: he is, in short, the man we observe, not the man we conceptualize.

But this does not mean that conceptualization has no role here. Consider the team production example once more. Aren't some sort of altruistic preferences sufficient to explain the otherwise anomalous contribution levels and doesn't this mean that Post Walrasian man is just *homo economicus* with a few more arguments in his preference function? And wouldn't another argument or two, intended to model the "taste for revenge," also explain punishment?

The answer to all three questions is no. As Bowles and Gintis (2000) observe, the experimental evidence suggests that strong reciprocators are not outcome-oriented but do condition on norm adherence, neither of which is consistent with simple altruism or, for that matter, "enlightened self-interest." Furthermore, no combination of altruism and revenge can explain both outgroup punishment and the punishment differential across groups (Carpenter and Matthews, 2005). And last, to paraphrase Matthew Rabin (1993), the simple transformation of material outcomes in experimental (or other) games on the basis of altruistic preferences is *overdeterministic*: "bad equilibria" are often eliminated in the process, which runs counter to the Post Walrasian notion that economic environments (often) have multiple equilibria in which the "selection problem" cannot be dismissed.

For the theorist, then, the representation of prosocial preferences is not a trivial exercise. Furthermore, he/she should then be able to rebut the "as if" argument that neoclassicals have used, to great rhetorical effect, ever since Armen Alchian (1950): wouldn't some sort of "natural selection" weed out those who contribute rather than free ride, who expend personal resources on norm enforcement, who do not behave, in other words, "as if" endowed with self-interested preferences?[4] As it turns out, the answer is once more "no." The emergence of reciprocal behavior in team production or public goods games, whether strong or social, can be rationalized in terms of an evolutionary dynamic based on the vertical and/or lateral transmission of preferences. This need not be "evolution" in the sense that sociobiologists use the term, however: as Camerer and Loewenstein (2004, p. 40) observe, "we believe in evolution ... but we do not believe that behavior of intelligent, modern people immersed in socialization and cultural influence can be understood *only* by guessing what their ancestral lives were like and how their brains might have adapted genetically." The establishment of prosocial preferences can be understood, in other words, as the product of

---

[4] To be fair, this is a bowdlerized version of Alchian's (1950) argument. On the other hand, so are most other versions, not least those to which students are often introduced.

gene-culture *co-evolution* (Bowles and Gintis, 2000). In some cases, the requisite laws of motion can even be derived on the basis of simple learning models (Carpenter and Matthews, 2004).[5]

Because strict Nash equilibria will also be stable under most dynamics, it comes as no surprise that for some initial conditions, behavior in the team production game will tend toward no contribution/no punishment. For the reasons mentioned earlier, however, Post Walrasians should see this as a desirable feature of the model.

The theory of psychological games, the invention of John Geanakoplos, David Pearce, and Ennio Stachetti (1989), provides another perspective on behavior in team production and other experiments. Their premise, if not its implementation, is a simple one: utilities are allowed to be functions of both outcomes and (hierarchies of) coherent beliefs and in equilibrium, these beliefs are fulfilled. As manifest in the more familiar work of Rabin (1993) and later behavioralists, the notion of a psychological Nash equilibrium was specialized and became the *kindness* (or reciprocal) *equilibrium* that is consistent with observed behavior in these experiments. It was not until the recent work of Martin Dufwenberg and Georg Kirchsteiger (2004), however, that Rabin's framework was extended to sequential games.

The possible role of *intention* in psychological games, a feature that distinguishes this framework from more outcome-oriented models of social preferences, calls for particular attention from Post Walrasians. Experimentalists have known for some time that intention matters: Sally Blount's (1995) often cited paper, for example, shows that rejection rates in ultimatum games are significantly higher when (human) responders believe the proposals to be computer-generated. For macroeconomists, an awareness of intention could contribute to a better understanding of wage and price rigidities. As the work of Daniel Kahneman, Jack Knetsch, and Richard Thaler (1990) reminds us, for example, the firm that sells bottled water to hurricane victims is perceived to be unfair — and in some jurisdictions, prosecuted for price gouging — but one that increases its price because its costs have risen is not. The surprise, as Camerer and Loewenstein (2004) observe, is how little macroeconomists have made of this observation. In a similar vein, when I have sometimes asked non-economists, including students, to explain the "morale differential"

---

[5] There is in fact considerable debate about what "evolution" should — and should not — mean in economics, but almost no disagreement that the preferences of Post Walrasian man are sustainable.

between nominal wage reductions and price increases, the most common response is that the firm's intentions make the former more "personal."

The notion of a psychological game is broader than Rabin's (1993) specialized model hints, however, even if the literature devoted to alternative applications remains thin. Geanakoplos (1996) himself, for example, has proposed psychological game theoretic solutions to two outstanding problems in decision theory, the Hangman's Paradox and Newcomb's Paradox. In principle, this framework can accommodate a Post Walrasian man who is sometimes surprised – an impossible state of mind, it should be added, in Walrasian models with a complete set of spot and future markets – or disappointed or even furious. Though much research remains to be done, it could also be consistent with prosocial behavior other than that manifest in a kindness equilibrium. Furthermore, Rabin (1993) was careful to underscore that in the games he considered, the transformation of material outcomes is not "trivial" – i.e., self-interested preferences are not replaced with altruistic ones – so that there are multiple psychological Nash equilibria. If there is bad news here, it is that reliable field data on even first order beliefs are scarce, so that the burden of empirical research falls on the experimentalists.

(As an historical aside, it is important that Post Walrasian macro-economists recognize that the search for better psychological/behavioral microfoundations did not start with them. Almost four decades ago, for example, James Tobin and Trenary Dolbear [1963, p. 679] lamented the fact that "economics has sought to be neutral with respect to the sources of preferences, but it has purchased this neutrality at the cost of substantive content" and provided several examples. In the case of consumption, for example, "the disregard of social interdependence ... contradict[ed] everyday observation as well as the presumptions of sociology and social psychology" [Tobin and Dolbear, 1963, p. 679]. In fact, their call for the use of more, and better designed, surveys intended to link the psychological characteristics of respondents and their economic decisions still resonates.)

For those who concede that *homo economicus* is not well, but are not prepared to bid him farewell, some if not most of the behavior in team production experiments is better explained as a *quantal response equilibrium* in which experimental subjects best respond to one another's anticipated "trembles." Charles Holt and a number of co-authors have turned to *stochastic game theory* to rationalize all sorts of experimental anomalies, from behavior in traveler's dilemma, coordination, and signaling games (Jacob Goeree and Charles Holt, 2001) to the public goods game considered here (Simon Anderson, Jacob Goeree, and Charles

Holt, 1998). Whether or not this research program should be considered Post Walrasian is perhaps a matter of taste. On the one hand, its economic actors are purposeful in the traditional (that is, Walrasian) sense of the word and are not boundedly rational per se but instead self-consciously nervous, *homo economicus* in need of a long vacation. On the other hand, it would be foolish to insist that Post Walrasian man never trembles or that he doesn't know, even account for, this. Furthermore, the equilibria of such models are the result of a particular sort of expectations-based social interaction.

THE VIEW FROM THE FIELD

To all of this the resolute Walrasian could still respond, "So what?" A theoretical paradigm that broadens our sense of how rational economic actors *could* behave and the observation of such behavior in controlled — but sterile? — lab environments is not evidence, he will counter, that Post Walrasian man lives where it matters, in the wild. Even the recent wave of "field experiments" has failed to convince the skeptics: the fact that subjects outside the lab with (often) substantial amounts on the line exhibit the same behavior as their counterparts in the lab does not mean, it is sometimes said, that either will reach similar decisions in the hurly-burly of everyday life. To provide a concrete example, the fact that neither well-to-do undergraduates nor the much less affluent participants in the "fifteen small-scale societies" project (Joseph Henrich et al., 2001) resemble *homo economicus* in public goods experiments does not mean that both will resist the temptation to free ride in the "real world." (Because I do not want to misrepresent the results of this exceptional achievement, I hasten to add that there were substantial differences across the fifteen societies. In the Ache [Paraguay] and Tsimané [Bolivia] groups, for example, there were fewer free riders *and* fewer full cooperators than in most North American or European subject pools, a reminder that the character of Post Walrasian man is not independent of his environment.)

One strict approach to external validation requires that behavior observed in experimental settings predict behavior or outcomes in nonexperimental ones. Given the practical difficulties involved, there are few examples of such tests, but the little evidence that does exist is encouraging. Abigail Barr and Peter Serneels (2004), for example, find that for Ghanian manufacturing workers, experimental measures of reciprocal behavior were correlated with wages, *ceteris paribus*, but concede that it is not clear from the data in which direction the causal arrow points. In a similar vein,

Jeff Carpenter and Erika Sakei (2004) find that among the Japanese fishermen in Toyama Bay, the more prosocial individual crew members were in a public goods experiment with monitoring, the more productive their boat was, controlling for the size and speed of the boat, the number of crew members, the experience of the captain, and so on. So while there is much work to be done − there are few studies of Western workers, for example − there is also reason to believe that it will bear Post Walrasian fruit.

But what about field data that does not come from an experiment and cannot be linked to one, the sort of data that applied econometricians are most familiar with? Can social preferences or, in broader terms, interaction effects even be identified in such data? Few have done more to answer these questions − and in the process illuminate some of the shortcomings with standard interpretations of experimental data − than Charles Manski, whose initial statement of the *reflection problem* (Manski, 1993) should be considered part of the Post Walrasian canon. In it he distinguishes three broad categories of interaction effect − endogenous, contextual and correlated − and shows that in the linear-in-means model, a simple but natural specification, the endogenous effects in which Post Walrasians will be interested cannot be separated from contextual ones. The intuition, as Manski (2000, p. 25) himself later described it, is that because "mean behavior in the group is itself determined by the behavior of group members ... data on outcomes do not reveal whether group behavior actually affects individual behavior, or group behavior is simply the aggregation of individual behaviors."

The immediate lesson for Post Walrasians is *not* that interaction effects are undetectable in nonexperimental data. For one thing, the reflection problem complicates the interpretation of experimental data too, a fact that experimentalists themselves have been (too) slow to appreciate. But as the recent work of Michael Carter and Marco Castillo (2004) demonstrates, careful attention to experimental design allows such effects to be identified even in the linear-in-means model. (For the record, Carter and Castillo do find evidence of "emulation effects" in field experiments conducted in 30 rural Honduran communities.) And a number of enterprising researchers have recognized that some natural experiments can facilitate identification: Bruce Sacerdote's (2001) clever paper, for example, exploits the random assignment of roommates at Dartmouth College to demonstrate the existence of significant peer effects.

Since the reflection problem was first posed, we have also learned that functional form − in particular, the introduction of "reasonable nonlinearities" — can solve the identification problem, at least in those cases where the researcher knows the boundaries of the reference group and its characteristics. William Brock and Steven Durlauf (2001a), for example, show that in discrete choice models with interaction effects, an extension of the logit model is a natural specification.

Alas, even in those cases where the existence of some sort of interaction can be identified, the econometric models in Manski (2000) or Brock and Durlauf (2001b) cannot tell us much about the source of the *social multiplier*. For those interested in the character of Post Walrasian man, however, the difference between expectations-driven interactions and preference-driven ones is fundamental. For this and other reasons, and despite all that has been achieved over the last decade, Post Walrasian macroeconomists still have much to do.

PART II

EDGING AWAY FROM THE DSGE MODEL

5

Social Interactions and Macroeconomics

William A. Brock and Steven N. Durlauf[*]

Political economy ... finds the laws underlying a mass of contingent occurrences.
It is an interesting spectacle to observe here how all of the interconnections have
repercussions on others, how the particular spheres fall into groups, influence
others, and are helped or hindered by these. This interaction, which at first sight
seems incredible since everything seems to depend on the arbitrary will of the
individual, is particularly worthy of note ...
    G. W. F. Hegel, *Elements of the Philosophy of Right*

Within economics, social interactions research constitutes a growing area
of study. This research represents a good faith attempt to introduce
substantive sociological factors into economic modeling. As such, this work
represents a significant departure from the sorts of market-mediated
interdependences between individuals that one finds in general equilibrium
theory. While the substantive ideas underlying this work may be found in
now-classic papers such as Loury (1977), the modern social interactions
literature is quite young. Despite this, there are now an impressive range
of applications of social interactions models in microeconomic contexts.
Examples of phenomena where empirical evidence of social interactions
has been found include (1) crime (Glaeser, Sacerdote, and Scheinkman
[1996], Sirakaya [2003]), (2) welfare and public assistance use (Aizer and
Currie [2004], Bertrand, Luttmer, and Mullainathan [2000]), (3) fertility
(Brooks-Gunn et al. [1993], Rivkin [2001]), (4) housing demand and
urban development (Irwin and Bockstaed [2002], Ioannides and Zabel
[2003a,b]), (5) contract determination (Young and Burke [2001, 2003]),

* We would like to thank the National Science Foundation, John D. and Catherine
T. MacArthur Foundation, Vilas Trust, and University of Wisconsin Graduate School for
financial support. Ethan Cohen-Cole and Giacomo Rondina have provided outstanding
research assistance as well as helpful suggestions.

(6) employment (Oomes [2003], Topa [2001], Weinberg, Reagan, and Yankow [2004]), (7) cigarette smoking (Krauth [2003], Nakajima [2003]), (8) school performance (Boozer and Cacciola [2001], Graham [2005]) and even (9) medical techniques (Burke, Fournier, and Prasad [2004]).

While the importance of social interactions has been argued for a range of interesting behaviors, far less attention has been paid to the role of social interactions in aggregate phenomena. The one partial exception to this claim is the use of social interactions to study inequality and the aggregate cross-section income distribution and/or dynamics of inequality (Bénabou, 1996; Durlauf, 1996). There has yet to be any systematic examination of whether social interactions may help explain the standard macroeconomic phenomena: growth and fluctuations, although elements of the existing literature may be connected to social interactions.

In this chapter, we attempt to accomplish two things. First, we review some of the theory and econometrics of social interactions. This part of the chapter will represent a brief synthesis of a large literature; more extensive surveys include Brock and Durlauf (2001b) and Durlauf (2004). Second, we consider how this body of work may be related to macroeconomics. This discussion is necessarily speculative. Our objective is to stimulate further work on social interactions that moves the field towards the consideration of aggregate phenomena.

SOCIAL INTERACTIONS: THEORY

A Baseline Model

We first describe the general structure of social interactions models. We follow the approach we have taken in previous work (Brock and Durlauf, 2001a,b, 2004a,b). Consider a group of I individuals who are members of a common group g. Individual i makes a choice ω_i. The description of the decision problem facing agent i is used to construct a conditional probability measure for ω_i in which the conditioning variables reflect different individual and social influences on the choice. The conditional probability measures that describe individual choice embody the micro-foundations of the model. The set of conditional probability measures for each individual is then used to construct a conditional probability measure for the vector of choices of all the members of the group, which we denote as ω_g. Equilibrium in a social interactions model may be understood as the consistency between the individual-level probability measures and the joint probability measure.

In modeling individual decisions, there are four distinct factors that determine individual and, hence, group behavior. Distinguishing among these factors is important in terms of both the development of the theory and its econometric implementation. These factors are:

X_i: deterministic (to the modeler) individual-specific characteristics associated with individual i,

ε_i: random individual-specific characteristics associated with i,

Y_g: predetermined (with respect to ω_g) group-level characteristics, and

$\mu_i^e(\omega_{g,-i})$: a subjective probability measure that captures the beliefs individual i possesses about behaviors of others in the group.

Two of these factors, Y_g and $\mu_i^e(\omega_{g,-i})$, capture how membership in a group affects an individual. Following Manski (1993), Y_g measures what are known as contextual effects and $\mu_i^e(\omega_{g,-i})$ captures what are known as endogenous effects; the key difference between the two is that endogenous effects capture how the behaviors of others in a group affect an individual whereas contextual effects capture how the characteristics of others in a group affect him. The endogenous effect is typically determined by the equilibrium of the model whereas contextual effects are typically modeled as predetermined. A typical endogenous effect is the expected average behavior of others whereas a typical contextual effect is the average of some individual characteristics of others, such as age. We model endogenous effects as beliefs rather than as outcomes, that is, individuals are affected by what they think others will do rather than what they actually do. By allowing beliefs to mediate endogenous effects, substantial analytical convenience is achieved. The appropriateness of this assumption will depend on context; presumably for small groups, such as friendship trios, individuals know the actual behavior of others whereas for larger groups, such as ethnicity, beliefs about behavior are what matters.

While this abstract description of social interactions as either contextual or endogenous effects is useful for formal modeling, we should note that it obscures the actual mechanisms by which social interactions may occur. Within the social interactions literature, there has been interest in peer effects (in which individuals imitate others due to a direct utility benefit), information effects (in which the behavior of others provides information on the payoffs to a person's choices), role model effects (in which the previous behavior of some individuals affects the current choices of group members), social norms (the emergence of rules by which individuals are punished by others for certain behaviors), etc. There has yet to be much integration of these types of direct sources of interdependences in decisions into formal social interactions models; such integration would be quite valuable, particularly for questions such as counterfactual evaluation of policy.

In our baseline model, individual decisions follow standard micro-economic analysis in that they represent those choices that maximize an individual payoff function $V(\cdot)$, which, given the factors we have described, means that each individual choice ω_i is defined by

$$\omega_i = \arg\max_{\omega \in \Omega_i} V\big(\omega, X_i, \varepsilon_i, Y_g, \mu_i^e(\omega_{g,-i})\big). \tag{1}$$

The solution to this problem for all members of the group produces a set of conditional probability measures

$$\mu\big(\omega_i | X_i, Y_g, \mu_i^e(\omega_{g,-i})\big), \tag{2}$$

which describes how observable (to the econometrician) individual-specific and contextual effects as well as unobservable (to the econometrician) beliefs influence the likelihood of the possible choices.

Under our assumptions, moving from the specification of individuals to group behavior is straightforward. Since the errors are independent, the joint probability measure of decisions will equal the product of the conditional probability measures

$$\mu\big(\omega_g | Y_g, X_1, \mu_1^e(\omega_{g,-1}), \ldots, X_I, \mu_I^e(\omega_{g,-I})\big) = \prod_i \mu\big(\omega_i | X_i, Y_g, \mu_i^e(\omega_{g,-i})\big). \tag{3}$$

To complete this model, it is necessary to specify how beliefs are formed. The benchmark in the literature is that beliefs are rational in the sense that the subjective beliefs an individual possesses about others corresponds to the actual probability measure that describes those behaviors given the information available to the individual. We assume that this information set comprises the deterministic characteristics and beliefs of others X_j and $\mu_j^e(\omega_{-j})$, so that subjective beliefs obey

$$\mu_i^e(\omega_{g,-i}) = \mu\big(\omega_{g,-i} | Y_g, X_1, \mu_1^e(\omega_{g,-1}), \ldots, X_I, \mu_I^e(\omega_{g,-I})\big). \tag{4}$$

While recent developments in behavioral economics suggest the importance of moving beyond this notion of rationality in describing beliefs, the self-consistency embedded in Eq. (4) is a key baseline in understanding the properties of social interactions models.

Together, Eqs. (1)−(4) represent a complete description of behavior within a group. The main technical issues that arise in the study of such models is the demonstration that a joint probability measure exists which satisfies Eqs. (3) and (4); the mathematical techniques for developing such proofs are discussed in Blume (1993), Brock (1993), Durlauf (1993), Bisin, Horst, and Ozgur (2004), and Horst and Scheinkman (2004). One should also note the early work by Föllmer (1974) and Allen (1982), which anticipated the modern social interactions approach. These early papers are useful in making clear the links among social interactions models and models of statistical mechanics that appear in physics and models of random fields that appear in probability theory.

Properties

The interesting properties of social interactions models occur when these models exhibit strategic complementarities in behavior. The key idea underlying the notion of complementarity is that incentives exist to behave similarly to others. Formally, let μ^{high} and μ^{low} denote two probability measures such that for any fixed vector $\bar{\omega}$, $\mu^{\text{high}}(\omega_{-i,g} \geq \bar{\omega}) \geq \mu^{\text{low}}(\omega_{-i,g} \geq \bar{\omega})$; this condition means that higher values of $\omega_{-i,g}$ are more likely under μ^{high} than μ^{low}. Let $\omega^{\text{high}} > \omega^{\text{low}}$ denote two possible levels of ω_i. The payoff function V exhibits strategic complementarities if

$$V(\omega^{\text{high}}, \varepsilon_i, X_i, Y_g, \mu^{\text{high}}) - V(\omega^{\text{low}}, \varepsilon_i, X_i, Y_g, \mu^{\text{high}}) > \\ V(\omega^{\text{high}}, \varepsilon_i, X_i, Y_g, \mu^{\text{low}}) - V(\omega^{\text{low}}, \varepsilon_i, X_i, Y_g, \mu^{\text{low}}). \tag{5}$$

Equation (5) captures the idea that when others are expected to make relatively high choices, the relative attractiveness of a high choice is increased for each individual.

Complementarity in individual payoffs has important implications for the aggregate equilibrium in social interactions models. The following properties are among those found in social interactions models.[1]

Multiple equilibria
When complementarities are sufficiently strong, multiple equilibria can exist. This means that more than one joint probability measure for the

---

[1] This discussion borrows from Durlauf (2001).

vector of choices ω_g are compatible with the conditional probabilities that describe the individual choices. Intuitively, complementarities mean that each individual has incentives to behave similarly to others, that is, conformity effects are present. When this conformity effect is sufficiently large relative to other influences, this introduces a degree of freedom in aggregate behavior: individuals in equilibrium behave similarly to one another, but this does not uniquely determine what they will do.

Phase transition

Phase transitions exist when small changes in a parameter of a system can induce qualitative changes in the system's equilibrium. Phase transitions are common in physical contexts. A standard example in physics concerns the relationship between the state of water and its temperature. When the temperature of water moves from slightly above 32°F to below 32°F, the water undergoes a transition from liquid to solid. In social interactions models, phase transitions occur via the interplay of endogenous social interactions and other influences. Suppose there is a parameter that measures the strength of endogenous social interactions; this is the case in Brock and Durlauf (2001a,b, 2004a), for example. When this parameter is zero, then the equilibrium is unique. Suppose that when this parameter is infinity, all agents behave the same as one another, as the payoff loss from not doing so is unbounded, inducing multiple equilibria. Then, as this parameter is increased from zero to infinity, at some point the number of equilibria will change. A phase transition occurs when this change is discontinuous.

Social multipliers

Regardless of the number of equilibria, social interactions models will typically exhibit social multipliers, which means that the equilibrium effect of a change in Y_g on individual m_g increases with the level of complementarity in the system. The basic idea is that when there are complementarities in behavior, a change in Y_g affects each person both directly as in Eq. (2) and indirectly, via the effect of the change in Y_g on the behavior of others, that is, $\mu^e(\omega_{g,-i})$, as captured in Eq. (4).

These properties are not necessarily present in social interactions models, but they typically arise depending on the level of the complementarities embedded in the individual payoff functions.

SOCIAL INTERACTIONS: ECONOMETRICS

In this section, we briefly review some of the econometric issues that arise in trying to bring social interactions models to data. Our focus will be on identification problems, that is, the extent to which socioeconomic data can provide evidence of social interactions given alternate explanations for individual outcomes. As such, we will review the main econometric work that has been accomplished for the study of social interactions. It is important to note that many outstanding issues remain, such as how to account for the lack of prior knowledge about the identity of the group that affects individuals in a given data set or how to allow for different strengths of interactions across members of a given group. Manski (2000) discusses many such issues.

Identification and the Reflection Problem

The first difficulty in identifying social interactions concerns the distinction between contextual and endogenous effects. Manski (1993), in a classic analysis, indicates how it may be impossible to disentangle these different effects in a linear model.

To see why this is so, consider the linear-in-means model of social interactions, which Manski studied:

$$\omega_i = k + cX_i + dY_g + Jm_g^e + \varepsilon_i, \tag{6}$$

where m_g^e denotes the subjective expected value of the average choice in group g. Relative to the general formulation, this model assumes all endogenous effects work through this average. For now, we assume that $E(\varepsilon_i | X_i, Y_g, i \in g) = 0$, so that the model residuals are uncorrelated with the model regressors and no self-selection effects are present.

As discussed earlier, under self-consistency, the subjective expected average equals the actual expected average, m_g, which is defined by

$$m_g = \frac{k + cX_g + dY_g}{1 - J} = \frac{k + dY_g}{1 - J} + \frac{cX_g}{1 - J}, \tag{7}$$

where X_g is the average of X_i across members of group g. Comparing Eqs. (6) and (7), it is easy to see why an identification problem can arise. Unless $cX_g/(1 - J)$ is linearly independent from Y_g, one cannot distinguish between endogenous and contextual effects. Put differently, endogenous social interactions are linearly dependent on the contextual effects; this is what is meant by the reflection problem. The reflection problem indicates the importance of prior information for identification in linear models. For example, suppose that one does not have any basis for distinguishing individual and contextual variables, in other words, that a researcher has no basis for arguing that for certain elements of X_i the corresponding values in the group average X_g are not elements of Y_g. This would imply that $X_g = Y_g$ so identification fails. This is precisely Manski's insight.

The reflection problem is specific to linear regressions. To see this, following Brock and Durlauf (2001b), consider the nonlinear model

$$\omega_i = k + cX_i + dY_g + J\lambda\left(m_g^e\right) + \varepsilon_i, \tag{8}$$

where $\lambda(\cdot)$ is an invertible function with $\lambda'' \neq 0$, that is, the second derivative of the function is nonzero. Defining $\psi(\cdot) = 1 - J\lambda(\cdot)$, the self-consistent expected average choice equals

$$m_g = \psi^{-1}\left(k + cX_g + dY_g\right). \tag{9}$$

Even if $X_g = Y_g$, Eq. (9) indicates that m_g cannot be linearly dependent on Y_g, so long as Y_g has a large enough support.

Similar reasoning indicates why the reflection problem does not arise in discrete choice or duration data models; see Brock and Durlauf (2001b, 2004a,b) for formal proofs. This is straightforward to see for a discrete choice model where the expected percentage of individuals in a group that make a particular choice is the measure of endogenous effects associated with the choice. Because these percentages must lie between zero and one, they cannot be linear functions of Y_g.

Relatively little work has been done on the estimation of nonlinear social interactions models; exceptions include Bisin, Moro, and Topa (2002), Krauth (2004), and Sirakaya (2003). This is an important area for future analysis if the identification results for such models are to be useful in practice and is ready to proceed given the results on identification that are now available.

Self-selection

The assumption is that $E\left(\varepsilon_i \mid X_i, Y_g, i \in g\right) = 0$ is unappealing in contexts where group memberships are endogenous, as occurs in cases such as residential neighborhoods. Following Heckman's (1979) classic formulation, one can think of self-selection as an omitted-variables problem, in the sense that the appropriate linear regression model in the presence of self-selection is

$$\omega_i = cX_i + dY_g + Jm_g + E(\varepsilon_i | X_i, Y_g, i \in g) + \xi_i. \tag{10}$$

It is easy to see why failing to account for self-selection can induce spurious evidence of social interactions. Consider the question of identifying social interaction effects on academic performance of students. If relatively ambitious parents self-select into neighborhoods with higher student achievement, the failing to account for this self-selection can lead one to the appearance of social interactions effects when none are in fact present. The potential importance of self-selection is indicated by Evans, Oates, and Schwab (1992), who show that instrumental variables estimates of social interactions, designed to overcome self-selection, can eliminate statistically significant evidence of social interactions. Rivkin (2001), using similar instruments, produces an analysis in which the instrumental variables produce much larger evidence of social interactions than when instruments are not used. We concur with Rivkin's interpretation that his results show that it is problematic to identify valid instruments in social interactions contexts; Brock and Durlauf (2001c), while discussing a very different issue (economic growth), provide some general reasons why finding persuasive instrumental variables is extremely hard for theories (such as social interactions) that are "open-ended," that is, theories whose internal logic does not exclude alternative theories of behavior from operating simultaneously.

This is one reason we prefer the explicit modeling of self-selection when analyzing social interactions. Self-selection does not represent an insuperable problem in drawing inferences on social interactions; as is well understood in the microeconometrics literature, consistent model estimates can be achieved in a variety of circumstances so long as self-selection is accounted for.

From the perspective of social interactions work, the new idea that emerges when accounting for self-selection, and our second reason for advocating explicit modeling of self-selection, is that it can help with identification. Specifically, Brock and Durlauf (2001b) show that if one can model the self-selection correction, self-selection can contribute to identification by addressing aspects of the reflection problem.

To understand why this is so, consider the original linear-in-means model. Suppose that $X_g = Y_g$ so that if $E(\varepsilon_i | X_i, Y_g, i \in g) = 0$ identification fails because of the reflection problem. As shown in Brock and Durlauf (2001b), self-selection may allow identification for this same linear-in-means model for two distinct reasons, depending on the structure of $E(\varepsilon_i | X_i, Y_g, i \in g) = 0$. First, if $E(\varepsilon_i | X_i, Y_g, i \in g) = \phi(m_g)$, that is, self-selection is determined by the expected average behavior of the neighborhood, then the selection correction induces nonlinearity into the model, thereby eliminating the possibility of a reflection problem outside of hairline cases.

Alternatively, if $E(\varepsilon_i | X_i, Y_g, i \in g) = \phi(X_i)$, then the selection correction is an example of an individual-specific variable whose group-level analog does not appear in the Y_g variables. The average of $E(\varepsilon_i | X_i, Y_g, i \in g)$ within g will function as an additional X_g variable that is not an element of Y_g; the average value of $E(\varepsilon_i | X_i, Y_g, i \in g)$ does not appear as a contextual effect in the model specification. Intuitively, self-selection provides additional information on an agent's behavior which may be used to uncover the role that social interactions may have in influencing his decisions.

While Brock and Durlauf (2001b) develop this general argument in the context of self-selection with respect to a binary choice, this idea can be generalized to multiple groups, as in Brock and Durlauf (2004a) and Ioannides and Zabel (2003b). The potential for using self-selection to facilitate the identification of social interactions is illustrated in Ioannides and Zabel (2003b), who use selection corrections for residential neighborhoods to identify interdependences in housing demand.

So far, analyses of self-selection corrections as facilitators of identification have all employed parametric corrections, that is, strong assumptions are made on the error distributions in both the selection equation and the behavioral model. An important next step in this work is the analysis of semiparametric selection corrections. Another useful extension is the linking of this approach to identification with hedonic modeling, in which prices for group memberships such as residential housing presumably contain information on social interactions. Methods to extract such information may be found in Ekeland, Heckman, and Nesheim (2002, 2004) and Nesheim (2002).

Unobserved Group Effects

A second important issue in social interactions models concerns the possibility of unobserved group effects. Suppose that the correct behavioral model is

$$\omega_i = k + cX_i + dY_g + Jm_g + \alpha_g + \xi_i \tag{11}$$

where α_g is a fixed effect. Without any restrictions on α_g, it is obvious that Eq. (11) is not identified, since for a given model one can always rewrite this original equation with $\alpha_g^* = \alpha_g + dY_g + Jm_g$, $d = 0$, $J = 0$ and perfectly replicate the behavior of ω_i. As in the case of self-selection, it is easy to identify cases where unobserved group effects are likely to matter, so that ignoring them will lead to noncredible inferences. For example, if one wants to identify endogenous social interactions in a classroom, one needs to account for unobserved differences in teacher quality.

Unobserved group effects appear to be somewhat more difficult to address than self-selection since there is no natural way to model the effects using economic theory. One possible solution is to employ panel data and eliminate the fixed effects through differencing; this approach is suggested in Brock and Durlauf (2001b) and pursued in detail by Graham and Hahn (2004). While differencing can solve the fixed effects problem in principle, it is not clear that the sorts of fixed effects associated with groups are necessarily time-invariant. For example, teacher quality may vary across time due to changes in experience, health, etc. Another route to achieving identification for this model is to assume that α_g may be modeled as a random effect; this approach is developed in Graham (2005). This assumption is relatively appealing in contexts such as random assignment of teachers to classrooms, as is studied by Graham.

For nonlinear models, it is possible to achieve partial identification even in cross sections. This is shown for binary-choice models in Brock and Durlauf (2004b). The basic idea of this approach is to ask whether there are shape restrictions one may place on the cross-group distribution function for α_g, F_α, that would allow for the data to reveal the presence of social interaction effects. What Brock and Durlauf (2004b) show is that for binary-choice models where the endogenous social interactions parameter is large enough to induce multiple equilibria across groups, such shape restrictions exist. While the specific arguments are complicated, the basic ideas are relatively intuitive. For example, one version of this approach is to identify restrictions on F_α that imply that m_g (as before, the expected average choice in a group) is monotonically increasing in Y_g when $J = 0$. One can then derive evidence by comparing expected average choices between pairs of groups, g and g'. If one then observes cases where

$m_g > m_{g'}$ whereas $Y_g < Y_{g'}$, this can only be explained by g and g' coordinating at equilibria that allow such a "pattern reversal." Another version of this approach involves exploiting the role of multiple equilibria in producing bimodality of the conditional distribution of m_g given Y_g, which extends and makes rigorous ideas that appear in Glaeser, Sacerdote, and Scheinkman (1996). Pattern-reversal findings of this type represent a form of partial identification (Manski, 2003) in that their presence does not provide an estimate of the value of J, but rather implies that it is non-negative and large enough to induce multiple equilibria.

MACROECONOMIC APPLICATIONS

In this section, we consider some possible uses of social interactions models in macroeconomic contexts. To some extent, the arguments here will echo previous analyses that have claimed an important role for complementarities in aggregate analysis; Cooper (1999) provides a valuable survey of this perspective. One feature that distinguishes our discussion is the emphasis on complementarites as a manifestation of social forces. Further, our probabilistic formulation of social interactions creates a natural way to move from theory to empirical work, since the equilibrium joint probability measures in our social interactions models may be interpreted as likelihood functions from the econometric perspective.

Economic Growth

One area where we believe social interactions may have important aggregate consequences is in terms of long term economic growth. Within growth economics, there is a small but growing body of work that has focused on the role of "culture" in explaining cross-country growth differences. On the empirical side, work of this type has focused on factors that range from trust (Knack and Keefer, 1997) to religious views (Barro and McCleary, 2003). These papers are suggestive, but suffer from complicated identification problems (Brock and Durlauf, 2001c; Durlauf, Johnson, and Temple, 2004). In essence, these findings are difficult to interpret because of the model uncertainty that plagues cross-country growth regressions with respect to the choice of variables and the measurement of social factors. We believe that aggregate studies of this type are a useful starting point, but feel they need to be supplemented with studies using disaggregated data that permits a resolution of these types of problems. We therefore interpret these aggregate studies as indicating that more careful analysis of social forces and growth is warranted.

A second source of evidence on the role of social factors in growth derives from economic history. Landes (1998) provides a broad argument in favor of this perspective with many suggestive examples. Other studies represent careful empirical delineations of particular historical episodes or comparisons. Important evidence of a role for social interactions in growth has been developed in Clark (1987); additional findings of this type appear in Wolcott and Clark (1999). This paper compares productivity differences between cotton mills in New England versus those in Great Britain, Greece, Germany, Japan, India, and China for the period around 1910. This comparison is especially interesting as the technology for cotton weaving did not differ across these countries and so one can engage in relatively straightforward comparisons of factories. Clark finds immense productivity differences between textile workers; around 1910, output per textile worker in New England was 1.5 times greater than in Great Britain, 2.3 times greater than in Germany, and 6 times greater than in Japan.

How can one interpret such a finding? One possibility, which is the basis of Clark's analysis, relates to social norms and effort. Clark is able to argue persuasively that these differences are not due to managerial or worker quality, but are due to what he calls "local culture." This type of analysis is a natural candidate for a formal social interactions-type analysis. Work such as Lindbeck, Nyberg, and Weibull (1999), which provides a model of social norms and welfare/work decisions, could be readily adapted to this. More generally, we see social interactions as providing an underpinning for efforts to formally model culture. For example, it seems reasonable to suppose that culture is to some extent a manifestation of how individuals define their identities, in the sense of Akerlof and Kranton (2000) or Fang and Loury (2004). To the extent that social interactions-type phenomena such as peer influences or conformity effects help determine which identities become salient in a population, social interactions can play a role in producing cultural differences. Social interactions approaches would be of particular interest if one could identify substantial within-country variation in productivity, so that the cultural differences identified by Clark are in fact generated locally.

Moving to new growth theory, one can identify a number of models that have social interactions components. One class of models focuses on the formation of trading networks that link different economic actors and the concomitant implications for industrialization and development. By way of background, Kirman (1983a, b) was the first to show that small differences in the process by which direct bilateral connections between economic actors form can produce, when markets represent groups of actors that are directly or indirectly linked, either economy-wide markets or many groups of small markets; the implications of these different market sizes for macroeconomic outcomes such as overall levels of risk-sharing are explored in Ioannides (1990). These ideas have proven useful in understanding the expansion of market size and its implications for economic development. A particularly interesting analysis is due to Kelly (1997) who models the takeoff to industrialization as a type of phase transition. Alternatively, one can use social interactions-type models to understand how local spillover effects can affect growth. This approach is taken in Durlauf (1993), where sector-specific spillovers can produce a phase transition from underdevelopment to industrialization in response to small increases in productivity.

In considering the roles of social norms and trading networks as mechanisms explaining industrialization and growth, we are led to conjecture that one can develop a vision of the development process in which social or cultural norms and preferences diffuse because of trading relationships and eventually dominate a population. To be clear, one needs to be careful about what this process encumbers. De Vries (1994) has argued that, in understanding the Industrial Revolution, one needs to account for the "industrious revolution" by which labor supply dramatically increased in England beginning in the 1600s. De Vries' claim has been challenged by Voth (1998) who finds that increases in hours worked occurred in the middle 1700s rather than earlier and by Clark and van der Werf (1998) who find little evidence of increased work rates in England before 1850. We are sympathetic with Clark's focus on effort while working as opposed to hours worked per se. But for either measure, one can envision the diffusion of new work attitudes and behaviors as a dynamic social interaction process. And we regard the debates over the industrious revolution as indicative of a role for more formal identification analysis in disentangling different types of social interactions that may be present. While we of course have no reason to think that there exist historical data sets that would allow estimation of the models we have described, the identification results provide clues as to what sort of evidence could help in resolving disagreements. In fact, we believe that the development of a complete evaluation of evidence for social interactions may well require considerable attention to evidence sources such as historical ones that are not amenable to full econometric analysis; of which Clark's work is an outstanding example.

Fluctuations

At first glance, it is less clear how social interactions approaches can influence the study of economic fluctuations. One perhaps trivial reason for this is that the primary body of dynamic stochastic general equilibrium (DSGE) models that are used in current macroeconomic theory have not been developed in ways in which there are natural routes for embodying social interactions. While recent work on DSGE models has made important advances in modeling individual heterogeneity (Krusell and Smith (1998) is an exemplar), DSGE models have not generally developed in directions where social interactions are a natural addition to existing microfoundations.

That being said, there are important strands of the modern macroeconomic literature where social interactions models may prove to be useful. As well reviewed in Cooper (1999), there has been considerable work in macroeconomics that has attempted to use the idea of complementarities in a range of contexts. One strand concerns the role of increasing returns to scale in propagating aggregate fluctuations. As developed for example in Benhabib and Farmer (1994), increasing returns to scale may lead to indeterminacy in the equilibrium paths of macroeconomic aggregates, this means that a given specification of the microeconomic structure of the economy, while leading to a unique balanced growth path, is consistent with multiple paths for output, consumption, etc. One important implication of increasing returns and indeterminacy is that business cycle fluctuations may be induced by self-fulfilling expectations. Focusing specifically on the "animal spirits" of investors, Farmer and Guo (1994), engage in a number of calibration exercises to demonstrate that these effects can capture a number of observed dynamic relationships in the U.S. economy.

We conjecture that the introductions of social interactions into some aspects of business cycle models can strengthen the microfoundations for these types of results. At one level, we would argue that social interactions models can help to elucidate the microfoundations that have already been identified. For example, suppose there are social interactions in the labor force participation decision. If so, then the potential for phase transition in social interactions models can induce nonconvexities in the aggregate supply schedule.

Alternatively, to the extent that one wishes to understand animal spirits of investors, work such as Brock (1993) suggests that a natural way to understand shifts in investor beliefs is via the interdependences in these beliefs; formal mechanisms for this are described in Brock and Hommes (1997). In our view, understanding waves of optimism and pessimism in the macroeconomy is critical in understanding short term and medium term fluctuations. We further believe that interdependence of beliefs play an essential role in generating these waves. Put differently, phenomena such as "irrational exuberance," to employ Robert Shiller's (2001) term, emerge, we would argue, precisely because individual beliefs are highly interdependent, so that small outside changes can be magnified up into large fluctuations on average.

Indeed the whole literature on "sunspot" effects (that is, effects of "extrinsic uncertainty") could benefit from the introduction of social interactions. A problem with the sunspots literature is that while one can demonstrate theoretically that sunspot effects can have macro level effects, existing sunspot models do not demonstrate why a cross sectional form of the law of large numbers might not apply to "wash out" the effects of such sunspots at the macro level. To put it another way, if there do not exist social interactions linking individual beliefs, there seems to be no reason why each individual micro agent would condition on the same sunspot variable when there is no intrinsic fundamental reason why that particular variable should matter. But methods such as Brock (1993) and Brock and Durlauf (2001a,b, 2004a) should be adaptable to produce tractable macro models where the cross sectional law of large numbers breaks down and where tiny outside effects cause explosive shifts in macro aggregates. We believe, for example, that this could be one way to give plausible microfoundations to the emergence of lock-in to one particular sunspot variable even though there is no intrinsic fundamental reason that particular sunspot variable should command economy-wide attention. It could also be a useful way to model the emergence and persistence of irrational exuberance.

The potential for social interactions to induce correlated behaviors in a population suggests a second area where the approach may have value in understanding business cycles: the role of individual-specific shocks in affecting aggregate outcomes. The possibility that interdependences in individual decisions can convert individual-shocks into aggregate fluctuations was originally studied in Jovanovic (1987), who identified the key role of complementarities in such a transformation, but this idea has not been nearly as much developed as we think is appropriate. Horvath (1998, 2000), using log linear models of the type pioneered by Long and Plosser (1983), extended this type of analysis by focusing on input/output-type relationships between sectors of the economy and showed how it is possible for sector-specific shocks to affect aggregate output; calibration evidence showed this approach can match various moments of aggregate U.S. data. The marginal value of this approach in understanding fluctuations has been criticized by Dupor (1999) who provides a number of observational equivalence theorems between one sector and multi-sector models of fluctuations.

We see a role for social interaction in elucidating the aggregate implications of sector-specific shocks. Social interactions can provide mechanisms by which individual sectors are interrelated. We would imagine that animal spirits are subject to various intersectoral dependences that mimic the technological interdependences that lie at the heart of Horvath's analysis. Further, the social interactions models we have described have the important feature that they are intrinsically nonlinear. Nonlinearities should, we believe, break the observational equivalence that Dupor has identified and as such may lead to sector-specific shocks generating aggregate fluctuations quite different from their aggregate shock counterparts. Of course, it may be that nonlinear single sector models can reestablish Dupor's observational equivalence result.

Recent work on the aggregation of idiosyncratic shocks is close to our vision of how research of this type might proceed. In a very interesting paper, Gabaix (2004) shows that in a world of fat-tailed firm size distributions, idiosyncratic firm-level shocks can aggregate up to nontrivial aggregate fluctuations at the GDP level, whereas in a world of thin-tailed firm size distributions, this cannot happen. He argues that idiosyncratic shocks to the 100 largest firms account for about 40% of U.S. output volatility. Gabaix uses the statistical theory behind fat-tailed distributions to get a factor of $1/\log N$ for the scaling of aggregate volatility rather than the usual scaling of $1/N^{1/2}$. One can see that $1/\log N$ "diversifies away" idiosyncratic fluctuations at a much slower rate than does $1/N^{1/2}$. While this is very speculative, we conjecture that it may be fruitful for future research in macroeconomics to couple a mechanism like Gabaix's with the presence of social interactions at various levels in the macroeconomy in order to get a more complete understanding of how idiosyncratic shocks can aggregate to macroeconomic volatility via the emergence of fat-tailed distributions at various levels of disaggregation. For example, intrafirm shocks may, via intrafirm social interactions, produce the fat tails needed for Gabaix's interfirm analysis. We believe this research route may be promising because we have already shown how social interactions can magnify very small shocks into large ones (Brock, 1993; Brock and Durlauf, 2001a,b; see also Glaeser, Sacerdote, and Scheinkman [1996]) who describe links between social interactions and excess volatility of averages) and so regard social interactions as a natural source for fat-tailed distributions.

Third, we see a potential role for social interactions in understanding what is still the major business cycle event of the modern economy — the Great Depression. While the idea of the Great Depression as a bad equilibrium has longstanding lineage, beautifully analyzed in Leijonhufvud (1968), with a few exceptions, notably Cooper and Ejarque (1995) and Dagsvik and Jovanovic (1994), this interpretation has fallen out of current macroeconomic discourse. The state-of-the art analysis of the Great Depression is arguably Cole and Ohanian (2004) which focuses on the role of bad government policies in generating persistence in the Depression; coordination failure/multiple equilibrium issues do not arise in their treatment. We believe that social interactions models, by providing a rigorous mathematical foundation for modeling how heterogeneous populations can exhibit phase transitions into locally stable, collectively undesirable equilibria, can help develop an approach to understanding the Great Depression in line with the Leijonhufvud vision. Whether this vision is empirically viable, of course, remains to be seen. For our purposes, what matters is that there has yet to be a quantitative delineation of the coordination failure view that can be compared to approaches such as Cole and Ohanian. The formal statistical mechanical models that have appeared in the social interactions literature provide a possible way of producing such a comparison and perhaps even an integration of these differing perspectives.

Finally, we would observe that social interactions have a role to play in understanding the interactions of business cycles and income distribution and as such can contribute to the research program developed in Krusell and Smith (1998) and elsewhere. One case where this seems plausible concerns the distribution of unemployment across different groups. As shown in theoretical work such as Montgomery (1990) and Oomes (2003), group heterogeneity will emerge in unemployment rates via network effects; the empirical importance of these effects is shown in Topa (2001). In this regard, Conley and Topa (2002) is of particular interest in its efforts to empirically compare different types of groups — spatial, ethnic, etc. — as the relevant group in which social interactions are created.

More generally, we think the sorts of factors that underlie social interactions models — peer effects, information spillovers, social norms, etc. — are an important complement to the imperfect risk sharing that is generally at the heart of macroeconomic models of income inequality. There is a dichotomy between macroeconomic models of inequality, with their emphasis on complete modeling of the evolution of the income distribution with relatively narrow views of the determinants of individual decisionmaking, and microeconomic models of inequality which contain richer conceptions of individual choice, but do so at the expense of less developed ways of modeling populations. The mathematical models underlying social interactions analysis have the potential to combine these two perspectives.

CONCLUSIONS

While we have great confidence in the importance of social interactions in explaining a range of socioeconomic phenomena, we wish to re-emphasize that this case has yet to be established by a consensus of empirical evidence. The empirical literature on social interactions is young and has not fully incorporated the insights of the relevant econometric literature. So one cannot make overly strong empirical claims for the importance of social interactions even in the microeconomic contexts in which social interactions seem most plausible.

Still, we strongly believe that in many macroeconomic contexts, social interactions plausibly matter and can affect how one thinks about the generative mechanisms underlying both long run and short run macroeconomic outcomes. At this stage, our claims are, to repeat, essentially speculative. Whether this belief is correct can only be resolved through new research. What we have tried to argue here is that expected payoff from this research warrants its undertaking.

6

Macroeconomics and Model Uncertainty

William A. Brock and Steven N. Durlauf

"The owl of Minerva begins its flight only with the onset of dusk."
G. W. F. Hegel, *Elements of the Philosophy of Right*

This chapter provides some reflections on the new macroeconomics of model uncertainty. Research on model uncertainty represents a broad effort to understand how the ignorance of individuals and policymakers about the true structure of the economy should and does affect their respective behaviors. As such, this approach challenges certain aspects of modern macroeconomics, most notably the rational expectations assumptions that are generally made in modeling aggregate outcomes. Our goal is to explore some of the most interesting implications of model uncertainty for positive and normative macroeconomic analysis. Our discussion will suggest directions along which work on model uncertainty may be fruitfully developed; as such it is necessarily somewhat speculative as we cannot say to what extent these directions are feasible.

Our interest in model uncertainty is certainly not unique; in fact, within macroeconomics, studies of model uncertainty have become one of the most active areas of research. Much of this new work was stimulated by the seminal contributions of Hansen and Sargent of which (2001, 2003a,b) are only a subset of their contributions. Hansen and Sargent's work explores the question of robustness in decision making. In their approach, agents are not assumed to know the true model of the economy, in contrast to standard rational expectations formulations. Instead, agents are modeled as possessing the more limited information that the true model lies within a model space that is defined as all models local to some baseline. This approach in turns leads to their adoption of minimax methods for decisionmaking; an agent chooses an action that works best under the assumption that the least favorable model (for the agent) in the model space is in fact the true one. This approach has been shown to have important implications for the equilibrium trajectory of macroeconomic aggregates.

Our discussion will consider both local and nonlocal forms of model uncertainty. Thus for much of our analysis, rather than consider spaces of models defined relative to some baseline, we consider the incorporation of model uncertainty into environments where the potential models are quite different. As such, this approach will be complementary to robustness analyses. We do not claim our approach is better than the robustness one; assumptions about the type of model uncertainty that is present cannot be assessed outside the objectives of the researcher and the particular economic environment under study.

Model uncertainty has also become a major area of research in statistics and econometrics. Draper (1995) is a conceptual analysis that lays out many of the implications of model uncertainty for data analysis. As Draper observed, many of the implications of model uncertainty for empirical practice are present in Leamer (1978) and had (and still have) yet to be fully integrated into empirical work. One area where statistical methods that account for model uncertainty are now well-developed is the determination of regressors in linear models. Raftery, Madigan, and Hoeting (1997), and Fernandez, Ley, and Steel (2001a) present a range of methods for implementing empirical analyses that account for uncertainty in control variable choice in evaluating regression coefficients.

These tools have been used in a range of empirical contexts in economics, especially economic growth; contributions include Brock and Durlauf (2001), Brock, Durlauf, and West (2003), Doppelhofer, Miller, and Sala-i-Martin (2000), and Fernandez, Ley, and Steel (2001b). This work has shown that many of the claims in the empirical growth literature concerning the predictive value of various aggregate variables in cross-country growth regressions do not hold up when one accounts for uncertainty in the control variables that should be included in the regression. On the other hand, this approach has also strengthened certain claims; for example, the negative partial correlation between initial income and growth, also known as β-convergence, has proven strongly robust with respect to variable choice, see Durlauf, Johnson, and Temple (2004) for a summary of this evidence.

The growing class of theoretical and empirical studies of model uncertainty does not lend itself to ready summary. Our intent in this essay is to provide a discussion of the broad themes that one finds in this literature. The section, "Model Uncertainty and Total Uncertainty" of this chapter describes the relationship between model uncertainty and total uncertainty with respect to predicting an unobserved variable such as a future macroeconomic aggregate. The section, "Implications for Macroeconomic Theory" discusses some implications of model uncertainty for macroeconomic theory. The section, "Model Uncertainty and Policy Evaluation" discusses the relationship between model uncertainty and policy evaluation. The section, "An Example" provides an extended example of how model uncertainty can be incorporated into an abstract modeling framework and how its presence affects the conclusions one draws from the model. The section, "Conclusion" offers some conclusions.

MODEL UNCERTAINTY AND TOTAL UNCERTAINTY

General Ideas

In this section, we consider the ways in which model uncertainty affects the formal description of uncertain economic outcomes. Our goal in this section is to integrate model uncertainty into a standard characterization of uncertainty. At an abstract level, we work with

θ = vector of outcomes of interest
d = data representing history of the economy
η = innovations that affect outcomes; these are independent of d
m = model of the economy, element of model space M

Conventional macroeconomic modeling may be abstractly understood as producing probability descriptions of the vector θ, given a model of the economy, its history, and various shocks. Abstractly, one can think about a data generating process

$$\theta = m(\eta, d). \tag{1}$$

For our purposes, we assume that the probability measure describing η is known and that the model m is associated with a set of parameters β_m. Hence, one can think of a given model producing probability statements about θ of the form

$$\mu(\theta | m, \beta_m, d). \tag{2}$$

The uncertainty associated with this probability is fundamental as it is exclusively driven by lack of knowledge of η.

As a description of the uncertainty about θ, Eq. (2) fails to properly account for the degree of uncertainty that a modeler faces at time $t-1$. The first level at which this is so is that the parameter vector β_m is generally not known. Hence, it is more natural to describe uncertainty about outcomes via

$$\mu(\theta|m, d). \tag{3}$$

In contrast to Eq. (2), the probabilities about outcomes described by Eq. (3) are conditioned only on the model and the available data. In standard (frequentist) practice, the data are used to construct estimates of β_m. The analysis of the differences between Eqs. (3) and (2) is an important question in the forecasting literature: West (1996) is a well-known example of an analysis that considers how forecast distributions need to account for parameter uncertainty. For questions of using conditional probabilities to compare policies, on the other hand, parameter uncertainty is not commonly evaluated; exceptions whose findings call into question this standard practice include Giannoni (2001) and Onatski and Williams (2003).

Model uncertainty extends this type of reasoning to eliminate the assumption that a modeler knows the form of the true data generating process. In other words, in evaluating model uncertainty, one attempts to construct

$$\mu(\theta|d). \tag{4}$$

How does one do this? The key insight, initially recognized in Leamer (1978) and subsequently developed in Draper (1995), is that model uncertainty may be treated like any other unobservable. Specifically, one thinks of the true model as lying in some space M over which probabilities are defined. The probability assigned to an element m of M may be thought of as the probability that model m is the true one.[1] Under the assumption that the space is countable, one uses Bayes' rule to eliminate the dependence of Eq. (3) on a specific model, thereby producing Eq. (4). Formally,

$$\mu(\theta|d) = \sum_{m \in M} \mu(\theta|d, m)\, \mu(m|d). \tag{5}$$

---

[1] We will later address some issues that arise when none of the models in the space is the correct one.

This conditional probability introduces a new argument into macro-economic analysis, $\mu(m|d)$, the probability that a given model is the correct one given the available data. By Bayes' rule, this probability in turn can be decomposed as

$$\mu(m|d) \propto \mu(d|m)\mu(m),\qquad(6)$$

where $\propto$ means "is proportional to." The probability of a model given the data thus depends on two factors: $\mu(d|m)$, the probability of the data, given the model; and $\mu(m)$, the prior probability of the model. The first term summarizes the implications of the data for the relative likelihoods of each model; the second term embodies the prior information that exists on which model is correct.

Macroeconomics and Forecast Errors

These calculations suggest a possible hierarchy for understanding the uncertainty that exists for macroeconomic outcomes, an argument made in Brock, Durlauf, and West (2004). Let the vector Y_{t+1} denote a macroeconomic outcome of interest. Suppose that the data generating process for this vector depends on information available at time t, d_t, and η_{t+1}, information that is realized between $t+1$ and t. In parallel to Eq. (1), the data generating process for Y_{t+1} is

$$Y_{t+1} = m(d_t, \eta_{t+1}, \beta_m),\qquad(7)$$

for some model m. This data generating process suggests different levels of prediction errors. The intrinsic uncertainty that is associated with future data realizations produces prediction errors of the form

$$Y_{t+1} - E\big(Y_{t+1}|d_t, m, \beta_m\big).\qquad(8)$$

Parameter uncertainty leads to a definition of prediction errors when predictions are conditioned only on the model and data, that is

$$Y_{t+1} - E(Y_{t+1}|d_t, m).\qquad(9)$$

Finally, model uncertainty means that prediction errors should be defined by

$$Y_{t+1} - E(Y_{t+1}|d_t).\qquad(10)$$

Implications for Empirical Practice

The probability statements we have described provide predictive statements about unknowns when one only conditions on the data. As such, when applied to data analysis, they represent a different way of reporting empirical results. One way to think about the bulk of standard empirical practice is that it involves reporting results that are model-specific whereas the analysis we have provided argues that these probability statements should integrate our dependence on a particular model. What does this mean in practice? For a Bayesian, the answer is straightforward, since Bayesian statistics is based on the reporting of conditional probability statements that map knowns (the data) to unknowns (θ or Y_{t+1}). Accounting for model uncertainty is straightforward for Bayesians since one simply averages over the model-specific probabilities using posterior model probabilities. For frequentists, the answer is less clear since frequentist statistics report probabilities of knowns (the data or transformations of the data, e.g. a parameter estimate) conditional on unknowns (the true parameter, for example).

That being said, one can certainly construct frequentist estimates that account for model uncertainty. Doppelhofer, Miller, and Sala-i-Martin (2000) do this in the context of cross-country growth regressions; Brock, Durlauf, and West (2003) argue that this is possible generally. Suppose that one has a frequentist model-specific estimate $\hat{\theta}_m$. In principle, one can always construct

$$\hat{\theta} = \sum_{m \in M} \hat{\theta}_m \hat{p}_m, \tag{11}$$

where $\hat{p}_m$ is a proxy for a posterior model probability. One candidate for these proxies is a Bayesian Information Criterion-adjusted (normalized) likelihood statistic for each model. This approach may be interpreted as treating each model as equally likely. Alternatively, one can modify these adjusted likelihoods to allow for greater prior weight for certain models. Some authors have made proposals to do this. Doppelhofer, Miller, and Sala-i-Martin (2000), for example, argue that less-complex models deserve greater prior weights. Brock, Durlauf, and West (2003) in contrast argue that economic theory should be used to account for similarities in the model space when assigning probabilities. This is an inadequately researched area.

For a Bayesian, these frequentist calculations are incoherent as they mix probability statements about observables and unobservables. However, we do not regard this as an important criticism with respect to empirical work. We believe that what is critical in an empirical exercise is that a researcher establishes clear procedures for analyzing data and that the procedures be interpretable relative to the objective of the data exercise. This "pseudo-frequentist" approach does this.

Our discussion of empirical practice has been somewhat too facile in that it has not addressed the issue of how to interpret model averaging results when the true model is not an element of the model space; Bernardo and Smith (1994) call this the *M*-open case. There is an extensive literature on maximum likelihood estimation of misspecified models which suggests that for model weighting schemes such as one based on BIC-adjusted likelihoods, asymptotically, the averaging procedure will place all weight on the model that in a Kullback-Leibler sense best approximates the data, see Brock and Durlauf (2001) for more discussion.

Further, our analysis has treated the model space as fixed. Of course, part of the evolution of empirical work is defined precisely by the evolution of the models under consideration. The question of how inferences will evolve in response to an evolving model space has yet to be researched as far as we know, despite its obvious importance.

IMPLICATIONS FOR MACROECONOMIC THEORY

In this section we identify some areas where model uncertainty may prove to have interesting implications for macroeconomic theory. In particular, we believe that model uncertainty raises a number of issues related to modeling individual behavior that can enrich standard macroeconomic formulations.

Expectations

Model uncertainty calls into question the ways in which expectations are formulated in macroeconomic theory. The dominant rational expectation paradigm in macroeconomics assumes that agents possess common knowledge of the model of the economy in which they operate. Efforts to generalize the rational expectations assumption include allowing for learning; these are well-surveyed in Evans and Honkapohja (2001). These commonly assume that the structure of the economy is known even if the values of the parameters of the structural model need to be learned. Model uncertainty introduces issues of expectations formation that are quite different from the standard learning paradigm. One reason, recognized by

Hansen and Sargent in (2003a,b) and elsewhere, is that model uncertainty raises questions of how one even defines rational expectations. My beliefs about the model of the economy will depend on what your beliefs are etc., which requires that I have information about your prior about models, etc.

The incorporation of model uncertainty in macroeconomic modeling can have important implications for understanding the historical record. Cogley and Sargent (2004) explore the implications of theory uncertainty for understanding Federal Reserve behavior. They show that uncertainty on the part of the Fed in determining the correct model of inflation can explain monetary policy during the 1970s even when evidential and theoretical support for the conventional Phillips curve had begun to disintegrate.

If one treats parameter uncertainty as a form of model uncertainty (albeit of a localized nature), one can further this claim. Weitzman (2004) shows how a range of asset price puzzles, notably the equity premium puzzle and excess volatility of stock prices may be resolved using parameter uncertainty. Specifically, he shows that if economic actors did not know the parameters of the relevant dividends process for stock returns and instead, were learning about the parameters following Bayesian updating rules, these puzzles no longer exist. Weitzman's results are very striking because they so strongly reverse various claims about the inadequacy of dynamic representative agent general equilibrium modeling for understanding asset markets simply by considering how agents will behave in the presence of a narrow type of model uncertainty.

Further, model uncertainty introduces two additional factors in the mapping of individual characteristics into equilibrium aggregate outcomes: the formation of initial beliefs and the ways in which these initial beliefs are updated. As indicated by our analysis, aggregate equilibria will depend on the distribution of $\mu_i(m)$ across i. One can easily imagine cases where this distribution is nontrivial. For example, in transitions for high inflation to low inflation regimes, it seems natural to expect substantial heterogeneity in beliefs as to whether the change has occurred. This is the sort of event that available data cannot adjudicate. And unlike cases in which individuals have heterogeneous valuations of a common object, there is no market mechanism to facilitate aggregation, nor is it clear how agents would react to information about the beliefs of others. In the asset case, the implications of one agent's beliefs about the value on the beliefs of another presupposes a model of how the other agent's beliefs are determined, which itself is subject to model uncertainty. Nor is this question resolved by recourse to the interesting work on rational beliefs initiated by Kurz (1997) since the issue here is not what types of heterogeneity are consistent with long-term data properties. Rather our concern is with the heterogeneity of prior beliefs when the data are not sufficiently informative to impose long run restrictions, at least in the sense that the data do not reveal the true model of the economy.

Beyond the issue of priors, model uncertainty suggests the importance of determining how agents acquire information about the economy. If an agent is confident that he knows the true model of the economy, he is presumably going to treat the costs and benefits of information acquisition differently than when the true model is unknown. Put differently, the value to an agent of superior information may depend on the degree of model uncertainty. This seems particularly relevant when the economy moves across regimes, which in our context may be interpreted as shifting across models.

Brock and Hommes (1997) suggest some ways to think about this problem by modeling environments in which agents make discrete choices about what sorts of information to acquire before forming expectations. They show how these decisions will correlate across individuals and induce interesting aggregate price dynamics. Brock and Hommes (1997) introduce an information cost for the acquisition of structural rational expectations in contrast to a zero cost for acquisition of backwards-looking expectations. Once one introduces costly rational expectations versus costless backwards expectations, then it is natural to introduce a notion of past net profit to having used either expectational scheme. Each agent chooses an expectational scheme according to a discrete choice mechanism which puts more probability weight on an expectational scheme the higher the accrued profits measure for that scheme. Dynamics emerge naturally.

To see how this mechanism can matter for macroeconomic contexts, consider inflation dynamics. If inflation has been stable for a long enough time, the net gain of acquiring rational expectations over simple backwards expectations will become negative. Hence the economy eventually moves to a state where most people are choosing backwards looking expectations. This state will persist until substantial shocks hit the economy (either exogenous or endogenous) which will cause the net benefit measure to shift in favor of rational expectations. If the economy goes through another "quiet" period then the net benefit measure will shift in favor of backwards expectations and the whole story repeats. Such a perspective is very much what one would expect when agents experience shifting degrees of model uncertainty, in this case with respect to the prevailing inflation regime.

If the economy goes through a period like that discussed in Sargent (1999a) where people got "fooled" by the government in the late 1960s and early 1970s, most agents will switch to rational expectations under the Brock and Hommes (1997) mechanism. But after a sustained episode of price stability, more and more agents will rationally become "inert," i.e. they will use backwards-looking expectations in order to economize on expensive rational expectations.

We believe that generalizing the usual Taylor rule and related monetary policy analysis to settings, where the dynamics of the distribution of prediction schemes across agents is endogenously determined by model uncertainty, and which further takes into account the simultaneity between the monetary rule chosen and the predictor dynamics is an important direction for future research. It would be an approach to "endogenizing" at least part of the model uncertainty we have been discussing in this paper. It could also lead to an approach to defining which parts of the model space that are more probable or less probable conditional upon the economy's history. For example, the theory above suggests that one should expect most of the economy's mass to be on expectational schemes close to rational expectations following a history of recent price inflation.

One reason why economists have found the rational expectations assumption appealing is that it imposes powerful discipline on modeling; in contrast, when expectations are not anchored by the logic of a model or some other well-defined rule, then it is difficult to empirically falsify a model. Hence, the introduction of nontrivial model space priors and rules for information acquisition into macroeconomic modeling will require disciplining as well, in order to avoid a situation where any set of empirical findings may be explained by ad hoc choices of prior beliefs and updating behavior.

Preferences

The analysis in the section, "Model Uncertainty and Total Uncertainty," treated model uncertainty in a fashion that is equivalent to other forms of uncertainty faced by a policymaker. This assumption may not be appropriate. One reason for this is strictly positive: individual preferences do not necessarily treat model uncertainty in this fashion. Evidence of this claim comes from experiments such as those that generated the classic Ellsberg Paradox. The Ellsberg Paradox comes from the following experimental observation. Suppose individuals are asked to compare bets in which there is a given payoff based on having correctly chosen the color of a ball drawn from an urn. In case one, the urn contains an equal number of red and black balls. In case two, the proportions in the urn are unknown before the individual is allowed to choose the color. Individuals systematically prefer the bet where they know the urn proportions to the bet where they do not, despite the fact that there is no expected payoff difference between them. This sort of finding has helped motivate recent efforts to axiomatize Knightian uncertainty in the economic theory literature, cf. Gilboa and Schmeidler (1989) and Epstein and Wang (1994). In this work, Knightian uncertainty is represented as a situation in which probabilities cannot be assigned to a set of unknowns. The absence of these probabilities leads to minimax types of behavior on the part of an agent. One may think of this Knightian uncertainty as representing model uncertainty.

These considerations suggest that model uncertainty affects preferences differently from other types of uncertainty. This idea may be formalized by considering how an agent makes a choice a from some set A in the presence of model uncertainty. Suppose that the agent's payoff is represented by a loss function $l(a, \theta)$ which depends on the action and an unknown θ. If the agent is a standard expected loss minimizer, he will make a choice in order to minimize

$$\int_{\Theta} l(a, \theta) \mu(\theta|d) d\theta, \tag{12}$$

where the conditional probability $\mu(\theta|d)$ accounts for model uncertainty in a way symmetric to all other sources of uncertainty, as is done in the derivation of Eq. (4) via the argument described by Eq. (5). How can these preferences account for ambiguity aversion? One way to do this is to follow the approach taken by Epstein and Wang (1994) and model preferences so that additional weight is placed on the least favorable model in M beyond the weight that is assigned in the expected loss calculation. Formally, preferences may be modeled as

$$(1-e) \int_{\Theta} l(a, \theta) \mu(\theta|d) d\theta + e \left(\sup_{m \in M} \int_{\Theta} l(a, \theta) \mu(\theta|d, m) d\theta \right). \tag{13}$$

In this equation, e measures the degree of ambiguity aversion. If $e = 0$, then Eq. (13) reduces to the expected loss calculation; if $e = 1$, then the policymaker exhibits minimax preferences with respect to model uncertainty.

The minimax case has been studied in the growing literature on robustness in macroeconomic analysis, a literature which we have noted was launched by Hansen and Sargent. This approach assumes that the model space is local in the sense described at the beginning of this chapter. Beyond the work of Hansen and Sargent, standard references now include Giannoni (2002); Marcellino and Salmon (2002); Onatski and Stock (2002); and Tetlow and von zur Muehlen (2001). This work has yielded a number of valuable insights. For example, Giannoni (2002) provides a comprehensive analysis of how ambiguity aversion increases the aggressiveness of optimal stabilization policies in the sense that the magnitudes of the sensitivity of changes in control variables to lagged states may increase for a minimax policymaker when model uncertainty is present. Brock, Durlauf, and West (2003) provide some simple examples of this behavior. That paper notes that ambiguity aversion is different from risk aversion in the sense that it is a first-order phenomenon rather than a second-order one. What this means is that if one starts with an environment with no model uncertainty and then defines an $O(\varepsilon)$ term that represents model uncertainty, the effects are $O(\varepsilon)$ whereas for the classic Arrow–Pratt analysis of risk, the introduction of risk in a risk free environment produces effects of $O(\varepsilon^2)$. The reason for this is that minimax preferences imply that the least favorable model is always assumed for the model space, hence the element that embodies uncertainty always has nonzero expected value (modulo hairline cases) whereas in risk aversion analysis it is assumed that the risk term has an expected value of zero.

As indicated for Eq. (13), minimax preferences are a special case of a more general ambiguity aversion formulation. We would argue that for nonlocal model spaces it is important to model ambiguity aversion where $e \neq 1$. One basic problem for nonlocal model spaces is that it is natural to worry that highly implausible (low prior probability) models will completely control decisionmaking. (For local model spaces, one typically does not think that the models will differ greatly in terms of prior probability.) Beyond this, there is a widespread belief that minimax preferences are inappropriately risk averse; in fact Hurwicz (1951) proposed loss functions similar to Eq. (13) specifically to reduce the implicit risk aversion involved in the minimax formulation. For these reasons, we believe a valuable direction is the exploration of behavioral rules for preferences where $e \neq 1$.

A move away from minimax preferences towards less extreme forms of ambiguity aversion raises the issue of how e is determined. It seems unsatisfactory to treat the degree of ambiguity aversion as a deep parameter. We regard this as an important next step in research. Further, it seems important to study alternative ways to account for model uncertainty in preference specification. Manski (2004) suggests the use of minimax regret for the study of treatment effects, an approach that may prove interesting in other contexts as well. However, minimax regret is not a panacea. Brock (2004) shows that minimax regret preferences will also exhibit significant sensitivity to implausible models, although not to the extent that is possible with minimax preferences. Minimax regret also suffers from the problem that it does not obey independence of irrelevant alternatives; specifically, the ordering between two models as to which is less may be affected under minimax by the presence of a third, see Chernoff (1954). We conjecture that further work on preferences will need to consider ways to avoid highly implausible models from dominating behavioral decisions.

There are good reasons to believe that the evaluation of macroeconomic policy rules will be especially sensitive to the interaction of model uncertainty and policymaker preferences. For many macroeconomic models, it is possible for policy rules to induce instability, e.g. infinite variances for outcomes that one wants to stabilize. Hence a policy rule that is optimal under one model may produce instability under other models. Instability is naturally associated with very high losses for a policymaker. This leads to the question of whether a rule should be rejected because it produces instability for models with very low posterior probabilities. The tradeoff of high losses and low model probabilities is the precise case where the deviations from expected loss calculations matter. This situation arises in Brock, Durlauf, and West (2004) which we discuss below.

MODEL UNCERTAINTY AND POLICY EVALUATION

How does model uncertainty affect the evaluation of macroeconomic policies? Suppose that a policymaker is interested at time t in influencing the level of Y_{t+1} using a policy p, which lies in some set P. Assume that the policymaker's preferences are associated with the loss function

$$l(Y_{t+1}, p, d_t). \tag{14}$$

Note that we do not work with a loss function that extends over periods beyond t; this is done strictly for convenience. In standard policy evaluation exercises, each policy is associated with an expected loss

$$E(l(Y_{t+1}, p, d_t)|d_t, m) = \int_Y l(Y_{t+1}, p, d_t)\mu(Y_{t+1}|d_t, m). \tag{15}$$

The optimal policy choice is therefore defined by

$$\min_{p \in P} \int_Y l(Y_{t+1}, p, d_t)\mu(Y_{t+1}|p, d_t, m), \tag{16}$$

where the conditional probability $\mu(Y_{t+1}|p, d_t, m)$ explicitly reflects the dependence of outcomes at $t + 1$ on the policy choice. Accounting for model uncertainty simply means replacing these formulas with

$$E(l(Y_{t+1}, p, d_t)|p, d_t) = \int_Y l(Y_{t+1}, p, d_t)\mu(Y_{t+1}|d_t), \tag{17}$$

and

$$\min_{p \in P} \int_Y l(Y_{t+1}, p, d_t)\mu(Y_{t+1}|p, d_t). \tag{18}$$

For our purposes, the important observation to make about Eqs. (17) and (18) is that there is no model selection involved. In response to ignorance of the true model of the economy, a policymaker does not first, evaluate potential models and then determine which best fits the data (subject to some penalty for model complexity, in order to ensure the selection rule does not reward overfitting) and second, evaluate policies conditional on that selection. Rather, policies should be evaluated according to their effects for each model, with the model-specific performances averaged. This may be seen explicitly when one rewrites Eq. (17) as follows:

$$\int_Y l(Y_{t+1}, p, d_t)\mu(Y_{t+1}|d_t) = \int_Y l(Y_{t+1}, p, d_t)\left(\sum_{m \in M} \mu(Y_{t+1}|d_t, m)\mu(m|d_t)\right)$$

$$= \sum_{m \in M}\left(\int_Y l(Y_{t+1}, p, d_t)\mu(Y_{t+1}|d_t, m)\right)\mu(m|d_t) \tag{19}$$

In fact, one could go so far as to argue that for a policymaker, model selection has no intrinsic value. This is true even if the payoff function is generalized to be model dependent, i.e. the loss function is written as $l(Y_t, p, d_{t-1})$. From the perspective of Eqs. (17–19), it is reasonable to conclude that model selection is generally inappropriate for policy analysis. Conditioning on a model in essence means replacing the correct posterior model probabilities with a degenerate posterior (all probability assigned to the selected model). Such a substitution thus amounts to using incorrect posterior model probabilities. As argued in great detail by Draper (1995), ignoring this source of uncertainty can lead to very inaccurate model assessments.

Levin and Williams (2003) provide a very valuable analysis of the robustness of different monetary policy rules in the presence of model uncertainty. They evaluate simple policy rules using standard forward-looking, backwards-looking, and hybrid (both forward- and backwards-looking) models. The exercise uses parameters that appear to be reasonable given previous studies and further weight all models equally, so in this sense their exercise is more theoretical rather than empirical. Interestingly, they find that no rule in the class they study[2] performs well across all models when a policymaker is only concerned about stabilizing inflation; on the other hand, when a policymaker places substantial weight on both inflation and output stabilization, robust rules do exist.

The implications of model uncertainty for monetary policy rule evaluation is explored in an empirical context in Brock, Durlauf, and West (2004). In one exercise, they compare the stabilization properties of the classic Taylor rule with an interest rate rule in which current interest rates are determined by a linear combination of lagged interest rates, lagged inflation, and lagged output (measured as a deviation from trend). The optimized three-variable interest rate rule substantially outperforms the Taylor rule for most models (and indeed almost all models if their posterior probabilities are summed) in a model space characterized by uncertainty in lag structure for the IS and Phillips curves. However, the space also contains models for which the optimized rule induces instability where the Taylor rule does not. This suggests a rationale for the Taylor rule, robustness to instability, which would never have been apparent had model selection been done prior to policy evaluation. It turns out that the models

---

[2] Levin and Williams (2003) study rules in which the nominal interest at time $t+1$ depends on t levels of the interest rate, inflation, and output relative to trend; different rules correspond to different parameters for the time t variables.

for which instability occurs for optimized models versus the Taylor rule have posterior probabilities of less than 1%, which is why the specification of the policymaker's preferences with respect to model uncertainty is so important.

AN EXAMPLE

To illustrate the power of the model uncertainty perspective, we summarize an analysis in Brock and Durlauf (2004b) that explores the role of local model uncertainty in the choice of optimal controls. Consider a general state equation for some outcome of interest Y_{t+1} where a policymaker has available some control variable u_t:[3]

$$Y_{t+1} = A(L)Y_t + Bu_t + \xi_{t+1}. \tag{20}$$

ξ_{t+1} is an unobservable, zero-mean component of the equation and is assumed to have an invertible moving average representation

$$\xi_{t+1} = w(L)v_{t+1}. \tag{21}$$

A policymaker chooses a feedback rule of the form

$$u_t = -F(L)Y_t. \tag{22}$$

We assume that the policymaker is interested in minimizing EY^2_{t+1}, the unconditional variance of Y_{t+1}. When this feedback rule is substituted into the state equation, one has the following representation of the state:

$$Y_{t+1} = (A(L) - F(L)B)Y_t + w(L)v_{t+1}. \tag{23}$$

In order to understand how different feedback rules affect EY^2_{t+1}, it is useful to contrast the system we have described to one where there is no control, i.e.

$$Y^{NC}_{t+1} = A(L)Y^{NC}_t + \xi_{t+1}. \tag{24}$$

The variable Y^{NC}_{t+1} is known as the free dynamics of the system. Stabilization policy may be thought of as transforming the free dynamics

---

[3] See Kwaakernak and Sivan (1972) for a detailed description of linear feedback systems of this type.

in such a way as to minimize the unconditional variance of Y_{t+1}. In order to understand the properties of this transformation, we work in the frequency domain. One advantage of the frequency domain is that it allows one to think about the variance components of fluctuations that occur for different cycles. In terms of notation, for any lag polynomial $C(L)$, let $C(e^{-i\omega}) = \sum_{j=-\infty}^{\infty} C_j e^{-ij\omega}$ denote its Fourier transform. One can show (see Brock and Durlauf [2004b] for a complete argument) that

$$EY_{t+1}^2 = \int_{-\pi}^{\pi} |S(\omega)|^2 f_{YNC}(\omega) d\omega, \qquad (25)$$

where

$$S(\omega) = \frac{1}{1 + (e^{i\omega} - A(e^{-i\omega}))^{-1} BF(e^{-i\omega})}. \qquad (26)$$

The function $S(\omega)$ is known as the sensitivity function and illustrates an important idea: a feedback rule transforms the spectral density of the free dynamics by altering the variance contributions of the individual frequencies. The effect of the feedback rule is produced by its effect on the sensitivity function. One can therefore think of the design problem for controls as asking how a policymaker will want to transform the spectral density of the free dynamics.

From the perspective of designing optimal stabilization policies, it is therefore essential to know what constraints exist on the possible sensitivity functions that a policymaker may implicitly shape by the choice of a feedback rule. An important result in the control theory literature, known as the Bode integral constraint characterizes these restrictions. Under the assumption that the system has no explosive roots, the constraint may be written (using a discrete time version due to Wu and Jonckheere [1992]) as

$$\int_{-\pi}^{\pi} \ln\left(|S(\omega)|^2\right) d\omega = 0. \qquad (27)$$

This form implies that a policymaker cannot set $|S(\omega)|^2 < 1$ for all frequencies; hence all stabilization policies necessarily tradeoff higher volatility at some frequencies for lower volatility at others. This is a *fundamental* tradeoff that all policymakers face as any sensitivity function that a policymaker wishes to produce via the choice of feedback rule must fulfill (Eq. [27]). This constraint has powerful implications; for example, it indicates how a policy designed to minimize low (high) frequency fluctuations will necessarily exacerbate some high (low) frequency fluctuations. See Brock and Durlauf (2004a) for a discussion of its implications in a range of macroeconomic contexts.

The Bode integral constraint allows one to prove an extremely interesting result concerning model uncertainty and robustness. Suppose that the spectral density of the innovations is not known, but rather that it lies in some set defined around a baseline spectral density $\bar{f}_\xi(\omega)$

$$\int_{-\pi}^{\pi} \left(f_\xi(\omega) - \bar{f}_\xi(\omega)\right)^2 d\omega \leq \varepsilon^2 \tag{28}$$

Equation (27) implies that a policymaker does not know the true time series structure of the state equation. This form of model uncertainty is also studied in Sargent (1999b) and is one way of capturing Friedman's (1948) concern about long and variable lags in the relationship between monetary policy and aggregate activity. One can show that for a policymaker who wishes to minimize EY_{t+1}^2, the least favorable spectral density among those in the set defined by Eq. (28) is

$$f_\xi^*(\omega) = \bar{f}_\xi(\omega) + \varepsilon \frac{\bar{f}_\xi(\omega)^{-1}}{\left\|\bar{f}_\xi(\omega)^{-1}\right\|} + O(\varepsilon) \tag{29}$$

where for any function $g(\omega)$, $\|g(\omega)\| = \left(\int_{-\pi}^{\pi} g(\omega)\overline{g(\omega)} \, d\omega\right)^{1/2}$. Equation (29) defines the spectral density that a policymaker will assume is true when choosing a feedback rule. As such, the policymaker behaves in a way that follows Wald's (1950) idea that minimax preferences may be interpreted as the Nash equilibrium of a noncooperative game, an idea that is critical in the development of the modern macroeconomic robustness research program.

To understand the least favorable spectral density for the policymaker, notice that relative to the baseline, the term $\bar{f}_\xi(\omega)^{-1}/\|\bar{f}_\xi(\omega)^{-1}\|$ is large (small) when $\bar{f}_\xi(\omega)$ is small (large). This means that when there is model uncertainty, the least favorable model is the one that "flattens" the spectral density, i.e. shifts the spectral density closer to white noise. This makes intuitive sense as a policymaker can never minimize the effects of white noise shocks when he is constrained to follow policy rules that set the policy variable before the white noise shocks are realized, as occurs with rules of the form of Eq. (22); put differently, v_{t+1} is the component of Y_{t+1} that cannot be affected by the choice of feedback rule.

We conjecture that this general result may help to explain the presence of various deviations of aggregate time series from the behavior implied by the absence of model uncertainty. Intuitively, if an agent guards against the least favorable model by choosing the one that is closest to white noise, this suggests that the state variable will have more persistence in it than would be expected to occur if the true model were known. This type of finding may be relevant for empirical rejections of models because of violations of Euler equation or other first order conditions that imply some combination of time series should be white noise; if agents react to model uncertainty by optimizing relative to the least favorable model in the way we have described, then it seems clear that violations of white noise conditions will be generated.

CONCLUSIONS

The new macroeconomics of model uncertainty has shown itself to be a fruitful direction for theoretical and empirical research. In one sense, this direction would seem to be an inevitable one, given the absence of resolution of so many macroeconomic debates, debates that include the role of incomplete markets in aggregate outcomes, the degree of price rigidity in the economy, the importance of increasing returns to scale in the aggregate production function in producing cycles and growth, etc.[4] An appealing aspect of this new program is the interconnected development of theory and empirics, a path of development that contrasts, for example, with the modern economic growth literature where theory and empirics have to a large extent evolved in parallel (see Durlauf, Johnson, and Temple [2004] for a defense of this claim). We therefore expect substantial progress in this area over time.

---

[4] Of course, much of what we have discussed about model uncertainty applies to any branch of economics, not just macroeconomics. That being said, macroeconomics seems particularly likely to benefit from this perspective.

7

Restricted Perceptions Equilibria and Learning in Macroeconomics

William A. Branch[*]

Since the 1970s, Rational Expectations (RE) has become the dominant paradigm in macroeconomics. One reason for its popularity is the consistency it imposes between beliefs and outcomes. Under RE agents' subjective probability, distribution coincides with the true distribution for the economy. Not surprisingly, a large literature objects to RE on the grounds that it requires agents to possess unreasonable information and cognitive abilities. Instead many researchers (e.g. Evans and Honkapohja [2001]) replace RE with an econometric forecasting model and ask under what conditions the forecasts converge to RE. The validity of RE is not just theoretical curiosa, Branch (2004) and Carroll (2003) demonstrate persistent heterogeneity in survey data on inflation expectations. Such phenomena cannot be explained by RE models. Papers such as Brock and Hommes (1997) generate heterogeneity by assuming agents make conscious choices between costly predictor functions, thereby, hypothesizing that deviations from rationality come from a weighing of benefits and costs.

These drawbacks, though, do not imply that there are no valid insights from the RE approach. In Muth's original formulation of the rational expectations hypothesis, he advocated for subjective expectations that coincide with the true distribution. His argument rested on the joint determination of beliefs and the economy. This is the self-referential feature of most dynamic models: the economy depends on expectations that *should* depend on the structure of the economy. If agents' subjective beliefs did not take account of the economic structure, then their forecasts

* I am greatly indebted to George Evans and Bruce McGough for many valuable discussions. I would also like to thank participants of the Middlebury Conference on Post Walrasian Macroeconomics, May 1–2, 2004.

would consistently perform badly. The great insight of the RE approach is that it hypothesizes an equilibrium to this self-referential process. Economic outcomes should not completely contradict the beliefs that generated these outcomes. If agents form their expectations by conditioning on the distribution (itself a function of those beliefs) then beliefs and outcomes are mutually consistent. The *Rational Expectations Equilibrium* (REE) is at the very heart of competitive or Walrasian equilibria.[1]

However, conditional expectations, or RE, are not the only form of beliefs which may lead to a fixed point of this self-referential property. A burgeoning literature argues that beliefs that satisfy a least squares orthogonality condition are also consistent with Muth's original hypothesis.[2] The least squares orthogonality condition in these models imposes that beliefs generate forecast errors that are orthogonal to an agent's forecasting model; that is, there is no discernible correlation between these forecast errors and an agent's model. Perhaps one should imagine agents' actions taking place in an economy but their beliefs (which generate the actions) exist in a perceived economy. Under this interpretation, the orthogonality condition guarantees that agents perceive their beliefs as consistent with the real world. Thus, agents can have misspecified (that is, not RE) beliefs but within the context of their forecasting model they are unable to detect their misspecification.[3] An equilibrium between optimally misspecified beliefs and the stochastic process for the economy is called a *Restricted Perceptions Equilibrium* (RPE).[4]

This survey advocates for Restricted Perceptions Equilibria. We argue that RPE is a natural alternative to REE because it is consistent with Muth's original hypothesis and it allows for bounded rationality. One way this article advocates for RPE is by demonstrating the generality of RPE as it encompasses many forms of misspecified beliefs. We develop most of our arguments in the context of a linear stochastic self-referential economy driven by an exogenous vector autoregressive (VAR) process. Misspecification in this setting implies agents underparameterize by omitting variables and/or lags of the VAR process in their forecasting

---

[1] See Ljungqvist and Sargent (2000) and Colander (1996).

[2] See, for example, Anderson and Sonnenschein (1985), Evans, Honkapohja, and Sargent (1993), Evans and Honkapohja (2001), Hommes and Sorger (1998), Branch and McGough (2005), Branch and Evans (2004), and Sargent (1999b).

[3] Of course, if agents step out of their forecasting model they might notice some structure to their forecast errors.

[4] The name Restricted Perceptions Equilibrium was given by Evans and Honkapohja (2001).

model. To demonstrate generality we highlight the connection between Sargent's (1999) Self-Confirming Equilibrium and RPE. We further demonstrate that the Consistent Expectations Equilibrium in Hommes and Sorger (1998), where agents have linear beliefs in a nonlinear model, is also an RPE.

Misspecification is an important part of a complex and data rich environment such as a macroeconomy. VAR forecasters purposely limit the number of variables and/or lags because of degree of freedom and computational limitations. Economists and econometricians routinely take linear approximations to nonlinear relations. In fact, White (1994) argues that all econometric models are necessarily misspecified. In applied work, there is disagreement about the true structure of the economy. So we should expect agents and policymakers to take actions based on misspecified models of the economy. An RPE simply requires that outcomes do not consistently contradict agents' beliefs.

We also advocate for RPE by demonstrating its implications. We show the implications in the context of Branch and Evans's (2004, 2005) *Misspecification Equilibrium* (ME). In a Misspecification Equilibrium, agents underparameterize their forecasting model but only choose the best-performing statistical models. An ME is an RPE with agents endogenously choosing their form of misspecification. We argue for this approach since the nature of the economy dictates the appropriate form of misspecification. The advantage of ME is that it makes the point that misspecification and economic outcomes are mutually dependent. We survey the main finding of Branch and Evans (2004) that in an ME agents can have heterogeneous expectations. The survey then shows how multiple equilibria can arise as in Branch and Evans (2005).

Finally, we present an example that shows that in a simple multivariate ad hoc macro model with optimal monetary policy, the basins of attraction between multiple equilibria switch. The basins of attraction are determined by the interaction of expectation formation effects and the underlying exogenous stochastic process. Optimal monetary policy takes agents' beliefs as a given and then counters the exogenous process. Policy alters the direct effect of these exogenous factors thereby causing a switch to another equilibrium.

TOWARDS AN EQUILIBRIUM CONCEPT CONSISTENT WITH MUTH

This section surveys the concept of a *Restricted Perceptions Equilibrium* (RPE). We argue that the RPE is consistent with Muth's Rational

Expectations Hypothesis, and, because it captures reasonable cognitive and computational limitations of agents, is a natural alternative to the Rational Expectations Equilibrium.

It will prove useful to have a common economic framework for discussion. We consider economies that have a reduced-form with the following recursive expectational structure:

$$x_t = \text{FE}^*_{t-1} x_t + \gamma' z_t, \tag{1}$$

where z_t has the vector autoregressive structure (VAR),

$$z_t = A z_{t-1} + \varepsilon_t.$$

The operator E^*_{t-1} is an expectations operator; the superscript $*$ highlights that expectations may not be rational. Under rational expectations $E^* = E$, where E_{t-1} denotes the mathematical expectation conditioned on all available information through time $t - 1$. We assume that z_t is a stationary VAR process and we will restrict attention to stationary solutions to Eq. (1).[5] In this paper we consider where x_t is both uni- and bivariate. There are many models in dynamic macroeconomics that have a reduced-form like Eq. (1). Examples include the cobweb model, the Lucas model, and the Sargent-Wallace ad hoc model. We abstract from specific formulations at first to illustrate the generality of RPE. Below, we highlight implications in specific economic applications.

The expectations formation effect of an economy is parameterized by F. The parameter F governs the self-referential feature because it determines the effect expectations have on the state. We often differentiate between positive and negative feedback models. A positive feedback model is one where the state moves in the same direction as expectations. Conversely, a negative feedback model has the state move in an opposite direction. The cobweb model is a univariate reduced-form system with negative feedback, that is, $F < 0$. The negative feedback arises because there is a lag from production to the market so that firms will forecast future prices when making supply decisions. If firms expect prices to be low, they produce little and equilibrium prices will actually be high; hence, the negative feedback from expectations. This particular self-referential feature

---

[5] Though, one implication of Misspecified Equilibria is that learning dynamics that surround these stationary equilibria may not be stationary.

generates expectations-driven oscillations. In business cycle models, though, the feedback is typically positive.[6]

Muth's Rational Expectations Hypothesis

Muth (1961) is credited with the development of the Rational Expectations Hypothesis. Later, in works by Lucas and Sargent, among others, RE became the dominant paradigm in dynamic macroeconomics. One aspect of RE that appealed to researchers was that in a REE, agents' subjective beliefs coincide with the true probability distribution of the economy. The REE is a deep equilibrium concept that rests on the self-referential feature of the model. In an REE, there is a sense of self-fulfilling prophesy. Agents form beliefs by conditioning on the true distribution which, itself, depends on these beliefs. The obvious objections to the RE then are the strong informational and cognitive assumptions required. RE assumes agents know the true distribution of the economy and are able to form conditional expectations with this information. The learning literature (e.g. Evans and Honkapohja, 2001) examines under what conditions agents can learn this distribution if it was unknown. Moreover, it strains credulity to imagine a large economy populated by agents all coordinating on the precisely correct distribution. It is to these objections, while preserving the essence of Muth's argument, that we propose overcoming with an RPE.

It is worth emphasizing the relationship between subjective beliefs and actual outcomes in an REE for it is this insight that RPE exploits while allowing for bounded rationality. This connection is made most clearly by the approach of Evans and Honkapohja (2001). Their approach conjectures subjective beliefs and finds the conditions under which these beliefs are supported by the actual stochastic process. For simplicity, assume x_t is univariate and z_t is an $(n \times 1)$ VAR (Eq. [1]). Suppose agents believe the economy is a linear function of the exogenous processes:

$$x_t = a + b'z_{t-1} + c\varepsilon_t. \tag{2}$$

Evans and Honkapohja (2001) refer to such an equation as a Perceived Law of Motion (PLM) because it summarizes agents' subjective distribution. Agents take conditional expectations of the PLM:

$$E_{t-1}x_t = a + b'z_{t-1}. \tag{3}$$

---

[6] When x is bivariate, we say that there is positive (negative) feedback when F is positive (negative) semi-definite.

Given these beliefs, the actual law of motion (ALM) is computed by plugging Eq. (3) into Eq. (1):

$$x_t = Fa + Fb'z_{t-1} + \gamma'Az_{t-1} + \gamma'\varepsilon_t.$$

The parameters $(a, b, c)'$ summarize agents' subjective beliefs. In an REE, these beliefs are reinforced so that a should coincide with Fa, b'coincide with $(Fb' + \gamma'A)$, etc. There exists a map from the space of beliefs to outcomes:

$$T\begin{pmatrix} a \\ b \\ c \end{pmatrix} = \begin{pmatrix} Fa \\ (Fb' + \gamma'A)' \\ \gamma \end{pmatrix}.$$

The connection between beliefs and outcomes is seen clearly in the ALM, suitably rewritten,

$$x_t = T([a, b, c]')'(1, z_{t-1}, \varepsilon_t)'. \tag{4}$$

Rational expectations are beliefs $(a, b, c)'$ that are consistent with the model's actual parameters. Thus, an REE occurs under the fixed point $(a, b, c)' = T([a, b, c]')$. The mapping T will be referred to as the "T-map." In this instance, the unique REE satisfies

$$x_t = (1 - F)^{-1}\gamma'Az_{t-1} + \gamma'\varepsilon_t.$$

It is worth emphasizing that in an REE, the agents' expectations are unbiased. This implies an orthogonality between their forecasting model and the actual stochastic process. Throughout we exploit mappings from beliefs to outcomes in self-referential models to find alternative equilibrium concepts that preserve the consistency between the model and expectations.

The learning literature as typified by Evans and Honkapohja (2001) studies whether agents could start with arbitrary values of (a, b, c) and learn the REE of $(0, (1 - F)^{-1}\gamma'A, \gamma')$. Evans and Honkapohja note that, in many models, the E-stability Principle determines if an REE is learnable. E-stability places a condition on how beliefs are adjusted and filtered through the T-map.

Now that we have highlighted the connection between beliefs and outcomes in an REE, we ask whether other equilibrium concepts can be consistent with Muth's original objectives while easing the strong information assumptions of RE. Muth (1961) states his objective to be

"...a theory of expectations and to show that the implications are — as a first approximation — consistent with the relevant data." (p. 316) He goes on to phrase his hypothesis a bit more precisely as

... expectations of firms (or, more generally, the subjective probability distribution of outcomes) tend to be distributed, for the same information set, about the prediction of the theory (or the "objective" probability distributions of outcomes). (p. 316)

This definition of Rational Expectations is the one that the literature has focused on: subjective expectations conditional on the true distribution of outcomes. To Muth, the only reason expectations might depart from outcomes is the occurrence of unforecastable events.

However, we argue that this theory of expectation formation is not the only definition consistent with Muth's stated hypothesis. After phrasing the REH, Muth then makes three assertions:

... (1) Information is scarce, and the economic system generally does not waste it. (2) The way expectations are formed depends specifically on the structure of the relevant system describing the economy. (3) A 'public prediction'... will have no substantial effect on the operation of the economic system (unless it is based on inside information). (p. 316)

Muth's hypothesis that agents' expectations are consistent with the underlying model is in the sense that: (1) agents do not (freely) dispose of useful information; (2) beliefs reflect the nature of the economy; and (3) beliefs and outcomes are directly related so that outcomes do not contradict beliefs. A "public prediction" to Muth is a published forecast of a future event that depends on individual beliefs. The lack of an effect of a public expectation is as we state in point (3) — expectations should be based on all available information. Clearly, RE satisfies these assertions: under RE, agents use all information available, the subjective distribution of beliefs coincides with the true economic distribution, and in an REE, there is a correspondence between beliefs and outcomes.

We argue, though, that other expectation formation schemes are consistent with Muth's hypothesis. It is the contention of this chapter that Muth's hypothesis is satisfied whenever each agent's forecast errors are uncorrelated with their forecasting model. An alternative way to think about a self-referential economy is that agents only understand the economy so far as their own subjective model; it is through this subjective model that they pass actual observations. Agents and their actions exist in economic models but their beliefs reside in forecasting models.

Under Muth's assertion (2) forecasting models must reflect, in some dimension, the true time-series structure of the economy. If agents' beliefs within their forecasting model are not contradicted by actual outcomes, then agents cannot be freely disposing of useful information. There also has to be a correspondence between beliefs and outcomes since agents' beliefs are supported by the structure of the economy. It follows that *any* forecasting model that produces forecast errors uncorrelated with that same forecasting model is consistent with Muth's hypothesis.[7] In the equilibria we present below, we exploit this orthogonality between forecast errors and forecast models to derive an alternative equilibrium. This alternative to REE is in the spirit of Muth but, as we will see below, incorporates bounded rationality.

Misspecification Consistent with the Model: Restricted Perceptions Equilibrium

The previous subsection argued that agents exist conceptually inside forecasting models. The Muth hypothesis requires that these forecasting models be consistent with the underlying economic model only in the sense that agents are unable to tell that their model is distinct from the actual stochastic process. An RPE, first defined by Evans and Honkapohja (2001), formalizes the notion that agents' beliefs come from misspecified forecasting models but agents cannot detect their misspecification.[8]

To illustrate, we again consider the univariate self-referential model in the previous subsection. In an RPE, agents form beliefs via a restricted version of the PLM in (2). Forecasting models are restricted from (2) by restricting the dimension of the vector of exogenous variables: by restricting the size of the set of explanatory variables we impose that agents underparameterize their forecasting models. The set of underparameterized forecasting models is:

$$\mathscr{F} = \left\{ x_t = a + b'\hat{z}_{t-1} + \varepsilon_t : \dim(\hat{z}) < \dim(z) \right\}. \tag{5}$$

---

[7] We are really arguing for consistent expectations. Simon suggested labeling RE "model consistent" expectations.

[8] The first development of an RPE was by Anderson and Sonnenschein (1985) who called their equilibrium a Rational Expectations Equilibrium with Econometric Models. Other early RPE models include Marcet and Sargent (1989), Sargent (1991), Evans, Honkapohja, and Sargent (1993).

An object in the set $\mathscr{F}$ is a PLM that must omit at least one variable or lag.[9] For the purposes of defining an RPE, we assume that all agents select one of these underparameterized models. Below, we describe a mechanism for allowing agents to choose only the best performing statistical models from this set.

Underparameterization is a reasonable approach to expectation formation. In VAR forecasting, many professional forecasters limit the number of variables and/or lags in their statistical models. Because of degrees of freedom restrictions, computational costs, etc. it may be necessary to forecast based on a parsimonious specification. The Muth hypothesis requires that agents construct these forecasts so that they are unable to detect their underparameterization within the context of the forecasting model. In other words, the parameters (a, b') are formed as the optimal linear projection of the forecasting model on the state x.[10] That is, (a, b') must satisfy the least-squares orthogonality condition:

$$E\hat{z}_{t-1}\{x_t - (a + b'\hat{z}_{t-1})\} = 0. \tag{6}$$

The condition (6) requires agents' forecast errors, $x_t - (a + b'\hat{z}_{t-1})$, to be uncorrelated with the forecasting model $\hat{z}_{t-1}$. Within agents' perceived world they are unable to improve on their forecast. Clearly, this is consistent with Muth's hypothesis.

A solution to Eq. (6) is nontrivial because the model is self-referential. When beliefs are underparameterized so that $E_{t-1}x_t = a + b'\hat{z}_{t-1}$, then the actual law of motion for the economy is

$$x_t = Fa + Fb'\hat{z}_{t-1} + \gamma'Az_{t-1} + \gamma'\varepsilon_t. \tag{7}$$

Agents' beliefs (a, b') affect the actual law of motion that, in turn, feeds back onto agents' beliefs via the orthogonality condition (6). An RPE is a fixed point to this mapping. This is the sense in which the model is self-referential; an equilibrium requires beliefs to be consistent. The RPE is distinct from the REE because the PLM does not include RE as a special case; it is not possible for agents' beliefs to coincide with the actual distribution of the economy.

---

[9] z can represent the stacked form of a VAR(1) so that omitting an element of z could be either a variable or a lag.
[10] Because the ε_t are iid zero-mean omitting the parameter c has no bearing on our definition.

The RPE is a reasonable equilibrium outcome because it accounts for realistic departures from RE. In dynamic models it is likely that agents will restrict their information sets. An RPE restricts information sets in a way that is consistent with the true economic structure. The remainder of this survey describes economic implications of this alternative to REE.

Related Equilibrium Concepts

We turn to a brief discussion of the connection between RPE and other closely related equilibrium concepts.

Sargent (1999) shows existence of a SCE in a simple dynamic macroeconomic model.[11] In Sargent's model, the economy is governed by the natural rate hypothesis — an expectations-augmented Phillips curve implies there is no long-run tradeoff between inflation and unemployment. The government, though, (mistakenly) believes the economy follows a statistical Phillips curve with a long-run tradeoff between inflation and unemployment. The government sets inflation by solving an optimal control problem with their statistical Phillips curve as one constraint. The actual time-series of the economy is determined by the government's misperceptions and the expectations-augmented Phillips curve. In Sargent's model, the SCE has the government exploit their misspecified Phillips curve, thereby producing excessive inflation.

Like the model above, decisions in Sargent's model are based on a misperceived forecasting model. Muth's hypothesis requires that the government not be able to detect its misspecification. Sargent defines an SCE exactly as we define an RPE: the government's beliefs must be uncorrelated with its forecast errors. The primary difference, though, between the RPE and the SCE is that the SCE can correspond with the REE while the RPE cannot. In the RPE, rational expectations cannot be nested within the set of restricted PLMs. In Sargent's SCE, it is possible that the data exactly confirm the governments beliefs and the economy is in an REE.

One reason the SCE in Sargent's model coincides with the REE is that agents in his model have rational expectations. In other models, such as Williams (2003), it is assumed that the private agents have restricted

---

[11] SCE were first developed by Fudenberg and Levine (1998) and applied in game theoretic settings. In an SCE players correctly guess opponents' play, however their assumptions on play out of equilibrium may be wrong.

perceptions, of the type in Eq. (5), and in that case the SCE and the RPE exactly coincide.[12]

Most dynamic macroeconomic models are actually nonlinear. The infinite-horizon representative agent model, overlapping generations model, and dynamic stochastic general equilibrium models, all produce dynamic equations that are nonlinear. Frequently, these nonlinear laws of motion come from Euler equations, which govern how the representative consumer will (optimally) choose her consumption sequence. Analytic solutions to these nonlinear models are difficult to obtain. Instead the predominant solution method takes a linear approximation to the nonlinear model.[13] These approximations bound the stochastic process to a neighborhood of a steady-state. So long as the noise has sufficiently small support, the system will stay bounded in this neighborhood and the linearization is reasonable.

Unfortunately, a number of papers cast doubt on whether economies stay bounded in a neighborhood of a unique steady-state. For example, Grandmont (1985), Grandmont, Pintus, and DeVilder (1998), Cazavillan, Pintus, and Lloyd-Braga (1998), Benhabib and Rustichini (1994) and Benhabib, Schmitt-Grohé, and Uribe (2001) show that the dynamics in many standard models may be quite complicated and not restricted to neighborhoods of the steady-states. Hommes and Sorger (1998) are motivated along these lines to assume agents have linear beliefs in a nonlinear world. They ask whether these beliefs can be consistent with the nonlinear model just as the RPE shows underparameterized models can be consistent with the economy. This is a compelling question since most economists construct linear solutions to these models and most econometric forecasting is based on linear models. If agents are boundedly rational then they should also form linear forecasts.

A Consistent Expectations Equilibrium (CEE) is a stochastic process and a set of beliefs such that agents use a linear forecasting rule and are unable to detect that the true model is nonlinear. Take, as an example, the model in Branch and McGough (2005) who suppose that the true model is

$$x_t = G(x^e_{t+1}, \eta_t),$$

[12] In Adam (2004), an RPE exists (with an additional stability condition) where agents choose between two models, one of which is consistent with RE. Adam finds that additional persistence from economic shocks arises and such a model can explain key covariance relationships of the U.S. economy.

[13] There are, on the other hand, a number of approaches to computing higher-order Taylor expansions. See Judd (1998).

but beliefs are formed according to the linear forecasting rule

$$x_t = bx_{t-1} + \varepsilon_t.$$

The function G can arise from an Euler equation. A CEE occurs when the autocorrelation coefficients of the perceived model align with the actual autocorrelation coefficients from the data $\{x_t\}$:

$$b^j = \text{corr}(x_t, x_{t-j}).$$

It can be shown that for the case where $j = 1$ this also satisfies an orthogonality condition:

$$Ex_{t-1}(x_t - bx_{t-1}) = 0.$$

Again, because of the self-referential feature of the model $- x_t$ depends on bx_{t-1} – existence of such equilibria are nontrivial. Hommes, Sorger, and Wagener (2003) provide an interesting example where a CEE exists in the Overlapping Generations Model of Grandmont (1985).

The intuitive properties of a CEE can be illustrated graphically. Figure 7.1, excerpted from Branch and McGough (2005), shows a nonlinear function symmetric about an (unstable) steady-state. The line running through G is the linear belief function. Given these linear beliefs, and realizations of the random variable η_t, the function G produces outcomes denoted by the circles. As the figure illustrates these realizations are scattered about the linear beliefs of the agents. Without knowing that G is nonlinear, agents will think they have represented the stochastic process well with their trend line. The orthogonality condition shows that this is an example of an RPE where agents have their functional form incorrect; within the context of their forecasting model agents are unable to detect their misspecification. A CEE, though, also requires that higher-order autocorrelations coincide with agents' beliefs. It is this restriction which differentiates a CEE and RPE. A CEE imposes stronger restrictions than an RPE.

EXTENDING THE RPE: MISSPECIFICATION EQUILIBRIUM (ME)

One criticism of the RPE as a suitable alternative to REE is that the form of misspecification is ad hoc. Branch and Evans (2004, 2005) develop an extension of the RPE called a Misspecification Equilibrium (ME) that endogenizes the underparameterization. The set F in Eq. (5) consists of all underparameterized forecasting models. A more restricted set of models

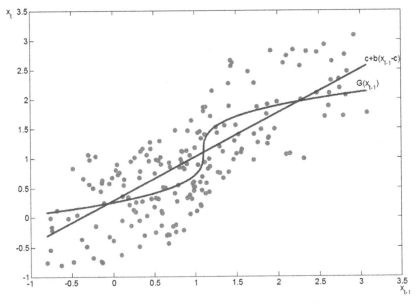

Figure 7.1. Consistent Expectations Equilibrium. (Excerpted from Branch and McGough [2005].)

would consist of all underparameterized forecasting models in F where the parameters are computed via the least squares orthogonality condition. An equilibrium most consistent with Muth's hypothesis will have agents only choose the best performing statistical models from the set of all underparameterized models. Of course, since these models are self-referential, "best performing" is dependent on how many agents forecast with a given model. By allowing agents to endogenously choose their forecasting model we can search for a Nash equilibrium in forecasting models.

Denote u^j as a selector matrix that picks out those elements of z_t used by the predictor indexed by j.[14] If there are K predictors then there exists a $K \times 1$ vector of predictor proportions $n' = (n_j)_{j=1}^K$; where n_j is the proportion of agents who use predictor j. Expectations in a reduced-form model such as Eq. (1) are a weighted average of underparameterized predictors,

$$E_{t-1}^* x_t = \sum_{j=1}^K n_j b^j u^j z_{t-1}.$$

Attached to each predictor j is a fitness measure EU^j.

---

[14] u^j consists of zeros and ones so that if one wanted to pick out the first element of z then $u = (1, 0, \dots, 0)$.

To close the model we need a method for determining the proportions n_j. Here, we follow Brock and Hommes (1997) in assuming that predictor choice is given by a discrete choice among the (optimal) forecasting functions.[15] In Brock and Hommes (1997), agents choose between rational and naive expectations with the probability that they will choose a given predictor given by a multinomial logit (MNL) law of motion. The MNL approach to discrete decision making has a venerable history in economics, and is discussed extensively in Manski and McFadden (1981). In Branch and Evans (2004, 2005) we specify:

$$n_j = \frac{\exp(\alpha EU^j)}{\sum_{k=1}^{K} \exp(\alpha EU^k)}. \tag{8}$$

Below, we consider several applications of this setup where fitness is defined as unconditional mean profits or mean square forecast error. In either case the fitness measures EU^j, $j = 1, \ldots, K$ depend on the stochastic process x_t. Because the model is self-referential, the data x_t also depend on the choices n_j. From this logic, it follows that predictor fitness measures depend on n and so we can define the function $G_j(n) = EU^j$.[16] The predictor proportions in Eq. (8) depend on $G_j(n)$ and, hence, on n itself. Rewriting Eq. (8),

$$n_j = \frac{\exp(\alpha G_j(n))}{\sum_{k=1}^{K} \exp(\alpha G_k(n))}. \tag{9}$$

A Misspecification Equilibrium is a vector n which is a fixed point of the mapping defined by Eq. (9). An ME is an RPE where agents only choose the best of the best misspecified models. An ME is a powerful equilibrium concept because it is most consistent with Muth's hypothesis but also allows for bounded rationality. As we will see in the remainder of this survey the ME makes several important implications.

Below we survey three applications. The first shows how heterogeneity may arise as an equilibrium outcome, the second explores the existence of multiple equilibria, and the third examines the joint determination of optimal monetary policy and misspecification.

---

[15] Brock and Durlauf (2001) examine discrete choices dependent on expectations of the actions of peers. They find that multiple equilibria can arise.
[16] This function maps from the unit simplex into the set of real numbers.

Cobweb Model

Heterogeneity in expectations is an element of most surveys such as the University of Michigan's Survey of Consumers (see Branch [2004]). However, models with fully optimizing agents have been unable to derive heterogeneous expectations endogenously. In Branch and Evans (2004), heterogeneity arises in an ME with agents split between underparameterized models. Branch and Evans (2004) call heterogeneity that arises in a Misspecification Equilibrium as $\alpha \to \infty$ *Intrinsic Heterogeneity*. The parameter α is often called the "intensity of choice." It plays a key role in the stability and bifurcation analysis of Brock and Hommes (1997). Because the discrete choice is based on a random utility model, the parameter α is inversely related to the variance of the noise in the random utility term. The neoclassical case has $\beta = \infty$. This is "neoclassical" because no agent will ever choose a predictor that performs poorly relative to the opportunities. We focus on the properties of ME as $\alpha \to \infty$ because this is where all agents only choose best performing statistical models. We highlight the results in Branch and Evans (2004) by focusing on the case where z_t is bivariate.

The cobweb model is a simple framework of supply and demand where supply has a one-period production lag. Branch and Evans (2004) adapt the cobweb model of Muth (1961):

$$D(p_t) = H - Bp_t + \delta'z_t, \tag{10}$$

$$S(E^*_{t-1}p_t) = CE^*_{t-1}p_t, \tag{11}$$

where z_t is bivariate and follows

$$z_t = Az_{t-1} + \varepsilon_t.$$

The equilibrium price process is

$$p_t = -\frac{C}{B}E^*_{t-1}p_t + \frac{\delta'}{B}z_t, \tag{12}$$

where H has been normalized to zero. Equilibrium price (12) has the same reduced form as Eq. (1) with $F = -C/B$, $\gamma' = \delta'/B$. In the cobweb model, $F < 0$ implies "negative feedback." Expectations produce a movement in price in the opposite direction. It is this self-referential feature of the cobweb model that makes heterogeneity possible as an equilibrium outcome.

In the cobweb model, the appropriate fitness measure for forecasting is expected profits $E\pi^j$. The forecasting models for the bivariate case are:

$$E^1_{t-1}x_t = b^1 z_{1,t-1}, \tag{13}$$

$$E^2_{t-1}x_t = b^2 z_{2,t-1}. \tag{14}$$

Aggregate beliefs are:

$$E^*_{t-1}x_t = nb^1 z_{1,t-1} + (1-n)b^2 z_{2,t-1},$$

where n is the proportion incorporating z into their beliefs. Given these beliefs, plugging expectations into the equilibrium price equation leads to the following reduced form for the economy:

$$x_t = \xi_1 z_{1,t-1} + \xi_2 z_{2,t-1} + v_t, \tag{15}$$

for appropriately defined ξ_1, ξ_2 and zero-mean iid v_t.[17] Note that ξ_1, ξ_2 depend on n. The form of Eq. (15) highlights the dual effects of z_t. z_t has a direct effect given by $\gamma' A$, but it also has an indirect expectation formation effect. It is this tension that produces interesting implications of an ME. The parameters b^1, b^2 are computed according to the orthogonality condition above and using the reduced-form (15) are given by

$$b^1 = \xi_1 + \xi_2 \rho, \tag{16}$$

$$b^2 = \xi_2 + \xi_1 \tilde{\rho}, \tag{17}$$

where $\rho = Ez_1 z_2 / Ez_1^2$ and $\tilde{\rho} = Ez_1 z_2 / Ez_2^2$ are correlation coefficients.[18]

A couple of brief notes are useful. These expectations take into account the correlation between the forecasting model and the omitted variable. Optimal projections will "tease" out of the price process as much information about z_t as is statistically possible. Note also how an RPE arises in Eqs. (16–17), given predictor proportions n: ξ_1, ξ_2 depend on b^1, b^2 which depend on ξ_1, ξ_2. An ME yields, in addition to the RPE, an equilibrium in n.

Given the reduced-form and the RPE belief parameters b^j, $j = 1, 2$, it is straightforward to compute mean profits.[19] We follow Brock and

---

[17] $\xi_1 = \gamma_1 a_{11} + \gamma_2 a_{21} + nb^1, \xi_2 = \gamma_1 a_{12} + \gamma_2 a_{22} + (1-n)b^2$.
[18] See Branch and Evans (2004) for details.
[19] The Muth cobweb model assumes a quadratic cost function.

Hommes (1997) in making a convenient reduction in the size of the state when there are only two predictors. Define $\tilde{G}(n) = E\pi^1 - E\pi^2$ as the relative profit differences as a function of n. For heterogeneity to arise, this function must be positive at $n = 0$ — so that agents have an incentive to deviate from the consensus forecast — and negative at $n = 1$. Brock and Hommes (1997) illustrated that it is possible to define the mapping for n in terms of the profit difference $\tilde{G}$:

$$n = \frac{1}{2}\tanh\left[\frac{\alpha}{2}\tilde{G}(n)\right] + \frac{1}{2}.$$

This function maps the unit interval into itself.[20] Since the tanh is continuous, Brouwer's theorem guarantees that there exists at least one misspecification equilibrium. Moreover, if $\tilde{G}(n)$ is a monotonically decreasing function then n will also be monotonically decreasing and there will exist a unique ME. Figure 7.2 illustrates one possibility.

Figure 7.2 plots the profit difference function (bottom panel) and the predictor proportion mapping (top panel). This is for a particular parameterization presented in Branch and Evans (2004). Notice that because the profit difference is positive at $n = 0$, an agent would have an incentive to use model 1 since it returns higher mean profits. The opposite is true at $n = 1$ where agents will want to mass from predictor 1 to predictor 2. These forces imply that the only equilibrium is where both predictors fare equally well in terms of average profit. Both predictors return the same mean profit at the proportion where $\tilde{G}$ crosses the horizontal axis. This intuition is demonstrated in the top panel. It plots the aggregate best-response mapping for agents. This panel plots the predictor proportion mapping for various values of the "intensity of choice" α. As $\alpha \to \infty$, the equilibrium proportion of agents tends to the point where both predictors fare equally well.

That agents only choose the best performing models was the motivation for an ME. Here we illustrate that it is possible for agents to be split across multiple models. In a model, such as the cobweb, where there is negative feedback from expectations the equilibrium dynamics of the model push each predictor to have the same average return; agents will be split heterogeneously across these predictors. The existence of heterogeneity is a significant result in Branch and Evans (2004) because previous models

---

[20] The tanh is continuous, increasing, symmetric about the origin and asymptotes at -1 and 1.

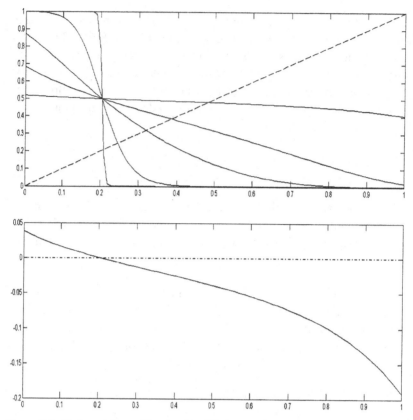

Figure 7.2. Unique Misspecification Equilibrium and Intrinsic Heterogeneity in the cobweb model. (Excerpted from Branch and Evans [2004].)

were unable to generate heterogeneity across predictors without assuming a finite "intensity of choice." That heterogeneity arises as an equilibrium outcome illustrates how small deviations from full rationality can lead to observationally important phenomena.

Lucas Model

In this subsection we present an overview of Branch and Evans (2005). The Lucas-type monetary model, adapted from Evans and Ramey (2003), shares the same reduced-form as the cobweb model. However, in this model $0 < F < 1$ so that there is "positive feedback" from expectations to the state. Positive feedback suggests coordination and the possibility of multiple equilibria.

The Lucas model is based on a general equilibrium framework where firms make signal extractions of local versus global price shocks. The model consists of an aggregate demand (AD) and aggregate supply (AS) relationship:

$$AS: q_t = \phi(p_t - E^*_{t-1}p_t) + \beta_1 z_t \tag{18}$$

$$AD: q_t = m_t - p_t + \beta_2 z_t + w_t \tag{19}$$

$$m_t = p_{t-1} + \delta' z_t + u_t \tag{20}$$

$$z_t = A z_{t-1} + \varepsilon_t \tag{21}$$

where $z_t \in \mathbb{R}^2$ is a vector of exogenous disturbances that hit the economy, w_t is white noise, and m_t is the money supply. The reduced-form of this model is

$$\pi_t = \frac{\phi}{1+\phi} E^*_{t-1}\pi_t + \frac{(\delta + \beta_2 - \beta_1)'}{1+\phi} z_t + \frac{1}{1+\phi}(w_t + u_t)$$

where $\pi_t = p_t - p_{t-1}$. This again takes the same reduced-form as Eq. (1).

The details of the model are identical to the cobweb model with the exception of the sign of F.[21] Additionally, we define predictor fitness in terms of mean square error:

$$EU^j = -E(x_t - b^j z_{j,t-1})^2, \quad j = 1, 2.$$

The positive feedback implies that agents' expectations are reinforced by the stochastic process. The coordinating forces suggests that multiple equilibria may be present.

A necessary condition for multiple equilibria is that the function $\tilde{G}(n_1) = EU^1 - EU^2$ takes the values $\tilde{G}(0) < 0$ and $\tilde{G}(1) > 0$. Under these conditions, agents have an incentive to stick with the consensus forecasts. Figure 7.3 illustrates this case for a particular parameterization of Branch and Evans (2005). The bottom panel shows that $\tilde{G}$ is monotonically increasing and crosses the horizontal axis. The top panel illustrates how this translates into the MNL mapping. Here, there are three equilibria: two homogenous expectations equilibria and a third interior equilibrium. The

---

[21] Beliefs are again of the form Eqs. (16–17).

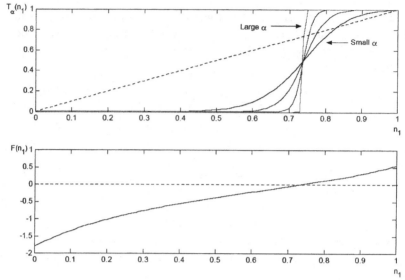

Figure 7.3. Multiple Misspecification Equilibria in the Lucas Model. (Excerpted from Branch and Evans [2005].)

outside equilibria, at $n = 0, 1$, are stable in the sense that the mapping is (locally) contracting at those points. This implies that under a learning rule the system will tend to be confined to neighborhoods of these two points.

This result is interesting because it suggests that there can be a coordinating incentive in misspecified models. Even though agents are free to choose their misspecification, the equilibrium forces of the model drive them to the same model. Of course, one hallmark of Post Walrasian macroeconomics is the assertion that the economy may not have institutions capable of coordinating on such an equilibrium. Branch and Evans (2005) explore this issue by replacing optimal linear projections with recursive least squares estimates. That paper shows that under certain learning rules, the economy may generate endogenous dynamics that switch between neighborhoods of these two stable equilibria. This occurs under a type of weighted least squares called constant gain learning. Constant gain learning has agents place greater weight on recent than distant observations. So a particularly large shock to the economy (by an omitted variable) may lead agents to believe the other forecasting model is superior. Because the asymptotic stochastic properties of each equilibria are distinct, it is shown that endogenous volatility in inflation and output can arise; this is an important finding because one empirical regularity is that inflation volatility has declined considerably in the United States since the mid 1980s. The next section explores how optimal monetary policy might interact with these coordinating Misspecification Equilibria.

POLICY IMPLICATIONS

The intuition for the ME results in the cobweb model and Lucas model surround the dual effects that exogenous disturbances have on recursive expectational models. An exogenous stochastic process has a direct effect (γ') on the state (x_t) but it also has an indirect expectation formation effect (F and b^j). The papers in Branch and Evans (2004, 2005) highlight the tension between these dual effects. If there is a negative feedback in the model, then the indirect effect may work to counteract the influence of the direct effect. In the Lucas model, where there is positive feedback, the indirect and direct effects work in tandem.

Many business cycle models also depend on a government control, such as monetary or fiscal policy. If this policy is conducted optimally (e.g. Woodford [2003]) then one would expect the government to counteract the direct effect of exogenous disturbances. This opens the possibility for a third effect of exogenous disturbances: policy feedback. Given the parameters of the model, optimal policy prescribes a reaction for the government's control (say nominal interest rates) to exogenous disturbances. This reaction must take into account the expectations of agents and how they are distributed across misspecified forecasting models: the indirect effect has bearing on the policy effect.[22] But the policy effect alters how the exogenous disturbances are correlated with the state x_t, so policy also influences the predictor proportions. This intuition suggests that a fully specified model will have a joint determination of optimal policy and a Misspecification Equilibrium. We explore this issue by presenting a highly stylized model as an example. A formal model is being developed in work in progress.

A Simple Model

To illustrate how optimal policy may affect the Misspecification Equilibrium we consider a slight alteration of Eq. (1):

$$x_t = FE^*_{t-1}x_t + \gamma'z_t + Pi_t \tag{22}$$

$$z_t = Az_{t-1} + \varepsilon_t \tag{23}$$

---

[22] We assume that the policy authority is able to commit to such a policy.

We assume x_t is bivariate and that it consists of output and inflation. Notice that Eq. (22) now depends on the nominal interest rate, which is under the control of the central bank. We continue to assume z_t is a stationary bivariate VAR(1). Then F, γ' are (2×2). This model is inspired by the Sargent–Wallace model, where expectations affect both an IS and AS curve. Expectations are multivariate and so misspecification can occur in multiple dimensions. To keep the analysis close to the previous section, we assume that agents underparameterize by omitting a component of z but their beliefs have the same form for both components of x_t:[23]

$$E^1_{t-1}x_t = b^1 z_{1,t-1},$$ (24)

$$E^2_{t-1}x_t = b^2 z_{2,t-1}.$$ (25)

Now b^j is (2×1). In an RPE, these expectations are set so that the forecast errors are orthogonal to the forecasting model. Before such an equilibrium can be computed we require a specification for optimal policy.

As before, the law of motion can be rewritten in the form:

$$x_t = \xi_1(n)z_{1,t-1} + \xi_2(n)z_{2,t-1} + Pi_t + \gamma'\varepsilon_t$$ (26)

where the ξs have been written to emphasize their dependence on the predictor proportion n. The government's problem is to choose a sequence $\{i_t\}_{t=0}^{\infty}$ in order to maximize its objective function subject to the law of motion for the economy, taking n as given.[24] We assume that policymakers care about minimizing inflation and output variance:

$$\min_{\{i_t\}} -E_0 \sum_{t=0}^{\infty} \beta^t \left(\pi_t^2 + \omega y_t^2 \right)$$

so that $x_t = \xi_1(n)z_{1,t-1} + \xi_2(n)z_{2,t-1} + Pi_t + \gamma'\varepsilon_t$.

Optimal policy in this case takes the form:

$$i_t = -G'z_{t-1},$$ (27)

---

[23] One could assume alternatively that z_1 is used to forecast inflation and z_2 to forecast output.

[24] In equilibrium, policy and beliefs, n, are jointly determined.

where G is (2×1).

Then the law of motion is:

$$x_t = \xi_1(n)z_{1,t-1} + \xi_2(n)z_{2,t-1} + PG'z_{t-1} + \gamma'\varepsilon_t. \tag{28}$$

In an RPE, beliefs must satisfy the orthogonality condition:

$$Ez_{j,t-1}(x_t - b^j z_{j,t-1}) = 0. \tag{29}$$

In this model, the effect of the exogenous disturbances depends on the direct effect $(\gamma'A)$ but also on the policy effect (PG').

As in the Lucas model, we assume that predictor fitness is measured by mean square error. Mean square error is now with respect to two state variables. In this survey article we are providing an illustration and so we choose the simplest case: agents care equally about inflation and output variance. The "intensity of choice" is now a vector $\alpha = (\alpha_1, \alpha_2)'$. Fix $\alpha_1 = \alpha_2$ and denote $\tilde{G}(n) = EU^1 - EU^2$ as the (2×1) vector of mean forecast errors. Predictor choice is governed by

$$n = \frac{1}{2}\tanh\left[\frac{\alpha'}{2}\tilde{G}(n)\right] + \frac{1}{2}$$

Misspecification Equilibrium with No Policy

We illustrate our results by picking parameters and computing the fitness difference $\tilde{G}$ and the best-response mapping for n. We set the parameters to be:

$$F = \begin{bmatrix} 0.7 & -0.3 \\ 0.2 & 0.8 \end{bmatrix}, \quad A = \begin{bmatrix} 0.2 & 0.2 \\ 0.2 & 0.7 \end{bmatrix},$$

$$\gamma = \begin{bmatrix} 0.1 & 0.01 \\ 0.01 & 0.8 \end{bmatrix}, \quad P = \begin{bmatrix} 0.1 \\ 0.05 \end{bmatrix}.$$

We choose z_t so that the asymptotic stochastic properties are $Ez_1^2 = 0.6161$, $Ez_2^2 = 7.0689$, $Ez_1z_2 = 1.3589$. These were chosen not for an insightful economic interpretation but to illustrate policy implications of Misspecification Equilibria.

Figure 7.4 plots the predictor proportion mapping when policy is set to zero, that is interest rates have no effect on the model. The figure

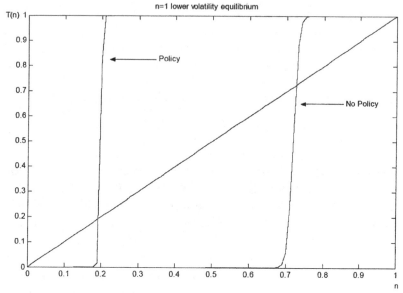

Figure 7.4. Multiple Misspecification Equilibria with and without optimal policy. The $n = 0.7$ ME is when there is no policy, $n = 0.2$, is for optimal policy.

demonstrates that because of the positive feedback of expectations there are again two stable coordinating equilibria at $n = 0$ and $n = 1$. Because the z_2 component has much higher variance, the basin of attraction is much higher for the $n = 0$ equilibrium than the $n = 1$ equilibrium. If we were to replace optimal linear projections with an adaptive learning rule the economy would spend, asymptotically, more time near the high variance equilibrium. It is possible, though, that agents will coordinate at times near the low variance equilibrium.

Misspecification Equilibrium with Optimal Policy

Our interest with optimal policy is what effect there is on the equilibrium properties when the government chooses its control by taking into account expectations and model misspecification. To explore this issue we present the same plot above, except now we include the predictor proportion mapping when policy is non-zero and takes account of n.

Figure 7.4 again includes the predictor proportion mapping for the no-policy case but also includes the mapping for the policy case. As the figure illustrates, the value for the interior equilibrium switches with the addition of optimal policy. The two stable coordinating equilibria still exist and will always exist regardless of policy in this model. The coordinating equilibria are a result of the positive feedback.

That the value of the unstable equilibrium will switch under optimal policy may not seem significant because the point is unstable. We focus on stable equilibria because under a suitable learning process we expect the system to spend most of its time near one of these equilibria. However, as discussed above, where the unstable equilibrium lies governs the "size" of the basin of attraction. When the interior equilibrium switched from a relatively high value of n to a relatively low value of n, the basin of attraction increased for the $n = 1$ equilibrium. This equilibrium is also the low volatility equilibrium. Under an adaptive learning rule, the asymptotic variance of the economy under optimal policy which takes expectations into account will be lower than when not taking expectations into account.

This finding is intuitive when placed in the context of the tension between indirect and direct effects of exogenous disturbances. When policy counteracts exogenous disturbances, the result is that z_t will have the opposite effect as when there is no policy. Thus, if without policy agents find model 2 more appealing under optimal policy they will now find model 1 more appealing. Clearly, these results are stylized and informal. As work progresses, we develop the details formally and in a less rigged model.

CONCLUSION

This survey summarizes and argues in favor of RPE as a boundedly rational alternative to Rational Expectations. Misspecification is a reasonable assumption in macroeconomics. We focus on cases where agents underparameterize their forecasting models by omitting a variable and/or a lag. In data rich environments it is likely that agents will underparameterize. In fact, most VAR forecasters purposely limit the number of variables and lags. In an RPE, agents underparameterize optimally in the sense that they are unable to detect their misspecification within the context of their forecasting model. We argue that such an equilibrium is consistent with Muth's original hypothesis. In self-referential models, consistency between beliefs and outcomes is a desirable feature. It turns out that Rational Expectations are not the only type of beliefs that are consistent with the underlying model. This chapter demonstrates that in an RPE, beliefs are also consistent with the data generating process.

We explore the implications of RPE by reviewing the ME (Branch and Evans, 2004, 2005). In an ME, agents endogenously choose their form of misspecification so that they only choose best performing statistical models.

In a model with negative feedback from expectations, like the cobweb model, agents may be distributed heterogeneously across forecasting models. In business cycle models, such as a Lucas-type or Sargent–Wallace ad hoc model, there are positive feedback and multiple Misspecification Equilibria.

Besides highlighting results on RPE in the literature, this paper also argues that there are important policy interaction effects. We provided an example where policy, taking the form of misspecification as given, alters the stochastic properties of the economy. By altering the stochastic properties of the economy agents, endogenous choice of misspecified model will also change. A fully specified equilibrium prescribes a joint determination of policy and misspecification. Future work intends to explore this implication more formally. In particular, the literature on monetary policy during the 1970s highlights two alternative explanations of the stagflation: misspecification on the part of agents (e.g. Orphanides and Williams [2003a]) and misspecification on the part of the government about the structure of the economy (see Sargent [1999] and Bullard and Eusepi [2005]).The approach advocated in this chapter suggests that an additional form of misspecification may be empirically important: agents optimally choose underparameterized forecasting models and policymakers form incorrect assumptions about the form of misspecification. The story in mind is that policymakers during the 1970s, by assuming agents were not coordinating on oil prices, accommodated supply shocks that altered the effects of oil prices to the extent that agents would then incorporate oil prices into their forecasting models. In the 1980s, though, policymakers correctly realized that agents were predominantly reacting to supply shocks; then they optimally responded to those shocks, altering the effects of the shocks and leading agents to coordinate on other forecasting models. Such a story can explain why oil price shocks lost their potency during the 1990s.

8

Not More So: some Concepts Outside the DSGE Framework

Masanao Aoki[*]

The macroeconomic models in the dynamic stochastic general equilibrium (DSGE) framework are certainly an improvement over earlier models, but they are still too simplistic to take seriously as policy advice because they fail to meet Albert Einstein's "Not More So" criterion. In the tradeoff between analytic tractability and relevance to macro problems, they err on the side of tractability. This chapter provides a brief introduction to some analytic tools and techniques that can make macro models more useful by incorporating agent interdependence. These include notions of exchangeability, exchangeable agents, random partitions of sets of agents, distribution of sizes of clusters of agents, and ultrametrics. These tools have been developed outside the economics profession in such disciplines as population genetics, combinatorial stochastic processes, and statistical physics, as they have struggled to deal with problems with structures similar to those with which macroeconomists are struggling, and they are important building blocks of what is being called Post Walrasian macroeconomics.

Specifically, I discuss tools that allow one to go beyond two assumptions that characterize almost all DSGE models: (1) the two clusters of agents in fixed proportions assumptions,[1] replacing them with general random partitions and random clusters of agents of various sizes; and (2) the uniform arrangement of agents on a unit interval assumption, replacing it with ultrametric distances between clusters.[2]

* The author wishes to acknowlege Hiroshi Yoshikawa for his insights and discussions, and thank David Colander for his helpful suggestions.

[1] See Carroll (2002), for example.
[2] See Ramal and Toulouse (1986). Aoki (1996, Sections. 2.5 and 7.1) has short descriptions and some elementary economic applications.

Ultrametric distances allow one to express relations among clusters of agents (firms or sectors) rather than simply among agents. They also allow one to discuss dynamics of clusters on trees with continuous-time Markov chains with transition rates (probabilities) that are functions of ultrametric distances among clusters, thereby providing a model that can explain sluggish aggregate responses. The notion also allows one to introduce one- and two-parameter Poisson–Dirichlet distributions and residual allocation models (Ewens, 1990) which are important for discussion of distributions of sizes of several clusters of agents for power-law behaviors of cluster sizes. The chapter is simply an introduction to these tools, but in it I give a sense of their power and how they might be used within the more general Post Walrasian model.

Since the chapter is about very abstract tools and notions, in the first section of the chapter I relate a model incorporating these notions with a case study of some very practical policy advice, demonstrating how reliance on "too simple" models led to inappropriate policy. The case study is the Japanese economy of the 1990s and it concerns policy advice given to the Bank of Japan on how to pull the Japanese economy out of its stagnation. The advice was based on models that incorporated the notion of the liquidity trap, models that assumed away certain combinatorial effects of interactions among agents in uncertain environments. But because the models used assumed-away cluster effects, they arrived at estimates of interest elasticity that were inappropriate to the period. Had the models incorporated cluster effects, they would likely have fit the period much better. Incorporating cluster effects, the models exhibit not only a liquidity trap, but also an *uncertainty* trap, and it was that uncertainty trap that was central to the Japanese economy.[3] Then in the second part of the chapter, I introduce the reader to some of the other analytic techniques that are likely to become central to the Post Walrasian toolkit.

This chapter first addresses the question: Why did policy advice offered to the Bank of Japan by several prominent macroeconomists fail to get the Japanese economy out of the long stagnation during the 1990s? The case study of the Japanese economy during this period reveals that the mainstream macroeconomists who gave this advice relied on the liquidity trap notion. Unfortunately they all ignored or did not fully grasp the implications for policy effectiveness of the uncertainty that pervaded the Japanese economy during this period, nor did they consider certain combinatorial effects that are crucial in assessing policy effects

---

[3] See Aoki and Yoshikawa (2003).

in circumstances in which economic agents are uncertain about the consequences of their decisions.

EFFECTS OF UNCERTAIN CONSEQUENCES OF CHOICES WITH EXTERNALITY

Suppose that there are a large number of agents. Assume that there are a fixed number N of them. Each agent makes one of two possible choices. Agents can change their minds at any time. We can accommodate this by using continuous-time Markov chains for dynamics of their choice patterns. The set of agents then separate into two subgroups or clusters: n of them prefer choice 1 and the rest, $N - n$ of them, prefer choice 2. We assume that the consequences of their choices are only imperfectly known to the agents when they choose. A crucial complicating factor is that their choices are interdependent. One agent's choice affects the desirability of other agents' choices. We use fraction $x = n/N$ as our basic variable.

Agents know that there is externality, that is, consequences or advantages of their choices are influenced by the fraction x, that is, how many have chosen choice 1.

Given that a fraction x of agents have made choice 1, denote the probability that choice 1 is better than choice 2 by

$$\eta(x) = \Pr(V \geq 0|x),$$

where V is some random variable that embodies relative advantages of the two choices. A positive value of V means choice 1 is better than choice 2.

We denote the mean of V, conditional on x by

$$g(x) = E(V|x).$$

This is the expected amount of the advantages associated with choice 1, given fraction x have chosen it.

If we assume that V is a normal random variable with conditional mean $g(x)$ and standard deviation σ, then η is known to be expressible in terms of the error function. Even when V is not a conditionally normal random variable, there is an approximation proposed by Ingber (1982) that allows:

$$\eta(x) = \frac{e^{\beta g(x)}}{Z},$$

where Z is the normalization $Z = e^{\beta g(x)} + e^{-\beta g(x)}$, and β is a constant proportional to $1/\sigma$. Large values of σ, that is, small values of β, indicate more uncertainty of the consequences of agent decisions than when σ is small, that is, β is large.

With this set-up we next show that relative merits of the two choices become less clear cut. As the value of β becomes small, the model becomes less responsive to changes in $g(\cdot)$. Put differently, if some government agency tries to affect the fraction of agents favoring choice 1 by increasing the conditional mean $g(\cdot)$ to favor choice 1, the fraction x will barely respond, when β is near zero, hence the term uncertainty trap.

This model is also useful in demonstrating that combinatorial consideration, in the number of ways n agents favoring choice 1 can be chosen out of N agents, is crucial in demonstrating the uncertainty trap effect via the Shannon entropy. See Eq. (3) below.

The dynamics of the model involve a random walk on the line segment $\{0, 1, \ldots, N\}$, which may be thought of a birth-death process. We model it as a continuous-time Markov chain with transition rate from n to $n+1$

$$r_n := (N - n)\eta(x) = N(1 - x)\eta(x), \tag{1}$$

and the rate from n to $n-1$

$$l_n := n(1 - \eta(x)) = Nx(1 - \eta(x)). \tag{2}$$

Equation (1) defines the transition rate for a rightward move by a step in the random walk model. This expresses the event that one of the agents with choice 2 switches to choice 1. Equation (2) is the transition rate to the left by one step, when an agent with choice 1 switches to choice 2.

Without the factor η, this is a basic random walk or birth−death model in many elementary stochastic process textbooks in which agents are assumed to be independent. The factor η expresses the effects of externality among agents belonging to a different cluster. Unlike the model in these textbooks, agents' choices in our model are dependent.

It is known that the probability $\Pr[n(t)]$, that is, the probability that $n(t)$ agents have choice 1, is governed by the Chapman−Kolmogorov equation, which converges to a stationary distribution as time goes to infinity. Let $\pi(n)$ be the stationary equilibrium probability that η agents reach choice 1. Balancing the inflow of probability flux with that of outflow, we obtain

$$\pi(n)r_n = \pi(n + 1)l_{n+1}.$$

This is called the detailed balance condition in the statistical physics literature. It can be solved recursively to give

$$\pi(n) = A \prod_{j=1}^{n} \frac{r_{j-1}}{l_j},$$

where A is a normalizing constant. After substituting Eqs. (1) and (2) into the transition rates, we obtain

$$\pi_n = AC_{N,n} \prod_{r=1}^{n} \frac{\eta[(j - 1/N)]}{[1 - \eta(j/N)]}.$$

Note the combinatorial effects $C_{N,n} = N!/n!(N - n)!$ in the stationary probability expression.

It is convenient to rewrite the above expression as

$$\pi_n = \frac{1}{Z} \exp\left\{-\beta N U\left(\frac{n}{N}\right)\right\},$$

where we introduce a function U, which physicists call potential, by

$$U(x) = -\frac{2}{N} \sum_{j=1}^{n} g\left(\frac{j}{N}\right) - \frac{1}{\beta} H(x) + O\left(\frac{\ln N}{N}\right),$$

where $H(x) = -x \ln x - (1 - x)\ln(1 - x)$ arises by using Stirling's formula to approximate the expression $C_{N,n}$. This is the Shannon entropy term.

Letting N become very large, we approximate the sum by the integral to obtain

$$U(x) = -2 \int^{x} g(y)dy - \frac{1}{\beta} H(x). \tag{3}$$

The maximum probability of $\pi(x)$ is achieved at the minimum of this potential.

When agents know with more confidence that choice 1 is better than choice 2, that is, when less uncertainty surrounds the outcomes or consequences of their decisions, parameter β tends to infinity because the standard deviation is getting very small. The entropy term becomes insignificant and the potential $U(x)$ is maximized at

$$0 = U'(\phi) = -2g(\phi),$$

where ϕ denotes the zero of $g(x)$. Thus the value of ϕ can be manipulated by changing $g(\cdot)$, that is, the mean of the distribution of the random variable V.

With a large degree of uncertainty, σ is large and β becomes small. This causes the entropy term to become dominant in determining the position of the maximum potential

$$0 = U'(\phi) = -2g(\phi) + \frac{1}{\beta}\ln\frac{\phi}{1-\phi}.$$

In the case where the second term on the right side is much larger than the first term $g(\phi)$, the effect of the first term will be insignificant in determining the maximum of the potential.

Multiple Equilibria

Any significant degree of uncertainty (small β) creates various problems. Even if the conditional mean of V, $g(x)$, has a unique stable root, the derivative of the potential, $U(x) = 0$, may have multiple stable roots.[4] Aoki (1995, 1996; Section 5.10) presents a numerical example in which two stable roots exist for

$$U'(x) = -2g(x) + \frac{1}{\beta}\ln\frac{x}{1-x} = 0.$$

To summarize the results so far, suppose that $g(x)$ is such that the model has a unique stable equilibrium. When uncertainty is negligible (β is large), the potential has a unique minimum. When uncertainty becomes significant, however, we cannot ignore the combinatorial aspect of the problem, as expressed as the Shannon entropy term $H(x)$.

A sufficiently small value of β, that is, a sufficiently large degree of uncertainty, causes the potential $U(x)$ to possess multiple minima.

---

[4] For example, see histograms of the simulation results in Aoki (1996, Figs. 5.1–5.3). As shown in Fig. 5.5 of that simulation the potential has two local minima.

Consequently, the economy has multiple equilibria. In the next sub-section we show that with small β, changing g has little effect on the economy.

Ineffectiveness of Conventional Macroeconomic Policy

In the context of this model, "policy" is a change in the g function in our model. Shifting $g(x)$ to $g(x) + h$ by some constant amount changes ϕ by

$$\delta\phi = \frac{2\beta h}{\left[\phi(1 - \phi)^{-1}\right] - 2\beta g'(\phi)}.$$

Note that with β nearly zero, the effect of a shift in g is nearly canceled out, and x does not move.

The Conventional Wisdom

Japan suffered from decade-long stagnation in the 1990s. After a series of recessions, the interest rate had fallen to zero by the late 1990s. The Bank of Japan lost control of the interest rate because of the absolute low boundary for the interest rate.

Krugman (1998) argued that caught in the liquidity trap, the Bank of Japan should create expected inflation to lower the real interest rate to get the economy out of this trap, and he offered a theoretical model to support his proposal. However, his model had a simple representative consumer maximization of discounted utility stream which is converted to a two-period model between present and future, and he assumed that the future is not caught in the liquidity trap and the quantity equation holds. In that model an increase in the money supply in the future will raise the equilibrium price level if the public really believes that the future money stock will increase.[5] Following Krugman's lead, Blanchard (2000b),[6] Bernanke (2000), Rogoff (2002), and Svensson (2001) all basically proposed a large increase in the supply of money coupled with inflation targeting.

Although there are some minor differences among the advice offered by these economists, their advice focused on changing the g function, and totally ignored effects of uncertainty and the associated combinatorial

---

[5] See Aoki and Yoshikawa (2006, Chapter 4) for detailed assessment of his model.
[6] Blanchard recommended that the Bank of Japan jump the stock of base money initially. This is effectively what the Bank of Japan did during 1997–2002.

factor. The analysis of uncertainty trap in this chapter suggests that the inflation targeting would not work in an economy with significant degree of uncertainty.

That Japan faced a significantly greater degree of uncertainty than the United States can be demonstrated in several ways. One is the time series of the coefficient of variation (standard deviation/mean) of quarterly GDP from, say, 1990 to 2001. This is the time series of the inverse of β. From mid 1990s to the beginning of 2000, the Japanese GDP had very significantly larger coefficient of variation than the U.S. GDP. Another suggestive piece of evidence is the time series of the standard error of regression of an AR(2) fit of the GDP. The rolling SER divided by the mean rose significantly for Japan during the 1990s.

My point is that when the degree of uncertainty is large, we must drop the representative consumer assumption and seriously consider the simple fact that the macroeconomy consists of a large number of interdependent economic agents. The combinatorial aspects discussed in this chapter play a crucial role, and have important policy implications. Specifically, once the economy falls into this "uncertainty trap," conventional macroeconomic analysis cannot be relied on.

Does the model presented above satisfy the "Not More So" principle? Yes. Without the introduction of parameter β, mainstream macroeconomic policy will not focus on the effects of uncertainty nor on the importance of the number of possible microeconomic configurations compatible with macroeconomic situations.

DISTRIBUTION OF CLUSTER SIZES, AND ENTRIES BY NEW TYPES OF AGENTS OR GOODS

The above *was only one example* of the tools necessary for at least a chance of dealing with the problem of agent interdependency. There are more, and the problem of theoretical macro is not that it is too mathematical; it is that it is not mathematical enough in subject areas that matter. If you are going to theorize, you need to use the mathematics necessary to capture the salient features of the reality you are trying to describe. There are many more such tools that I have explored in Aoki (1996, 2002), and in the remainder of this chapter I will briefly discuss a couple of them.

I begin with some recent advances in combinatorial stochastic processes, in particular one- and two-parameter Poisson–Dirichlet distributions,[7]

---

[7] See Antoniak (1969) and J. Pitman (2002).

and how their relation to residual allocation models can be used to model entries by new types of agents or new goods.[8]

Some rudimentary analysis with two clusters of agents of fixed proportion is conducted in DSGE models, such as Carroll (2002). More explicit considerations of distribution of sizes of clusters of agents must be injected into macroeconomic models that take account of recent advances in combinatorial stochastic processes. The importance of the combinatorial factor is illustrated in the first section of this chapter. Growth may be modeled in cluster dynamics, and entries of new types of agents (creation of new sectors) or invention of new goods may also be modeled analogously. The importance of introducing new goods or new types of agents in growth models has been illustrated in Aoki (2002, Section 8.6) and Aoki and Yoshikawa (2002, 2006).

In the first section we had two endogenously formed groups or clusters of agents, depending on their choices. In many economic phenomena we need more than two clusters. In DSGE models, it is routinely assumed that agents are uniformly distributed on the unit interval, or they are treated as if they are at equal "distance" from each other.[9]

Ultrametrics

In more realistic analysis it is necessary to recognize some groups or clusters that are closer together than others. For example, in a multi-sector model with employed and laid-off workers, the pool of laid-off workers from all sectors is not homogeneous. When a firm wishes to increase its labor force, the probability that it hires back some of its laid-off workers will be higher than that of hiring from pools of industries or firms that are not closely related to the hiring firms. This aspect can be modeled by using ultrametrics. Similar comments can be made about differentiating by human capital, length of unemployment, and so on to incorporate into models the fact that the total pool of unemployed may consist of several clusters of more homogeneous agents.

---

[8] See Kingman (1978), Aldous (1985), Zabell (1992), Ewens (1990), and Pitman (2002) for further detail, and Aoki (2002, Chapter 8) for elementary applications to macroeconomics. See Derrida (1994) and Solomon and Levy (1996) on power-laws.

[9] See Aoki (2002, Chapter 9) where this arrangement of agents on the unit interval was dropped in discussing the Diamond search model, Diamond (1982). As one of the results of this choice, we obtain information on the variance of unemployment rates and more informative analysis of the equilibria. The well-known work by Taylor on staggered wage contracting by unions is another example. He did not differentiate distance between unions; they are treated alike. Taylor (1979, 1980).

We need some notion of distance to measure similarity or dissimilarity of clusters, and to organize the whole pool of unemployed into tree structure. Correlations do not work since they are not transitive.[10]

The distance between two clusters called i and j is denoted by $d(i, j)$ which satisfies not the usual triangle inequality but

$$d(i,j) \leq \max_k\{d(i,k), d(k,j)\}.$$

For further references see Aoki (1996, Section 2.5, Chapter 7).

Clusters may be organized into an upside down tree. The leaves of a tree correspond to clusters, composed of agents who are similar or the same in some characteristics within a collection of agents.

Stochastic dynamics on trees have many applications. Labor markets may be regarded as segmented, that is, with clusters of firms with different productivity coefficients; clusters (pools) of unemployed with ultrametric distances between them to model the assumption of sectoral differentiated coefficients of productivity; and heterogenous unemployed agents. We can rework Okun's law and the Beveridge curves in this more general setting.[11] We can also show that these more realistic models depend on the GDP, and demand policies are effective to increase GDP. The models that show no effect of aggregate demand do so because they are too simple; for analytical tractability, they eliminate the paths through which demand is most likely to affect GDP. We can use the tree-structured clusters to explain why aggregate price index is sluggish.

CONCLUDING REMARKS

This chapter has focused on the importance and applicability to macro-economics of some concepts from statistical physics and combinatorial stochastic processes. The mathematics to analyze these alternative models may look strange and complicated, but are straightforward, even though they may look exotic at first sight. Many noneconomists and even some mathematical macroeconomists may reject the approaches to macro-economics proposed in this chapter on the ground that they are unnecessary abstractions or technicalities. This chapter discusses the likelihood that without what initially may appear to be unnecessary technical

---

[10] See Feigelman and Ioffe (1991, p. 173). Instead, we use the notion of ultrametrics originally introduced by physicists to study spin glasses.
[11] See Aoki and Yoshikawa (2005, 2006; Chapters 6 and 7).

complications important new insights in macroeconomics cannot be obtained.

Models ought to be simple to clarify how insights about or understanding of macroeconomics are produced. However, there is a point beyond which simplification of models destroys the very insights or points being made by the new approaches to macroeconomics. We need to heed Albert Einstein's "Not More So" criterion.

I argue that this chapter represents the minimum degree of complication beyond the mainstream models to better capture the essence of real-world economy. The examples in this chapter are brief, but are chosen to provide a short guided tour to the concepts and methods that are developed outside mainstream macroeconomics but should be in the toolkits of macroeconomists.

PART III

LEAPING AWAY FROM THE DSGE MODEL

9

Agent-based Computational Modeling and Macroeconomics

Leigh Tesfatsion[*]

How should economists model the relationship between macroeconomic phenomena and microeconomic structure? Economists have been struggling to answer this question for decades. Nevertheless, the Walrasian equilibrium model devised by the nineteenth century French economist Leon Walras (1834–1910) still remains the fundamental paradigm that frames the way many economists think about this issue. Competitive models directly adopt the paradigm. Imperfectly competitive models typically adopt the paradigm as a benchmark of coordination success. Although often critiqued for its excessive abstraction and lack of empirical salience, the paradigm has persisted.

As detailed by Katzner (1989) and Takayama (1985), Walrasian equilibrium in modern-day form is a precisely formulated set of conditions under which feasible allocations of goods and services can be price-supported in an economic system organized on the basis of decentralized markets with private ownership of productive resources. These conditions postulate the existence of a finite number of price-taking profit-maximizing firms who produce goods and services of known type and quality, a finite number of consumers with exogenously determined preferences who maximize their utility of consumption taking prices and dividend payments as given, and a Walrasian Auctioneer (or equivalent clearinghouse construct) that determines prices to ensure each

[*] With permission from Elsevier, this chapter is an abridged version of a study (Tesfatsion, 2006) first presented in preliminary form at the Post Walrasian Macroeconomics Conference held at Middlebury College in May, 2004.

market clears.[1] Assuming consumer nonsatiation, the First Welfare Theorem guarantees that every Walrasian equilibrium allocation is Pareto efficient.

The most salient structural characteristic of Walrasian equilibrium is its strong dependence on the Walrasian Auctioneer pricing mechanism, a coordination device that eliminates the possibility of strategic behavior. All agent interactions are passively mediated through payment systems; face-to-face personal interactions are not permitted. Prices and dividend payments constitute the only links among consumers and firms prior to actual trades. Since consumers take prices and dividend payments as given aspects of their decision problems, outside of their control, their decision problems reduce to simple optimization problems with no perceived dependence on the actions of other agents. A similar observation holds for the decision problems faced by the price-taking firms. The equilibrium values for the linking price and dividend variables are determined by market clearing conditions imposed through the Walrasian Auctioneer pricing mechanism; they are not determined by the actions of consumers, firms, or any other agency supposed to actually reside within the economy.

What happens in a standard Walrasian equilibrium model if the Walrasian Auctioneer pricing mechanism is removed and if prices and quantities are instead required to be set entirely through the actions of the firms and consumers themselves? Not surprisingly, this "small" perturbation of the Walrasian model turns out to be anything but small. Even a minimalist attempt to complete the resulting model leads to analytical difficulty or even intractability. As elaborated by numerous commentators, the modeler must now come to grips with challenging issues such as asymmetric information, strategic interaction, expectation formation on the basis of limited information, mutual learning, social norms, transaction costs, externalities, market power, predation, collusion, and the possibility of coordination failure (convergence to a Pareto-dominated equilibrium).[2] The prevalence of market protocols, rationing rules, antitrust legislation, and other types of institutions in real-world macroeconomies is now better

[1] The colorful term "Walrasian Auctioneer" was first introduced by Leijonhufvud (1967). He explains the origins of the term as follows (personal correspondence, May 10, 2004): "I had come across this statement by Norbert Weiner, made in the context of explaining Maxwell's Demon to a lay audience, to the effect that 'in the physics of our grandfathers' information was costless. So I anthropomorphized the tâtonnement process to get a Walras's Demon to match Maxwell's."

[2] See, for example, Akerlof (2002), Albin and Foley (1992), Arrow (1987), Bowles and Gintis (2000), Clower and Howitt (1996), Colander (1996), Feiwel (1985), Hoover (1992), Howitt (1990), Kirman (1997), Klemperer (2002a,b), and Leijonhufvud (1996).

understood as a potentially critical scaffolding needed to ensure orderly economic process.

Over time, increasingly sophisticated tools are permitting macroeconomic modelers to incorporate more compelling representations for the public and private methods governing production, pricing, trade, and settlement activities in real-world macroeconomies. Some of these tools involve advances in logical deduction and some involve advances in computational power.[3]

This essay provides an introductory discussion of a potentially fruitful computational development for the study of macroeconomic systems, *Agent-based Computational Economics* (ACE). Exploiting the growing capabilities of computers, ACE is the computational study of economic processes modeled as dynamic systems of interacting agents.[4] Here "agent" refers broadly to bundled data and behavioral methods representing an entity constituting part of a computationally constructed world. Examples of possible agents include individuals (e.g. consumers, workers), social groupings (e.g. families, firms, government agencies), institutions (e.g. markets, regulatory systems), biological entities (e.g. crops, livestock, forests), and physical entities (e.g. infrastructure, weather, and geographical regions). Thus, agents can range from active data-gathering decision-makers with sophisticated learning capabilities to passive world features with no cognitive functioning. Moreover, agents can be composed of other agents, thus permitting hierarchical constructions. For example, a firm might be composed of workers and managers.[5]

---

[3] See, for example, Albin (1998), Anderson et al. (1988), Arifovic (2000), Arthur et al. (1997), Axelrod (1997), Brock et al. (1991), Clark (1997), Day and Chen (1993), Durlauf and Young (2001), Evans and Honkapohja (2001), Gigerenzer and Selten (2001), Gintis (2000), Judd (1998), Krugman (1996), Mirowski (2004), Nelson (1995), Nelson and Winter (1982), Prescott (1996), Roth (2002), Sargent (1993), Schelling (1978), Shubik (1991), Simon (1982), Witt (1993), and Young (1998).

[4] See http://www.econ.iastate.edu/tesfatsi/ace.htm for extensive online resources related to ACE, including readings, course materials, software, toolkits, demos, and pointers to individual researchers and research groups. A diverse sampling of ACE research can be found in Leombruni and Richiardi (2004) and in Tesfatsion (2001a,b,c). For surveys and other introductory materials, see Axelrod and Tesfatsion (2006), Batten (2000), Epstein and Axtell (1996), Tesfatsion (2002), and Tesfatsion and Judd (2006).

[5] A person familiar with object-oriented programming (OOP) might wonder why "agent" is used here instead of "object," or "object template" (class), since both agents and objects refer to computational entities that package together data and functionality and support inheritance and composition. Following Jennings (2000) and other agent-oriented programmers, "agent" is used to stress the intended application to problem domains that include entities capable of varying degrees of self-governance and self-directed social interactions. In contrast, OOP has traditionally interpreted objects as passive tools in the

The first section of this essay explains more fully the basic ACE methodology. The second section starts by setting out a relatively simple Walrasian equilibrium model for a two-sector decentralized market economy. The Walrasian Auctioneer is then removed from this model, and the circular flow between firms and consumers is reestablished through the introduction of agent-driven procurement processes. The resulting "ACE Trading World" is used in the following section to illustrate how ACE modeling tools facilitate the provision of empirically compelling microfoundations for macroeconomic systems. Concluding remarks are given in the final section.

THE BASIC ACE METHODOLOGY

A system is typically defined to be *complex* if it exhibits the following two properties (for example, see Flake [1998]):

- The system is composed of interacting units;
- The system exhibits *emergent* properties, that is, properties arising from the interactions of the units that are not properties of the individual units themselves.

Agreement on the definition of a complex *adaptive* system has proved to be more difficult to achieve. The range of possible definitions offered by commentators includes the following three nested characterizations:

Definition 1: A *complex adaptive system* is a complex system that includes *reactive* units, that is, units capable of exhibiting systematically different attributes in reaction to changed environmental conditions.[6]

Definition 2: A *complex adaptive system* is a complex system that includes *goal-directed* units, that is, units that are reactive and that direct at least some of their reactions towards the achievement of built-in (or evolved) goals.

---

service of some specific task. Consider, for example, the following description from the well-known Java text by Eckel (2003): "One of the best ways to think about objects is as 'service providers.' Your goal is to produce ... a set of objects that provides the ideal services to solve your problem."

[6] For example, this definition includes simple Darwinian systems for which each unit has a rigidly structured behavioral rule as well as a "fitness" attribute measuring the performance of this unit relative to the average performance of other units in the current unit population. A unit ceases to function if it has sufficiently low fitness; otherwise it reproduces (makes copies of itself) in proportion to its fitness. If the initial unit population exhibits diverse behaviors across units, then the fitness attribute of each unit will change systematically in response to changes in the composition of the unit population.

Definition 3: A *complex adaptive system* is a complex system that includes *planner* units, that is, units that are goal-directed and that attempt to exert some degree of control over their environment to facilitate achievement of these goals.

The ACE methodology is a culture-dish approach to the study of economic systems viewed as complex adaptive systems in the sense of Definition 1, at a minimum, and often in the stronger sense of Definition 2, or Definition 3. As in a culture-dish laboratory experiment, the ACE modeler starts by computationally constructing an economic world comprising multiple interacting agents (units). The modeler then steps back to observe the development of the world over time.

The agents in an ACE model can include economic entities as well as social, biological, and physical entities (e.g. families, crops, and weather). Each agent is an encapsulated piece of software that includes data together with behavioral methods that act on these data. Some of these data and methods are designated as publicly accessible to all other agents, some are designated as private and hence not accessible by any other agents, and some are designated as protected from access by all but a specified subset of other agents. Agents can communicate with each other through their public and protected methods.

The ACE modeler specifies the initial state of an economic system by specifying each agent's initial data and behavioral methods and the degree of accessibility of these data and methods to other agents. As illustrated in Tables 9.1–9.4, an agent's data might include its type attribute (e.g. world, market, firm, consumer), its structural attributes (e.g. geography, design, cost function, utility function), and information about the attributes of other agents (e.g. addresses). An agent's methods can include socially instituted public behavioral methods (e.g. antitrust laws, market protocols) as well as private behavioral methods. Examples of the latter include production and pricing strategies, learning algorithms for updating strategies, and methods for changing methods (e.g. methods for switching from one learning algorithm to another). The resulting ACE model must be *dynamically complete*. As illustrated in Table 9.5, this means the modeled economic system must be able to develop over time solely on the basis of agent interactions, without further interventions from the modeler.

In the real world, all calculations have real cost consequences because they must be carried out by some agency actually residing in the world. ACE modeling forces the modeler to respect this constraint. An ACE model is essentially a collection of algorithms (procedures) that have been encapsulated into the methods of software entities called "agents."

Table 9.1. *A computational world*

---

agent World

{

   Public Access:

     //Public Methods

       The *World Event Schedule*, a system clock permitting World inhabitants to time and order their activities (method activations), including synchronized activities such as offer posting and trade;

       Protocols governing the ownership of stock shares;

       Protocols governing collusion among firms;

       Protocols governing the insolvency of firms;

       Methods for retrieving stored World data;

       Methods for receiving data.

   Private Access:

     //Private Methods

       Methods for gathering, storing, and sending data.

     //Private Data

       World attributes (e.g. spatial configuration);

       World inhabitants (e.g. markets, firms, consumers);

       Attributes and methods of the World's inhabitants;

       History of World events;

       Address book (communication links);

       Recorded communications.

}

Algorithms encapsulated into the methods of a particular agent can only be implemented using the particular information, reasoning tools, time, and physical resources available to that agent. This encapsulation into agents is done in an attempt to achieve a more transparent and realistic representation of real-world systems involving multiple distributed entities with limited information and computational capabilities.

Current ACE research divides roughly into four strands differentiated by objective.[7] One primary objective is *empirical understanding*: why have particular global regularities evolved and persisted despite the absence of centralized planning and control? ACE researchers pursuing this objective seek causal explanations grounded in the repeated interactions of agents

---

[7] See http://www.econ.iastate.edu/tesfatsi/aapplic.htm for pointers to resource sites for a variety of ACE research areas, including a site on multi-market modeling and macroeconomics.

Table 9.2. *A computational market*

---

agent Market
{

   Public Access:
    //Public Methods
      getWorldEventSchedule(clocktime);
      Protocols governing the public posting of supply offers;
      Protocols governing the price discovery process;
      Protocols governing the trading process;
      Methods for retrieving stored Market data;
      Methods for receiving data.
   Private Access:
    //Private Methods
      Methods for gathering, storing, and sending data.
    //Private Data
      Information about firms (e.g. posted supply offers);
      Information about consumers (e.g. bids);
      Address book (communication links);
      Recorded communications.

}

---

operating in realistically rendered worlds. Ideally, the agents should have the same flexibility of action in their worlds as their corresponding entities have in the real world. In particular, the cognitive agents should be free to behave in accordance with their own beliefs, preferences, institutions, and physical circumstances without the external imposition of equilibrium conditions. The key issue is whether particular types of observed global regularities can be reliably generated from particular types of agent-based worlds, what Epstein and Axtell (1996) refer to as the "generative" approach to science.

A second primary objective is *normative understanding*: how can agent-based models be used as computational laboratories for the discovery of good economic designs? ACE researchers pursuing this objective are interested in evaluating whether designs proposed for economic policies, institutions, and processes will result in socially desirable system performance over time. The general approach is akin to filling a bucket with water to determine if it leaks. An agent-based world is constructed that captures the salient aspects of an economic system operating under the design. The world is then populated with privately motivated agents with learning capabilities and allowed to develop over time. The key issue is the extent to which the

Table 9.3. *A computational firm*

---

agent Firm
{

   Public Access:
     //Public Methods
       getWorldEventSchedule(clocktime);
       getWorldProtocol(ownership of stock shares);
       getWorldProtocol(collusion among firms);
       getWorldProtocol(insolvency of firms);
       getMarketProtocol(posting of supply offers);
       getMarketProtocol(trading process);
       Methods for retrieving stored Firm data;
       Methods for receiving data.
   Private Access:
     //Private Methods
       Methods for gathering, storing, and sending data;
       Method for selecting my supply offers;
       Method for rationing my customers;
       Method for recording my sales;
       Method for calculating my profits;
       Method for allocating my profits to my shareholders;
       Method for calculating my net worth;
       Methods for changing my methods.
     //Private Data
       My money holdings, capacity, total cost function, and net worth;
       Information about the structure of the World;
       Information about World events;
       Address book (communication links);
       Recorded communications.

}

---

resulting world outcomes are efficient, fair, and orderly, despite attempts by agents to gain individual advantage through strategic behavior.

A third primary objective is *qualitative insight and theory generation*: how can economic systems be more fully understood through a systematic examination of their potential dynamic behaviors under alternatively specified initial conditions? Such understanding would help to clarify not only why certain global outcomes have regularly been observed, but also why others have not.

Table 9.4. *A computational consumer*

---

agent Consumer
{

  Public Access:
    //Public Methods
      getWorldEventSchedule(clocktime);
      getWorldProtocol(ownership of stock shares);
      getMarketProtocol(price discovery process);
      getMarketProtocol(trading process);
      Methods for retrieving stored Consumer data;
      Methods for receiving data.
  Private Access:
    //Private Methods
      Methods for gathering, storing, and sending data;
      Method for determining my budget constraint;
      Method for determining my demands;
      Method for seeking feasible and desirable supply offers;
      Method for recording my purchases;
      Method for calculating my utility;
      Methods for changing my methods.
    //Private Data
      My money holdings, subsistence needs, and utility function;
      Information about the structure of the World;
      Information about World events;
      Address book (communication links);
      Recorded communications.

}

A fourth primary objective is *methodological advancement*: how best to provide ACE researchers with the methods and tools they need to undertake systematic theoretical studies of economic systems through controlled computational experiments, and to validate experimentally generated theories against real-world data? ACE researchers are exploring a variety of ways to address this objective ranging from careful consideration of methodological principles to the practical development of programming, visualization, and validation tools.

ACE can be applied to a broad spectrum of economic systems ranging from micro to macro in scope. This application has both advantages and disadvantages relative to more standard modeling approaches.

Table 9.5. *World dynamic activity flow*

```
main () {
    initWorld();              //Construct a world composed of agents
                              //(markets, firms, consumers, ...).
    configWorld();            //Configure the world and its constituent
                              //agents with methods and data.
    For (T = 0, ..., Tmax) {  //Enter the World Event Schedule:
        postOffers();         //Firms select supply offers and
                              //publicly post them.
        seekOffers();         //Consumers seek supply offers in accordance
                              //with their needs and preferences.
        match();              //Firms and consumers determine trade
                              //Partners and record transaction costs.
        trade();              //Firms and consumers engage in trade
                              //interactions and record trade outcomes.
        update();             //Firms and consumers update their methods
                              //and data based on their search and trade
                              //experiences.
    }
}
```

On the plus side, as in industrial organization theory (Tirole [2003]), agents in ACE models can be represented as interactive goal-directed entities, strategically aware of both competitive and cooperative possibilities with other agents. As in the extensive-form market game work of researchers such as Albin and Foley (1992), Rubinstein and Wolinsky (1990), and Shubik (1991), market protocols and other institutions constraining agent interactions can constitute important explicit aspects of the modeled economic processes. As in the behavioral game theory work of researchers such as Camerer (2003), agents can *learn*, that is, change their behavior based on previous experience; and this learning can be calibrated to what actual people are observed to do in real-world or controlled laboratory settings. Moreover, as in work by Gintis (2000) that blends aspects of evolutionary game theory with cultural evolution, the beliefs, preferences, behaviors, and interaction patterns of the agents can vary endogenously over time.

One key departure of ACE modeling from more standard approaches is that events are driven solely by agent interactions once initial conditions have been specified. Thus, rather than focusing on the equilibrium states of a system, the idea is to watch and see if some form of equilibrium develops over time. The objective is to acquire a better understanding of a system's entire phase portrait, that is, all possible equilibria *together* with corresponding basins of attraction. An advantage of this focus on process rather than on equilibrium is that modeling can proceed even if equilibria are computationally intractable or nonexistent.

A second key departure presenting a potential advantage is the increased facility provided by agent-based tools for agents to engage in flexible social communication. This means that agents can communicate with other agents at event-driven times using messages that they, themselves, have adaptively scripted.

However, it is frequently claimed that the most important advantage of ACE modeling relative to more standard modeling approaches is that agent-based tools facilitate the design of agents with relatively more autonomy; see Jennings (2000). Autonomy, for humans, means a capacity for self-governance.[8] What does it mean for computational agents?

Here is how an "autonomous agent" is defined by a leading expert in artificial intelligence, Stan Franklin (1997a):

An *autonomous agent* is a system situated within and part of an environment that senses that environment and acts on it, over time, in pursuit of its own agenda and so as to effect what it senses in the future.

Clearly the standard neoclassical budget-constrained consumer who selects a sequence of purchases to maximize her expected lifetime utility could be said to satisfy this definition in some sense. Consequently, the important issue is not whether agent-based tools permit the modeling of agents with autonomy, per se, but rather the degree to which they usefully facilitate the modeling of agents exhibiting substantially more autonomy than permitted by standard modeling approaches.

What degree of agent autonomy, then, do agent-based tools permit? In any purely mathematical model, including any ACE model in which agents do not have access to "true" random numbers,[9] the actions of an agent are ultimately determined by the conditions of the agent's world at the time of

---

[8] See the "Personal Autonomy" entry at the Stanford Encyclopedia of Philosophy site, accessible at http://plato.stanford.edu/entries/personal-autonomy/.

[9] Agent-based modelers can now replace deterministically generated pseudo-random numbers with random numbers generated by real-world processes such as atmospheric noise and radioactive decay; for example, see http://www.random.org. This development has potentially interesting philosophical ramifications.

the agent's conception. A fundamental issue, dubbed the First AI Debate by Franklin (1997b), is whether or not the same holds true for humans. In particular, is Penrose (1989) correct when he eloquently argues there is something fundamentally noncomputational about human thought, something that intrinsically prevents the algorithmic representation of human cognitive and social behaviors?

Lacking a definitive answer to this question, ACE researchers argue more pragmatically that agent-based tools facilitate the modeling of cognitive agents with more realistic social and learning capabilities (hence more autonomy) than one finds in traditional *Homo economicus*. As suggested in Tables 9.3–9.4, these capabilities include: social communication skills; the ability to learn about one's environment from various sources, such as gathered information, past experiences, social mimicry, and deliberate experimentation with new ideas; the ability to form and maintain social interaction patterns (e.g. trade networks); the ability to develop shared perceptions (e.g. commonly accepted market protocols); the ability to alter beliefs and preferences as an outcome of learning; and the ability to exert at least some local control over the timing and type of actions taken within the world in an attempt to satisfy built in (or evolved) needs, drives, and goals. A potentially important aspect of all of these modeled capabilities is that they can be based in part on the internal processes of an agent, that is, on the agent's *private* methods, which are hidden from the view of all other entities residing in the agent's world. This effectively renders an agent both unpredictable and uncontrollable relative to its world.

In addition, as indicated in Tables 9.3–9.4, an agent can introduce structural changes in its methods over time on the basis of experience. For example, it can have a method for systematically introducing structural changes in its current learning method so that it learns to learn over time. Thus, agents can socially construct distinct persistent personalities.

Agent-based tools also facilitate the modeling of social and biological aspects of economic systems thought to be important for autonomous behavior that go beyond the aspects reflected in Tables 9.1–9.5. For example, agents can be represented as embodied (e.g. sighted) entities with the ability to move from place to place in general spatial landscapes. Agents can also be endowed with "genomes" permitting the study of economic systems with genetically-based reproduction and with evolution of biological populations. For extensive discussion and illustration of agent-based models incorporating such features, see Belew and Mitchell (1996), Epstein and Axtell (1996), and Holland (1995).

What are the disadvantages of ACE relative to more standard modeling approaches? One drawback is that ACE modeling requires the construction of *dynamically complete* economic models. That is, starting from initial conditions, the model must permit and fully support the playing out of agent interactions over time without further intervention from the modeler. This completeness requires detailed initial specifications for agent data and methods determining structural attributes, institutional arrangements, and behavioral dispositions. If agent interactions induce sufficiently strong positive feedbacks, small changes in these initial specifications could radically affect the types of outcomes that result. Consequently, intensive experimentation must often be conducted over a wide array of plausible initial specifications for ACE models if robust prediction is to be achieved.[10] Moreover, it is not clear how well ACE models will be able to scale up to provide empirically and practically useful models of large-scale systems with many thousands of agents.

Another drawback is the difficulty of validating ACE model outcomes against empirical data. ACE experiments generate outcome distributions for theoretical economic systems with explicitly articulated microfoundations. Often these outcome distributions have a multipeaked form suggesting multiple equilibria rather than a central-tendency form permitting simple point predictions. In contrast, the real world is a single time-series realization arising from a poorly understood data generating process. Even if an ACE model were to accurately embody this real-world data generating process, it might be impossible to verify this accuracy using standard statistical procedures. For example, an empirically observed outcome might be a low-probability event lying in a relatively small peak of the outcome distribution for this true data-generating process, or in a thin tail of this distribution.

FROM WALRASIAN EQUILIBRIUM
TO ACE TRADING

For concrete illustration, this section first presents in summary form a Walrasian equilibrium modeling of a simple two-sector economy with price-taking firms and consumers. The Walrasian Auctioneer pricing mechanism is then removed, resulting in a dynamically incomplete economy. Specifically, the resulting economy has no processes for determining how production and price levels are set, how buyers are to

---

[10] This point is discussed at some length by Judd (2006).

be matched with sellers, and how goods are to be distributed from sellers to buyers in cases in which matching fails to result in market clearing.

One possible way to complete the economy with agent-driven procurement processes is then outlined, resulting in an *ACE Trading World.*[11] The completion is minimal in the sense that only procurement processes essential for re-establishing the underlying circular flow between firms and consumers are considered. As will be elaborated more carefully below, these processes include firm learning methods for production and pricing, firm profit allocation methods, firm rationing methods, and consumer price discovery methods.

In the ACE Trading World, firms that fail to cover their costs risk insolvency and consumers who fail to provide for their subsistence needs, face death. Consequently, the adequacy of the procurement processes used by these firms and consumers determines whether they survive and even prosper over time. The critical role played by procurement processes in the ACE Trading World highlights in concrete terms the extraordinarily powerful role played by the Walrasian Auctioneer pricing mechanism in standard Walrasian equilibrium models.

Walrasian Bliss in a Hash-and-Beans Economy

Consider the following Walrasian equilibrium modeling of a simple one-period economy with two production sectors. The economy is populated by a finite number of profit-seeking firms producing hash, a finite number of profit-seeking firms producing beans, and a finite number of consumers who derive utility from the consumption of hash and beans. Each firm has a total cost function expressing its production costs as a function of its output level. Each consumer is endowed with an equal ownership share in each firm as well as an exogenous money income.

At the beginning of the period, each firm has expectations for the price of hash and the price of beans. Conditional on these price expectations, the firm selects a production level to maximize its profits. The solution to this profit-maximizing problem gives the optimal output supply for the firm as a function of its price expectations and its cost function. At the end of the period, all firm profits are distributed back to consumers as dividends in proportion to their ownership shares.

---

[11] A detailed technical presentation of the ACE Trading World can be found in Tesfatsion (2006).

At the beginning of the period, each consumer has expectations regarding the dividends she will receive back from each firm, as well as expectations for the price of hash and the price of beans. Conditional on these expectations, the consumer chooses hash and bean demands to maximize her utility subject to her budget constraint. This budget constraint takes the following form: the expected value of planned expenditures must be less than or equal to expected total income. The solution to this utility maximization problem gives the optimal hash and bean demands for the consumer as a function of her dividend expectations, her price expectations, her tastes (utility function), and her exogenous money income.

Definition: A specific vector e^* comprising each consumer's demands for hash and beans, each firm's supply of hash or beans, non-negative prices for hash and beans, expected prices for hash and beans, and consumer expected dividends is said to be a *Walrasian equilibrium* if the following four conditions hold:

(a) *Individual Optimality*. At e^*, all consumer demands are optimal demands conditional on consumer expected prices and consumer expected dividends, and all firm supplies are optimal supplies conditional on firm expected prices.

(b) *Correct Expectations*: At e^*, all expected prices coincide with actual prices, and all expected dividends coincide with actual dividends calculated as consumer shares of actual firm profits.

(c) *Market Clearing*. At e^*, aggregate supply is greater than or equal to aggregate demand in both the market for hash and the market for beans.

(d) *Walras' Law (Strong Form)*: At e^*, the total value of excess supply is zero; that is, the total value of all demands for hash and beans equals the total value of all supplies of hash and beans.

Conditions (c) and (d) together imply that any consumption good in excess supply at e^* must have a zero price. If consumers are nonsatiated at e^*, meaning they would demand more of at least one type of good if their incomes were to increase, their budget constraints must be binding on their purchases at e^*. Given nonsatiation together with conditions (a) and (b), a summation of all consumer budget constraints would then reveal that the total value of excess supply must necessarily be exactly zero at e^*, that is, Walras' Law in the strong sense of condition (d) necessarily holds. Finally, given consumer nonsatiation together with conditions (a) through (c), the

First Welfare Theorem ensures that any hash and bean consumption levels supportable as optimal consumer demands under a Walrasian equilibrium will be a Pareto efficient consumption allocation (see Takayama [1985]).

Plucking Out the Walrasian Auctioneer

The fulfillment of conditions (b) through (d) in the above definition of Walrasian equilibrium effectively defines the task assigned to the Walrasian Auctioneer. This task has three distinct aspects, assumed costless to achieve. First, all prices must be set at market clearing levels conditional on firm and consumer expectations. Second, all firms must have correct price expectations and all consumers must have correct price and dividend expectations. Third, consumers must be appropriately matched with firms to ensure an efficient set of trades.

To move from Walrasian to agent-based modeling, the Walrasian Auctioneer has to be replaced by agent-driven procurement processes. This replacement is by no means a small perturbation of the model. Without the Walrasian Auctioneer, the following types of agent-enacted methods are minimally required in order to maintain a circular flow between firms and consumers over time:

Terms of Trade: Firms must determine how their price and production levels will be set.

Seller-Buyer Matching: Firms and consumers must engage in a matching process that puts potential sellers in contact with potential buyers.

Rationing: Firms and consumers must have procedures in place to handle excess demands or supplies arising from the matching process.

Trade: Firms and consumers must carry out actual trades.

Settlement: Firms and consumers must settle their payment obligations.

Shake-Out: Firms that become insolvent and consumers who fail to satisfy their subsistence consumption needs must exit the economy.

Attention thus shifts from firms and consumers optimizing in isolation, conditional on expected prices and dividends, to the interaction patterns occurring among firms and consumers over time as they attempt to carry out their trading activities.

The ACE Trading World outlined below illustrates one possible completion of the hash-and-beans economy with procurement handled by the agents themselves rather than by a Walrasian Auctioneer. The resulting process model is described at each point in time by the configuration of data and methods across all agents. A partial listing of these data and methods is schematically indicated in Tables 9.1–9.4. As indicated in Table 9.5, all outcomes in the ACE Trading World are generated through firm and consumer interactions played out within the constraints imposed by currently prevalent structural conditions and institutional arrangements; market clearing conditions are not imposed. Consequently, in order to survive and even prosper in their world, the firms and consumers must learn to coordinate their behaviors over time in an appropriate manner.

The ACE Trading World

Consider an economy that runs during periods $T = 0, 1, \ldots, \text{TMax}$. At the beginning of the initial period $T = 0$, the economy is populated by a finite number of profit-seeking hash firms, a finite number of profit-seeking bean firms, and a finite number of consumers who derive utility from the consumption of hash and beans.

Each firm in period $T = 0$ starts with a non-negative amount of money and a positive production capacity (size). Each firm has a total cost function that includes amortized fixed costs proportional to its current capacity. Each firm knows the number of hash firms, bean firms, and consumers currently in the economy, and each firm knows that hash and beans are perishable goods that last at most one period. However, no firm has prior knowledge regarding the income levels and utility functions of the consumers or the cost functions and capacities of other firms. Explicit collusion among firms is prohibited by antitrust laws.

Each consumer in period $T = 0$ has a lifetime money endowment profile and a utility function measuring preferences and subsistence needs for hash and beans consumption in each period. Each consumer is also a shareholder who owns an equal fraction of each hash and bean firm. The income of each consumer at the beginning of period $T = 0$ is entirely determined by his/her money endowment. At the beginning of each subsequent period, each consumer's income is determined in part by his/her money endowment, in part by his/her savings from previous periods, and in part by his/her newly received dividend payments from firms.

At the beginning of each period $T \geq 0$, each firm selects a *supply offer* consisting of a production level and a unit price. Each firm uses a *learning method* to make this selection, conditional on its profit history and its cost attributes. The basic question posed is as follows: Given I have earned particular profits in past periods using particular selected supply offers, how should this affect my selection of a supply offer in the current period? Each firm immediately posts its selected supply offer in an attempt to attract consumers. This posting is carried out simultaneously by all firms, so that no firm has a strategic advantage through asymmetric information.

At the beginning of each period $T \geq 0$, each consumer costlessly acquires complete information about the firms' supply offers as soon as they are posted. Consumers then attempt to ensure their survival and happiness by engaging in a *price discovery process* consisting of successive rounds. During each round, the following sequence of activities is carried out. First, any consumer unable to cover his/her currently unmet subsistence needs at the currently lowest posted prices immediately exits the price discovery process. Each remaining consumer determines his/her utility-maximizing demands for hash and beans conditional on his/her currently unspent income, his/her currently unmet subsistence needs, and the currently lowest posted hash and bean prices. He/she then submits his/her demands to the firms that have posted these lowest prices. Next, the firms receiving these demands attempt to satisfy them, applying if necessary a *rationing method*. Consumers rationed below subsistence need for one of the goods can adjust downward their demand for the remaining good to preserve income for future rounds. Finally, actual trades take place, which concludes the round. Any firms with unsold goods and any rationed consumers with unspent income then proceed into the next round, and the process repeats.

This period-T price-discovery process comes to a halt either when all firms are stocked out or when the unspent income levels of all consumers still participating in the process have been reduced to zero. Consumers who exit or finish this process with positive unmet subsistence needs die at the end of period T. Their unspent money holdings (if any) are then lost to the economy, but their stock shares are distributed equally among all remaining (alive) consumers at the beginning of period $T + 1$. This *stock share redistribution method* ensures that each alive consumer continues to own an equal share of each firm. At the end of each period $T \geq 0$, each firm calculates its period-T profits. A firm incurs positive (negative) profits if it sells (does not sell) enough output at a sufficiently high price to cover its total costs, including its fixed costs. Each firm then calculates its period-T net worth (total assets minus total liabilities). If a firm finds it does not have a positive net worth,[12] it is declared *effectively*

---

[12] As detailed in Tesfatsion (2006, Appendix), a valuation of each firm's capacity is included in the calculation of its net worth. Consequently, a zero net worth implies a firm has no capacity for production.

insolvent and it must exit the economy. Otherwise, the firm applies a state-conditioned *profit allocation method* to determine how its period-T profits (positive or negative) should be allocated between money (dis)savings, capacity (dis)investment, and (non-negative) dividend payments to its shareholders.

In summary, the ACE Trading World incorporates several key structural attributes, institutional arrangements, and behavioral methods whose specification could critically affect model outcomes. These include: initial numbers and capacities of hash and bean firms; initial number of consumers; initial firm money holdings; consumer money endowment profiles; initial firm cost functions; consumer utility functions; market price discovery and trading protocols; world protocols regarding stock ownership, firm collusion, and firm insolvency; firm learning methods; firm rationing methods; and firm profit allocation methods.

The degree to which the ACE Trading World is capable of self-coordination can be experimentally examined by studying the impact of changes in these specifications on micro behaviors, interaction patterns, and global regularities. For example, as detailed in Cook and Tesfatsion (2006), the ACE Trading World is being implemented as a computational laboratory with a graphical user interface. This implementation will permit users to explore systematically the effects of alternative specifications, and to visualize these effects through various types of run-time displays.

Defining "Equilibrium" for the ACE Trading World

Definitions of equilibrium appearing in scientific discourse differ in particulars depending on the system under study. All such definitions, however, would appear to embody the following core idea: a system is in *equilibrium* if all influences acting on the system offset each other so that the system is in an unchanging condition.

It is important to note the absence in this core definition of any conception of uniqueness, optimality, or stability (robustness) with regard to external system disturbances. Once the existence of an equilibrium has been established, one can further explore the particular nature of this equilibrium. Is it unique? Does it exhibit optimality properties in any sense? Is it locally stable with respect to displacements confined to some neighborhood of the equilibrium? If so, what can be said about the size and shape of this "basin of attraction"?

The ACE Trading World is a deterministic system.[13] The state of the system at the beginning of each period T is given by the methods and data of all of the agents currently constituting the system. The methods include all of the processes used by agents in period T to carry out production, price, trade, and settlement activities, both private behavioral methods and public protocols. These methods are schematically indicated in Tables 9.1–9.4 and presented in detail in Tesfatsion (2006). The data include all of the exogenous and period-T predetermined variables for the ACE Trading World; a complete listing of these variables is provided in Tesfatsion (2006).

Let $X(T)$ denote the state of the ACE Trading World at the beginning of period T. By construction, the motion of this state follows a first-order Markov process. That is, $X(T+1)$ is determined as a function of the previous state $X(T)$. This function would be extremely difficult to represent in explicit structural form, but it could be done.[14] For expository purposes, let this state process be depicted as

$$X(T+1) = S(X(T)), \quad T = 0,1,\ldots,\text{TMax}. \tag{1}$$

If in some period $\bar{T} \geq 0$, all firms were to become insolvent and all consumers were to die for lack of goods sufficient to meet their subsistence needs, the ACE Trading World would exhibit an "unchanging condition" in the sense of an unchanged state,

$$X(T+1) = X(T) \quad \text{for} \quad T = \bar{T} + 1, \ldots, \text{TMax}. \tag{2}$$

Apart from this dire situation, however, the ACE Trading World has four features that tend to promote continual changes in the data components of $X(T)$: (a) the firms' use of choice probability distributions to select supply offers; (b) firm learning (updating of choice probability distributions); (c) changing firm capacity levels in response to changing profit conditions; and (d) resort by firms and consumers to "coin flips" to resolve indifferent choices. Consequently, although a stationary-state

---

[13] Each firm and consumer in the ACE Trading World implementation by Cook and Tesfatsion (2006) has access to its own method for generating "random numbers." However, as usual, these methods are in actuality pseudo-random number generators consisting of systems of deterministic difference equations.

[14] See Epstein (2006) for a discussion of the recursive function representation of ACE models.

equilibrium in the sense of condition (2) is possible, it is too restrictive to be of great·interest.

More interesting than this rarefied stationary-state form of balance are conceptions of equilibrium for the ACE Trading World that entail an "unchanging condition" with regard to more global world properties. Some of these possible conceptions are listed below.

- The economy exhibits an *unchanging carrying capacity*, in the sense that it supports an unchanged number of solvent firms and viable consumers over time.

- The economy exhibits *continual market clearing*, in the sense that demand equals supply in the markets for hash and beans over time.

- The economy exhibits an *unchanging structure*, in the sense that the capacity levels (hence fixed costs) of the hash and bean firms are not changing over time.

- The economy exhibits an *unchanging belief pattern*, in the sense that the firms' choice probability distributions for selection of their supply offers are not changing over time.

- The economy exhibits an *unchanging trade network*, in the sense that who is trading with whom, and with what regularity, is not changing over time.

- The economy exhibits a *steady-state growth path*, in the sense that the capacities and production levels of the firms and the consumption levels of the consumers are growing at constant rates over time.

Finally, it is interesting to weaken further these conceptions of equilibria to permit approximate reflections of these various properties. Define an idealized *reference path* for the ACE Trading World to be a collection of state trajectories exhibiting one (or possibly several) of the above-listed global properties. For example, one might consider the set E^* of all state trajectories exhibiting continual market clearing. For any given tolerance level τ, define a τ-neighborhood of the reference path E^* to be the collection of all state trajectories whose distance from E^* is within τ for some suitably defined distance measure.[15] Given any initial specification for the ACE Trading World, one can then conduct multiple experimental runs using multiple pseudo-random number seed values to

---

[15] For example, a state trajectory might be said to be within distance τ of E^* if, for all sufficiently large tested T values, the discrepancy between period-T aggregate demand and period-T aggregate supply is less than τ in absolute value for both hash and beans.

determine the (possibly zero) frequency with which the ACE Trading World enters and remains within this τ-neighborhood.

ACE MICROFOUNDATIONS FOR MACROECONOMICS

Decentralized market economies are complex adaptive systems. Large numbers of micro agents engage repeatedly in local interactions, giving rise to macroregularities such as employment and growth rates, income distributions, market institutions, and social conventions. These macroregularities in turn feed back into the determination of local interactions. The result is an intricate system of interdependent feedback loops connecting microbehaviors, interaction patterns, and macroregularities.

This section briefly discusses how ACE modeling tools might facilitate the provision of empirically compelling microfoundations for macroeconomic systems taking the form of decentralized market economies. Six issues are highlighted: namely, constructive understanding; the essential primacy of survival; strategic rivalry; behavioral uncertainty and learning; procurement support; and the complex interactions among structural attributes, institutional arrangements, and behavioral dispositions.[16] The ACE Trading World outlined in the previous section is used to motivate key points.

CONSTRUCTIVE UNDERSTANDING

If you had to construct firms and consumers capable of prospering in a realistically rendered macroeconomy, how would you go about it? For example, in the ACE Trading World, how should firms co-learn to set their supply offers (production and price levels) over time, and how should consumers search across these supply offers?

My macroeconomic students are generally intrigued but baffled when presented with this type of constructive exercise. They find it difficult to specify production, price, trade, and settlement processes driven solely by agent interactions, and they are unsure how to define a compelling testable conception of "equilibrium" for the resulting macroeconomic system. Yet the key issue is this: If economists cannot carry out this type of exercise, to what extent can we be said to understand the microsupport requirements for actual macroeconomies and the manner in which such macroeconomies might achieve an "unchanging condition"?

---

[16] See Tesfatsion (2006) for a more extended discussion of these issues.

ACE modeling permits economists and economics students to test their constructive understanding of economic processes essential for the functioning of actual real-world macroeconomies.

The Essential Primacy of Survival

The most immediate, dramatic, and humbling revelation flowing from the ACE modeling of macroeconomic systems is the difficulty of constructing economic agents capable of *surviving* over time, let alone prospering. When firms with fixed costs to cover are responsible for setting their own production and price levels, they risk insolvency. When consumers with physical requirements for food and other essentials must engage in a search process in an attempt to secure these essentials, they risk death. Every other objective pales relative to survival; it is lexicographically prior to almost every other consideration.

ACE modeling permits economists to test their ability to construct firms and consumers·capable of surviving and prospering in realistically rendered macroeconomies for which survival is by no means assured.

Strategic Rivalry

In macroeconomies organized on the basis of decentralized markets, each firm is necessarily in rivalry with other firms for scarce consumer dollars. For example, in the ACE Trading World, the production and price choices of the hash and bean firms are intrinsically linked through consumer budget constraints and preferences. A firm's production and price choices can help attract consumers for its own output by making its output relatively cheap, or by making its output relatively abundant and hence free of stock-out risk. In addition, the production and price choices of the firms producing one type of good can help to counter the relative preference of consumers for the other type of good.

Similarly, each consumer is necessarily in rivalry with other consumers for potentially scarce produced goods. For example, in the ACE Trading World, the hash and bean firms currently offering the lowest prices can suffer stock-outs, hence a consumer formulating his/her demands conditional on receiving these lowest posted prices has no actual guarantee that his/her demands will be realized. If a stock-out results in a consumer's demand being rationed below his/her subsistence needs, preserving income for future purchases to secure these needs becomes a critical survival issue.

ACE modeling permits economists to explore the extent to which strategic behaviors by individual agents can potentially affect the determination of macroeconomic outcomes.

Behavioral Uncertainty and Learning

Tractability problems have made it difficult to incorporate individual learning behaviors in analytical macroeconomic models in an empirically compelling manner. In current macroeconomic theory, it is common to see the problem of learning short-circuited by the imposition of a rational expectations assumption. Rational expectations in its weakest form assumes that agents on average make optimal use of their information, in the sense that their subjective expectations coincide on average with objectively true expectations conditional on this information. Moreover, economists typically apply rational expectations in an even stronger form requiring optimal usage of information *plus* the inclusion in this information of *all* relevant information about the world.

Whatever specific form it takes, the rational expectations assumption requires uncertainty to be ultimately calculable for all agents in terms of "objectively true" conditional probability distributions as an anchor for the commonality of beliefs. Expectations can differ across agents conditioning on the same information only by noise terms with no systematic relationship to this information, so that these noise terms wash out when average or "representative" expectations are considered. This rules out the dynamic study of strategic multi-agent environments such as the ACE Trading World in which a major source of uncertainty is *behavioral uncertainty*, that is, uncertainty regarding what actions other agents will take, and the focus is on interactive learning processes rather than on equilibrium per se.

ACE modeling, particularly in parallel with human-subject experiments, could facilitate the study of behavioral uncertainty and learning in macroeconomic systems.

Procurement Support

In the Walrasian equilibrium model, the fictitious Walrasian Auctioneer pricing mechanism ensures buyers are efficiently matched with sellers at market clearing prices. In the real world, it is the procurement processes implemented by firms, consumers, and other agents actually residing within the world that drive economic outcomes. These procurement processes must allow for a wide range of contingencies in order for economies to function properly. In particular, buyers and sellers must be able to continue on with their production, price, trade, and settlement activities even if markets fail to clear.

The ACE Trading World illustrates the minimal types of scaffolding required to support orderly procurement in macroeconomic systems despite the occurrence of excess supply or demand. As seen in the previous section, this scaffolding includes insolvency protocol, price discovery protocol, profit allocation methods, and rationing methods.

Interactions among Attributes, Institutions, and Behaviors

Anyone who has had hands-on experience with the construction of ACE models, and hence with the specification of data and methods for multiple agents in a dynamic social setting, is sure to have encountered the following modeling conundrum: everything seems to depend on everything else.

Consider, for example, the complicated feedbacks that arise even for the firms and consumers in the relatively simple ACE Trading World. It is generally not possible to conclude that a particular attribute will give a firm or consumer an absolute advantage over time, or that a particular method is optimally configured for a firm or consumer in an absolute sense. The advantage or optimality accruing to an attribute or method at any given time generally depends strongly on the current configuration of attributes and methods across firms and consumers as a whole.

This modeling conundrum is not simply a methodological defect; rather, it is reflective of reality. Empirical evidence strongly indicates that structural attributes, behaviors, and institutional arrangements in real-world macroeconomic systems have indeed co-evolved. For example, McMillan (2002) uses a variety of case studies to argue that markets have both evolved from below and been designed from above, with necessary support from rules, customs, and other institutions that have co-evolved along with the markets.

Given these complex interactions among attributes, institutions, and behaviors, and the growing ability to model these interactions computationally, it seems an appropriate time to re-examine the standards for good macroeconomic modeling. Taking the broad view of "agent" adopted in ACE modeling, institutions and structures as well as cognitive entities can be represented as recognizable and persistent bundles of data and methods that interact within a computationally constructed world. Indeed, as schematically depicted in Tables 9.1−9.4, the ACE Trading World includes a structural agent (the world), institutional agents (markets for hash and beans), and cognitive agents (firms and consumers). In short, agent-based tools provide tremendous opportunities for economists and other social scientists to increase the depth and breadth of the "representative agents" depicted in their models.

A key outstanding issue is whether this ability to consider more comprehensive and empirically compelling taxonomies of representative agents will ultimately result in better predictive, explanatory, and exploratory models. For example, for the study of decentralized market economies, can the now-standard division of cognitive agents into producers, consumers, and government policymakers be usefully extended to include brokers, dealers, financial intermediaries, innovative entrepreneurs, and other forms of active market-makers? Similarly, can the traditional division of markets into perfect competition, monopolistic competition, duopoly, oligopoly, and monopoly be usefully replaced with a broader taxonomy that better reflects the rich diversity of actual market forms as surveyed by McMillan (2002)?

CONCLUDING REMARKS

The defining characteristic of ACE models is their constructive grounding in the interactions of agents, broadly defined to include economic, social, biological, and physical entities. The state of a modeled system at each point in time is given by the data and methods of the agents that currently constitute the system. Starting from an initially specified system state, the motion of the state through time is determined by endogenously generated agent interactions.

This agent-based dynamical description, cast at a less abstract level than standard equation-based economic models, increases the transparency and clarity of the modeling process. In particular, macroeconomists can proceed directly from empirical observations on the structural conditions, institutional arrangements, and behavioral dispositions of a real-world macroeconomic system to a computational modeling of the system. Moreover, the emphasis on process rather than on equilibrium solution techniques helps to ensure that empirical understanding and creative conjecture remain the primary prerequisites for useful macroeconomic model design.

That said, ACE modeling is surely a complement, not a substitute, for analytical and statistical macroeconomic modeling approaches. As seen in the work by Sargent (1993), ACE models can be used to evaluate macroeconomic theories developed using these more standard tools. Can agents indeed learn to coordinate on the types of equilibria identified in these theories and, if so, how? If there are multiple possible equilibria, which equilibrium (if any) will turn out to be the dominant attractor, and why? ACE models can also be used to evaluate the robustness of these theories to relaxations of their assumptions, such as common knowledge, rational expectations, and perfect capital markets. A key question in this regard is the extent to which learning, institutions, and evolutionary forces might substitute for the high degree of individual rationality currently assumed in standard macroeconomic theories.

More generally, as elaborated by Axelrod (2006), ACE modeling tools could facilitate the development and experimental evaluation of integrated theories that build on theory and data from many different related fields. For example, using ACE modeling tools, macroeconomists can address growth, distribution, and welfare issues in a comprehensive manner encompassing a wide range of pertinent economic, social, political, and psychological factors. It is particularly intriguing to re-examine the broadly envisioned theories of earlier economists such as Adam Smith, Joseph Schumpeter, John Maynard Keynes, and Friedrich von Hayek, and to consider how these theories might now be more fully addressed in quantitative terms.

Another potentially important aspect of the ACE methodology is pedagogical. ACE models can be implemented by computational laboratories that facilitate and encourage the systematic experimental exploration of complex economic processes. Students can formulate experimental designs to investigate interesting propositions of their own devising, with immediate feedback and with no original programming required. This permits teachers and students to take an inductive open-ended approach to learning. Exercises can be assigned for which outcomes are not known in advance, giving students an exciting introduction to creative research. The modular form of the underlying computational laboratory software also permits students with programming backgrounds to modify and extend the laboratory features with relative ease.[17]

A number of requirements must be met, however, if the potential of ACE for scientific research is to be realized. ACE researchers need to focus on issues of importance for understanding economic processes. They need

---

[17] See http://www.econ.iastate.edu/tesfatsi/syl308.htm for an ACE course relying heavily on computational laboratory exercises to involve students creatively in the course materials. Annotated pointers to other ACE-related course preparations can be found at http://www.econ.iastate.edu/tesfatsi/teachsyl.htm.

to construct models that capture the salient aspects of these issues, and to use these models to formulate clearly articulated theories regarding possible issue resolutions. They need to evaluate these theories systematically by means of multiple controlled experiments with captured seed values to ensure replicability by other researchers using possibly other platforms, and to report summaries of their theoretical findings in a transparent and rigorous form. Finally, they need to test their theoretical findings against real-world data in ways that permit empirically supported theories to cumulate over time, with each researcher's work building appropriately on the work that has gone before.

Meeting all of these requirements is not an easy task. One possible way to facilitate the task is interdisciplinary collaboration. Recent efforts to advance collaborative research have been encouraging. For example, Barreteau (2003) reports favorably on efforts to promote a *companion modeling* approach to critical policy issues such as management of renewable resources. The companion modeling approach is an iterative participatory process involving stakeholders, regulatory agencies, and researchers from multiple disciplines in a repeated looping through a three-stage cycle: field work and data analysis, model development and implementation, and computational experiments. Agent-based modeling and role-playing games constitute important aspects of this process. The objective is the management of complex problems through a continuous learning process rather than the delivery of definitive problem solutions.[18]

Realistically, however, communication across disciplinary lines can be difficult, particularly if the individuals attempting the collaboration have little or no cross-disciplinary training. As elaborated by Axelrod and Tesfatsion (2006), economists and other social scientists interested in agent-based modeling should therefore ideally acquire basic programming, statistical, and mathematical skills together with suitable training in their desired application areas.

---

[18] See Janssen and Ostrom (2006) for applications of the companion modeling approach to the study of governance mechanisms for social-ecological systems. Koesrindartoto and Tesfatsion (2004) advocate and pursue a similar approach to the design of wholesale power markets.

10

Multi-agent Systems Macro: A Prospectus

Robert L. Axtell

While macroeconomics has never denied the essentially microeconomic character of most economic activity, it is only in the past 30–40 years that the quest for microeconomic foundations for macro has assumed center stage. There appear to be myriad motivations for this quest, from logical necessity to ultimate completeness to elements of the "Lucas critique." While no single motivation is universally cited, few would argue with the general notion that a macroeconomics with microfoundations would be at least as useful as macro without microfoundations.

Unfortunately for macro today, the quest for microfoundations has taken on quixotic proportions, with little sign of the quarry on the horizon and the conquistadors constantly jousting among themselves concerning the most fertile direction to turn their pursuit.

In this chapter I argue that the quest for microfoundations is desirable, even admirable, but that doing so via analytical and numerical techniques is surely very difficult. In lieu of such conventional formulations, it is today feasible to instantiate relatively large populations of purposive agents in software and study their dynamics and evolution without need for the heroic assumptions and gross simplifications that are the norm in macroeconomics today.

Today very little is known about how to actually build agent models directly relevant to macroeconomic concerns, and so in place of results I substitute statements about feasibility and potential. But history is on our side in this quest, providing us exponentially more powerful machinery over time, and virtually guaranteeing that at some point somewhere this quest will succeed.

IN SEARCH OF MICROFOUNDATIONS: ANALYTICAL MACRO AND REPRESENTATIVE AGENTS

It is natural that the initial attempts to develop microfoundations were very simple, viewing the macroeconomy as simply a N-agent replica of a single individual decision-maker. But this abstraction of the "representative agent," nominally derivative of Marshall's "representative firm" (Marshall, 1920), suffers from a variety of important pathologies (Kirman, 1992). Along with preference aggregation difficulties, and the leap of faith entailed in imagining that a population of utility maximizing agents implies collective rationality, the well-intentioned notion that models should be responsive to the strategic reactions of investors to policy changes is far from satisfactorily accounted for by use of the representative agent.

If there were modeling techniques and technologies available to dispatch with the representative agent then macroeconomists would surely want to use them, so problematical is the representative agent. I describe below relatively new computational tools that may indeed permit economists to dispense with all manner of representative agents (consumers, firms, governments). Such techniques are being rapidly developed and assimilated in other fields where high fidelity micromodels are seen as important to understanding phenomena on a social or aggregate level (e.g. traffic models, Nagel and Paczusik [1995]).

SOME PHILOSOPHY OF EMERGENCE: RESULTANT VS. EMERGENT

Modern conceptions of micro—macro linkages typically distinguish two modes, so-called *resultant* and *emergent*. By *resultant* is meant that the macro structure is simply a magnification of the micro, a simple linear combination of micro entities having properties that result directly from aggregation.

Emergent macrostructures are different. They have properties that are not present — possibly not even well-defined — for the components (agents) in the system (economy). Examples of this in noneconomics settings include individual molecules possessing energy but not temperature, while for the gas in a room its temperature is meaningful; similarly, the overall function of an ant colony, while of course the result of the efforts of many individual ants, involves qualitatively different activities than any specific type or representative ant can do; obversely, schools of fish cannot swim and flocks of birds cannot fly, as swimming and flying are behaviors of individuals. In economics, examples of this are myriad: individuals do not make profit but the firms they work in do; individuals *qua* individuals do not make policy but the institutions they manage do; prices in markets are defined for both individual transactions and as the overall value of financial instruments (resultant property), but the risk-sharing feature of modern markets is not a property that can be summarized by inspecting the state of any individual issue or portfolio.

This position on emergent macrophenomena is closely related to the philosopher's dual fallacies of composition and division, and the statistician's concern with ecological inference (Achen and Shively, 1995). It is also closely associated with attacks on reductionism, particularly the position of *pragmatic anti-reductionism*, which does not deny reductionism in principle but rather asserts that it is often less useful than alternatives (Darley, 1994; Faith, 1998). There has been a great deal written about the relationship between reductionism and emergence in complex adaptive systems (Simon, 1996), including popular accounts (Johnson, 2001). Much of what today passes as the scientific content of emergence is quite close to what in physics is called *self-organization* (Haken, Mikitani and Posen, 1987), and to the *invisible hand* (Smith, 1976) and *spontaneous order* in economics (Hayek, 1937, 1945, 1964).

Economics of our time features highly developed models of production through firms, and distribution through markets. These are, in the main, probably largely correct, but unsatisfactory as a theory of economic structure and function. For we lack today credible accounts of how these multi-agent institutions came into being, how they evolved, and how they are likely to unfold over time. That is, we need a coherent theory of the genesis of economic organization and complexity. Agent computing, with its "grow it" mentality and distributed perspective, is ripe for contributing to such theorizing.

MAS AS MICROFOUNDATIONS

Multi-agent systems (MAS) refers to a sub-branch of computer science, derivative of artificial intelligence (AI) and distributed AI (DAI), in which autonomous and semi-autonomous agents are given more or less well-defined sense of self-interest, and then allowed to interact in some social environment. The applications of MAS are quite varied; see Weiss (1999) for an overview. It has become quite common recently for MAS researchers to draw upon economic and game theoretic concepts to motivate, build, and solve the agent systems they create. Somewhat curiously, the intrinsically equilibrium character of conventional economic and game theoretic solution concepts (e.g. Walrasian equilibrium, Nash equilibrium) have been largely embraced by this research community. Only recently have the essentially dynamic character of MAS models been shown to be in conflict with the simplistic equilibrium conceptions so pervasive in formal social science, leading to reconsideration of the early enthusiasm for such formalisms. Interestingly, software agents of the kind being developed by MAS researchers, who can be designed to be arbitrarily rational, up through constraints on deliberation time, may be the single most applicable environment for many economic and game theoretic notions, since the failings of human decision-making (Tversky and Kahneman, 1986) are not relevant.

The application of MAS technology to economics has been around for approximately a decade, the first generation of such models being utilized to relax some single assumption of conventional neoclassical models. These early efforts were further characterized by relatively small number of agents, typically 10–1000, having very simple decision rules.

Today much richer models are feasible, from much more elaborate agent decision-making – e.g. neural nets (LeBaron, 2001a) – to very large numbers of simple agents (Axtell, 2002). Continued exponential increase in computer hardware promises to dramatically increase the range of feasible models for at least a generation, this being computing power that MAS economics can easily harness, in contrast to more conventional numerical economics (Axtell, 2003).

There have been some nascent attempts to apply agent-based computing (aka MAS) to macroeconomic problems. These typically have the flavor of fairly neoclassical set-ups with few agents (Bullard and Duffy, 2001). Behaviorally in these models, agents are still trying to maximize the exponentially discounted sum of utilities over their lifetimes. The problems with these approaches are that they are too little different from the mainstream and fail to take advantage of the strengths of MAS.

An alternative approach is to use very large-scale MAS to create high-fidelity models that closely simulate actual economies. To date this has not been systematically undertaken, although some early voyages of discovery have been attempted (Basu and Pryor, 1997). In this chapter I describe what seems to me like a fertile research plan for developing very large-scale MAS models relevant to macroeconomic dynamics. After going through the components of such a model in the next section, I then survey the model overall, and end this prospective exercise by considering how the output of such a model is likely to differ, conceptually, from conventional analytical macroeconomic models.

COMPONENTS OF A MAS MACRO MODEL

The main ways that MAS can be used to relax conventional neoclassical assumptions have been described in some detail elsewhere (Axtell, 2000). These are summarized in this section, with special reference to their application to questions of macroeconomics. Interestingly, within micro-economics today, there exist research programs that actively work to relax usual assumptions along one of these dimensions. However, in none of these branches of microeconomics does one find attempts to relax along *all* dimensions. While MAS makes it possible to do so, and the broad scope of macroeconomics seems to demand it, one might justifiably question the extent to which it makes good scientific sense to completely lose sight of known research terrain in pursuit of an unknown, uncharted continent, when the belief that riches await stems primarily from the probably false notion that more realism is always better in modeling. Indeed, Occam's razor seems to suggest rather the opposite – paraphasing Thomas Schelling, a model is done not when nothing else can be added but when nothing else can be taken away, while preserving the results.[1]

Agent Heterogeneity, Parametric and Behavioral

The difficulties of the representative agent have been thoroughly described (Kirman, 1992) and are well-understood. These difficulties extend to both the theory of the consumer and the theory of the firm. The primary barriers for incorporating arbitrary heterogeneity into macromodels are analytical and are too well-understood.

The workarounds for these difficulties are not obvious, although if all agents have the same structure to preferences then at least numerical progress is usually possible. However, if agents with many distinct types of preferences are present then even numerical progress can be hard to come by. This *structural* diversity, as opposed to mere *parametric* diversity, represents a significant challenge for all extant economic modeling paradigms today.

However, agent-based computational models are well-equipped to handle such variety, essentially because no attempt is made to aggregate preference relations. Rather, agent behaviors are what are summed up, in

---

[1] Remark made at the news conference of October 18, 1996, at the Brookings Institution in Washington DC, upon publication of *Growing Artificial Societies* (Epstein and Axtell, 1996). Note the similarities to Einstein's remark that "a model should be as simple as possible but no simpler."

order to compute a market-clearing price, for instance, and so it is a relative triviality to handle arbitrarily diverse populations. The key is that each agent has within itself the computational machinery necessary to figure out how it should behave in particular environments. Conveniently, such computational methods are a natural part of an agent specification when implemented in software as an *object.*

The empirical question as to just how heterogeneous economic agents really are remains to be uncovered. Economic experiments seem to universally reveal significant decision-making heterogeneity. How such results map into useful parameterizations of behavior is an important question for future research.

Behavioral Realism: Taking Experimental Economics to the Social Level

For the better part of two generations, economists have paid lip service to bounded rationality (BR) (Simon, 1997); its importance little doubted, its implementation virtually unknown. A key difficulty with integrating bounded rational notions into neoclassical economics is that it is analytically messy to do so (Rubinstein, 1998). For the results of experiments are never as precise and smooth as the real analysis foundations of microeconomics would have them.

This lack of any coherent parameterization of BR has many other implications. For instance, the pregnant field of *neuroeconomics* (Glimcher, 2003) is likely to reveal many interesting connections between decision-making and neurophysiology. But without a satisfactory, user adjustable, representation of BR there is simply no way to leverage these new results in any formal way. Now some computer and cognitive scientists will put significant weight on purely computational representations of cognitive behavior, such as the SOAR model, but much work remains to be done to empirically validate such models against, for example, behavioral alternatives such as prospect theory (Kahneman and Tversky, 1979).

A somewhat different attack on mainstream rationality specifications is due to Kirman (1993), who argues that certain conceptual features of the neoclassical model of behavior are inherently flawed. He uses the example of ant foraging behavior to motivate a re-evaluation of the marginal physical productivity (MPP) conception of production. Given well-accepted data on how ants forage among multiple food sources — that they systematically exhaust one supply before beginning to exploit another — leads him to ask why, if ant colonies have been (ostensibly) so finely honed by natural selection to function effectively, do they not jointly exploit each food source, the way a rational choice microeconomics would have them. Perhaps there is some "bird-in-the-hand" type rationale in effect at the colony level, a kind of hyperbolic discounting that reflects the highly variable character of Nature. Alternatively, perhaps there are certain economies of scale of which we are not aware — e.g. the positive feedback associated with pheromone signaling — that lead the ants to the behavior we observe. In any case, the MPP theory of production, standing as it does on shaky to nonexistent *empirical* foundations, independently from the undeniably desirable logical/formal status it occupies, is one which seems to be falsified by simple creatures like ants, so could it possibly hold for complex organisms like us?

Assume that there develops some consensus way to represent human decision-making powers with reasonable empirical fidelity. With high probability, this will be a computational implementation, primarily for the simple reason that most scientists working on such problems are wont to build such computer-enabled representations. Now let us say we want to build an entire population of decision-makers having such abilities. Presumably, the only way to coherently realize such a research program — the only way to go from the micro- to the macrolevel with such a messy cognitive model — is through computational agents.

Direct Interaction: Peers, Neighborhoods, Networks

Conventional economics assumes, either implicitly or explicitly, that agents interact only indirectly, through economic variables like prices and interest rates, instead of directly with one another through social networks (Kirman, 1997). This is clearly an empirically false feature of conventional models, but possibly a useful, practical abstraction. Indeed, it can be analytically difficult to deal with in direct network interactions, and only recently has significant mathematical progress been made on this subject (Watts, 1999; Newman, Watts et al., 2002; Barabasi, 2002). However, the neglect of network effects with economics, ostensibly necessary for the continued reign of the individual utility maximizer view of human behavior, has served to bias economic models away from peer and neighborhood effects, despite the fact that these often turn out to be important (e.g. Topa [2001]).

In MAS it is straightforward to treat social networks, either in the idealized form of a regular graph or, to the extent that reliable network data exist, by connecting the agents via empirically significant graphs. There are many examples of this including Bell (1997), Young (1998, 1999), Axtell and Epstein (1999), and Wilhite (2001).

SKETCH OF A MAS MACRO MODEL

Imagine a population of interacting agents who are both consumers and producers, working at (self-organized) firms and holding financial assets in an artificial equity market. The essential pieces of this picture we describe next, followed by some discussion of the kinds of output such a model might yield.

Putting the Pieces Together

The artificial stock market piece of this picture is the most mature, the most well-developed agent-based application to date (Arthur, Holland et al. [1997], LeBaron [2001a,b,c], LeBaron [2002a,b], Lux [1998], Lux and Marchesi [1999]. In these models, a population of agents perpetually allocate and reallocate their resources over time to a riskless, low-return asset and a risky, speculative asset. Each agent has a more or less idiosyncratic price forecast function that evolves over time. The character of this forecast function determines the agent's type: agents who utilize only market fundamentals are so-called fundamentalist traders, while those who look for patterns in price time series and neglect (relatively) the fundamentals are called chartists or technical traders. The agents in such models are reasonably viewed as adaptive, not rational, insofar as none possess a complete model of the financial market overall and so there is essentially no way for any agent to compute, for example a rational expectations equilibrium (REE). While these models may exhibit approximately REE behavior in certain limiting cases, for example all long horizon traders in the case of LeBaron, such behavior is exceptional in these models. Rather, the generic behavior of agent-based financial market models seems to be perpetual co-evolution of the agents' trading strategies, with prices characterized by many empirically salient features, for example heavy-tailed returns, clustered volatility, long memory of absolute autocorrelations, volume—volatility correlations.

We imagine the consumer side of the model to closely follow that of Allen and Carroll (2001). Theirs is a model of consumption in which agents learn how to adjust savings vs. consumption rates by imitating their peers. In their model, incomes are stochastic, and so the imitation process leads to quite noisy dynamics and behavior that can deviate significantly from optimality. Specifically, in many configurations of their model, agents overconsume since they end up copying agents who have gotten fortuitous draws from the income distribution. This leads to behavior in their model of too little buffer savings in the stationary state and related empirically relevant features. Most importantly for our purposes, theirs is a *social interactions* picture of consumption, not one grounded on autonomous optimization. As such, it fits naturally into the heterogeneous agent, boundedly rational, social network connected picture of an economy we are developing here.

Lastly, we dispense with all manner of representative firms and substitute multi-agent firms, as in Axtell (2002). Various motivations for relaxing the profit-maximizing view of firms are described there. Here we merely summarize the model in order for the reader to gain some intuitive understanding of its interworking, and also because it will serve as the basis for subsequently motivating the need to have a very large number of agents in our MAS macrospecification.

A population of agents in an increasing returns-to-scale (team production) environment will always find it advantageous to work together in groups. When the agents have heterogeneous preferences for income and leisure, then the groups that form will also be heterogeneous. Permitting the agents to dynamically adjust (adapt) their effort levels to those of the other agents in their group creates a group-level adjustment process that may or may not settle down to, say, the Nash equilibrium. Further, permitting agents to migrate out of poorly performing groups in search of welfare improvements leads to potentially complicated intra- and inter-group dynamics − multi-level dynamics − for which equilibrium configurations may or may not exist, depending on the number and types of agents present. Agent-based computational realizations of this model closely reproduce many more or less well-known empirical regularities associated with U.S. business firms, such as skew firm size distributions, approximately constant returns to scale at the aggregate level, Laplace distributed growth rates, and wages that increase with firm size. This model, like agent-based financial markets and social interactions models of consumption, is inherently bottom-up, with all aggregate structures arising as a result of direct agent−agent interactions.

So the architecture for a simple, primitive MAS macromodel is as follows:

1. Agents derive income from working in firms and consume goods made by firms; they also own shares of firms.

2. Firms employ workers and make goods and are owned by the agents.

This is shown graphically in Figure 10.1:

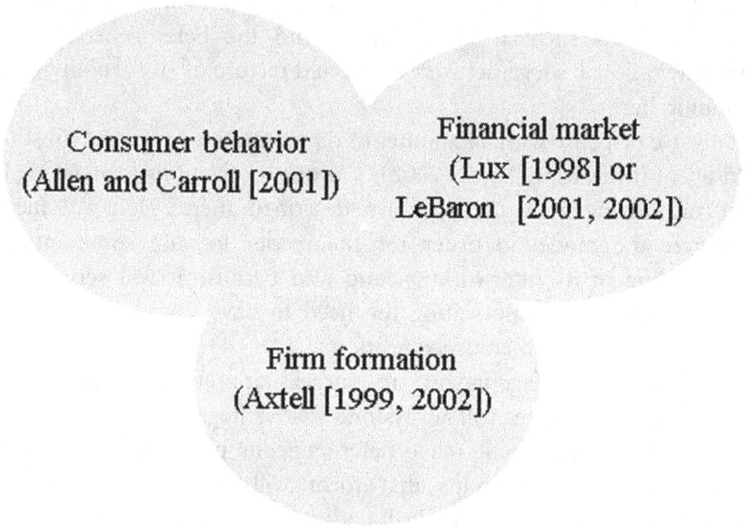

Figure 10.1. Schematic of the model.

Since each of these models exist in code, at present it is a relatively straightforward matter to integrate them. The income stream in the Allen and Carroll model results from their employment in the Axtell model. The firm performance in the Axtell model plays a role in the fundamentals employed by trader agents in the Lux finance model. The income that the agents earn by trading is used for consumption. This is basic economics, but as one can imagine, the coupling of three complex models might magnify this complexity, so much so that the overall dynamics might be unintelligible. Alternatively, other processes of self-organization may be at work to limit the complexity of the overall economy. Only time will tell which of these scenarios is actually the case.

Emergence: Multi-Agent Norms, Conventions, Institutions

In the previous discussion of emergence, we characterized the kinds of macrophenomena that are *qualitatively different* from their underlying components (agents). Examples of such emergence in economics include the invisible hand (Vriend, 2002) and the emergence of money (Weatherford, 1997), while in game theory similar phenomena are obtained (Young [1993, 1996, 1998], and Axtell, Epstein and Young [2001]). Specifically, in MAS models in which the agents' behaviors become correlated in some way, it is reasonable to say that such correlation is emergent. Examples include the establishment of norms of behavior in MAS, the development of conventions of, say, behavior, and the formation of multi-agent institutions, such as reasonably long-lived multi-agent firms.

Coordination at the macrolevel may occur in conventional macro-models, but when it does, it is not because individual agents have stumbled into such a configuration, but rather because the modeler has stipulated in advance that such a situation must hold. This is very different from the bottom-up approach for at least two related reasons. First, the kinds of ordered macrostates that are considered in traditional models are those that the analyst can imagine and, having imagined them, can justify game theoretically or otherwise. Second, traditional models do not tell stories for how their economies get into such configurations. As such, these have rather more the flavor of "just so" stories and we might reasonably expect that they are more or less implausible as actual equilibria.

Emergence: Macroregularity, Microadaptation

A specific kind of emergence of this type occurs when the agents never really settle down to either a fixed point or periodic oscillations, but rather constantly adjust their behavior to adapt to the social or economic situation. This kind of "groping" is much more plausible behaviorally than conventional rationality. It also means that conventional game theoretic solution concepts and their refinements are essentially wrong-headed, for it is clear that they are sufficient but not necessary.

Consider a labor market situation. A particular worker is either employed or not. If the former, then he/she conducts job searches with low intensity, while if the latter, a more high intensity search is pursued. It is not the case that the worker, over his/her spells of employment and unemployment, continually seeks new employment with uniform prob-ability, that is, following some kind of mixed Nash equilibrium. Rather, the state of being employed (or not) determines his/her near-term behavior, and the shocks that send his/her from one state to another may or may not depend much on his/her strategies. However, at the level of the population of workers there may exist something like a steady-state number of job pursuers or resume writers. This would mean that while there is constant flux into and out of the unemployed pool at the agent level, as agents perpetually adapt to the state in which they find themselves, there is a more or less fixed amount of job search activity going on.

This situation is closely analogous to the distinctions between population and individual processes in evolutionary game theory as developed by biologists. From a general perspective, it argues against what we might call the *Nash program* of conventional game theory, which hopes to locate all social phenomena in equilibrium behavior at the agent level. Our labor market example demonstrates that the Nash program is clearly not necessary in order to explain social regularities, like the constant search for new jobs.

The Need for Very Large-Scale MAS

Since a major component of the MAS macromodel sketched above is multi-agent firms, it is instructive to consider the number and kind of such firms that would be needed for a model having significant versimilitude. That the empirical distribution of firm sizes is very skew has been well-known for a long time (Gibrat [1931], Simon and Bonini [1958], Steindl [1965]), and recently confirmed through analysis of comprehensive U.S. data (Axtell, 2001).

I have recently reviewed the scale of MAS models in the social sciences utilized over the past decade, and made some prognostications about the near future (Axtell, 2003). While models having 100−1000 agents were state-of-the-art at the end of the twentieth century, models of up to 100K agents are relatively easy to create and manipulate today. Over the next few years models on the scale of 10 million agents will become commonplace. Such models call out for application to macroeconomics!

Specifically, in order to model large firms in the economy, large numbers of agents are needed. The largest firm in the United States today, Wal-Mart, has more than 1 million employees, representing just under 1% of the U.S. workforce of some 125 million people. Given the highly skewed nature of the U.S. firm size distribution, the only credible way to get very large firm sizes arising from multi-agent firm models is to have lots and lots of agents present in the model. With 1 million agents, firms of size 10K can be grown. The work I have done with 10 million agent models has demonstrated that firms having hundreds of thousands of workers can be formed. It is becoming feasible to build models with huge numbers of agents, suggesting that MAS macro is just around the corner.

Table 10.1. *Near-term prospects for the feasibility of building large-scale MAS macromodels, given continued exponential growth in computer hardware*

Model	Feasible by	Agents
Small country macroeconomy	2002−2004?	$O(10^7)$
Industrial country macroeconomy	2004−2006?	$O(10^8)$
U.S. macroeconomy	2006−2008?	$O(10^9)$
World economy	2008−2010?	$O(10^{10})$

For example, for a small country of say 10−20 million people having 5−10 million workers, it would be possible today to fully represent each and every citizen in a MAS macromodel. Medium sized countries of 20−50 million people are just around the corner. Large countries having more than 100 million people are just a generation of hardware or two away, while a model of the entire world macroeconomy will have to wait for another generation or two beyond that. These considerations are summarized in Table 10.1. It should be emphasized that these calculations are for relatively simple agents running on state-of-the-art workstations in MAS codes written in low-level languages (e.g. C, C++). Much of the work in agent-based computational economics is of just this type. However, use of complex agents or higher level languages (e.g. Java) surely pushes back these frontiers by further generations. Therefore, one could well imagine that it might not be until 2020 that one can fully represent 10 billion economic actors on a desktop computer in a high-level, user-friendly way. But the main point is that such a day will surely come, and will do so in something like one scholarly generation.

However, the main impediment to fully implement the MAS macro research program is not hardware but software. Today, we know *very* little about how to program agent systems in order to make them relevant for macroeconomics. I have sketched out a crude, zeroth-order model above, but far from being either definitive or the last word on the subject it is surely the exact opposite − a starting point, one possible point of departure. Any attempt to suggest that "there is more word to be done" sounds like gross understatement; all the work needs to be done!

MAS MACRO VS. ANALYTICAL MACRO

Aside from the obvious differences in approach between MAS macro and conventional analytical macro, several other distinctions are clear upon contrasting the output of such models. These we summarize in this section.

Emergence One More Time

In the same sense that the macroeconomy is not just a magnification of a single representative agent economy, the kinds of economic structures that can emerge in MAS-type models may have a different character than any of the components of the model. These *emergent* structures are problematical for analytical macros in that they are assumed away.

One important way that such emergent structures might manifest themselves in MAS macro is through *unintended consequences*. That is, imagine a MAS macromodel, featuring rich and poor agents, hard-working and lazy ones, rapacious and gentle creatures, and all manner of other agent types that one finds in the real world. Now, imagine that we want to study the effect of some kind of policy change, perhaps one that will soon come into law, perhaps a prospective one. Conventional macromodels may tell an analyst much about the changes in *quantities* likely to be associated with such a policy shift. But it is silent on how the *character* of the economy is likely to be altered. Here, the agent model, populated as it is with agents of all different types, may turn up that certain agents begin to exploit the new law in unplanned and previously unforeseen ways. Such exploitation may either circumvent the benefits hoped for by the policymakers, or it may create a need for an entire new class of laws meant to curb the exploitation. It is hard to see how any aggregate model could possibly tease out such delicate yet important effects, but not too hard to see how they could arise in the MAS setting.[2]

Estimating MAS Macromodels

An objection might be raised against the MAS macro research program I have outlined here that until a systematic way to estimate such models is developed there is no way to make such models truly relevant empirically, at least on a level with conventional macromodels. A different way to express this is that in the space of all possible models that can be created in software, only one or at most a few matter empirically, and until methods

---

[2] A good example of this occurs in the MAS model of the NASDAQ (Darley, Outkin et al., 2001), where an evolutionary model of behavior revealed that so-called "small-order execution system" (SOES) agents (aka bandits) might be able to exploit certain features associated with alteration of the NASDAQ tick size.

are developed that determine these from data, the MAS macro will be more a speculative enterprise than a scientific undertaking.

One approach to this problem that to some extent turns the matter on its head is to simply note that the Lux (1998) and Lux and Marchesi (1999) model of financial markets, for example, is much more capable of reproducing the known facts of financial markets than any neoclassical model. Similarly, for my model of firm dynamics (Axtell, 2002), one would hope that a large model formed from empirically significant components would yield correct empirical regularities at the aggregate level. However, the situation is surely more complicated than this. In many ways the Lux model, for all its realism, remains highly idealized — e.g. single speculative asset, fixed number of traders — similar to the model of firm formation, in which neither prices nor fixed capital manifest themselves in any significant way. Therefore, both for internal reasons of the component models themselves, as well as for the "glue" code needed to hook them all together, the macroeconometrician's critique is salient. Happily, a reasonably well-developed solution to this problem exists.

"Estimation by simulation" is a relatively new technique for rigorously estimating numerical and other analytically-intractable models. Application of this technique involves searching parameter spaces for values that minimize the difference between model output and the aggregate data. In principle, it is directly applicable to agent-based computational models, but this appears to have been rarely applied. The only example of which I am aware comes from beyond economics (Axtell, 2002).

SUMMARY: WHITHER ANALYTICAL MACRO?

I have argued above that an alternative to analytical macroeconomics exists, one that utilizes state-of-the-art computational techniques to model economies in a highly distributed, decentralized fashion. Large-scale agent-based computational models are today becoming feasible, involving millions of agents. As of today, little is known about the gross character such models will have, whether it will be an easy matter to build empirically relevant models, and whether such models might serve as robust engines for policy analysis.

I have sketched out perhaps the simplest large-scale MAS model that might have some minimal relevance to macroeconomics, and suggested that the kinds of results that are likely to emanate from it will almost surely be qualitatively different from conventional macromodels. The role of *emergence* in MAS models has been highlighted. The ability of MAS macro to represent the incentives faced by all agents in an economy, and to then study the agent behavior that results along with the macrostructure that arises, is seen as the primary strength of the new tool vis-à-vis analytical macro.

While the ultimate significance of MAS macro is opaque, and will no doubt require a generation or two of research to assess, let us imagine alternative scenarios and speculate on their implications for conventional macroeconomic practices. Specifically, consider a research frontier in which MAS macro has grown and evolved to be as capable as analytical macro for conventional specifications of preferences, endowments, rationality, and so on, but for alternative specifications − e.g. bounded rationality − it is essentially the only way to realize credible models. In such a world what would be the relation between analytical and MAS macro? This is the question we take up presently.

Agent Computing: Substitute or Complement?

In assessing the relation of numerical economics to mainstream neo-classical economics, Judd (1997) argues that the main role for computation is as complementary to conventional theory. That is, given the analytical difficulties of solving all but the simplest models in closed form, the main contribution of computation to economics is to provide numerical solutions to otherwise intractable sets of equations. For such models, one may have theorems to the effect that solutions exist or are stable under a wide range of conditions, but the actual solution − whether needed for policy purposes or simply for illustration − may be available only by numerical analysis, and sometimes heroic numerics at that.

I have argued elsewhere that while agent computing can play a complementary role to conventional rational choice economics, it is more powerfully utilized as a *substitute* for mainstream analysis (Axtell, 2006). This is so because the kinds of models that one ultimately constructs using MAS technology, while nominally specializable to a conventional structural and behavioral specification, are normally exercised in regions of parameter space that put them outside the narrow conventions of neoclassical economics. As such, there is no natural way for analytical models to reproduce the results generated by MAS models, and therefore the latter is essentially a substitute for the former. MAS-style models that take "baby steps" away from conventional models may indeed have much more of the character of complements to conventional specifications, but I do not believe that this is where the most fertile area of application of the new technology lies.

Continuity or Abrupt Change?

Should MAS models come to reproduce analytical results while being capable of yielding conceptually different ones, one might rightly wonder what role there is for analytical macroeconomics in the long run. Perhaps a different way to ask this is "To what extent is there an abrupt discontinuity in methodology on the horizon?," one roughly analogous to the kinds of fundamental breaks that have occurred in other sciences (Kuhn, 1962). Will the kind of transition that looms on the generational horizon be one in which there is a sudden alteration in methodology, as exemplified in the relatively rapid transition to quantum mechanics over a 30-year time-span in physics, from Einstein and Planck to Schroedinger? Or will there be a more gradual transition, in which mathematical specifications continue to play a role but with progressively less significance over time?

Elements of both kinds of transitions are currently on display within the economics profession, and it would probably be foolish to try to handicap the contest. Suffice it to say that the main determinant of whether the transition is rapid or drawn-out may lie in how the current generation of economists adapts to the new methodology, and whether or not they train the next generation of students in these new methods.

Reform or Revolution?

A rather different way to say all this involves the related speculation as to how historians of economic thought will characterize such a transition. Perhaps, the most generous interpretation of the coming migration from analytical through numerical and ultimately to MAS techniques will simply suggest that the current chaotic state of macro was the logical consequence of having the wrong tool for the job. If you are forced to hunt without modern weapons you will of necessity rely on natural implements that you use for other tasks (that is, mathematics), tricks that have worked before (that is, solution techniques), and superstition (that is, economic "doctrines," e.g. the law of one price, Say's law). Your hunting will be woefully inefficient but will not fail to turn up some results occasionally. Its just that much of the time spent hunting is time spent minding the inappropriate tools and seeking out new tricks and superstitions, as opposed to actually felling prey.

A rather less generous perspective of the historians of thought – perhaps more likely to follow from an abrupt, discontinuous transition – would characterize the present efforts with analytically focused macroeconomics as essentially wrong-headed, lacking in behavioral realism and therefore sub-scientific, uninteresting mathematically despite its analytical pretensions, and so weakly connected to empirics as to be more like cultural anthropology than physical anthropology. Should this interpretation carry the day there might arise a normative stance in which MAS macro is seen as *reforming* today's macroeconomic practice. Coupled with an abrupt transition, the monicker of *revolution* might also be used to describe the history of this subject.

In any case, the movement of macroeconomic modeling away from unrealistic agent-level specifications of behavior and toward a more *emergent* view of macroeconomic quantities can only have an invigorating effect on the practice of macroeconomics. For in the end, the goal of macroeconomic theorizing is the synthesis of effective macroeconomic policy, and there can be little doubt today that the current generation of models is so badly misspecified and inappropriately solved that they are little more than caricatures of any real economy. MAS macro holds out the promise of an entirely new way of doing business. Only time will tell whether it succeeds or fails as a methodology.

In the future the combination of ever-greater computing power with increased knowledge of how to build useful MAS will lead to MAS macromodels. Perhaps, the main unknown today is who will get there first. By rights it should be the economists, but as knowledge about the economy gives way to knowledge about techniques for solving models one has to wonder. Perchance, it will be the computer scientists given their superior knowledge of how to get large models running on "big iron." Or maybe it will even be the so-called econophysicists who have become enamored of financial processes, leaving one to wonder if macroeconomics can be far behind. Whoever wins the race, macroeconomics will likely be changed forever. Like the anxious father, unsure of the fate of his progeny in a rapidly changing world, we can only hope that the intellectual foundation we lay today for those who will come after us will permit them to follow the right course.

11

Agent-based Financial Markets: matching Stylized Facts with Style

Blake LeBaron[*]

The movements of financial markets, and their connections to the macro economy are one of the most difficult areas for traditional economic theories. This is true both from an empirical and a theoretical perspective. This chapter will concentrate on the empirical puzzles from finance that demand new approaches, such as agent-based financial markets. It will be argued that even when traditional modeling approaches fit some subset of empirical features, it comes with the cost of moving farther from economic believability and robustness. Agent-based approaches fit more features with frameworks that seem to make more intuitive sense for the functioning of real markets. Also, agent-based frameworks can be used as a testbed for drawing in behavioral results found in both experimental and microlevel financial markets. This is crucial for understanding when and where behavioral quirks of economic actors will appear at the macrolevel.

Many of the most puzzling results from finance deal with problems of behavioral heterogeneity, and the dynamics of heterogeneity. The study of market heterogeneity as a kind of complicated dynamic state variable that needs to be modeled is probably one of the defining features of agent-based models. Empirical features such as trading volume are directly related to the amount of heterogeneity in the market, and demand models that can speak to this issue. Other empirical features are probably indirectly related. Large moves, excess kurtosis, and market crashes, all probably stem from some type of strategy correlation that keeps the law of large numbers from functioning well across the market.

[*] International Business School, Brandeis University, 415 South Street, Mailstop 32, Waltham, MA 02453 - 2728, blebaron@brandeis.edu, www.brandeis.edu/~blebaron.

These changing patterns can only be explored in a framework that allows agent strategies to adapt and adjust over time, and more importantly, to respond to features of the aggregate population around them.

This chapter visits some of the empirical puzzles, and shows that many of these can be replicated in an agent-based model. It also compares and contrasts the Post Walrasian approaches of agent-based models with current research in behavioral finance. These two areas have some important overlaps, and also some important differences. It will be argued that agent-based approaches are necessary in understanding which behavioral features will have macropricing consequences.

The next section goes over some of the empirical finance puzzles. The section, Empirical Examples, looks at some of the empirical results from an agent-based example model. The section, Aggregation and Behavior, looks at some of the important connections between agent-based models and behavioral finance, and also emphasizes that the latter may be a critical tool in sorting out behavioral models. The final section concludes and discusses some policy implications.

EMPIRICAL FEATURES

Financial time series are arguably some of the most interesting data collected on the functioning of economic relationships. We have relatively long and clean series of financial prices. These prices are generated from well-organized financial markets that bring large numbers of investors, and trade goods which can be compared over time. They are also crucial in allocating investment funds, and therefore to the performance of the overall economy. Recently, market microstructure research has utilized data sets that often contain almost every trade on a given market. Although not available for very long periods, these detailed data afford an unprecedented view into the inner workings of large trading institutions. It is surprising that given the amount and quality of data we have on financial markets, many of their features remain somewhat of a frustrating mystery. Before looking into some of the results of agent-based financial markets, it will be important to document some of the major puzzles of financial markets.

Volatility is the most obvious and probably the most important puzzle in finance. Why do financial prices and foreign exchange rates move around so much relative to other macroseries both on a short term and long term basis? The difficulty of overall financial volatility was first demonstrated in Shiller (1981), and an update is in

Shiller (2003).[1] The issue has been that it is difficult to find financial or macroeconomic fundamentals that move around enough to justify the large swings observed in financial markets. As a potential policy problem, and an issue for long range investors, this might be the most important puzzle faced by financial modelers. This excess volatility could lead to reductions in welfare for savers and potential misallocations of resources for investors. The basic task is therefore to build a market that can take relatively stable fundamentals, and amplify their volatility into a fluctuating price series.

There are several puzzles related to financial volatility that may be at least as interesting as the simple level of volatility. First, financial volatility is extremely persistent. The persistence of volatility in many financial markets has led to an entire industry of models, and is an area of intense interest both in academic and commercial areas. However, although there is a lot of empirical activity, the underlying microeconomic motives for volatility persistence are still not well understood. There are very few models which have even tackled this problem. This is probably due to the fact that in a homogeneous agent framework this is simply a very difficult problem. There also may be something very interesting about the nature of this phenomenon. Volatility appears to be very persistent. It has autocorrelations which decay slowly out to almost a year or more. This is an indication of a long memory process. This may be a very interesting signature for return dynamics, and it sets a pretty high hurdle for any financial model to meet.

The second feature is excess kurtosis. Financial returns at relatively high frequencies (less than one month) are not normally distributed. There is not much of a strong theoretical reason that they need to be, but the hope has often been that some form of the central limit theorem should drive returns close to normality when aggregated over time. Recently, a new field, Econophysics, has appeared which stresses that returns also have additional structure that can be described using power laws.[2] The determination and testing of power laws remains a somewhat open area, and the set of processes that generate acceptable power law pictures is also

---

[1] A related paper is Hansen and Singleton (1982), which uses a very different methodology, but comes to similar conclusions. A simple macroeconomic variable, consumption, which should be able to explain the movements of returns in an intertemporal representative agent framework, simply doesn't move around enough to account for changes in returns. It also doesn't move in a way that is correlated with returns either, and this is also part of the problem.

[2] See Mantegna and Stanley (1999) for an introduction and examples.

not well understood.[3] It is also important to realize that most persistent volatility processes generate excess kurtosis, so there is a connection between these two phenomena. The connection between large moves and endogenous correlations, or reductions in heterogeneity in the population makes these a crucial fact for agent-based modelers. They are also an important practical fact to deal with for finance professionals in the risk management business.

Another broad empirical puzzle that has captured an enormous amount of attention is the equity premium puzzle, which considers the returns on stocks versus bonds. In most representative agent-optimizing models it is difficult to explain this return spread.[4] This remains a critical puzzle, though many explanations have been put forth. It is important to realize that in many ways this can't be separated from the volatility puzzle mentioned previously. If there are mechanisms that magnify market volatility that we don't quite understand, then the premium on equity might be reasonable to justify this extra risk component.

Finally, trading volume is a major issue that can only be tackled from a heterogeneous agent perspective. Most traditional financial models remain completely silent on this issue. This is troubling since it often appears that trading volume is too large to be explained with standard models. Daily foreign exchange trading volume is often well over a trillion dollars, which represents a large fraction of total U.S. annual GDP moving through the market each day. Beyond this, trading volume is very persistent. It is another time series which also might be a long memory process. This is more difficult to determine since many trading volume series also have persistent time trends in them, but there is some early evidence that volume is also a long memory process (Logato and Velasco, 2000). There is also interesting, and possibly related, evidence for long memory in Internet packet traffic (Leland et al., 1994). It would be fascinating if the Internet and trading volume mechanisms were similar.

EMPIRICAL EXAMPLES

This section presents some short examples of an agent-based model replicating many of the empirical features mentioned so far. The basic model structure is taken from LeBaron (2002a,b). Details are presented in these chapters, but a very brief sketch will be presented here.

---

[3] LeBaron (2001d) gives some examples of this issue.
[4] This result goes back to Mehra and Prescott (1988), and was surveyed more recently in Kocherlakota (1996).

The model is based on a single risky asset available in fixed supply, paying a dividend that follows a random walk growth process aligned with aggregate growth and volatility in U.S. dividends after World War II. It is simulated at weekly frequencies. There is a risk-free asset paying zero interest available in infinite supply. Agents in this model all maximize intertemporal constant relative risk aversion (CRRA) utility which is restricted to log preferences. This locks down the consumption as a constant fraction of agents' wealth and concentrates learning on determining optimal dynamic portfolio strategies.

Agents chose over a set of portfolio strategies that map current asset market information into a recommended portfolio fraction of wealth in the risky asset. This fraction can vary from zero to one since short selling and borrowing are not allowed. Information includes lagged returns, dividend price ratios, and several trend indicators. Agents must evaluate rules using past performance, and it is in this dimension where they are assumed to be heterogeneous. Agents use differing amounts of past information to evaluate rules. In other words, they have different memory lengths when it comes to evaluating strategies. Some agents use 30 years worth of data, while others might use only six months.[5] In this way, this model conforms to behavioral features. Agents are boundedly rational in that they do not attempt to determine the entire state space of the economy, which would be unwieldy if they attempted this. Also, they are assumed to have "small sample bias" since all of them do not choose to use as much data as possible. If it actually is better to use longer sample sizes, then wealth will shift to the longer memory agents, and the shorter memory types will steadily control less and less wealth, and will steadily be evolved to zero.[6] The set of trading rules is represented by a neural network, and is evolved over time using a genetic algorithm. The diverse set of strategies of the different agents are used to numerically form a market excess demand function. The equity is assumed to be in constant supply of one share, and the price is then determined by numerically clearing this market. It is a form of temporary Walrasian equilibrium.

Figure 11.1 compares the actual market price for a set of agents with many different memory lengths ranging from six months to 30 years. This will be referred to as the all memory case. The actual price is compared to a

[5] Formally, they try to find the rule that maximizes the log of their portfolio return following a dynamic strategy going into the past.

[6] This is also a type of constant gain learning as used in Sargent (1999a). It is also related to a form of "learning stationarity," in that agents need to know whether the time series they are looking at are stationary or not.

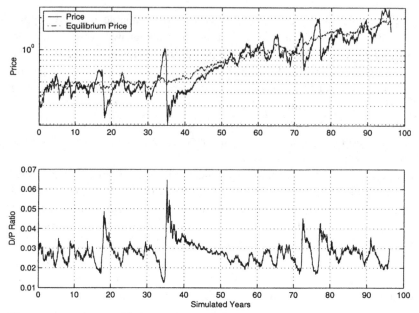

Figure 11.1. Price, equilibrium price, and *d/p* ratio for all memory case.

theoretical price derived by assuming the market has converged to a homogeneous equilibrium where agents hold all equity, and consume the dividends paid. The actual price takes large swings from the equilibrium and exhibits what appear to be large crashes. The bottom panel of the figure examines the dividend price ratio, which varies significantly over time.

A similar picture corresponding to the S&P 500 is shown in Fig. 11.2. This picture is drawn from the Shiller annual data, and uses Shiller's constant dividend discount price, P^*, as a comparison.[7] Obviously, there are many choices for a "rational price" in the actual data, but P^* is a good first comparison. The figure shows swings around P^* that are similar to the all memory simulation. The frequency of large price swings is a little smaller than in the actual data, but the patterns are similar. The lower panel displays the dividend yield again. This also shows large swings, which are slightly less frequent than in the simulation.

In the last price figure, agents are required to be of relatively long memory. They vary between 28 and 30 years in the data sets they use for decision making. This will be referred to as long memory. Figure 11.3 displays these results, which show a dramatic convergence to the

---

[7] See Shiller (1981, 2003) for a recent analysis.

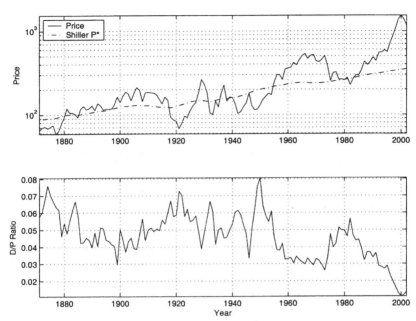

Figure 11.2. Price, Shiller P^*, and d/p ratio for S&P.

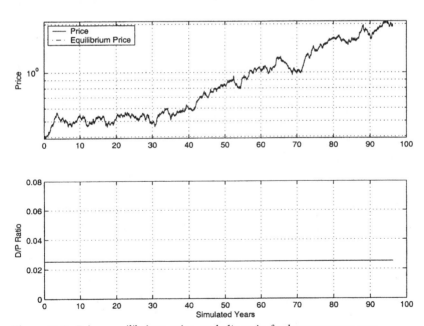

Figure 11.3. Price, equilibrium price, and d/p ratio for long memory case.

Table 11.1. *Weekly return summary statistics*

	Mean (%)	Std (%)	Skew	Kurtosis	1% VaR (%)	ARCH(5)	Volume
All Memory	0.114	2.51	−0.567	10.23	−7.47	315.3	0.065
Long Memory	0.083	0.75	−0.012	3.01	−1.69	2.7	0.053×10^{-8}
S&P (47-2000)	0.175	1.88	−0.380	5.92	−4.69	211.1	
S&P (28-2000)	0.140	2.56	−0.214	11.68	−7.38	738.6	

Simulation returns include dividends. S&P returns are nominal without dividends. 1% VaR is the Value-at-Risk at the one percent level, or the 1% quantile of the return distribution. ARCH(5) is the Engle test for ARCH using an autoregression of squared returns on five lags. It is distributed asymptotically χ^2_5 with 1% critical value of 15.1.

equilibrium price, where the dividend price ratio is constant. This benchmark demonstrates the importance of short memory strategies, and also confirms that without these strategies, the learning mechanism is able to find the homogeneous equilibrium.

Table 11.1 presents summary statistics for the generated weekly stock returns, and it compares the two different simulations with data from the S&P 500. The table shows that the heterogeneous memory framework amplifies volatility, and also generates leptokurtic returns, the same as in the actual market data. The long memory returns are close to Gaussian in terms of kurtosis. The column labeled VaR presents the value-at-risk, or one percent quantile level on returns, and again shows that the all memory runs correspond well to actual return distributions in terms of this simple property of the left tail. Finally, the column labeled ARCH performs Engle's test for the presence of conditional heteroskedasticity. This is not found for the long memory case, but is present for all the other series. The table also shows the impact of short memory traders on trading volume, which is larger in the all memory case.

This simple agent-based model has met several difficult hurdles presented in actual financial series. First, it has boosted volatility, and generates price series which go through persistent deviations from equilibrium prices, and violently crash. More precisely, the variance of returns is boosted to the level of actual variances, and returns show strong evidence for leptokurtosis and GARCH. This is far from the only model to show these features. Models such as Arifovic and Gencay (2000), Brock and Hommes (1998), Lux (1998), and Levy, Levy, and Solomon (2000) display similar features.

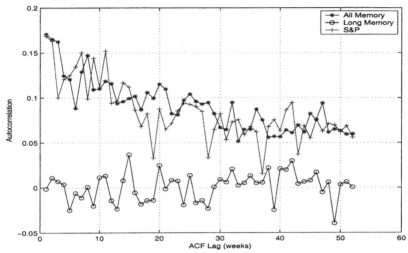

Figure 11.4. Absolute Return Autocorrelations: All Memory, Long Memory, S&P.

Figure 11.4 shows the persistence of volatility in more detail where it is represented by the autocorrelations of absolute values of returns. For the all memory case, and the actual S&P returns, the figure shows a large amount of persistence going out for more than 52 weeks. This kind of slow decay in autocorrelations is a characteristic of a long memory process, and the agent-based model can replicate this feature well.[8] The long memory only case generates no persistence.[9]

Figure 11.5 turns to the dynamics of trading volume. The actual level of trading volume in this model is not a reasonable number to compare to actual data, since volume must be affected by the fact that there is only one stock available. However, the dynamics of volume is equally as interesting as the dynamics of volatility. The autocorrelation patterns of trading volume in the various simulations are compared with trading volume from IBM from 1990–2000 in Fig. 11.5. The stock and the all memory simulation again show a very strong persistence pattern, which is similar to that presented for volatility. The persistence goes out for a long range, and the decay rate is very slow. Figure 11.6 looks at the connections between volume and volatility by displaying the cross correlations between trading

[8] Another model that is designed specifically to generate long memory is Kirman and Teyssiere (1998).
[9] Evidence for long memory in volatility can be found in papers such as Ding, Granger, and Engle (1993) and Baillie, Bollerslev, and Mikkelsen (1996). It is not clear why volatility shows such persistence, or persistence at all for that matter.

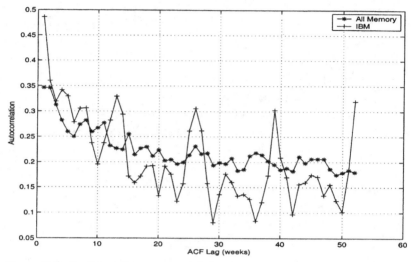

Figure 11.5. Trading volume autocorrelations.

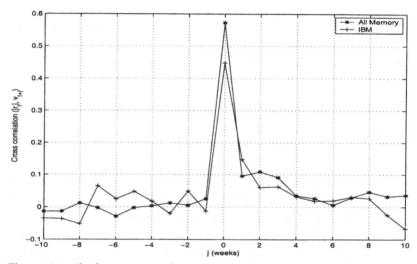

Figure 11.6. Absolute return–volume cross-correlations.

volume and absolute values of returns.[10] It displays the strong positive contemporaneous correlation which is clearly present in the IBM series as well. Also, there is an interesting asymmetry indicating a stronger

---

[10] Connections between volatility and trading volume have been extensively documented. See papers such as Gallant, Rossi and Tauchen (1993) and also Liesenfeld (2001).

Table 11.2. *Annual return summary statistics*

	Excess Return (%)	Return Std (%)	Sharpe Ratio	Kurtosis
All Memory	6.8	20.5	0.33	3.49
S&P 47-01	7.1	15.3	0.47	2.86
S&P 28-01	6.9	19.4	0.36	3.25
S&P 1871-2001	5.8	17.9	0.32	3.21

All returns include dividends and are excess of a T-bill. Simulation returns are compounded over 52 weeks, and are nonoverlapping.

impact from today's volatility into future trading volume than there is from today's trading volume into future volatility. This is another important feature replicated in both series.

Beyond short term dynamics, an important hurdle for agent-based markets is to replicate return properties at the long run. Table 11.2 displays simple summary statistics for the all memory market runs, and compares these with several examples drawn from a long horizon return series constructed by Robert Shiller.[11] The simulated markets are in a reasonable range for all of the annual return numbers. This includes the reduction in leptokurtosis that is observed in all long horizon return series. Another important measure is the Sharpe ratio, which looks at the excess return over the risk-free rate divided by the return standard deviation. This level of the risk reward ratio is another important fact from the actual data that has been traditionally difficult to match.[12]

Traditional models have had difficulty in matching many of these facts. Also, most have only concentrated on a subset of this set of features. Financial economists often prefer the realm of pricing anomalies such as the equity premium, while physicists prefer to look at distribution tails and power law-related features. A recent paper that tries to look at returns at many horizons and performs detailed calibration is Campbell and Cochrane (1999). This is a representative agent framework that faithfully matches many of these empirical features. It does this by implementing a representative agent with habit persistent preferences. The form of the habit persistence is carefully designed to make the model work. It is not clear

---

[11] These are used in Shiller (2000) and are available on his website.

[12] It is directly related to Hansen and Jagannathan bounds as shown in Hansen and Jagannathan (1991), and Cochrane and Hansen (1992). The generally large magnitude of estimated Sharpe ratios puts a lower bound on the volatility of risk measures in a standard representative agent asset pricing world.

how robust the model might be to other forms of habit, and our knowledge of the habit structure is probably small. It is not clear how a diverse set of agents might aggregate up into a representative agent with habit preferences. Also, many of the features listed here are not touched in their framework. They do not deal with the extreme persistence of volatility, and its possible long memory behavior. Finally, since it is a representative agent model, it cannot deal with any issues related to trading volume.

Incomplete markets and idiosyncratic risks are another major explanation for asset pricing anomalies. Mankiw (1986) is an early example of how an incomplete market with uninsurable risks hitting individuals might impact the aggregate risk level, and aggregate asset pricing. This has been explored in detail in Constantinedes and Duffie (1996). Similar to some of the other explanations, this one also may not be all that robust. It requires that shocks be persistent, and they must be heteroskedastic with countercyclical conditional variance. This explanation still has not attempted to explain heteroskedasticity in overall price levels, or excess kurtosis, and it also does not attempt to explain trading volume.

This chapter's main point is that most of these rational/equilibrium based models will have a difficult time replicating these features.[13] In the next section, attention turns to more behavioral approaches. These need to be treated with some care, since many of their foundations have overlaps with agent-based approaches. The relationship between the two is interesting, and it is likely to be complementary, since the tools of heterogeneous agent modeling will be necessary to help sort out some of the aspects of behavioral models.

AGGREGATION AND BEHAVIOR

Agent-based models and Post Walrasian approaches both deviate from more traditional approaches based on complete rationality in a well understood equilibrium environment. Recently, the field of behavioral finance has weakened strict restrictions on rationality in economics.[14] Dynamic models of interacting boundedly rational agents are behavioral in that the agents do not optimize their behavior and do follow rules of thumb. However, they often do not take on all the behavioral quirks

---

[13] A recent survey that explores recent rational explanations is Constantinides (2002).

[14] These restrictions often include the entire mechanism of intertemporal expected utility maximization. Many surveys on behavioral finance have appeared including Mullainathan and Thaler (2000). Also, Thaler (1993) is a good early collection.

suggested in the psychology literature. They form an important test bed for exploring behavior outside of the standard rationality paradigm.

There are several reasons individual micro irrationality might not appear in aggregate financial prices.[15] The first is related to aggregation. Will features beyond rationality and optimality appear at the macrolevel? This is a difficult question, and much of the behavioral finance literature ignores this. Should one expect to see loss aversion, or regret at the aggregate level?[16] In many cases, these modified preferences depend critically on a reference point where a stock is purchased defining gains and losses. If a heterogeneous population has loss aversion preferences, but also makes equity purchases at different prices, then what will be the impact on aggregate returns? This would need to be answered in an explicitly heterogeneous agent framework. It is possible that certain types of behavior will not appear in the aggregate, and explicit microlevel modeling is necessary to make this determination. Ideas from complex systems, which often deal with how and when individual components in a system become correlated, suggest that this will not be an easy problem.

A second reason for aggregate behavior to appear more rational than individual psychology would suggest that less than rational strategies may not survive in an evolutionary race.[17] If certain strategies are less than rational, they will eventually be eliminated by market selection forces. Evolution is a very powerful and important idea in both economics and finance, but whether it works as this conjecture states is a difficult problem. There are several dimensions to this. First, in markets that are not in an equilibrium, the determination of which strategy is "rational" is very difficult, if not impossible, since rationality must be defined relative to a current population of strategies. Second, the evolutionary dynamic in a multi-agent setting is very complex in that strategies are all evolving against each other, and there is no guarantee of a simple dynamic converging to a homogeneous equilibrium. The model used in the previous section is a good example of this. There are agents who, *ex ante*, appear rational and less than rational. The market allows wealth to shift between these different types, and therefore select for the "best" strategy. This dynamic doesn't settle down, and the short-memory agents are not driven out of the market. Therefore, they demonstrate a type of behavior that

---

[15] Some of these are mentioned in recent critiques of the behavioral finance literature as in Rubinstein (2001).

[16] An example of a representative agent model of this is in Benartzi and Thaler (1996) or more recently, Barberis, Huang, and Santos (2001).

[17] This idea goes back at least as far as Alchian (1950) and Friedman (1953b).

withstands two restrictions. First, they are observable at the aggregate level, and also they are not eliminated by evolution.

A final restriction on behavior concerns institutions that can often play a key role in coordinating behavior.[18] Financial markets are constrained by their institutional structure, and are not free from this argument. A good example of this is Gode and Sunder (1993), which shows that markets with nearly random behavior can still be very efficient in the sense of making trades. Once again, the use of an agent-based approach can be important in analyzing behavior when the outcome of institutions in a heterogeneous world is not completely obvious.[19]

CONCLUSIONS

Agent-based financial models can be fit to a large range of empirical features from financial markets. Some of these facts have been tackled by more traditional models. However, these models are fine tuned to carefully fit the facts, and it is not clear how reasonable their preference structures are for a representative consumer. Beyond standard setups, behavioral finance may offer some promise for understanding some of the empirical puzzles of modern finance. However, these approaches will need the addition of an agent-based, or Post Walrasian, approach to markets to make sense of which aspects of individual psychology remain relevant at the macrolevel.

At the moment agent-based markets can match many features of finance in a fairly "stylized manner." They do this by setting forth agents who in some ways are quite simple. Trying to do the best they can in a complex world, and working hard to adjust, adapt, and maximize relatively simple objectives. These approaches are still new, often involving computational tools that are still not well understood by agent-based modelers and the economics profession. Also, the construction of heterogeneous economics models still remains uncharted territory. This should not be a major concern, since the field and its tools are still very young.[20]

There are many policy questions that can be answered by well constructed agent-based models. As we move toward models taking

---

[18] Colander (1996) comments on the importance of institutions in a Post Walrasian setting. Also, cognitive psychologists such as Clark (1997) stress the importance of institutions in guiding behavior.
[19] Gode and Sunder (2004) is an example of this, using nonbinding price controls which should have no impact in an equilibrium price setting world.
[20] It might be compared to the early stages of experimental economics.

greater license with rationality, the importance of many policy choices, and quantitative modeling will increase. In financial markets, questions about institutions and trading become more important in a Post Walrasian setting where institutions can have a profound impact on outcomes, and restrictions that might appear inefficient in a market clearing setting can be beneficial in these out of equilibrium settings.[21] Applied economists and consultants have already entered this area in advising several institutions on how to deal with financial trading. An example is NASDAQ's questions about decimal trading.[22] More questions like this will certainly follow.

While there are problems that need Post Walrasian approaches in all of economics, the problems in finance have some of the most pressing empirical questions. The data in these markets appear extremely far from the usual economic worlds of stability and equilibrium. Agent-based models make more progress than other frameworks in explaining these features due to the fact that at their core is a world of people who process information differently, and try hard to continually adjust and adapt their behavior over time. This market may never reach anything that looks like an equilibrium efficient market, but it is in a continual struggle toward this. The range of facts these models explain, and the robustness of their explanations to different structures and parameters, is impressive. At the moment, no other models can capture so many facts with this kind of simplicity and style.

---

[21] An example might be trading halts which would seem to be a kind of constraint on the agents' trading abilities.
[22] See Meyer and Davis (2003) for examples.

PART IV

LETTING THE DATA GUIDE THEORY

12

The Past as the Future: the Marshallian Approach to Post Walrasian Econometrics

Kevin D. Hoover

The popular image of the scientific revolution usually pits young revolutionaries against old conservatives. Freeman Dyson (2004, p. 16) observes that, in particle physics in the mid twentieth century, something had to change. But in the revolution of quantum electrodynamics, Einstein, Dirac, Heisenberg, Born, and Schödinger were *old revolutionaries*, while the winners, Feynman, Schwinger, and Tomonaga, were *young conservatives*. Post Walrasian economics is not a doctrine, but a slogan announcing that something has to change. Most of the self-conscious efforts to forge a Post Walrasian economics are due to old radicals. Here I want to explore the space of the young conservative: the future is past, particularly in the methodology of Alfred Marshall's essay, "The Present Position of Economics" (1885). The radical approach identifies the problem as Walrasian theory and seeks to replace it with something better and altogether different. The conservative approach says that theory is not the problem. The problem is rather to establish an empirical discipline that connects theory to the world.

Marshall's methodology places the relationship between theory and empirical tools on center stage. In North America, if not in Europe, the dominant tools of macroeconometrics are the vector autoregression (VAR) and calibration techniques. These techniques reached their current status as the result of two nearly simultaneous reactions to the Cowles Commission program, which dominated macroeconometrics during the two decades 1950–70. These are the famous Lucas critique, and the practically influential, if less storied, Sims critique. I will briefly consider the nature of these two critiques and, then, the competing Walrasian and Marshallian visions of the role of theory in econometrics. I conclude with some suggestions about how to do Marshallian macroeconometrics.

TWO CRITIQUES

The Cowles Commission Program

Econometrics rose to self-consciousness in the 1930s in part as the result of the founding of the Econometric Society. Its manifesto called for a discipline that combined economic theory and statistics as the basis for empirical economics (Frisch, 1933). Whose rites would be used to solemnize this marriage was a fraught question during the two decades after 1933.[1] Spanos (1995) argues that there were two models of statistics for economics to draw on.

The first, the *theory of errors*, was developed for applications in the physical sciences. It presumed a well articulated, and unquestioned, underlying theoretical model. The statistical problem arose because repeated observations, which were never exact, had to be combined to measure unknown parameters in astronomical and geodesic applications (Stigler, 1986, Chapter 1).

The second was R. A. Fisher's statistical approach to *experimental design*. Fisher envisaged repeated experiments in which carefully deployed controls permitted a phenomenon to be isolated except for random and unsystematic influences. The statistical problem was to identify the significance of a phenomenon against the background of this random variation.

Both the theory of errors and experimental design were clear about the sources of the random processes characterized through their statistics. Both were secure in their applications of probability theory because they dealt with repeated observations of what they could convincingly argue were the same phenomena. The problem for economics, especially for macroeconomic time-series data was that there were no repeated observations or repeated experiments; there was only a single history.[2]

Spanos argues that Haavelmo's (1944) "Probability Approach in Econometrics" represented a kind of union of the theory of errors and Fisher's experimental approach. Economic theory was used to *identify* the relevant causal factors in economic structures viewed as a system. The complete articulation of the relevant factors stood in the place of experimental controls.[3] The economic structure could then be seen as mechanism

---

[1] Morgan (1990) provides the best general history of econometrics in this period.

[2] The term "macroeconomics" appeared at roughly the same time as "econometrics," though it is rarely found in the early econometrics literature, even when it clearly deals with what we now regard as macroeconomic data.

[3] Also see Morgan (1990, Chapter 8) who emphasizes identification as a substitute for controlled experiment.

in which each datum is a realization of a single process, much like the position of the moon measured at different times, rather than as observations from a constantly changing and incommensurable economic reality.

The Cowles Commission, particularly in its monographs of the late 1940s and early 1950s (Koopmans, 1950; Hood and Koopmans, 1953) developed the theory of identification to the canonical form that can still be found in econometrics textbooks. It set the stage for later developments in the techniques of structural estimation. The Cowles Commission approach placed great weight on more or less complete theoretical knowledge. In the classic example, data on prices and quantities are some impossible-to-disentangle mixture of supply and demand. It is only when theory can convincingly discriminate between factors other than price that affect supply but not demand and vice versa that it is possible to estimate the price-elasticity of supply or of demand.

For all of its stress on the critical importance of a priori theory as the source of identification, the Cowles Commission was fairly agnostic with respect to just what the content of relevant economic theory would be. In particular, it was not thought obvious that the theory was Walrasian. Indeed, much of the theory lying behind structural models after the Cowles Commission was Keynesian in that it involved relations between aggregates at best loosely connected to explicit assumptions about individual economic behavior.

The measurement of free parameters and the identification of causes were run together in the notion of structural estimation. The Cowles Commission clearly saw econometric models as articulating causal structures (see especially Simon [1953], who explores the relationship between causality and identification). After the early 1950s, even while the Cowles Commission program flourished, causal language rapidly disappeared from econometric discourse (see Hoover [2004] for a discussion of the reasons).

The Lucas Critique

To borrow Jevon's assessment of Ricardo: with the publication of "Econometric Policy Evaluation: A Critique" (1976) that able but wrongheaded man, Robert Lucas, shunted the car of economic science onto a wrong line. He faulted the typical macroeconomic theory of the day for paying too little attention to the fact that the economy comprised intentional agents, who responded to incentives and formed plans on the basis of available information. The econometric models used for policy evaluation failed to account for the fact that policy followed patterns discernible by people in the economy. If policymakers used equations describing economic aggregates systematically to guide a change in policy, then as people's behavior responded to the new policy, the very equations used to predict its effects would no longer capture that behavior.

Lucas's initial point was neither new nor necessarily radical.[4] Since Lucas's illustrations attributed the principal source of the difficulty to the formation of expectations, a straightforward response was consistent with the Cowles Commission program: supplement the economic theory with a good model of aggregate expectation formation (e.g. the rational expectations hypothesis) and proceed in the usual manner.[5]

Lucas did, however, have a more radical program in mind. The first element of the program was at best hinted at in "Econometric Policy Evaluation" but was clearly articulated in "Understanding Business Cycles" (Lucas 1977) and in his lectures *Models of Business Cycles* (1987). The goal of economic theory is to provide an economic model that accurately mimics the economy. A good model is one that would pass the test of the Adelmans – a test similar to the Turing test for machine intelligence – if an econometrician having only the data from the model and the data from the economy cannot distinguish between the two, then the model is a good one (Adelman and Adelman, 1959).[6]

The second element stakes a claim to the particular theoretical base on which models should be built. Lucas seeks the economically invariant in the tastes and technology of the underlying agents in the economy. He argues that these should be analyzed as a complete Walrasian model. In practice, this means not a model of every agent in the economy, but a representative-agent model – one that takes the form of a Walrasian economy with only one agent or a few types of agents standing for all the rest. The case for adopting the representative-agent, Walrasian model is never made fully explicit. It is, in part, a technical one: this is the only model that theorists have worked out more or less completely. But the wholeheartedness of the embrace also has a religious quality to it. It is

[4] His precursors include Marschak (1953), one of the key players in the Cowles Commission program.

[5] This was the program implemented vigorously by Hansen and Sargent (1980). For later developments along these lines, see Ingram (1995).

[6] See Hoover (1995) for a methodological appraisal of calibration and Lucas's conception of modeling.

a leap faith. Modern economists, at least since Adam Smith, have agreed that economic behavior was shaped by individual human choices in the face of changing incentives and constraints. The Walrasian model was a particularly stark representation of that observation. Lucas conveys the feeling, that if we do not hold to the Walrasian creed, then what? Chaos, perhaps.

The third element is an ambition. The ideal model is Walrasian, judged by the test of the Adelmans', and is *complete*. Lucas (1980, p. 288) sees a model without free parameters as the perfect model. In this, he abandons the elements of Fisher's experimental method that are preserved in the Cowles Commission program and more or less completely embraces the theory of errors as the statistical basis for econometrics. Ideally, economics is about a perfect theoretical characterization in which errors of observation are shrunk to zero. It is this attitude that explains the rise of calibration, particularly in the work of Kydland and Prescott and their followers and Lucas's embrace of it.[7] Calibration takes theory to be paramount to the point of questioning the data before questioning the theory when there is a discrepancy (Prescott, 1986). It eschews statistical estimation of parameters. And it evaluates its success by matching simulated moments of the calibrated model to the moments of data in the same spirit as the test of the Adelmans.

The Sims Critique

In contrast to Lucas's call for redoubled devotion to a set of fundamentalist theoretical principles, Christopher Sims' (1980) "Macroeconomics and Reality" appears to be a Nietzschean declaration that the god of the Cowles Commission is dead. Sims' critique was straightforward: Structural estimation in the Cowles Commission program requires a priori theory to secure identification. Identification was largely achieved through the exclusion of variables from particular equations (zero restrictions). Such identification was literally "incredible" – that is, no one really believed that there were good theoretical grounds for the exclusions that were routinely made. The commitment to identification was little more than the empty forms of piety.

Honesty, Sims argued, requires that we give up on structural estimation and do what we can without unsupported identifying assumptions.

---

[7] Kydland and Prescott (1982); Lucas (1987). See also Hoover (1995), and Hartley, Hoover, and Salyer (1998).

He advocated analyzing vector autoregressions (VARs), which are equations of the form:

$$\mathbf{Y}_t = \mathbf{B}(L)\mathbf{Y}_{t-1} + \mathbf{U}_t, \tag{1}$$

where $\mathbf{Y}_t$ is an $n \times 1$ vector of contemporaneous variables, $\mathbf{B}(L)$ is a polynomial in the lag operator, L; and $\mathbf{U}_t$ is an $n \times 1$ vector of error terms with $\mathbf{U} = [\mathbf{U}_t]$, $t = 1, 2, \ldots, T$.

It is said that there are no atheists in the foxhole. The battle for the VAR analyst is to use it for policy analysis, and that requires theoretical commitments. The problem is that the elements of $\mathbf{U}_t$ are typically intercorrelated – that is, the covariance matrix $\mathbf{\Omega} = \mathrm{E}(\mathbf{UU}')$ is not diagonal. This means that the individual equations of the system are not causally distinct. They cannot be perturbed separately, which is what policy analysis requires. Sims initially dealt with this issue in an ad hoc fashion, suggesting that Eq. (1) could be orthogonalized using particular transformations (Choleski decompositions) without too much concern about which one. (His position reminds one of Dwight Eisenhower urging every American to worship ... at the church or synagogue of his choice.) Under criticism from Cooley and LeRoy (1985), and Leamer (1985), among others, Sims (1986) came to accept that some a-priori structure had to be imposed on Eq. (1). In particular, this required a choice of $\mathbf{A}_0$ such that

$$\mathbf{Y}_t = \mathbf{A}_0^{-1}\mathbf{A}(L)\mathbf{Y}_{t-1} + \mathbf{A}_0^{-1}\mathbf{E}_t = \mathbf{B}(L)\mathbf{Y}_{t-1} + \mathbf{U}_t, \tag{2}$$

where $\Sigma = \mathrm{E}(\mathbf{EE}')$ is diagonal. The equation

$$\mathbf{A}_0\mathbf{Y}_t = \mathbf{A}(L)\mathbf{Y}_{t-1} + \mathbf{E}_t, \tag{3}$$

is known as the structural VAR (SVAR).

Equation (1) can be estimated and, given $\mathbf{A}_0$, transformed into Eq. (3). From Eq. (3), it is possible to work out the response of the economy to various shocks. In general, there are many choices of $\mathbf{A}_0$ that will fulfill the conditions of Eq. (2). So, in general, an a-priori theoretical commitment remains necessary. But where the Cowles Commission program typically imposed identifying constraints on both $\mathbf{A}_0$ and $\mathbf{A}(L)$, SVARs place constraints only on the contemporaneous causal relationships among the variables (that is, on $\mathbf{A}_0$). The god of the Cowles Commission program is not, then, dead after all, but still remains on life support – not least because the charge of incredibility that Sims leveled against structural models identified in the Cowles Commission tradition applies equally to SVARs. The idea seems to be to have just enough faith to get you through the night.

An Uneasy Alliance

Both Lucas and Sims agree that the Cowles Commission program, at least as implemented in the macroeconometric models of the 1960s and 1970s, was deficient. Yet the Lucas critique calls for a renewed dedication to a microtheoretical basis for macroeconomics, while the Sims critique calls for an atheoretical macroeconomics. Surprisingly, the two methodologies stand in a kind of uneasy alliance. Many adherents to Lucas's methodological views nevertheless employ SVARs in their research.

The relationship is two-way. In one direction, the use of SVARs is conditioned by the Lucas critique. One argument for using the SVAR was suggested early on by Sims (1982). He conceded that Lucas's argument was correct; nonetheless, if in practice changes of policy regime were infrequent or if they could be modeled as part of a superregime in which the current regime was a realization of knowable switching process between regimes, then the SVAR could be a stable representation of the economy. This argument accounts for one of the most puzzling features of SVAR analysis – the obsessive concern for policy shocks.

Typically, the effect of monetary or fiscal policy is analyzed in an SVAR by calculating the impulse–response function – that is, by tracing out the effect of a random shock to the policy equation on all the variables of the system over time. What is odd about this is that we do not normally think of policymakers as crafting policy through the delivery of random shocks. And, in practice, the residuals of the policy equations, which give an estimate of the size of the shocks, are quite small. We normally think of policymakers as trying to affect the economy through systematic reactions to changing conditions. In a Lucasian world of rapidly clearing markets, continuous full employment, and rational expectations, systematic monetary policy would not have any effects – changing it would not matter – and shocks are the only thing that would have real effects. The world in which the SVAR is immune from the Lucas critique is also the world in which, from the policy point of view, it does not matter whether the equations of the SVAR are stable or not. Shock analysis is legitimate when it is useless.

Over time, however, even new classical macroeconomists have come to believe that markets do not clear perfectly or quickly and that there may be deviations from rational expectations. In theory, this gives policy a handle on the real economy. But then, if the Lucas critique is correct, any systematic change in the equations representing policy reactions should be reflected in structural breaks in other equations of the SVAR. When policy analysis is useful, the validity of the SVAR is questionable. Sims (1999) has conducted counterfactual experiments that amount to substituting one policy-reaction function for another in an SVAR. It is unclear, however, how that could be valid in the face of the Lucas critique.

The use of SVARs is conditioned by the Lucas critique. And in the other direction, users of calibrated models frequently turn to SVARs to validate the success of their models. An SVAR is estimated using the same variables as the calibrated model. Impulse–response functions are calculated from both the SVAR and the calibrated model. The model is judged a success if, qualitatively at least, it manages to mimic the impulse–response functions of the SVAR.

There is a strong element of casual empiricism in these exercises. Which variables are included in the SVAR depends not on which might be important in the world but on which happened to be elements for the calibrated model. Typically, these models are simultaneous, and do not possess a recursive causal ordering. Nevertheless, A_0 is typically chosen to be a triangular matrix – that is, to have a well-defined recursive causal ordering. This choice is usually arbitrary or justified by an appeal to considerations such as common-sense views on relative speeds of adjustment unrelated to the theoretical implications of the model. Such a lack of seriousness about how one should connect theoretical models to empirical methods shows how far away the VAR program is in practice from Fisher's experimental design. In that methodology, the omission of a control would result in an invalid experiment. In the Cowles Commission framework, identifying assumptions are meant to take the place of such controls. That requires a tight mapping between theory and econometric model. Here the mapping is extremely loose.

In the end the alliance between the VAR program and the Lucasian microfoundational program is essentially incoherent. The root of the problem is the reigning Walrasian methodology.

TWO VISIONS

Walrasian Methodology

When David Colander (1996; Introduction, this volume) calls for a Post Walrasian economics, he appears to react primarily to the Walrasian vision of what economic theory should be. This is the familiar conception of economic atoms, each maximizing its utility and/or profit subject to technological and resource constraints. The characteristic which most marks the Walrasian system is the completely generalized interdependence among competitive markets. This vision may or may not be a good starting point for a theoretical account of the economy. I am less inclined to attack it, than is Colander. Adherence to Walrasian theory in its commonly accepted sense, however, does not seem to me to be the root of the problem with macroeconometrics.

Instead, where macroeconometrics goes off the rails is in adhering to Walrasian *methodology* in something like the sense this term is used by Milton Friedman (1949, 1953a, 1955). Friedman characterizes Walrasian methodology as seeking photographic accuracy in its representation of reality. This may not be the most felicitous way to put the matter; for Walrasian theory is itself highly abstract. But one sees the point. The Walrasian approach is totalizing. Theory comes first. And when it is applied to econometrics, it is taken in at the ground floor. Empirical reality must be theoretically articulated before it can be empirically observed.[8] There is a sense that the Walrasian attitude is that to know anything, one most know everything. This attitude might be called *apriorism*. It is already present in the Cowles Commission program, so that in some sense reactions to the Lucas critique are a kind of Cowles Commission Puritanism.

Apriorism suffers from a fundamental problem. How do we come to our a priori knowledge? For Austrians, such as Mises (1966), it is not a problem, because economics is seen as a branch of deductive logic. But most macroeconomists expect empirical evidence to be relevant to our understanding of the world. If that evidence can be viewed only through totalizing a priori theory, it cannot be used to revise the theory.

Even though there is no necessary connection between the content of Walrasian theory and the Walrasian totalizing methodology, it is not accidental that the new classical macroeconomics wedded itself so thoroughly to Walrasian theory. If one must commit a priori to some theory, it is likely to be the one that captures the age-old concerns of economics – responses of self-interested individuals to incentives in markets – in the most tractable and highly developed form. The methodological Walrasian needs theoretical conviction in order to carry out his empirical agenda. The irony is that the representative-agent version of Walrasian theory is neither faithful to the underlying microeconomic theory nor coherent in

---

[8] Walras was not an empirical economist and, so, may not be truly responsible for the attitude that I am calling "Walrasian" as it shows up in econometrics.

its own right. In a sense, it suffers from its own Sims critique: the restrictions that would allow one to move from Walrasian microeconomics to an aggregate Walrasian model are literally incredible (more on this in the next section).

Marshallian Methodology

The distinction between Walrasian and Marshallian methodology has been promoted most notably by Friedman. We draw heavily on Friedman's view of what it means to be Walrasian, even as we qualify his characterization slightly. There is no need to qualify his characterization of Marshall, which is drawn nearly verbatim from Marshall's essay, "The Present Position of Economics" (1885).

Walras started his intellectual life as an engineer. The Walrasian vision is an engineering vision. The Walrasian wants to articulate the causal structures of the economy. The modern Walrasian macroeconomist wants microfoundations for macroeconomics. Here the metaphor of foundations is seen through the eyes of the engineer. The foundations are where we start building. If we do not get them right, the superstructure will be shaky.

The Marshallian also wants microfoundations. But the metaphor is a different one. The Marshallian approach is archeological. We have some clues that a systematic structure lies beneath the complexities of economic reality. The problem is to lay this structure bare, to dig down to find the foundations, modifying and adapting our theoretical understanding as new facts accumulate, becoming ever more confident in our grasp of the superstructure, but never quite sure that we have reached the lowest level of the structure.

The Marshallian approach is not atheoretical. Marshall writes:

[F]acts by themselves are silent. Observation discovers nothing directly of the action of causes, but only sequences in time [Marshall 1885, p. 166]... [T]he most reckless and treacherous of all theorists is he who professes to let the facts and figures speak for themselves... [p. 168]

Economic theory is "not a body of concrete truth, but an engine for the discovery of concrete truth" (Marshall, 1885, p. 159). Again, Marshall writes that economic theory provides "systematic and organized methods of reasoning" [p. 164] and an account of "manner of action of causes" [p. 171].

While theory is ideally universal – not unlike Lucas's vision of a theory without free parameters – theory is, in practice incomplete and probationary. Theory must be supplemented with particular facts to be useful. This is not, as some modern economists would have it, invidious ad hockery; it is an inevitable part of the process of acquiring empirical knowledge.

MARSHALLIAN MACROECONOMETRICS

Synthetic Microanalysis

Robert Lucas has profoundly shaped modern macroeconomics. Only the wildly heterodox dare express skepticism about the necessity for microfoundations for macroeconomics. What is surprising is just how flimsy the representative-agent microfoundations that macroeconomists commonly demand really are. Microeconomic theorists are well aware that the conditions needed to aggregate systematically to representative production, utility (or demand) functions are simply too stringent to be fulfilled in actual economies (see, for example, Kirman [1992], or Felipe and Fisher [2003]). Yet, support for such pseudo-microfoundations remains solid in the profession.

The appeal of microfoundations is largely ontological: everyone agrees that the economy is composed of individuals making choices subject to constraints. The operative question, however, is: can the aggregate outcomes be inferred from detailed knowledge of individuals? The practical answer is clearly no. No one has proposed an analysis of macroeconomic aggregates that truly begins with individuals. Who would know how? Is this because the problem is just too difficult? Or is it because it cannot be done in principle? The advocate of the representative-agent model implicitly believes the former. I have argued elsewhere that macroeconomic aggregates are emergent phenomena that belong to categories different than even similarly named microeconomic concepts, and that, in principle, one cannot reduce the macro to the micro (Hoover, 2001, Chapter 5).

The physicist-turned-philosopher, Sunny Auyang (1998), points out that economics and physics face analogous problems. Quantum physicists are reductionist. They typically believe that the microstructure of reality, revealed by particles in isolation, not only accounts for the existence of aggregate macrophysical phenomena, but that one could, at least in principle, work out the characteristics of the macrophysical phenomena from quantum principles. Solid state physicists, on the other hand, typically argue for the autonomy of their own macrophysical concepts and do not believe that reduction is possible. Auyang appeals to complexity theory to explain how the macrophysical reality could both be deterministically related to the microphysical reality and, yet, solid-state physics not be reducible, even in principle, to quantum physics.

Yet, Auyang believes that the gulf between the micro and the macro in physics or economics is not completely unbridgeable in the sense that what happens at the microlevel must matter for the macrolevel. She makes the case for what she refers to as *synthetic microanalysis.* Synthetic microanalysis essentially replaces the engineering, bottom-up approach of the microreductionist with an archeological, top-down approach. It is, in this sense, a Marshallian methodology. Macropheno-mena are analyzed into simpler components. That is microanalysis. But why "synthetic"? First, there is no reason to believe that the theoretical structures identified map onto the most fundamental ontological building blocks of reality. Theorizing is the construction of models for purposes. Models propose different ways of disjointing a seamless reality for different purposes. They emphasize some particularly important feature and look for ways to suppress complications that may be irrelevant to the problem at hand. They are not independent of empirical fact, but they can arrange the facts in ways that suit different purposes and that may sometimes appear to be incompatible with each other. Synthetic microanalysis is compatible with realism, but rejects what the philosopher Paul Teller (forthcoming) refers to as the "perfect-model model." There are good models and bad models, but models are literally ad hoc – that is built for the purpose at hand.

One need not accept that the gulf between the micro and macro is in principle unbridgeable to agree that it is so in practice. In that, the micro-reductionist quantum physicist, Richard Feynman agrees completely with Auyang. Feynman (1995, p. 114) argues that " 'solid-state physics' or 'liquid-state physics' or 'honest physics' " cannot be derived from elementary analysis of the constituent particles – their relationships are too many and too complex. Practically, economics is in the same boat, and it does little good to pretend that we can do so, in principle, and that, therefore, the representative-agent model, which mimics the mathematical methods of microeconomics, but which is not micro-economics in substance, should be regarded as the standard for macro-economics. If we wish to understand what lies beneath macroeconomic phenomenon, we need to adopt the attitude of synthetic microanalysis and dig.

Econometric Examples

What kind of macroeconometrics is compatible with synthetic micro-analysis? What might Marshallian econometrics look like? I will try to hint at an answer with some illustrations.

First, consider VAR analysis. As we saw in earlier sections, VAR analysis started off as an atheoretical approach – macroanalysis without any ambitions to connect to the microeconomic. It then discovered that it required minimal structure. Subsequently, the practices of VAR analysis have been heavily conditioned by the assumptions of Lucasian microfoundations, even when those have been abandoned by theoretical macroeconomists. John Cochrane (1998) points out the cognitive dissonance experienced by macroeconomists who believe that some agents follow rules of thumb or that prices are sticky and, yet, analyze SVARs as if the world were populated only by agents with rational expectations operating in clearing markets. Cochrane offers an example of synthetic microanalysis – a small step toward the underlying structural behavior behind the VAR without the pretense of bedrock individual tastes and technology.

Cochrane proposes an aggregate supply relationship:

$$y_t = \Psi(L)[\lambda m_t + (1 - \lambda)(m_t - E(m_t|\Omega_{t-1}))] + \mathbf{D}(L)\varepsilon_{wt}, \qquad (4)$$

where y_t denotes an output measure that belongs to a vector of nonmonetary variables $\mathbf{w}$, m_t denotes a monetary policy indicator, $E(\cdot|\cdot)$ is the conditional expectations operator, Ω_{t-1} is the information available at time $t-1$, and ε_{wt} is a vector of orthogonalized, nonmonetary innovations (which include the output innovation itself).[9] The term $\Psi(L)$ is a polynomial in the lag operator L (e.g. $L^\alpha x_t = x_{t-\alpha}$). $\mathbf{D}(L)$ is polynomial vector in the lag operator. The parameter λ takes values between 0 and 1.

When $\lambda = 0$, Eq. (4) is the famous Lucas surprise-only supply curve (see Hoover, 1988). In an economy with a Lucas supply curve, rational expectations, and clearing markets, systematic monetary policy does not affect output. When $\lambda = 1$, then Eq. (4) can be interpreted as the supply curve of an economy with rule-of-thumb consumers.[10] In such an economy, systematic monetary policy does affect real output. When λ takes any other value, systematic monetary policy matters, but to different degrees.

---

[9] The notation has been altered slightly from Cochrane (1998).

[10] Cochrane (1998) also develops an identifying model with sticky prices that has much the same practical consequences for the influence of systematic monetary policy as one with some rule-of-thumb consumers.

Cochrane (1998) shows – if we only knew the value of λ – how to relate the coefficients of Eq. (4) (embedded in the lag functions $\Psi(L)$ and $\mathbf{D}(L)$) to the estimated parameters of an SVAR such as Eq. (3) repeated here:

$$\mathbf{A}_0\mathbf{Y}_t = \mathbf{A}(L)\mathbf{Y}_{t-1} + \mathbf{E}_t. \tag{3a}$$

The effects of policy on the real economy differ, depending on the value of λ.

When $\lambda = 0$, a shift in policy parameters (the coefficients of the policy–reaction function that governs the behavior of m_t) would result in structural breaks in the output equation of the SVAR, Eq. (3). This is an example of the Lucas critique: macroeconometric relationships are not invariant in the face of policy shifts. But it really does not matter, systematic policy is ineffective, so the SVAR is not useful for policy anyway. When $\lambda = 1$, the parameters of the policy–reaction function will not play any part in the output equation of the SVAR, so that it remains stable in the face of a change in systematic policy and, in fact, measures the effect of policy on output. The irony is that the Lucas critique matters most when policy is least effective, and matters least when policy is most effective.

Cochrane (1998) argued that λ, the fraction of rule-of-thumb agents, could not be identified. Hoover and Jorda (2001) show how it can be identified from using information from distinct monetary-policy regimes. Such identification requires that Eq. (4) be accepted as an *a priori* identifying assumption.

The first thing to notice is that Eq. (4) lacks a microfoundation – it is not derived from optimization given deep tastes and technology, either from a disaggregated microeconomic model or from a representative-agent model. One could argue that, in principle, the coefficients of $\Psi(L)$ itself would be subject to the Lucas critique (see Cochrane [1998], p. 283). It does, however, take a step toward articulation of the structure underlying the VAR: it models the effects of a population of two classes of agents (those with rational expectations and those without) in a manner that would be compatible with a variety of particular models falling into broad classes.

Marshallian macroeconometrics in this case starts with some tentative theoretical presuppositions and asks, how well they do when confronted with the data? For example, the salience of the Lucas critique can be checked by examining the invariance or lack thereof of the estimated parameters of the model. Hoover and Jorda (2001) discovered some evidence for the Lucas critique in that they estimated value of $\lambda = 0.57$. Yet even at that value, which implies a close-to-even split between "rational" and rule-of-thumb agents, it can be shown through simulation that the economy would behave nearly the same as if it were completely populated by the rule-of-thumb agents.[11] The theoretical presuppositions help us to learn something about the data and to render it more useful for policy analysis, but the data also provide a check on those presuppositions. They may suggest areas in which the theory could be elaborated to better account for features of the data. For example, do either the formation of rules-of-thumb or of the ability to construct rational expectations depend on learning behavior?

Cochrane's analysis of the monetary policy highlights the interplay of a theoretical model (e.g. Eq. [4]) and a particular characterization of the data (e.g. Eq. [3]). North American macroeconomics has focused more on [developing theory subject to certain criteria] than on the quality of the characterization of the data. In contrast, Spanos (1995) argues for an approach to econometrics that he calls *probabilistic reduction*. The essential point is to maximize the salience of the econometric model by searching for a representation of the data that extracts the maximal amount of statistical information from it. That representation of the data then provides a better basis on which to exercise the interpretative transformations of economic theory.

The data side of Cochrane's analysis could be addressed in the spirit of Spanos's approach. We have already commented on the arbitrariness of the identifying assumptions of the structural VAR – i.e. the restrictions on $\mathbf{A}_0$. It is widely believed by VAR practitioners that these restrictions are arbitrary and must come from theory. But, in fact, there may be statistical grounds for selecting these restrictions, at least in some cases, based on the graph-theoretic analysis of causation.[12]

A simple example shows the key points. We can think of $\mathbf{A}_0$ as placing a set of restrictions on the variables in $\mathbf{Y}$. To illustrate, let

$$\mathbf{Y} = \begin{bmatrix} W \\ X \\ Y \\ Z \end{bmatrix}$$

and let

---

[11] Estrella and Fuhrer (1999) provide related evidence that the Lucas critique is not practically important.

[12] Hoover (2004b) provides a concise introduction to graph-theoretic methods of causal inference.

$$\mathbf{A}_0 = \begin{bmatrix} 1 & 0 & 0 & 0 \\ \alpha_{XW} & 1 & 0 & 0 \\ 0 & 0 & 1 & 0 \\ \alpha_{ZW} & 0 & \alpha_{ZY} & 0 \end{bmatrix},$$

where the α_{ij} can be thought of as the coefficients of regression equations, so that, for example, the last line corresponds to $Z = \alpha_{ZW}W + \alpha_{ZY}Z +$ error. A regression equation can be regarded as having the arrow of causation pointed from the right-hand to the left-hand side (see Hoover 2001, p. 39; Cartwright 1989, p. 18; Pearl, 2000). The causal relationships among the variables can be represented by a diagram (Figure 12.1) that is isomorphic to the relationships in $\mathbf{A}_0$.

Graph-theory has been applied to such diagrammatic representations of causal structure by Pearl (2000) and Spirtes, Glymour, and Scheines (2000) among others. They have established an isomorphism between causal relationships expressed in a graph and properties of statistical independence among data. In this case, X is an intervening cause between W and Z. If Fig. 12.1 is the complete relevant universe, then W and Z are statistical dependent when considered as a pair, but statistically independent conditional on X. In constrast, X and Y are statistically independent when considered as a pair, but statistically dependent conditional on Y. Causal search algorithms work backwards from these patterns of statistical independence to find the class of graphs (and therefore the restrictions on $\mathbf{A}_0$) that are consistent with them. Sometimes, the class has only a single member. In that case, data identify $\mathbf{A}_0$ without an appeal to prior theory. In other cases, the class has multiple members, but statistics may nonetheless reduce the work left for the identifying theory to do. Swanson and Granger (1997) show how to apply these methods to a VAR. Demiralp

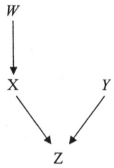

Figure 12.1. A Casual graph.

and Hoover (2004) extend Swanson and Granger's search method and provide a Monte Carlo analysis of its effectiveness.

Spanos sees his approach as tracing ultimately to the biometric tradition of Galton and Pearson. It is also closely related to what might be called the London School of Economics (LSE)–Copenhagen School. The LSE approach is often traced to the work of Denis Sargan, but is most clearly associated with David Hendry and a large number of co-workers (see Mizon [1995] for a survey). What I am calling the Copenhagen school is the approach exemplified in the work of Katarina Juselius and Søren Johanssen (see Juselius [1999, 2005] and Juselius and Johansen [Chapter 16] this volume for a methodological exposition).

Hendry has for many years advocated a "general-to-specific approach" to econometrics. The essence of his approach is to provide as broad a characterization of the data as possible – a *general* model – to be used as benchmark to test down to a *simple* model that carries the irreducible statistical information of the general model in a more parsimonious form. An acceptable simple model must meet stringent statistical specification criteria (including desirable properties for residuals and stability of coefficients), and it must statistically encompass both the general model and alternative simplifications. Recently, Hendry and Krolzig (1999) have incorporated many of the practices of LSE econometrics into an expert system, *PCGets* (Hendry and Krolzig, 2001).[13]

The Copenhagen approach has focused on the characterization of the long-run properties of time-series data – its *integration* and *cointegration* properties. It has long been known that the statistics typically used in econometrics up to the 1980s was not suitable to nonstationary data. The Copenhagen approach is again a species of probabilistic reduction, decomposing time-series data into variables which move together in the long run (cointegrate) and the common trends that drive them.

There are many detailed connections between the LSE and Copenhagen approaches in their history; and their practices are strongly complementary. It is natural, therefore, to group them together. Where typically both approaches impose less prior theory than the approach to SVARs illustrated by Cochrane's policy analysis, they insist on much stronger statistical criteria. They fit very nicely into a Marshallian methodology, because, by establishing much more highly defined characterizations of

---

[13] Hoover and Perez (1999), which initiated Hendry and Krolzig's development of *PCGets*, provides a Monte Carlo evaluation of a related expert system; see also Hoover and Perez (2004).

the data than does the typical VAR, they can place restrictions on what characteristics an acceptable theory must have. In some cases, they may allay theoretical concerns. The Lucas critique, for instance, can be seen as a possibility theorem: *if* the economy is structured in a certain way, then aggregate relations will not be invariant to changes in systematic policy. Tests of superexogeneity, based in LSE methods, have been used to test whether invariance fails in the face of policy change (for a survey, see Ericsson and Irons [1995]). That it does not in many cases provides information that the economy is not structured in the way that Lucas contemplates.

AFTER WALRASIAN ECONOMETRICS

It is easy to complain about the failures of orthodox macroeconomics and to lay the blame on its particular narrow Walrasian theoretical conception and to see progress in greater openness to a more realistic theory. But I suggest a different diagnosis. The problem is not in Walrasian theory, but in the Walrasian attitude of *apriorism*. The moral problem of science is how, in the phrase of the great pragmatist philosopher C. S. Peirce (1934–58), to fix belief. The failure of the Cowles Commission program in the 1970s was less from its supposed predictive failure or the failure of its models to be invariant to policy, than from a lack of conviction on the part of macroeconomists in the soundness of its identifying assumptions. Sims responded by trying to live without theoretical convictions, but with limited success. Lucas tried to find conviction in a zealous commitment to Walrasian theory. Lucas carried the day; but, as with other cases of zealotry, there is a gap between the ideal (a macroeconomics built from individual microeconomic behaviors) and the practice (a macroeconomics that mimics the forms of microeconomics, but never deals with individuals). This zealotry has been damaging to empirical macroeconomics because it dismisses particular, useful empirical investigations, not because they are not informative, but because they do not appear in appropriate dress.

I doubt, however, that a Post Walrasian program that replaces Walrasian theory with some supposedly richer or more realistic theory will do any better. A philosophy of "anything goes" and low expectations for the possibility of discriminating between competing conclusions on a principled basis are not calculated to produce conviction or fix belief. They cannot produce a stable economics – scientifically or sociologically.

Marshallian methodology seems more calculated to fix belief and to produce workable conviction. Yes, we must start with whatever theoretical understanding we have at the moment. But all theory is tentative. It must be rigorously confronted with data. Theory and data must be mutually adjusted. Marshallian econometrics is possible, either in the familiar North American VAR framework or in the European LSE–Copenhagen framework. It is not Walrasian, because it does not start with the premise that to know anything one must know everything. It is Marshallian, not because of its specific content, but because of its attitude: to know anything, you have to dig.

13

Old World Econometrics and New World Theory

Roger E. A. Farmer[*]

Since this volume is about Post Walrasian economics I must confess at the outset to feeling somewhat of an interloper. I take the defining characteristic of Walrasian economics to be the assumption that data can be well described by competitive markets with continuous market clearing. Much of my work over the past decade has been on the implications of indeterminacy and sunspots in Walrasian economies and, although the economies that I study are often not competitive, I have never felt confined by the assumption of continuous market clearing – on the contrary, in my view, market clearing is an irrefutable proposition once markets are defined broadly enough. I am nevertheless grateful to the organizers of the conference for the opportunity to collect together some ideas that I have been working on over the past few years in joint research with Andreas Beyer of the European Central Bank.

My work with Beyer begins with the observation that North American macroeconomists and European time-series econometricians often have difficulty communicating with each other. The main points of disagreement concern the way that theory should be confronted with data and the way that economists should treat expectations. Roughly speaking, the dominant paradigm in North America favors calibration and data is passed through a two-sided filter. The dominant trend in European econometrics points out that theoretical models often have rich implications for both low and high frequency components of the data; filtering data removes the low frequency component and throws away information that can potentially discriminate between competing theories. On this point my work comes

*I am grateful to Andreas Beyer for permission to extensively quote our joint unpublished work. Any opinions or factual errors that remain in the paper are, however, my sole responsibility. This research was supported by NSF grant SBR 0418174.

down squarely on the side of the Old World. But not all of my sympathies lie with the way that European econometricians have applied formal econometric methods. David Hendry (1995), for example, has argued that there is little merit in the rational expectations hypothesis. In contrast I see merit in the argument that expectations are forward looking and I see no difficulty with pushing this idea to its logical extreme and assuming that expectations are rational. My research agenda is to combine the general-to-specific methodology favored by the Hendry school of European econometrics with parsimonious theory-driven rational expectations models. This chapter summarizes the progress that Beyer and I have made in pursuit of this approach.

BACKGROUND

In the 1950s a group of economists at the Cowles Commission developed a framework for studying time-series data that dealt with the difficulty of conducting experiments. Cowles Commission methodology proposed a distinction between *structural models* that might involve systems of simultaneous equations and *reduced form* models in which each endogenous variable is explained as a function of predetermined and exogenous variables. The role of the theorist was to find a set of assumptions that would allow the econometrician to recover a unique structural model from estimates of the reduced form parameters.[1] This approach remained unchallenged for 20 years.

In the 1970s, Lucas (1976) published a critique of Cowles Commission methodology based on the proposition that agents' expectations are forward looking. He argued that the Keynesian identification assumptions that were commonly used in the 1960s were misspecified since they failed to account for cross-equation restrictions that arise naturally in models in which expectations are rational. He pointed out that although Keynesian models might fit well within a given sample, they should not be used to inform policy analysis since misspecified structural parameters would not remain invariant to a change in the rule followed by a policy maker.

Following the Lucas critique, macroeconomists moved in two directions. One group continued to construct structural models but made different

---

[1] See the collection of papers "Statistical Inference in Dynamic Economic Models," Koopmans, ed. (1950). The introduction, Marschak (1950), provides a particularly clear summary of the Cowles Commission approach.

identifying assumptions. Specifically, they assumed that the data is generated by a dynamic general equilibrium model (possibly with sticky prices) in which forward looking agents have rational expectations of future prices.

A second group of economists, following the arguments of Sims (1980), gave up entirely on structural models and concentrated on identifying the effects of policy shocks in reduced form vector autoregressions (VARs). This enterprise is very different from the goal of structural modelers who seek to design optimal policy rules by estimating the "deep parameters" of the "true structure" of the economy. Those on the side of VAR models sometimes defend their methodology by arguing for a kind of meta-model in which all possible changes in policy rules have already been rationally anticipated by agents and are built into expectations. A second defense, and perhaps a more persuasive one, is that identification is difficult or impossible in rational expectations models since there are no credible instruments.

In my work with Beyer, we are on the side of the VAR modelers in recognizing the difficulty of finding credible identifying restrictions. We explore this theme in Beyer and Farmer (2003b) and Beyer and Farmer (2004) in which we argue that the identifying assumptions used by rational expectations modelers are difficult to defend and that the lack of identification may have serious consequences for a research agenda that seeks to find an optimal policy rule. But although identification is difficult, it is not impossible. In Beyer and Farmer (2002, 2003a) we argue that occasional changes in policy regime can be used as a natural experiment to help to identify a subset of the parameters of a structural model.

STRUCTURE AND REDUCED FORM IN RATIONAL EXPECTATIONS MODELS

The Cowles Commission distinguished between a structural model that might involve simultaneous relationships between variables, and a reduced form model in which each endogenous variable has been reduced to a function of exogenous and predetermined variables. The purpose of this section is twofold. First, I will discuss the amendments to Cowles Commission methods that arise from the possibility that data may be nonstationary but cointegrated. Second, I will discuss the amendments to these methods that arise in rational expectations models as a consequence of the existence of forward looking expectations.

THE OLD WORLD APPROACH

My work has been conducted in the framework of U.S. monetary policy using quarterly data from 1970 through 1999 on the Fed funds rate, unemployment, and the inflation rate. Although many of the ideas I will discuss are more general, this environment is rich enough to introduce my main points and specific enough to make them with a minimum of notation.

Let $\{y_t\}_{t=1}^{T}$ be a vector-valued time series of three variables, partitioned as $\{y_t^s, y_t^p\}_{t=1}^{T}$. y_t^s is a 2-vector of private sector structural variables that consists of the first difference of the unemployment rate and the first difference of the inflation rate and y_t^p is a scalar that represents the first difference of the federal funds rate. I have separated the variables in this way because I will need a notation that allows me to discuss the behavior of an economic system in which a policymaker may design a rule that sets a policy variable – in my case this will be the federal funds rate – as a function of other variables in the system.

Because the data that I consider is nonstationary but cointegrated, I need a rich enough model to allow me to discuss the problems of inference that arise in this case. Let us begin with an approach that I call "Old World" econometrics since its major practitioners are European. An econometrician following this approach might construct the following structural model:

$$\underset{2\times 2}{\bar{A}_{11}} \underset{2\times 1}{y_t^s} + \underset{2\times 1}{\bar{A}_{12}} \underset{1\times 1}{y_t^p} = \underset{2\times m}{\bar{B}_1} \underset{m\times 1}{z_{t-1}} + \underset{2\times 1}{v_t^s}, \tag{1}$$

$$\underset{1\times 2}{\bar{A}_{21}} \underset{2\times 1}{y_t^s} + \underset{1\times 1}{y_t^p} = \underset{1\times m}{\bar{B}_2} \underset{m\times 1}{z_{t-1}} + \underset{1\times 1}{v_t^p}. \tag{2}$$

v_t is a 3-vector of iid shocks partitioned conformably as $\{v_t^s, v_t^p\}$ with covariance matrix Ω_v and z_{t-1} is an m-vector of exogenous and predetermined variables. z_{t-1} contains a constant, k lags of y_t, and the levels of the first lags of unemployment, inflation, and the federal funds rate.

I have separated the model into two blocks. The first, Eq. (1), represents the behavior of the private sector; the second, Eq. (2), is a policy reaction function. Although it is not necessary to break up the model in this way in order to discuss the relationship of structural and reduced form models, the partition of the model into a private sector block and a policy rule will play an important role in my discussion of identification.

The Cowles Commission economists assumed that the data they studied were stationary. More recently there has been an explosion of work on the properties of dynamic systems of nonstationary variables.[2] Recent advances in this area permit valid inferences to be made in structural and reduced form time series models when the level variables are nonstationary but cointegrated.

Any vector autoregression in levels has an equivalent representation as a Vector Error Correction Model (VECM). A VECM is a VAR in first differences in which first lags of the levels appear as additional explanatory variables. If the data are nonstationary but cointegrated then the matrix of level coefficients has reduced rank. If this matrix has full rank, the parameters of the VECM can be consistently estimated by ordinary least squares. But if it has reduced rank, the regressors will include nonstationary variables and statistical inference using classical methods will be invalid.

A solution to the problem of cointegrated regressors in systems of n equations was provided by Johansen (1995) who showed how to consistently estimate the rank of the cointegrating matrix, using a maximum likelihood approach. In Beyer and Farmer (2003a) we take a two-step approach to the problem of inference. In the first step we use Johansen's procedure to estimate the rank of the cointegrating matrix which we find to be equal to two for our U.S. data set. In the second step we replace the full set of three level variables, that might potentially be included in z_{t-1}, by two stationary linear combinations of these variables. The weights we use to construct these linear combinations are the cointegrating vectors estimated in step 1.

A NEW WORLD TWIST

The class of models described in Eqs. (1) and (2) is rich, but not rich enough to include the structural models of rational expectations econometrics. To allow for the influence of expectations, the system must be expanded by adding the date t vector $E_t[y_{t+1}]$ as an additional set of explanatory variables:

$$\underset{2\times2}{\bar{A}_{11}}\ \underset{2\times1}{y_t^s} + \underset{2\times1}{\bar{A}_{12}}\ \underset{1\times1}{y_t^p} + \underset{2\times3}{\bar{F}_1}\ \underset{3\times1}{E_t[y_{t+1}]} = \underset{2\times m}{\bar{B}_1}\ \underset{m\times1}{z_{t-1}} + \underset{2\times1}{v_t^s}, \tag{3}$$

$$\underset{1\times2}{\bar{A}_{21}}\ \underset{2\times1}{y_t^s} + \underset{1\times1}{y_t^p} + \underset{1\times3}{\bar{F}_1}\ \underset{1\times3}{E_t[y_{t+1}]} = \underset{1\times m}{\bar{B}_1}\ \underset{m\times1}{z_{t-1}} + \underset{1\times1}{v_t^p}. \tag{4}$$

---

[2] See the survey by Waston (1994) for a detailed exposition of these developments.

Since the three components of the vector $E_t[y_{t+1}]$ are endogenously determined at date t, one must add three additional equations to close the structural model. Under the rational expectations assumption, these equations define the one-step-ahead forecast errors of y_t,

$$\underset{3\times 1}{y_t} = \underset{3\times 1}{E_{t-1}[y_t]} + \underset{3\times 1}{w_t}. \tag{5}$$

The set of models defined by Eqs. (3)–(5) may be classified into two types, *determinate* or *indeterminate*, depending on the values of the model's parameters. Determinate models allow the economist to find a unique reduced form that describes the evolution of y_t as a vector autoregression driven by the vector of shocks v_t. The shocks v_t are called *fundamental* to distinguish them from the *nonfundamental* forecast errors w_t. In determinate models, the w_t are endogenously determined as a function of v_t as part of the solution procedure. In indeterminate models the properties of w_t must be independently chosen as part of the specification of the model. In this case the random variables w_t have the interpretation of nonfundamental shocks to agents' beliefs that may independently influence the evolution of y_t.

The following definitions of the variance–covariance parameters of w_t and v_t will provide us with a language that is general enough to cover both determinate and indeterminate models,

$$E[(v_t^s)(v_t^s)'] = \Omega_v^s, \ E[(v_t^p)^2] = \Omega_v^p, \ E(v_t^s v_t^p) = \Omega_v^{sp},$$
$$E[(w_t w_t')] = \Omega_w, \ E[(v_t w_t')] = \Omega_{vw}.$$

In the determinate case the parameters Ω_w and Ω_{vw} are endogenously determined as functions of the fundamental parameters. In the indeterminate case, these matrices may contain independent elements that index a particular reduced form. In either case, by including the possibility that Ω_w and Ω_{vw} may be prespecified as part of the definition of the structural model, there will be a unique mapping from the structure to the reduced form.

STRUCTURE AND REDUCED FORM

The model described by Eqs. (3–5) is well suited to the discussion of policy design. But to illustrate the concept of structure and reduced form it will help to simplify it in two ways. I will study a version of the model in which the data is stationary and in which only one lag appears on the right-hand side. The purpose of introducing this stripped-down model is to show that the classification into structural and reduced form models introduced by the Cowles Commission can also be applied to linear rational expectations models. It will also allow me to discuss a complication that occurs in rational expectations models but is not present in standard models. This arises from the possibility that a structural rational expectations model may be determinate or indeterminate.

Let upper case Y_t be a 3-vector of level data (I will retain lower case y_t for differenced data) and write the structural rational expectations model as follows:

$$
\overset{\tilde{A}}{\underset{\substack{3\times3 \ 3\times3 \\ 3\times3 \ 3\times3}}{\begin{bmatrix} A & F \\ I & 0 \end{bmatrix}}}
\overset{X_t}{\underset{\substack{3\times1 \\ 3\times1}}{\begin{bmatrix} Y_t \\ E_t[Y_{t+1}] \end{bmatrix}}}
=
\overset{\tilde{C}}{\underset{\substack{3\times1 \\ 3\times1}}{\begin{bmatrix} C \\ 0 \end{bmatrix}}}
+
\overset{\tilde{B}}{\underset{\substack{3\times3 \ 3\times3 \\ 3\times3 \ 3\times3}}{\begin{bmatrix} B_1 & B_2 \\ 0 & I \end{bmatrix}}}
\overset{X_{t-1}}{\underset{\substack{3\times1 \\ 3\times1}}{\begin{bmatrix} Y_{t-1} \\ E_{t-1}[Y_t] \end{bmatrix}}}
$$

$$
+
\overset{\tilde{\Psi}_v}{\underset{\substack{3\times3 \\ 3\times3}}{\begin{bmatrix} \Psi_v \\ 0 \end{bmatrix}}}
\underset{3\times1}{v_t}
+
\overset{\tilde{\Psi}_w}{\underset{\substack{3\times3 \\ 3\times3}}{\begin{bmatrix} 0 \\ I \end{bmatrix}}}
\underset{3\times1}{w_t} \, .
\tag{6}
$$

More compactly,

$$
\underset{6\times6}{\tilde{A}} \, \underset{6\times1}{X_t} = \underset{6\times1}{\tilde{C}} + \underset{6\times6}{\tilde{B}} \, \underset{6\times1}{X_{t-1}} + \underset{6\times3}{\tilde{\Psi}_v} \, \underset{3\times1}{v_t} + \underset{6\times1}{\tilde{\Psi}_w} \, \underset{3\times1}{w_t} \, .
\tag{7}
$$

In Cowles Commission methodology, the mapping from structure to reduced form is found by premultiplying (7) by the inverse of $\tilde{A}$ to give the following expression[3]

$$
\underset{6\times1}{X_t} = \underset{6\times6}{\Gamma^*} \, \underset{6\times1}{X_{t-1}} + \underset{6\times1}{C^*} + \underset{6\times3}{\Psi_v^*} \, \underset{3\times1}{v_t} + \underset{6\times3}{\Psi_w^*} \, \underset{3\times1}{w_t} \, .
\tag{8}
$$

A structural rational expectations model also has a reduced form represented by Eq. (8) although the mapping from the structural to the reduced form model is more complicated than in the Cowles Commission case. To derive the reduced form of a structural rational expectations

---

[3] This transformation requires that the matrix $\tilde{A}$ have full rank. Although it is not necessary to make this assumption in order to find the reduced form of the linear rational expectations model, I will maintain the assumption here for expository purposes.

model, one must eliminate the influence of unstable roots of the matrix $\tilde{A}^{-1}B$ by ensuring that the system always remains in the linear subspace associated with the stable roots of this matrix. This is achieved by allowing the endogenous random variables w_t to adjust in each period to offset the effect of the fundamental shocks v_t.

The classes of reduced form models that might be associated with the structural model can be indexed by the number of unstable roots of $\tilde{A}^{-1}B$. If this matrix has three unstable roots the solution is said to be determinate. In this case Γ^* has rank 3, Ψ_w^* is identically zero, and the endogenous errors w_t do not appear in the reduced form. At the other extreme, if all of the roots of $\tilde{A}^{-1}B$ are inside the unit circle, the model has three degrees of indeterminacy. In this case Γ^* has rank 6, Ψ_w^* has rank 3, and w_t is an arbitrary vector of shocks with zero conditional mean and arbitrary covariance matrix. The vectors v_t and w_t may also be correlated.

In addition to the determinate case and the case of three degrees of indeterminacy, the three equation linear rational expectations model may also have one or two degrees of indeterminacy. For example, the case of one degree of indeterminacy occurs when two roots of $\tilde{A}^{-1}B$ are outside the unit circle. In this case Γ^* has rank 4, Ψ_w^* has rank 1, and a one dimensional arbitrary nonfundamental shock w_t influences the behavior of the system. As in the case of complete indeterminacy, w_t has zero mean and may be correlated with v_t.

THE LUCAS CRITIQUE AND NEW WORLD THEORY

We now have the necessary notation in place to discuss how one might pursue an agenda that combines Old World econometrics with New World theory. Consider the class of linear rational expectations models represented by Eqs. (3–4) which we reproduce below:

$$\underset{2\times2}{\bar{A}_{11}} \underset{2\times1}{y_t^s} + \underset{2\times1}{\bar{A}_{12}} \underset{1\times1}{y_t^p} + \underset{2\times3}{\bar{F}_1} \underset{3\times1}{E_t[y_{t+1}]} = \underset{2\times m}{\bar{B}_1} \underset{m\times1}{z_{t-1}} + \underset{2\times1}{v_t^s}, \tag{9}$$

$$\underset{1\times2}{\bar{A}_{21}} \underset{2\times1}{y_t^s} + \underset{1\times1}{y_t^p} + \underset{1\times3}{\bar{F}_2} \underset{3\times1}{E_t[y_{t+1}]} = \underset{1\times m}{\bar{B}_2} \underset{m\times1}{z_{t-1}} + \underset{1\times1}{v_t^p}. \tag{10}$$

Following the critique of Lucas (1976) much of macroeconomic theory is conducted using a linear rational expectations model in this class as an organizing framework. But before a model like this can be calibrated or estimated, its parameters must be restricted through identifying assumptions.

One approach to identification proceeds by deriving restrictions from microeconomic theory. For example, a theorist might assume that data is generated by the actions of a representative agent with a time separable utility function defined over current consumption and the real value of money balances. This agent has access to a technology for producing commodities using labor and a fixed factor and the agent may hold money or government bonds as stores of wealth. The technology might use intermediate inputs produced by monopolistically competitive firms that face frictions in the adjustment of their prices. Government behavior might be modeled with the assumption that the central bank forms rational expectations of future inflation and responds to these expectations by raising or lowering the federal funds rate. If the modeler is sophisticated then the parameters of this rule will themselves be derived from the assumption of maximizing behavior on the part of the central bank.

It is often asserted that the approach described above is superior to the Cowles Commission methods that preceded it since the parameters of a linear rational expectations model, restricted in this way, represent the "deep economic structure" and they would not therefore be expected to change if the central bank were to change its policy rule. This argument is surely correct if the economist has identified the true structural model, but this is a very big if. It is more likely that the theorist has used false identifying restrictions and, if this is the case, the model he believes to be structural cannot be used to guide policy. The argument of Lucas (1976) against the use of Keynesian econometric models as guides to policy evaluation applies to any misspecified model, whether or not the model pays lip service to rational expectations by including expected future endogenous variables as right-hand-side variables. This is the point made in Beyer and Farmer (2003b, 2004) and, in the following section, I describe some of the examples we constructed in those papers to illustrate how serious the lack of identification may be.

LACK OF IDENTIFICATION AND ITS CONSEQUENCES

In central banks and universities throughout the world, researchers are engaged in an agenda that hopes to uncover the properties of a "good" monetary policy. The thrust of this agenda is to construct economic models that are based on solid microfoundations where microfoundations means that aggregate data can be modeled "as if" they were chosen by a set of identical representative agents operating in competitive markets with rational expectations of the values of future variables. The restrictions imposed by theory are used to identify the parameters of a linear model, similar to the one described by Eqs. (3)−(5). These parameters are given numerical values, either through calibration or through more formal estimation methods, and the resulting quantified model is used to inform policy analysis. Beyer and Farmer (2004) argue that this is a futile exercise for the following reason.

Using Eqs. (3)−(5) as a benchmark, consider the following partition of the model parameters into two sets. The elements of $\bar{A}_{11}$, $\bar{A}_{12}$, $\bar{F}_1$, $\bar{B}_1$, and Ω_v^s are parameters that describe private sector behavior: I will refer to them as θ^s.[4] Since we have already included future expectations as endogenous regressors, θ^s is determined by the specification of the technology, preferences, and endowments of the agents in a microfounded model. In the language of Lucas and Sargent (1981), the elements of θ^s are functions of the "deep structure." The elements of $\bar{A}_{21}$, $\bar{A}_{22}$, $\bar{F}_2$, $\bar{B}_2$, Ω_v^p and Ω_v^{sp} are parameters that describe the policy rule of the government: I will refer to them as θ^p. By definition, $\theta = \theta^s \cup \theta^p$ is a structural model.

Every structural model, θ, has a unique reduced form Γ^*; but the converse is not true. In Beyer and Farmer (2004) we construct an algorithm that finds equivalence classes of exactly identified models. We begin with a "true" model θ that we refer to as the data generating process (DGP) and we use our algorithm to find its associated reduced form $\Gamma^*(\theta)$. We feed the reduced form parameters to a fictional econometrician who supplements $\Gamma^*(\theta)$ with a set of linear restrictions, described by a matrix R and a vector r, that identifies some different model $\bar{\theta}$. Since θ and $\bar{\theta}$ both have the same reduced form, they obey the equivalence relationship,

$$\Gamma^*(\bar{\theta}) = \Gamma^*(\theta).$$

We call $\bar{\theta}$ the *equivalent model*. The equivalent model is identified by the restrictions

$$R\bar{\theta} = r.$$

Beyer and Farmer (2004) use this algorithm to construct four examples, each of which is progressively more destructive to a research agenda that hopes to design a "good" economic policy. The following two subsections discuss these examples in more detail.

---

[4] In the case of an indeterminate model, some or all of the elements of the matrices Ω_w and Ω_{vw} must also be included in this set.

LACK OF IDENTIFICATION IN DETERMINATE MODELS

The first two of Beyer and Farmer's examples exploit the fact that one cannot identify the unstable roots of a rational expectations model since the solution to the model is restricted to lie in a convergent subspace. To understand this idea, consider the following simple example,

$$y_t + f\, E_t[y_{t+1}] = by_{t-1} + v_t, \quad E[v_t] = \sigma_v^2. \tag{11}$$

If there is a unique solution to this model then its characteristic polynomial must have two roots, λ_1 and λ_2, that obey the inequality $|\lambda_1| < 1 < |\lambda_2|$ and the reduced form of the model will take the form:

$$y_t = \lambda_1 y_{t-1} + \psi v_t. \tag{12}$$

The econometrician can learn the value of λ_1 by regressing y_t on y_{t-1} but he can never recover the value of λ_2 unless he has prior knowledge of the variance of v_t. Although the reduced form parameter ψ is a known function of λ_2, it cannot be disentangled from σ_v^2. In Beyer and Farmer (2004) we draw two implications from this point. First, in simple New-Keynesian models, the parameters of the policy rule are unidentified. Second, this lack of identification extends to the private sector equations.

DISCRIMINATING BETWEEN DETERMINATE AND INDETERMINATE MODELS

One of the goals of the New-Keynesian agenda is to distinguish periods in which the policy regime led to a determinate outcome from periods when the outcome was indeterminate. It has been argued that central banks should avoid policy rules that induce indeterminacy since rules of this kind permit the influence of nonfundamental shocks to create additional undesirable uncertainty.[5]

Clarida, Gali, and Gertler (2000) use single equation methods to estimate a policy rule before and after 1980 and they claim that Fed policy before 1980 led to an indeterminate equilibrium that was influenced by non-fundamental shocks. After 1980, when Paul Volcker took over as chairman

---

[5] Michael Woodford puts the point this way: "... I demand that the policy rule be not merely consistent with the desired equilibrium, but also that commitment to the rule imply a *determinate* equilibrium, so that the rule is not consistent with other, less desirable equilibria." Woodford (2003), p. 536. (Emphasis in original.)

of the Board of Governors of the Fed, they find that there was a change in policy that led to a determinate equilibrium. Although the Clarida−Gali−Gertler paper has been criticized for use of single equation methods, subsequent studies using a full information approach (Boivin and Giannoni [forthcoming] and Lubik and Schorfheide [2003], have confirmed their result.

In Beyer and Farmer (2004) we construct two examples that demonstrate the fragility of the Clarida−Gali−Gertler findings. In each of our examples the DGP is a standard New-Keynesian model in which the Fed responds to its own expectations of future inflation by raising the interest rate by more than one percent for every one percent increase in expected inflation.[6] We present two equivalent models. The first is driven by a model of private sector behavior based on a model of supply due to Benhabib and Farmer (2000); this example is explained in more depth below. In our second example we present an equivalent model in which the econometrician is assumed to know the true structure of the private sector but he is unable to determine the exact form of the policy rule followed by the Fed. Although, in the DGP, the Fed responds to its expectation of future inflation, the econometrician incorrectly identifies an equivalent model in which the Fed responds to contemporaneous inflation. Both of our examples of equivalent models have reduced forms that are indistinguishable from the DGP, but in each case the structural model is indeterminate. Whereas the DGP is driven by three fundamental shocks, the equivalent models are driven by two fundamental shocks and one, possibly correlated, nonfundamental.

To understand the mechanism behind our two examples, consider the following one-equation model. Let the DGP be given by Eq. (11). This is a determinate model driven by a fundamental shock, v_t. Suppose that the economist mistakenly estimates the following equivalent model,

$$y_t + \tilde{f} E_t[y_{t+1}] = 0. \tag{13}$$

The equivalent model has a family of solutions:

$$y_t = \tilde{\lambda}_1 y_{t-1} + w_t, \tag{14}$$

---

[6] Following Leeper (1991), rules with this property are called *active*. If a one percent increase in expected inflation leads to a less than one percent increase in the federal funds rate the rule is called *passive*. In many simple New-Keynesian models an active rule is known to be associated with a determinate equilibrium while a passive rule leads to indeterminacy. Following Taylor (1999), the proposition that monetary policy should be active is referred to as the *Taylor Principle*.

indexed by $\tilde{\lambda}_1$ and the variance of the non-fundamental shock, σ_w^2. If $|\tilde{f}| < 1$ the model has a unique reduced form given by

$$y_t = 0.$$

This is a special case of Eq. (14) for which $\tilde{\lambda}_1 = 0$, and $\sigma_w^2 = 0$. If $|\tilde{f}| > 1$, the model has a family of reduced forms in which $\tilde{\lambda}_1 = 1/\tilde{f}$, and the value of σ_w^2 is arbitrary.

An economist using the methods of Lubik and Schorfheide (2003) would conclude that the model is determinate if the data follows the degenerate process $y_t = 0$ and indeterminate if it follows an AR (1). Their conclusion follows from an identifying restriction that excludes y_{t-1} from the structural model. If one is unwilling to make an assumption of this kind it is no longer possible to distinguish determinate from indeterminate models.

A MORE CONCRETE EXAMPLE

Although the one-equation example is useful for expository purposes, perhaps it is always possible to find identifying assumptions, based on sound microeconomic principles, that make the Lubik and Schorfheide method applicable. Unfortunately, this is not the case since there will typically be uncertainty as to the exact specification of the private sector equations.

In addition to the difficulty of finding the right equations for the private sector, there is a more fundamental problem that arises from the inability to identify the parameters of the policy rule. We show in Beyer and Farmer (2004), by means of an example, that the economist cannot distinguish a determinate from an indeterminate model, even if he knows the structure of the private sector. Our conclusion rests on the assumption that the economist does not know whether the Fed responded to current, past, or expected future values of inflation. We show that these three possibilities may lead to different conclusions for the question: Was the data generated by a determinate or an indeterminate model?

The following example, drawn from Beyer and Farmer (2004), illustrates that very different structural models may have the same reduced form. We assume that the DGP is a relatively standard three-equation model and we refer to the equations as the IS curve, the Phillips curve, and the policy rule. This terminology is inherited from Keynesian models but the theoretical structure of the New Keynesian model is based on a modification of an equilibrium model with a representative agent.[7]

The IS curve is given by the structural equation:

$$y_{1t} + a_{13}y_{3t} + f_{11}E_t[y_{1t+1}] + f_{12}E_t[y_{2t+1}] = b_{11}y_{1t-1} + c_1 + v_{1t}. \quad (15)$$

In this notation y_{1t} is unemployment, y_{2t} is inflation, and y_{3t} is the interest rate. The symbols a_{ij}, f_{ij} and b_{ij} represent coefficients on variable j in equation i. We use $[a_{ij}]$ to represent coefficients on contemporaneous variables, $[f_{ij}]$ for coefficients of expected future variables, and $[b_{ij}]$ to represent coefficients of lagged variables.

The second equation of the New Keynesian model is the Phillips curve also known as the New Keynesian aggregate supply curve (AS-curve). This equation takes the form:

$$y_{2t} + a_{21}y_{1t} + f_{22}E_t[y_{2t+1}] = c_2 + v_{2t}. \quad (16)$$

To close the New Keynesian model we assume that policy is generated by a reaction function of the form

$$y_{3t} + f_{32}E_t[y_{2t+1}] = b_{33}y_{3t-1} + c_3 + v_{3t}. \quad (17)$$

The Taylor principle, widely discussed by policymakers, is the condition $|f_{32}| > 1$. In simple forms of this model (when $b_{33} = 0$ and when there is no habit formation in preferences), the Taylor principle implies that there exists a unique equilibrium. In this case policy is said to be active.

In an alternative theory of the transmission mechanism, Benhabib and Farmer (2000) have argued that prices are slow to adjust because equilibria are typically indeterminate. The Benhabib-Farmer model has the same IS curve as the New Keynesian model, but a different supply curve that takes the form

$$y_{1t} + a_{23}y_{3t} = c_2 + b_{21}y_{1t-1} + v_{2t}. \quad (18)$$

In this model, the parameter a_{23} is negative and the mechanism by which the nominal interest rate, y_{3t}, influences unemployment, y_{1t}, operates through liquidity effects in production; a lower nominal interest rate causes agents to hold more money, measured in real units. The increase in

---

[7] For a more complete explanation of our use of these terms see Beyer and Farmer (2004).

the ratio of money to output causes an expansion in economic activity because, in the Benhabib–Farmer model, money is a productive asset. In a simple version of this model, with the additional simplifications of no habit formation, no lagged adjustment of the policy rule, and a policy rule of the form

$$y_{3t} + a_{32}y_{2t} = c_3 + v_{3t}, \tag{19}$$

equilibrium is determinate if $|a_{32}| < 1$ and indeterminate if $|a_{32}| > 1$. In this version of the policy rule, the Fed responds to current inflation and not to expected future inflation.

The Benhabib-Farmer model with a contemporaneous policy rule can be shown to lead to a reduced form of the same order as the New Keynesian model with a forward looking policy rule. However, in the Benhabib-Farmer (BF) model, the Taylor principle is reversed in the sense that active policy implies indeterminacy and passive policy implies determinacy.

In Beyer and Farmer (2004) we give a numerical version of this model. We compute its reduced form and combine the reduced form parameters with a set of linear restrictions that exactly identifies an observationally equivalent Benhabib-Farmer model. In our example, the DGP is given by the equations

$$y_{1t} = 0.5E_t[y_{1t+1}] + 0.5y_{1t-1} + 0.05(y_{3t} - E_t[y_{2t+1}]) - 0.0015 + v_{1t},$$
$$y_{2t} = 0.97E_t[y_{2t+1}] - 0.5y_{1t} + 0.0256 + v_{2t}, \tag{20}$$
$$y_{3t} = 1.1E_t[y_{2t+1}] - 0.012 + 0.8y_{3t-1} + v_{3t}.$$

This structural model has a unique equilibrium represented by Eq. (21).

$$X_t = \Gamma^* X_{t-1} + C^* + \Psi_v v_t. \tag{21}$$

The equivalent Benhabib–Farmer model is parametrized as follows:

$$y_{1t} = 0.5E_t[y_{1t+1}] + 0.5y_{1t-1} + 0.05(y_{3t} - E_t[y_{2t+1}]) - 0.0015 + v_{1t},$$
$$y_{1t} = 0.2038y_{3t} + 0.859y_{1t-1} - 0.0031 + v_{2t}, \tag{22}$$
$$y_{3t} = 0.0626y_{2t} + 0.7129y_{3t-1} + 0.0018 + v_{3t}.$$

We show that this equivalent model has a reduced form with identical parameters matrices Γ^* and C^* as the DGP. However, equilibria of the BF model are indeterminate and the model may be driven by a combination of fundamental and sunspot shocks. We were able to compute a variance-covariance matrix for the fundamental and nonfundamental shocks to the BF model such that the New Keynesian determinate model and the indeterminate Benhabib-Farmer model are observationally equivalent.

A considerable amount of recent literature in New Keynesian economics has been directed towards estimating either policy rules (Clarida, Gali, and Gertler [2000]) or private sector equations (Gali and Gerter [1999], Fuhrer and Rudebusch [2003], Fuhrer [1997]). The ultimate purpose of this literature is to draw inferences that can be used to design optimal economic policy rules. The argument made in Beyer and Farmer (2003b, 2004) is that much of this literature rests on identifying assumptions that are tenuous at best and it follows that policy conclusions drawn from New-Keynesian models should be treated with caution.

POLICY CHANGE AS A NATURAL EXPERIMENT

In an insightful early comment Sargent (1971) pointed out that identification is difficult or impossible if policymakers pursue a single policy regime. In Beyer and Farmer (2002, 2003a) we pursue the idea that it might be possible to make headway on the issue of identification by exploiting information from multiple regimes.

In those papers we argue that there are frequent instances of real world events in which macroeconomic data change at a discrete instant. Often, the change can credibly be attributed to an unanticipated change in economic policy regime. Examples include the collapse of the fixed exchange rate system in the 1970s or the change in chairmanship of the Fed in 1980 when Paul Volcker instigated a set of disinflationary policies. If one is willing to make the identifying assumption that these regime changes are exogenous unpredictable events, they may be used to identify other equations of the macroeconomic system.

Consider the model represented by Eqs. (3)−(5) that we reproduce below:

$$\underset{2\times2}{\bar{A}_{11}}\,\underset{2\times1}{y_t^s} + \underset{2\times1}{\bar{A}_{12}}\,\underset{1\times1}{y_t^p} + \underset{2\times3}{\bar{F}_1}\,\underset{3\times1}{E_t[y_{t+1}]} = \underset{2\times m}{\bar{B}_1}\,\underset{m\times1}{z_{t-1}} + \underset{2\times1}{v_t^s}\,, \qquad (23)$$

$$\underset{1\times2}{\bar{A}_{21}}\,\underset{2\times1}{y_t^s} + \underset{1\times1}{y_t^p} + \underset{1\times3}{\bar{F}_2}\,\underset{3\times1}{E_t[y_{t+1}]} = \underset{1\times m}{\bar{B}_2}\,\underset{m\times1}{z_{t-1}} + \underset{1\times1}{v_t^p}\,, \qquad (24)$$

$$\underset{3\times1}{y_t} = \underset{3\times1}{E_{t-1}[y_t]} + \underset{3\times1}{w_t}\,. \qquad (25)$$

The New Keynesian and the Benhabib-Farmer models that we discussed above are both special cases of this general linear structure. For the reasons discussed earlier, this model is not identified unless one is willing to place considerably more structure on the coefficients of Eq. (23). Several recent papers do exactly this by generating this equation from a primitive structural model based on optimizing behavior by forward looking agents. Examples include Boivin and Giannoni (forthcoming), Ireland (2001b), and Lubik and Schorfheide (2003).

Although we disagree with the identification methods of earlier authors, we do find evidence of a structural break in the data around 1980. In Beyer and Farmer (2003a) we argue, in the context of U.S. monetary data, that 1979 quarter four represents a natural break point and we show that it is possible to estimate two separate stable parameter VARs; one for a period from 1970 quarter one through 1979 quarter three and the second for the period 1979 quarter four through 1999 quarter four. We assume that this break in the parameters of the VAR was caused by a change in the parameters of Eq. (24) that we attribute to a change in the chairmanship of the Fed board of governors. In contrast, we assume that the parameters of Eq. (23) remained constant across the break. Using this assumption we define new variables that are equal to zero over the first sub-period and equal to $\{y_t\}$ over the second. We use these variables as instruments to identify a subset of the parameters of Eq. (23). The following section explains which parameters are identified by this assumption and which are not.

WHICH PARAMETERS ARE IDENTIFIED?

We defined a structural model to be the union of the private sector parameters, θ^s and the policy parameters θ^p. In Beyer and Farmer (2003a) we show that if there is a break in the parameters θ^p, one can identify a subset of the parameters of θ^s that are found by defining a rotation of the structure that we refer to as the quasi-reduced form.

To define the quasi-reduced form, premultiply Eq. (23) by the matrix $\bar{A}_{11}^{-1}$ to generate the equivalent model:

$$\underset{2\times1}{y_t^s} + \underset{2\times1}{A_{12}}\,\underset{1\times1}{y_t^p} + \underset{2\times3}{F_1}\,\underset{3\times1}{E_t[y_{t+1}]} = \underset{2\times m}{B_1}\,\underset{m\times1}{z_{t-1}} + \underset{2\times1}{\tilde{v}_t^s}, \qquad (26)$$

$$\underset{1\times2}{\bar{A}_{21}}\,\underset{2\times1}{y_t^s} + \underset{1\times1}{y_t^p} + \underset{1\times3}{\bar{F}_2}\,\underset{3\times1}{E_t[y_{t+1}]} = \underset{1\times m}{\bar{B}_2}\,\underset{m\times1}{z_{t-1}} + \underset{1\times1}{v_t^p}, \qquad (27)$$

$$y_t = E_{t-1}[y_t] + w_t,$$
$$\underset{3\times1}{} \quad \underset{3\times1}{} \quad \underset{3\times1}{} \tag{28}$$

We refer to the parameters of Eq. (26) as, $\bar{\theta}^s$, where the bar denotes the parameters of the quasi-reduced form. One can show that, although the quasi-reduced form has fewer parameters than the structural model, it is a member of the equivalence class of reduced forms; that is,

$$\Gamma^*\big(\bar{\theta}^s \cup \theta^p\big) = \Gamma^*(\theta^s \cup \theta^p).$$

The quasi-reduced form, $\bar{\theta}^s$, has two important properties. First, like the true structural model $\theta^s, \bar{\theta}^s$ is invariant in the sense of Engle, Hendry, and Richard (1983) to changes in θ^p. Second, $\bar{\theta}^s$ can be identified by changes in θ^p, whereas the DGP, θ^s, cannot.

To identify θ^s, the policymaker could change the way his instrument, the interest rate, responds to lagged variables and to current realizations of unemployment and inflation. By varying θ^p in this way he can elicit information about the way that unemployment and inflation respond to changes in the contemporaneous interest rate. Notice, however, that changes of this kind can never elicit information about the way that the unemployment rate responds to inflation in the IS curve or the way that inflation responds to unemployment in the Phillips curve. The parameters that describe how unemployment and inflation respond to the interest rate are elements of $\bar{\theta}^s$, the quasi-reduced form; these parameters can be identified through changing the policy rule. The parameters that describe how unemployment and inflation react to each other in the private sector equations are elements of θ^s, the deep structure; these parameters remain unidentified through experiments that are under the control of the policymaker.

CONCLUSION

The calibration methodology that dominates much of North American macroeconomics is an advance over the macroeconomic theory that preceded it since some quantitative discipline on the set of plausible theories is better than none. But if a calibrated model is to provide a suitable guide for the design of good policies, one must be certain that one has used the correct identifying assumptions to calibrate key parameters. In our view, the methods currently used to achieve identification are arbitrary at best. Although we have made this point in the context of New-Keynesian monetary models, it applies equally to any macroeconomic model based on dynamic stochastic general equilibrium theory.

If models cannot be identified through the choice of microfoundations then how is a quantitative macroeconomist to proceed? Our suggestion is inspired by the general-to-specific methodology promoted by David Hendry.[8] Like Hendry, we are in favor of beginning with a model that is rich enough to endogenously explain the key features of the dynamics that characterize the data. Unlike Hendry, we embrace the rational expectations revolution in macroeconomics and have no difficulty with models that include expectations of future variables among the set of endogenous regressors. In our work so far, we have shown how to exploit natural experiments to identify the parameters of a structural rational expectations model. In future work, we hope to exploit our identification method to help in the design of optimal policy rules.

[8] Hendry (1995).

14

Four Entrenched Notions Post Walrasians Should Avoid

Robert L. Basmann

Any hypothesis must be tested on all points of observational fact.
Patrick Hurley[1]

It takes two to speak the truth, — one to speak, and another to hear.
Henry David Thoreau[2]

The introduction to this volume on Post Walrasian macroeconomics takes me back to my graduate student days of the early 1950s. At that time, I was pursuing two research programs and formal studies towards doctoral degrees in agricultural economics and statistics. Inspired by Samuelson (1948, Chapter V, esp. pp. 117–22) on current prices affecting the parameters of indifference maps containing money as a commodity and by Scitovsky (1945), Lange (1940), Ichimura (1951) and Tintner (1952a) on shifts of demand produced by more general sorts of cause affecting indifference maps, I found much satisfaction in challenging the widely expressed fear that acceptance of such ideas would wreak havoc with economics, Scitovsky (1945, p. 100). The papers by Haavelmo (1947) and Girshick and Haavelmo (1947) drew my research in statistics into tackling some unsolved puzzles in the budding econometric statistics of macro-economics. In particular, Haavelmo (1947), on the marginal propensity to consume, revealed the forms of the exact finite sample distributions of maximum likelihood estimators and test statistics associated with the Keynesian consumption function, Basmann (1974, pp. 214–18).

The prospect suggested in the introduction of developing an adequate agent-based macroeconometrics is of special interest to me. In the 1950s,

---

[1] "The confirmation of continental drift," *Scientific American*, April, 1968. Reprinted in *Continents Adrift*, 1972.
[2] *A Week on the Concord and Merrimack Rivers* (Wednesday).

my dissertation supervisor, Gerhard Tintner, had taken an interest in problems of aggregating individual demand functions. In a casual discussion following my dissertation defense, Tintner and Leonid Hurwicz (University of Minnesota) who was on a short visit to Iowa State at the time, asked me to consider how randomly distributed individual consumer demands could be aggregated to form market demand functions that would satisfy the definitions required by the neoclassical theory of consumer demand. I suggested the hypothesis that the individual consumer demand quantities and total personal consumptions have joint statistical distributions with the multivariate *Beta I* or *Beta II* form and then proved that conditional expectations of market demand quantities, given total expenditure, would have the properties required of neoclassical demand functions.[3] It turned out that derived conditional expectations took the form of *linear expenditure functions*, which had been studied by Klein and Rubin (1947), Frisch (1954), and Houthakker (1960).

That's as far as I got with that research. It is not to be thought that any intuition of economic reality was involved in my solution of that mathematical puzzle. Of course, it would be a fundamental mistake to suppose that econometrics is no more than a mathematical puzzle. Intuition of economic reality is central to conducting good econometrics. A central argument in this essay is that any scientifically adequate Post Walrasian macroeconometrics derived from microeconomic behavior is going to be the rewarded efforts largely of many people with deep experience-based intuitions of various aspects of economic reality.[4] Thus, participants in the enterprise can well afford time to examine how and why the chief research choices of macroeconometricians since 1950 went wrong.

ENTRENCHED NOTIONS IN MACROECONOMETRICS

The infancy, childhood, and adolescence of nearly every science has been beset at one time or other by persisting unfounded beliefs so deeply entrenched that they cannot be extirpated. Consequently, much effort has to be expended on circumventing them, or development bogs down before scientific maturity can be attained. Economists and econometricians cannot

---

[3] The *Beta II* density of individual consumer demand quantities is displayed in Basmann, Battalio, and Kagel (1976, Section 4, pp 176–717. It is also displayed in Basmann, Molina, and Slottje (1983, pp 43–45). The general form of beta distribution is simply described in Gillespie (1951, p. 94).

[4] How academic departments are going to change themselves in order to supply a sufficient cadre of such researchers for the Post Walrasian enterprise is not readily foreseeable at this time.

escape that chore. Despite the many contributions to "hard" econometrics in the 1950s and 1960s, by the 1970s many very dubious notions about identifying assumptions had become deeply entrenched in opinions expressed by macroeconometricians.

Four major entrenched interdependent notions in macroeconometrics are listed below.

1. The notion that the Cowles Commission research program requires a priori theory to achieve identification in statistical estimation of structural equation systems.
2. The notion that pure economic theories are determinative of suitable a priori identifying restrictions.
3. The notion that exclusions of variables from structural equations are the only correct form of identifying restrictions.
4. The notion that *identifiability* is more than a property of sets of parameters of structural models, that identifiability is a property of the modeled economic reality itself.

Kevin Hoover's essay in this volume alludes to the effects of those entrenched beliefs in the macroeconometric thinking of the past 50 years. Hoover argues that

the failure of the Cowles Commission program in the 1970s was less from its supposed predictive failure or the failure of its models to be invariant to policy, than from a *lack of conviction on the part of macroeconomists in the soundness of its identifying assumptions.* (Italics mine. RLB)

Hoover summarizes Sims's criticism of identifying assumptions of large-scale econometric models in his influential 1980 *Econometrica* article, "Macroeconomics and Reality."

Sims's critique was straightforward: Structural estimation in the Cowles Commission program requires *a priori* theory to secure identification ... Such identification was literally "incredible" – that is no one really believed that there were good theoretical grounds for the exclusions that were made ... Honesty, Sims argued, requires that we give up on structural estimation and do what we can without unsupported identifying assumptions. (Hoover, this volume.)

In his essay Sims promised to develop the conclusion that "the identification claimed for existing large-scale models is incredible," Sims (1980, p. 1). Sims credited T. C. Liu (1960) with presenting convincing arguments for not taking modelers' claims for identification seriously, Sims (1980, p. 1n).

THE IMPORTANCE OF COMPREHENSIVE
TESTING OF MODELS

A central argument of this essay is that most of the failures of macroeconometrics are due to the macroeconometricians' lack of seriousness concerning the comprehensive testing of their models.[5] I hope to make clear how the entrenched notions listed above encouraged that lack of seriousness. The ideas can be conveyed in reference to two well-known econometric models from the late 1940s, which helped direct econometrics on its incorrect path. One of them, L. R. Klein's **Model I**, cf. Klein (1950, Chapter III), exemplifies identifying restrictions that most econometric statisticians of the 1950s would have agreed turned out to be incredible.[6] The other model, "Statistical analysis of the demand for food," Girshick and Haavelmo (1947) exemplifies identifying restrictions that would, on the data used in its estimation and test, turn out to be quite credible retrospectively since the *p-value* for the likelihood ratio test of its hypothetical restrictions turned out to be 0.979.

Klein's **Model I** exemplifies retrospectively incredible identifying restrictions. Statistically highly significant *p-values* have been calculated for Klein's hypothetical identifiability restrictions. Those *p-values* have ranged in statistical significance from large 0.000090 (Berndt, 1990, p. 554), to small of the order 10^{-16}. Basmann and Hwang (1990, p. 139) computed the FIML (full information maximum *likelihood*) ratio test for the overidentifying restrictions of **Model I**, which yielded a test criterion of 206.98 and *p-value* less than 10^{-16}. For LIML (limited information maximum likelihood) the likelihood ratio criterion was 94.85, yielding a *p-value* of $1.85(10^{-15})$.

Klein's **Model I** is not a large-scale model. Other 1950s econometric models might equally well exemplify what constitutes extremely poor agreement with data. However, such models were dedicated to expository purposes and — justifiably — focused on only one or two aspects of scientific modeling in economics. **Model I** is the only small one whose creator specifically proffered it as *asseverative*. That, and its description in several popular textbooks, constitute the sole reason for presenting it here. According to Klein, estimation of **Model I** tested, in some sense, the *Marxian* theory of effective demand. It was, he asserted

---

[5] Testing includes but, of course, is not limited to the statistical testing of identifying restrictions.

[6] My personal preference would be to say that the hypothetical restrictions were exceptionally lacking in respect of agreement with observation.

... more than a mere demonstration of various statistical methodologies. The calculations made for this model serve as a test of certain economic hypotheses. If the data were to refute this model, we should have grounds for questioning the validity of the Marxian theory of effective demand.[7]

Klein went on to assert that the test failed to refute that theory:

Since the data do not refute this model ... we can have more faith in it ... than would be the case if we made no tests at all." Klein (1950, p. 64).[8]

As far as I could tell in 1953, few, if any, of Klein's Cowles Commission colleagues would have agreed that the outcome of his test warranted the claim of increased plausibility of the Marxian theory of effective demand.[9] Klein, perhaps, was unaware then of the extremely poor agreement of **Model I** with observation. If that was so, it had to be because he did not avail himself of the likelihood ratio tests, which others made use of then and subsequently.

Cowles Commission authors Anderson (1950), Anderson and Rubin (1949a, 1949b), Koopmans (1949), Koopmans and Reiersøl (1950), Tintner (1952b, Chapter 7), Koopmans and Hood (1953) stressed the importance of performing and reporting of identifiability tests. Koopmans and Hood (1953, pp. 184–5) also stressed the practical importance of performing those tests as preliminary to computation of coefficient estimates.[10] Koopmans and Hood wrote:

It is natural to use the test of the set of restrictions on a given equation before proceeding to estimate its coefficients, which is a subsequent step in computational procedure. It is likewise natural to abandon without further computation a set of restrictions strongly rejected by the test. (Koopmans and Hood, 1953, p. 184.)

The turning point in the Cowles Commission program occurred with the abandonment of identifiability testing by L. R. Klein's *Economic*

---

[7] By "validity" he seems to mean "empirical truth."

[8] In Bodkin, Klein, and Marwah (1991), *A History of Macroeconometric Model-building*, no mention is made of criticisms of **Model I** that were made on the ground of its exceptionally poor agreement with observational data.

[9] In 1955–6, while at the University of Oslo, I "polled" Trygve Haavelmo, Ragnar Frisch, Herman Wold, Eraldo Fossati, and several other econometricians on this matter.

[10] In the 1950s, working through the Koopmans–Hood presentation of the limited information maximum likelihood estimators (LIML), it was impossible to miss the fact that the identifiability test statistic had to be determined before parameter estimates could be computed.

Fluctuations in the United States, 1921—1941 (1950).[11] In my opinion, the original Cowles Commission scientific program was never seriously pursued by many macroeconometricians after that time. Instead, in the late 1950s, failure to report *p-values* of tests of identifying restrictions (assuming that the tests were performed) began to dominate mainstream macroeconometric practice, especially in the presentation of large-scale econometric structural models.

The omission of testing macroeconometric models did not go unnoticed in the early days, however. Klein's 1950 monograph was soon followed by statistical tests of the identifying restrictions that were embedded in his **Model III**. The first of such tests were performed by Cowles Commission research consultants, Andrew Marshall and Carl Christ; cf. Christ (1951, p. 35, pp. 55—9). As in the case of **Model I**, outcomes of Carl Christ's tests of **Model III** uncovered very serious disagreement of that model with the data batch Klein employed. Table 4 in Christ (1951, p. 82) displays outcomes of ten identifiability tests (LIML) that he performed on structural equations of **Model III**. For only two structural equations (investment and rental housing) the outcomes are moderately favorable.[12] Thus, with two exceptions, the observed significance levels are clear signals that the underlying economic theory and assumptions of **Model III** are illusory and in serious need of rethinking before using the model for any asseverative purpose.

Puzzled by such failures a few econometric statisticians speculated concerning the rationale Klein and other macroeconometricians would have proffered for neglecting tests of identifying restrictions. Some relevant empirical research by Orcutt and Irwin (1948), Gartaganis (1954), Ames and Reiter (1961) foreshadowed a serious practical difficulty testing identifiability constraints that builders of large-scale econometric models would find especially daunting. It was plausible that large-scale models

---

[11] The current perception that the Cowles Commission program required a priori theory to secure identification is of slightly later origin. The current perception took hold probably because Klein's book was published as Cowles Commission Monograph No. 11. It is probable that many economists inferred that to be a sort of *imprimatur* of the Cowles Commission itself. Today the perception of the original program has become too deeply entrenched in academic conversation to be successfully uprooted.

[12] A computational mistake caused the *p-values* in Table 4 to seem much less unfavorable to **Model III** than their correct values. Since 2000 the *p-values* have been corrected in a recent reprinting of Carl Christ's monograph (Personal communication, C. F. Christ to author Jan. 1999). My own corrected *p-values* in 1999 were: Investment equation, 0.066. Inventory equation, 0.0178. Production equation, 0.00025. Private wages and salaries equation, 0.000015. Employment equation, 0.000041. Wage rate, 0.00021. Consumption, 0.0017. Owned housing, 0.000000000048. Rent, 0.000188. Rental housing, 0.20.

would often fail to pass the *rank condition* tests of identifying restrictions, especially in the case of large-scale models in which model-builders specify lagged endogenous variables as predetermined.[13] A large proportion of statistically insignificant estimates of the reduced-form coefficients signals the likelihood of encountering that difficulty.

The failure of **Model I** to pass the necessary and sufficient conditions for identifiability was foreshadowed by the failure of most of the *unrestricted reduced-form coefficient estimates* to be statistically significant. Table 10.4 in Berndt (1990, p. 555) displays those estimates together with their estimated asymptotic standard errors. Approximate *p-values* calculated for the ratios of coefficient estimates to their own standard errors are shown in Table 14.14.1.

Table 14.1. *Klein's model I* p-values *for unrestricted reduced-form coefficients*

Variable	pval_C	pval_I	pval_W
Constant	**0.03969**	0.178600	0.111200
P_{-1}	0.16046	**0.041500**	0.567400
K_{-1}	0.22650	0.061570	0.221100
E_{-1}	0.41490	0.621400	0.681200
T	0.36915	0.598200	0.274368
TX	0.39808	0.645080	0.106700
G	0.59754	0.750820	**0.016348**
W_2	0.93841	0.726006	0.830870

Variables: P, profits; W_1, wages earned in the private sector; W_2, wages earned in public sector; $W = W_1 + W_2$; I, investment, including net change of inventories; capital, K, where $K = I + K - 1$; TX, indirect business taxes; $Y = P + W$; private product E, where $E = Y + TX - W_2$, total product Y+TX. G, government demand.
Sources: Calculated from coefficient estimates by Goldberger (1964, p. 325) and standard errors by Berndt (1990, p. 555). *p-values* were calculated by the present author. *p-value* is the probability that the absolute value of *Student's t*, with *d.f.* = 13, exceeds the absolute value of the ratio of coefficient estimate to its standard error, on the null hypothesis that the true coefficient is zero.

Statistically significant *p-values* are shown in **boldface**. For purposes of this illustration let us assume that the economist has specified, for his purposes, that *p-values* greater than 0.05 are statistically nonsignificant.

It is important to recognize that a statistically nonsignifcant *p-value* does not deductively imply that the "true" value of the coefficient is actually zero

---

[13] For brief descriptions of the *rank condition* tests of identifying restrictions see Tintner (1952b, pp. 159–61, p. 184), Hood and Koopmans (1953, pp. 183–4).

or negligible. Nor is statistical nonsignificance dispositive of the matter of the coefficient's substantive nonsignificance. Nonetheless, on the evidence displayed in Table 14.1, it is reasonable to expect that real elements that are described by one or more of the specified predetermined variables have no significant substantive effect on those described by the endogenous variables represented in **Model I**.

Before proceeding on the initial identifying hypotheses to estimate the structural equations or discarding them, it is wise to apply methods of *step-wise regression* to the reduced-form equations and examine the result. This has not often been done in macroeconometric studies.[14] Here are results for **Model I**.

$$C = 21.31 + 1.22P_{-1} + 2.48W_2 + v_C; \qquad s_C = 2.01, R^2 = 0.923.$$
$$\quad (0.000) \ (0.000) \quad (0.000) \qquad\qquad A^2 = 0.118, pval = 0.390 (1a - c).$$
$$I = 24.91 + 0.745P_{-1} - 0.179K_{-1} + v_I; \qquad s_I = 1.53, R^2 = 0.833.$$
$$\quad (0.000) \ (0.000) \quad\ (0.000) \qquad\qquad A^2 = 0.488, \ pval = 0.200.$$
$$W_1 = 10.01 + 1.073P_{-1} - 1.935W_2 + 0.894G - 0.716TX + v_{w1};$$
$$\quad (0.000) \ (0.000) \quad\ (0.001) \quad\ (0.004) \quad\ (0.041)$$
$$s_{W1} = 1.69, R^2 = 0.943; \qquad\qquad A^2 = 0.436, \ pval = 0.129.$$

s_C, s_I, and s_W denote the standard errors of regression. The A^2 is Anderson-Darling test for normality. (The number in parentheses below a coefficient estimate is the *p-value* for a two-tailed test of the null hypotheses that the "true" coefficient is zero.) The likelihood ratio test statistic for the system (1a–c) against the unconstrained reduced-form is 16.9; the *p-value* is 0.203, calculated by 2 times $\Pr\{\chi^2_{13} \geq 16.9\}$. This outcome does not seriously disfavor the stepwise regression system in relation to the unrestricted regression system.

Notice that two predetermined variables do not appear in any of the stepwise regression Eqs. (1a–c), namely, the description of trend, T, and E, where E is defined by the identity $E =_{def} Y + TX - W_2$ (income plus taxes-government wage bill). E is a descriptive measure of private product.

---

[14] By MINITAB Release 10xtra. Stepwise regression is done more easily today by such programs than it was in the desktop machines available when Klein made the original computations of **Model I**. However, if a confirmation of the Marxian theory of effective demand was to be made, the ethos of the scientific profession obligated him to perform the task howsoever tedious it would be.

Klein (1950, p. 62) introduced the linear trend, T, as a description of the gradually increasing strength of unionization. The *p-values* in Table 14.1 and the failure of the trend to appear in the stepwise results (1a–c) raises a *substantive* issue concerning whether the linear trend is an adequate measure of the increasing strength of unionization. However, the failure of the variable T to be statistically significant does not deductively imply that increasing unionization is not a cause of the increase of labor's income.

Simultaneous equations systems with G endogenous variables, and L lagged endogenous variables and K exogenous variables are logically equivalent to a system of G ordinary difference equations of order n, where $n = G\chi L$.

$$y_{t+n,i} - a_1 y_{t+n-1,i} + a_2 y_{t+n-2,i} + \cdots + (-1)^n a_n y_{t,i} =$$
$$\sum_{h=1}^{G} \sum_{k=1}^{K} \sum_{j=1}^{n} C_{ikj} X_{t+n-j,h} + \sum_{h=1}^{G} \sum_{m=1}^{n} d_{ihm} \eta_{t+n-m,h} \tag{2}$$

The right-hand terms are, respectively, the elements of the systematic and stochastic parts of the *dynamical stochastic general equilibrium* path. Parameters $a_1, a_2, \ldots, a_n$, and the parameters on the nonhomogenous right-hand terms, are functions of, and only of, the parameters of the reduced-form system. Notice that statistically significant approximate unit roots of the characteristic equation

$$z^n - a_1 z^{n-1} + \cdots + (-1)^n a_n = 0 \tag{3}$$

signal the plausibility of inadequate specification of exogenous variables.

The relevance of the time-series studies of Ames and Reiter (1961) can now be appreciated. Ames and Reiter fit ordinary difference equations to 100 time-series randomly selected from the *Statistical Abstract of the United States*. They found that difference equations of low order *almost always* fit the time-series closely. If an ordinary difference equation of low order, e.g. m, fits the endogenous variables closely, then that fact foreshadows that $G\chi L$-m of the coefficients in the differences in Eq. (2) are approximately zero in magnitude. For instance, in a macroeconometric model with 50 equations and with each endogenous variable lagged only one period, Eq. (2) would be of order $G\chi L = 50$. Since the coefficients of the ordinary difference equation are functions of the structural coefficients, the result is that a large number of troublesome, algebraically complex restrictions are automatically imposed on the estimates of the reduced-form coefficients, or structural coefficients in the identifying restrictions.

CONCLUSION

The four entrenched notions listed near the beginning of this essay are all involved in one fashion or another in the matter of the nitty-gritty of incredible identifying restrictions. The entrenched notions that identifying restrictions must be exclusions only (No. 3) or that the property of identifiability is a property of economic reality itself (No. 4) usually occur when the asserter, for some reason, is not careful. The assertions occur at seminars and in print, cf. Klein (1960, p. 870) and Christ (1960, p. 843) where both assert that the design equations of Monte Carlo experiments are underidentified, cf. Basmann (1962).

The notion that the initial Cowles Commission research program required a priori identifiability (1) and the notion that economic theories supply sufficient independent and consistent restrictions to achieve identifiability (2) are still commonly held. They are wrong, and early Cowles researchers knew they were wrong as is evidenced by the Koopmans–Hood counsel quoted at the start of the essay. That counsel is not the counsel of researchers who thought identifying restrictions to be a priori in the technical sense — to have the character of, for example, the *Principle of Noncontradiction* or the *Axioms of Choice* and *Regularity*. In short, good econometric practice requires that identifying restrictions have to be tested for probable poor agreement with observation, and it is good to see that Post Walrasian macro is making that a central element of its econometric practice.

15

Confronting the Economic Model with the Data

Søren Johansen[*]

INTRODUCTION

Econometrics is about confronting economic models with the data. In doing so it is crucial to choose a statistical model that not only contains the economic model as a submodel, but also contains the data generating process. When this is the case, the statistical model can be analyzed by likelihood methods. When this is not the case, but likelihood methods are applied nonetheless, the result is incorrect inference. In this chapter, we illustrate the problem of possible incorrect inference with a recent application of a DSGE model to U.S. data (Ireland, 2004). Specifically, this chapter discusses two broad methodological questions.

- How should a statistical model be chosen to achieve valid inference for the economic model?
- Given a correctly chosen statistical model, can we rely on the asymptotic results found in the statistical literature for the analysis of the data at hand?

Using some simple examples, the chapter first discusses some unfortunate consequences of applying Gaussian maximum likelihood when the chosen statistical model does not properly describe the data. It also demonstrates that even when the correct statistical model is chosen, asymptotic results derived for stationary processes cannot be used to conduct inference on the steady state value for a highly persistent stationary process.

* I would like to thank David Colander, Massimo Franchi, Christian Groth, Henrik Hansen, Kevin Hoover, Katarina Juselius, Mikael Juselius and the members of the EFS-EMM network as well as the audiences in Rome and Helsinki for useful comments.

When taking an economic model to the data in order to conduct inference "we need a stochastic formulation to make simplified relations elastic enough for applications," to quote Haavelmo (1943). Thus, the relations derived from theory need to be supplemented by some extra error terms to describe the stochastic variation of the measurements. We thereby embed the economic model in a statistical model. But the statistical model must also be chosen so that it describes the variation of the data, that is, it has to contain the density of the data generating process. In this case the empirical model provides a platform for conducting valid inference on the relevant parameters of the economic model, see Kapetanios, Pagan, and Scott, (2004) or Altuğ (1989) among many others.

The papers by Söderlind (1999) and Ireland (2001a, 2004) suggest a particular method for taking a DSGE model to the data. The method is discussed in the next section, but can briefly be described as follows: the DSGE model delivers relations and first order conditions involving forward looking expectations, and the relations are linearized around their steady state values. This gives identities and stochastic difference equations driven by the technology shocks of the theoretical model. The identities are then made "more elastic" by adding an autocorrelated error term, thereby extending the economic model to a statistical model. The statistical model is formulated as a state space model and analyzed by Gaussian maximum likelihood methods using the Kalman filter to calculate the likelihood function. The method is then applied to U.S. data.

Most economists would find this approach appealing as it suggests a straightforward way of conducting inference on precisely defined economic relations and their coefficients. But, for this inference to be valid, and therefore reliable, one has to demonstrate that the statistical model adequately describes the stochastic variation of the data. The paper to be discussed did not demonstrate this, and therefore possibly provides misleading and irrelevant results.

EXTENDING THE DSGE MODEL TO A STATE SPACE MODEL

Let me begin by discussing some details of the method proposed and the findings by Ireland (2001a, 2004). He begins with a DSGE model that has a representative agent producing output Y_t with capital K_t and labor H_t, measured as hours worked, according to

$$Y_t = A_t K_t^{\theta} (\eta^t H_t)^{1-\theta}.$$

The coefficient $\eta > 1$ measures the "gross rate of labor-augmenting technological progress." The agent has preferences over consumption C_t and hours worked H_t and wants to maximize

$$E\left[\sum_{t=0}^{\infty} \beta^t(\ln C_t - \gamma H_t)\right],$$

with respect to $\{C_t, H_t\}_{t=0}^{\infty}$ subject to a number of constraints. The technology shocks A_t follow a stationary AR(1) process

$$\ln(A_t) = (1 - \rho)\ln A + \rho \ln(A_{t-1}) + \varepsilon_t, \quad |\rho| < 1.$$

The variables Y_t, K_t, C_t and investment I_t obey the identities

$$Y_t = C_t + I_t$$

and

$$K_{t+1} = (1 - \delta)K_t + I_t.$$

The first order conditions become

$$\gamma C_t H_t = (1 - \theta)Y_t,$$

and

$$1 = \beta E_t\left[\frac{C_t}{C_{t+1}}\left(\frac{\theta Y_{t+1}}{K_{t+1}} + 1 - \delta\right)\right].$$

The assumption of trend stationarity of the variables is added in order to linearize the solution of these equations around their steady state values. We define the means or steady states y, c, i, k, a, h of the variables Y_t/η^t, C_t/η^t, I_t/η^t, K_t/η^t, A_t, H_t respectively. For the observations Y_t, C_t, and H_t, expressed as deviations of their logarithm from their trend, the three variables

$$f_t = \begin{pmatrix} \log Y_t - t \log \eta - \log y \\ \log C_t - t \log \eta - \log c \\ \log H_t - \log h \end{pmatrix},$$

are introduced.

The two variables A_t and K_t are considered unobserved and define

$$s_t = \begin{pmatrix} \log K_t - t \log \eta - \log k \\ \log A_t - \log a \end{pmatrix}.$$

A linearization of the model equations around the steady state of the variables gives equations of the form

$$s_t = \mathscr{A} s_{t-1} + \mathscr{B} \varepsilon_t,$$
$$f_t = \mathscr{C} s_t.$$

Here the matrices $\mathscr{A}$, $\mathscr{B}$, and $\mathscr{C}$ and the steady state values are computable functions of the parameters of the model: $\beta, \gamma, \theta, \eta, \delta, \gamma, A, \rho, \sigma$.

Because $\mathscr{C}$ is 3×2 and $f_t = \mathscr{C} s_t$ there must be a vector ξ so that $\xi' \mathscr{C} = 0$, and hence $\xi' f_t = 0$. No such identity holds in the data, so the method suggested for taking the model to the data is to enlarge the system by an autoregressive noise term u_t:

$$s_t = \mathscr{A} s_{t-1} + \mathscr{B} \varepsilon_t,$$
$$f_t = \mathscr{C} s_t + u_t,$$
$$u_t = \mathscr{D} u_{t-1} + \xi_t,$$

where u_t is an unobserved AR(1) process with innovations ξ_t which are iid and distributed as $N_3(0, V)$. Thus the statistical model for the five variables, Y_t, K_t, C_t, H_t, and A_t are driven by four errors, $\varepsilon_t, \xi_{1t}, \xi_{2t}$, and ξ_{3t}. It is also assumed that ε_t is i.i.d. $N(0, \sigma^2)$, and independent of ξ_t. A model of this form can be written as a state space model and Gaussian inference can be conducted using the Kalman filter.

He then fits the model to U.S. data, see www2.bc.edu/~irelandp. The economic model is supplemented with the assumption that $\beta = 0.99$ and $\delta = 0.025$, as these coefficients were difficult to determine from the data. The main finding is that the model seems to predict well out of sample as compared to some competitors, a VAR(1) and a VAR(2) model and a model with diagonal D.

His finding, however, is based upon the assumption that the model is correctly identified. As a check for model misspecification, he finds that by comparing the estimated values of ε_t and ξ_t, the estimated correlations were rather small (-0.0634, 0.0133, 0.0010), so the assumption of independence seems reasonable. He also finds, using Wald tests, that the parameters of the economic model before and after 1980 have hardly been the same for the whole period. The estimated values of ρ (0.9987) and the largest eigenvalue of D (0.9399) are very close to one. These findings mean that the stationarity assumption is hard to justify. The data has also been investigated by Meeks (2005, personal communication) who showed by recursive estimation, that the assumption of constant parameters is indeed not possible to maintain.

Nevertheless, the conclusions of the paper are stated as if the model describes the data.

MODEL BUILDING AND THE ROLE OF MAXIMUM LIKELIHOOD

In order to discuss in more detail what are the consequences of not choosing a model that describes the data, we consider in this section a very simple example, where the (simulated) data is analysed by two different Gaussian maximum likelihood methods, but first we formulate two assumptions that need to be satisfied by the statistical model before we can apply the likelihood methodology.

The starting point for building a statistical model is that we have an economic model given by economic relations, which may include stochastic error terms. We call this the substantive model. We also have data $(x_1, \ldots, x_T)$, which we assume are measurements of the economic variables. Let the (unknown) data density be denoted by $f(x_1, \ldots, x_T)$. We choose a statistical model as a class of densities

$$p(x_1, \ldots, x_T, \theta), \quad \theta \in \Theta,$$

where Θ is the parameter space. We then need to make two important assumptions:

The substantive assumption: *The statistical model embeds the substantive model, that is, the economic relations are given by some parameter restrictions.*

The likelihood assumption: *We assume that the density $f(x_1, \ldots, x_T)$ of the data is a member of the statistical family to which we apply the methodology. This means that there is some parameter value θ_0, the true value, for which the density $p(x_1, \ldots, x_T, \theta_0)$ is the same as the density of the data:*

$$p(x_1, \ldots, x_T, \theta_0) = f(x_1, \ldots, x_T).$$

The first assumption is naturally satisfied if the statistical model is constructed as an extension of the economic model. It is the second assumption that will be discussed here. The likelihood function $L(\theta) = p(x_1, \cdots, x_T, \theta_0)$ is the density considered as a function of θ, and a submodel is defined by a subset $\Theta_0 \subset \Theta$. Thus, under the substantive assumption, the economic model is given as a submodel of the statistical model.

The method of maximum likelihood provides, under certain stationarity and regularity conditions, the following useful statistical results:

- The maximum likelihood estimator $\hat{\theta}$ is calculated by optimizing the likelihood function $L(\theta)$ over the parameter set Θ, and the estimator is consistent and asymptotically Gaussian.
- The observed information, $I(\hat{\theta}) = -d^2 \log L(\theta)/d^2\theta|_{\theta=\hat{\theta}}$, provides an estimate of the asymptotic variance of $\hat{\theta}$, given by $I(\hat{\theta})^{-1}$.
- The maximum likelihood estimator of $\theta \in \Theta_0$ is $\check{\theta}$, and the likelihood ratio test of $\theta \in \Theta_0$:

$$-2 \log \mathrm{LR}(\Theta_0|\Theta) = -2 \log(L(\check{\theta})/L(\hat{\theta}))$$

is asymptotically distributed as χ^2, when $\theta \in \Theta_0$.

Thus, once we can apply this methodology, we have general theorems from statistics and probability, which ensure that we have answers to a number of relevant questions in inference about the substantive model, without having to do more than finding a program to optimize the likelihood function and print out $\hat{\theta}, I(\hat{\theta})^{-1}$ and $L(\hat{\theta})$, for the various hypotheses we want to test.

This looks like a free lunch, but of course, the method has a price. To derive useful results from our statistical model, we have to choose a reasonable model on which to base our likelihood analysis, and it is in the art of model building that the cost involved in likelihood based inference is found.

In order to illustrate the implications of the likelihood assumption, we consider a very simple situation, where we have given some (simulated) data and have to choose between just two different statistical models from which to derive our inferences. One model satisfies the likelihood assumption and the other does not.

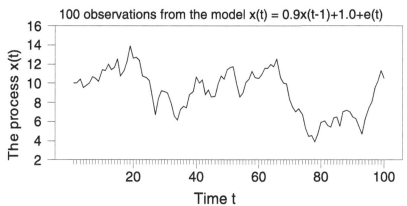

Figure 15.1. A simulation of 100 observations from the univariate AR(1) process (1).

A simple example of the role of the likelihood assumption
Consider data generated as a univariate time series by the equations:

$$x_t = 0.9x_{t-1} + 1.0 + \varepsilon_t, t = 1, \ldots, 100, \ x_0 = 10, \tag{1}$$

where ε_t are i.i.d. $N(0,1)$. Note that $E(x_t) = 1/(1 - 0.9) = 10$, and $\text{Var}(x_t) = 1/(1 - 0.9^2) = 5.263$. A sample of the data is shown in Figure 15.15.1.

Consider two different statistical models for conducting inference in the form of asymptotic confidence intervals on the mean of the process x_t. Both models give rise to a Gaussian likelihood, but inference based upon the two models is very different.

Model 1: We first model the data as

$$x_t = \mu + \varepsilon_t, \tag{2}$$

with ε_t iid $N(0, \sigma^2)$, so that $E(x_t) = \mu$. Let P_{μ,σ^2} be the probability measure for $(x_1, \ldots, x_T)$ determined by Eq. (2). We want to make inference on μ and find that the maximum likelihood estimator is the average $\hat{\mu}_1 = \bar{x} = T^{-1} \sum_{t=1}^{T} x_t = 9.138$, which is distributed as $N(\mu, \sigma^2/T)$, and $\hat{\sigma}_1^2 = T^{-1} \sum_{t=1}^{T} (x_t - \bar{x})^2 = 5.256$, so that $\text{Var}(\hat{\mu}_1) = T^{-1}\sigma^2$ is estimated by 0.0526. An asymptotic 95% confidence interval is given by

$$\hat{\mu}_1 \pm \frac{1.96}{\sqrt{T}} \hat{\sigma}_1 = 9.138 \pm 0.449,$$

so that, if x_t were generated by Eq. (2), then

$$P_{\mu,\sigma^2}\left\{\hat{\mu}_1 - \frac{1.96}{\sqrt{T}}\hat{\sigma}_1 < \mu < \hat{\mu}_1 + \frac{1.96}{\sqrt{T}}\hat{\sigma}_1\right\} \to 95\%. \qquad (3)$$

Model 2: We could also model the data as a stationary time series

$$x_t = \rho x_{t-1} + \mu(1 - \rho) + \varepsilon_t, \qquad (4)$$

where again with ε_t i.i.d. $N(0, \sigma^2)$ and $E(x_t) = \mu$, if $|\rho| < 1$. We let P_{μ,ρ,σ^2} denote the probability measure for the observations determined by Eq. (4). We find the estimates $\hat{\rho} = 0.923$ and

$$\hat{\mu}_2 = \bar{x} - \hat{\rho}T^{-1}(x_0 - x_T)/(1 - \hat{\rho}) = 9.123,$$

and $\hat{\sigma}_2^2 = T^{-1}\sum_{t=1}^{T}(x_t - \hat{\rho}x_{t-1} - \hat{\mu}_2(1 - \hat{\rho}))^2 = 0.774$. For $|\rho| < 1$, $\hat{\mu}_2$ has the same asymptotic distribution as the average $\bar{x}$, but now $\text{Var}(\hat{\mu}_2) \approx \sigma^2 T^{-1}(1 - \rho)^{-2}$, which is estimated as 1.314, so that we get a much wider asymptotic 95% confidence set for μ:

$$\hat{\mu}_2 \pm \frac{1.96}{\sqrt{T}}\frac{\hat{\sigma}_2}{1 - \hat{\rho}} = 9.123 \pm 2.247,$$

so that if x_t were generated by Eq. (4), then

$$P_{\mu,\rho,\sigma^2}\left\{\hat{\mu}_2 - \frac{1.96}{\sqrt{T}}\frac{\hat{\sigma}_2}{1 - \hat{\rho}} < \mu < \hat{\mu}_2 + \frac{1.96}{\sqrt{T}}\frac{\hat{\sigma}_2}{1 - \hat{\rho}}\right\} \to 95\%. \qquad (5)$$

In order to conduct Gaussian likelihood inference we have to choose between these two models, and in practice of course many more. If we choose the first model, we get a confidence interval which is smaller than if we choose the second model. Thus inference is different depending on the model we choose, even though in both cases we are interested in the same quantity, namely the mean of the process, and in both cases we base our inference on the Gaussian likelihood.

These simple examples demonstrate that using maximum likelihood does not in itself guarantee useful inference, as different methods can be derived this way depending on the model chosen. So one has to ask the question of which method leads to valid inference when applied to the data at hand.

Obviously the density of the data in Figure 15.15.1 corresponds to the parameter values $\rho = 0.9$, $\mu = 10$, $\sigma = 1$ in the AR(1) model, and hence the likelihood assumption is satisfied for Model 2, but there are no parameters (μ, σ^2) from the first model that correspond to the data density. Thus applying Model 2, we can use all the results of maximum likelihood, but with Model 1 we get a serious underestimate of the variance of the estimator (0.0526 instead of 1.314). Thus we cannot rely on the standard error of the estimate or the confidence interval when applying Model 1 to the data in Figure 15.1. In the process of checking the likelihood assumption above we are able to show that the model chosen for the first likelihood analysis does not satisfy the assumption that for some values of the parameters the model captures the density generating the data. More precisely, the residuals $\hat{\varepsilon}_t = x_t - \bar{x}$ based upon Model 1 will show autocorrelation, so that likelihood inference derived from Model 1, which assumes no autocorrelation, is useless for this particular data. In fact we find an estimate of the correlation between $\hat{\varepsilon}_t$ and $\hat{\varepsilon}_{t-1}$ to be 0.923, which is clearly different from zero, which is the value assumed by the first model. Thus we are warned by the misspecification test that the mathematical results of the likelihood based methods for Model 1 are not valid.

Note that the probability statement (3) involves a probability measure P_{μ, σ^2} which is irrelevant in view of the way the data is generated from (1) using $P_{10, 0.9, 1}$.

Thus, there is nothing wrong with either of the two models analyzed, they are both standard models. The problem is that, only the second model describes the data, the first does not. Hence, for the data at hand, application of the asymptotic results of maximum likelihood of the second method is valid and application of the asymptotic results for the first is not, even though both are simple applications of Gaussian maximum likelihood. Thus, unfortunately, it is the wider confidence interval 9.123 ± 2.247 which is the correct one for the simulated data.

Which Statistical Model to Choose?

In practice, there is obviously a serious problem with the method of maximum likelihood, because we can of course never know with certainty if we have the right model, and the likelihood assumption is difficult, not to say impossible, to check completely. But we can sometimes show that *it is not satisfied*, and this is a very useful piece of information, because it implies that *we cannot use the model considered for conducting inference*.

What we have to do in this case is of course to find a new and better statistical model by specifying a different and more flexible family of densities, which has a better chance of capturing the density of the data, while still embedding the economic model. Only then can we conduct valid inference on the parameters of the economic model. More constructively we should ask the question

• Which statistical model describes the data adequately?

If we want to analyse an economic model, it looks like a waste of time to spend too much effort on the above question, which is clearly a statistical question. But that depends on the purpose of the analysis.

If the idea is to test hypotheses on the parameters of the economic model and test the model itself, then we need to establish a sound statistical basis for doing so, that is, we need to embed the economic model in a statistical model that describes the data. This is then used as a platform for making inference on coefficients and relations.

In case we find that the statistical model does not allow for the restrictions on the parameter space as defined by the economic model, the explanation can be that the economic model is inadequate, or of course, that the data quality is not good enough. Whatever the case, the statistical model cannot be used for inference about the economic model, and we either have to rethink and extend the economic model, or check the quality and relevance of the data.

If the purpose of the analysis, however, is not to make inference on coefficients or model equations, but to apply an economic model that we believe firmly in with the purpose of making predictions, say, then perhaps it is enough to pick some likelihood method to get some estimates. But then, consistency of the estimators is not guaranteed, and standard errors derived from the likelihood theory, let alone t-statistics, should not be reported.

If we are in the first situation, that we want to make inference about our economic model from the data, there is no way we can avoid checking the many assumptions behind the likelihood methods. Thus, after we have suggested a statistical model that embeds the economic model, we should always ask the question

• How can we prove that this statistical model is incorrect?

For example, are the residuals uncorrelated? If they are not, then t-tests, χ^2-tests, and F-tests would no longer be valid. Are the parameters constant over the sample? If they are not, we cannot define the economic parameters and conduct inference on them.

Only after having confronted the statistical model with all possible misspecification tests and not having been able to reject the underlying assumptions, is it possible to be more confident in applying the general theory of likelihood. Of course, we still run the risk that someone else will analyze the data, and show that the model we have chosen is incorrect, and hence that the conclusions we have reached might need to be modified.

In the above illustration of the U.S. data by means of the DSGE model, which assumes constant parameters, it is impossible to give a meaning to a confidence interval based upon full sample estimates, when misspecification tests show that the data generating process does not have constant parameters.

In the next section, we assume that we have chosen the correct model and discuss the consequences of accepting that a very large (but less than one) root is indeed a stationary root. We conduct a simple simulation experiment and show that asymptotic inference can be seriously misleading, because the number of observations needed to make inference is excessively large.

HOW RELIABLE ARE ASYMPTOTIC RESULTS WITH A NEAR UNIT ROOT?

In this section we analyse, by simulation, the problem of making inference on the mean μ in the autoregressive process (4), when $|\rho| < 1$. We know that standard asymptotic inference applies as long as $|\rho| < 1$, but it is to be expected that with ρ close to one, the asymptotic results offer poor approximations to the finite sample distribution, which is needed for making reliable inference.

Simulations

The equations determining the univariate process x_t are

$$x_t = \rho x_{t-1} + (1 - \rho)\mu + \varepsilon_t, t = 1, \ldots, T \qquad (6)$$

where ε_t are iid $N(0, \sigma^2)$. Under the assumption of stationarity, the asymptotic distribution of the maximum likelihood estimator $\hat{\mu}$ is given by

$$T^{1/2}(\hat{\mu} - \mu) \xrightarrow{w} N\left(0, \frac{\sigma^2}{(1 - \rho)^2}\right).$$

The problem we want to discuss is how inference can be distorted when ρ is close to one. We see that, as the root ρ approaches one, the variance blows up and there is little information about the mean of the process. Not only does the variance blow up, the finite sample distribution deviates seriously from the asymptotic Gaussian distribution, so that inference of the type

$$\hat{\mu} \pm \frac{1.96}{\sqrt{T}} \frac{\hat{\sigma}}{1 - \hat{\rho}},$$

becomes highly misleading and tests on μ become unreliable. In order to illustrate this, we choose as simulation experiment the equation

$$x_t = \rho x_{t-1} + \varepsilon_t, \tag{7}$$

that is, we choose $\rho = 0.5$, 0.9, 0.99, and 0.999, take $\sigma^2 = 1$, and choose $\mu = 0$. We do 10,000 simulations for $T = 50$, 100, and 500. As a statistical method we choose Gaussian maximum likelihood inference based on model (6), which in this case happens to be the correct one because the likelihood assumption is satisfied for the statistical model chosen.

We simulate the distribution of the estimator of $\hat{\mu}(1 - \rho)\sqrt{T}$, which has been normalized to have asymptotic variance one. Figure 15.2 shows some histograms for different values of ρ, compared with the Gaussian distribution ($\rho = 0$), based upon 5,000 simulations of a time series with $T = 50$. Note that for $\rho = 0.5$ and $\rho = 0.9$, the asymptotic distribution describes the finite sample distribution quite well, but for larger ρ, the asymptotic distribution is far from the finite sample distribution, and inference, assuming it is Gaussian, is highly misleading.

In Table 15.1, we calculate the rejection probabilities of the likelihood ratio test that $\mu = 0$, using the asymptotic critical value of $\chi^2_{0.95}(1) = 3.84$. We see that even 500 observations are not enough for getting anywhere near a 5% test when ρ is 0.99 or 0.999. Thus one can insist that a root of 0.99 is a highly persistent stationary root so that variables have a well defined steady state value, but the price paid is that one cannot make inference on this steady state values using usual sample sizes. Thus when Ireland (2004) finds $\hat{\rho} = 0.9987$ and takes that to support that the variables are stationary, the consequence is that many more observations would be needed to make inference on the assumed steady state values of the variables.

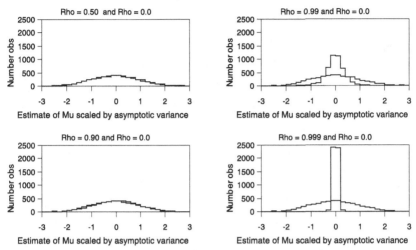

Figure 15.2. In the DGP(1), we simulate the distribution based upon 10,000 simulations of the estimator of μ scaled by the asymptotic standard error for $\rho = 0.0$, 0.5, 0.9, 0.99, and 0.999, and $T = 50$.

Table 15.1. *In the DGP(7) we simulate the rejection probability of the likelihood ratio test statistic for the hypothesis* $\mu = 0$, *for various values of* ρ *and* T *using the quantile* $\chi^2_{0.95}(1) = 3.84$. *The results are based on 10,000 simulations.*

	Rejection Probability in % for test of $\mu = 0$		
$\rho\backslash T$	50	100	500
0.5	6.1	5.8	5.4
0.9	11.9	9.3	6.1
0.99	24.6	22.4	12.4
0.999	27.6	27.4	25.1

CONCLUDING DISCUSSION

If the approaches being described in this chapter were limited to a few papers, one could perhaps see them as outliers. But, unfortunately, they are not. In efforts to bring models to the data researchers all too often fail to heed the two simple methodological rules given at the beginning of the paper. These rules place limits on which specifications can be reasonably used.

To summarize: when confronting an economic model with data in order to make inference on the parameters using likelihood methods it is not enough to use the Gaussian maximum likelihood methods. One has to specify a statistical model that not only contains the economic model but also the data generating process, so that the likelihood assumption is satisfied. This can be checked by misspecification tests. If the model is misspecified, one cannot rely on the results of the likelihood methods. Even if the assumptions are satisfied and a correct statistical model has been chosen, it may not be enough to rely on asymptotic methods for conducting inference. One must also check, by simulation or small sample corrections, how reliable the asymptotic results are. This is particularly the case for processes close to nonstationarity.

The failure to adequately confront the models with the data means that the development of economic theories cannot be given guidance from the data. The consequence is that the profession is likely to stick to theories which are no longer useful or even have become harmful. Even worse, the profession will fail to recognize new features in the data, which go against mainstream beliefs, which could signal a change in the underlying mechanism.

We should emphasize that the principles we have discussed in some detail have nothing specifically to do with the DSGE model, which was taken as an example of a mismatch between theory and evidence. We could consider many other examples, see for example the discussion in Juselius (2005).

What do these technical issues mean for policymakers? They mean that the macrodata available are highly unlikely to provide support for a model in the manner often attempted by macroeconometricians. If analysed correctly, however, the data can provide indications that certain assumptions do not work and hence guidance in choosing among alternative hypotheses, along the lines of the approach specified in Juselius and Johansen (chapter 16, this volume). Therefore the frequently observed mismatch of the models and the empirical evidence should be of serious concern for any scientist and policymaker.

16

Extracting Information from the Data: a European View on Empirical Macro

Katarina Juselius and Søren Johansen

INTRODUCTION

The last few decades have witnessed a revolution in the use of econometrics in empirical macroeconomics mostly due to the easy access to fast performing computers. Even though the use of new sophisticated techniques has been burgeoning the profession does not seem to have reached a consensus on the principles for good practise in the econometric analysis of economic models. Summers' (1992) critique of the scientific value of empirical models in economics seems equally relevant today.

The basic dilemma is that the reality behind the available macro-economic data is so *much more rich and complex* than the (often narrowly analyzed) problem being modeled by the theory. How to treat these "additional" features of the data (which often go against the *ceteris paribus* assumptions of the economic model) has divided the profession into the proponents of the so called "specific-to-general" and the proponents of "general-to-specific" approach to empirical economics.

The former, more conventional, approach is to estimate the parameters of a "stylized" economic model, while ignoring the wider circumstances under which the data were generated. These factors are then dumped into the residual term, causing its variance to be large. This practice has important implications for the power of empirical testing, often leading to a low ability to reject a theory model when it is false. As a result, different (competing) theory models are often not rejected despite being tested against the same data. Furthermore, the statistical inference in such models is usually based on a number of untested (and often empirically incorrect) *ceteris paribus* assumptions and the "significance" of estimated parameters may lack scientific meaning.

The "general-to-specific" approach to empirical economics represented by the VAR approach is a combination of induction and deduction. It recognizes from the outset the weak link between the theory model and the observed reality. For example, few, if any, theory models allow for basic characteristics of macroeconomic data such as path dependence, unit-root nonstationarity, structural breaks, shifts in equilibrium means, and location shifts in general growth rates.

These empirical features of economic data are at odds with the prevailing paradigm, which assumes a few (constant) structural parameters describing technology and preferences combined with model-based rational expectations (RE) as a description of how economic agents form expectations. These assumptions allow economists to rid their models of free parameters, and in doing so pretend that economics comes close to the precision of the natural sciences. Such models cannot be validly confronted with empirical time-series data as the link is too weak and, therefore, they continue to describe a "toy economy."

We will here focus on some basic principles for empirical research based on the (co-integrated) VAR approach and how it can be used to extract long-run and short-run information in the data by exploiting their integration and co-integration properties. The idea is to replace "simple stylized facts" such as correlations, graphs, etc. (which admittedly have inspired many new advances in theoretical economics) with more sophisticated facts better representing the nonstationary world of economic agents. In such a world, economic behavior is influenced by exogenous shocks pushing economic variables away from equilibrium, thereby activating adjustment forces that gradually pull the system back towards the equilibrium.

As an illustration of the potential strength of the co-integrated VAR approach, we will translate M. Friedman's claim (Friedman, 1970b) that "inflation is always and everywhere a monetary phenomenon" into a set of testable empirical hypotheses, building partly on Chapter 9, "Inflation and Monetary Policy," in D. Romer (1996). Using Danish monetary data we will then demonstrate that the co-integrated VAR model not just provides more efficient estimates of crucial parameters than conventional regression models, but also gives a conceptual framework for discussing the empirical content of many macroeconomic phenomena, and generates a set of robust empirical regularities characterizing economic behavior, the "new" stylized facts against which the empirical relevancy of theoretical results can be assessed.

Furthermore, the empirical analysis not only delivers a precise answer to whether a hypothesis is rejected (or accepted) but allows the researcher to see why it was rejected and how one can reformulate the hypothesis in the larger framework of the statistical model, thereby suggesting new hypotheses to be tested. Thus, by embedding the theory model in a broader empirical framework, the analysis points to possible pitfalls in macroeconomic reasoning, and at the same time generates new hypotheses for how to modify too narrowly specified theoretical models.

We believe that this empirical approach, which is Popperian in spirit, has a large potential for generating new empirically relevant hypotheses for macroeconomic behavior.

INFLATION AND MONEY GROWTH

A fundamental proposition in most macroeconomic theories is that growth in money supply in excess of real productive growth is the cause of inflation, at least in the long run. Here we will briefly consider some conventional ideas underlying this belief as described by Romer (1996).

The well-known diagram illustrating the intersection of aggregate demand and aggregate supply provides the framework for identifying potential sources of inflation as shocks shifting either aggregate demand upwards or aggregate supply to the left. See the upper panel of Figure 16.1.

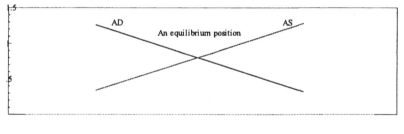

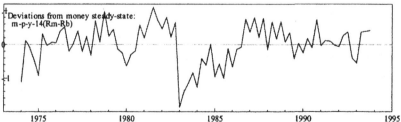

Figure 16.1. An equilibrium position of the *AD* and *AS* curve (upper panel) and deviations from an estimated money demand relation for Denmark: $(m - p - y)_t - 14.1(R_m - R_b)$ (lower panel).

As examples of aggregate supply shocks that shift the *AS* curve to the left Romer (1996) mentions: negative technology shocks, downward shifts in labor supply, and upwardly skewed relative-cost shocks. As examples of aggregate demand shocks that shift the *AD* curve to the right he mentions: increases in money stock, downward shifts in money demand, and increases in government purchases. Since all these types of shocks, and many others, occur quite frequently there are many factors that potentially can affect inflation. These shocks are isolated or auto-nomous in assuming that all other factors are kept constant. Some of these shocks may only influence inflation temporarily and are, therefore, less important than shocks with a permanent effect on inflation. Among the latter, economists usually emphasize changes in money supply as the crucial inflationary source. The economic intuition behind this is that other factors are limited in quantity, whereas money in principle is unlimited in supply.

More formally the reasoning is based on money demand and supply and the condition for equilibrium in the money market:

$$M/P = L(R, Y^r), \quad L_R < 0, L_y > 0, \tag{1}$$

where M is the money stock, P is the price level, R the nominal interest rate, Y^r real income, and $L(\cdot)$ the demand for real money balances. Based on the equilibrium condition, that is, no changes in any of the variables, Romer (1996) concludes, assuming that money causes prices, that the price level is determined by:

$$P = M/L(R, Y^r) \tag{2}$$

The equilibrium condition (1), is a static concept that can be thought of as a hypothetical relation between money and prices for fixed income and interest rate. The underlying comparative static analysis investigates the effect on one variable, say price, when changing another variable, say money supply, with the purpose of deriving the new equilibrium position after the change. Thus, the focus is on the hypothetical effect of a change in one variable (M) on another variable (P), when the additional variables (R and Y^r) are exogenously given and everything else is taken account of by the *ceteris paribus* assumption.

The empirical interest in money demand relations stems from basic macroeconomic theory postulating that the inflation rate is directly related to the expansion in the (appropriately defined) supply of money at a rate greater than that warranted by the growth of the real productive potential of the economy. The policy implication is that the aggregate supply of money should be controlled in order to control the inflation rate. The optimal control of money, however, requires knowledge of the "noninflationary level" of aggregate demand for money at each point of time, defined as the level of money stock, $M/P = L(R, Y^r)$, at which there is no tendency for prices to increase or decrease. Thus, from a practical point of view, the reasoning is based on the assumption that there exists a stable aggregate demand-for-money relation that can be estimated.

Theories of money demand usually distinguish between three different motives for holding money. The transactions motive is related to the need to hold cash for handling everyday transactions. The precautionary motive is related to the need to hold money to be able to meet unforeseen expenditures. Finally, the speculative motive is related to agents' wishes to hold money as part of their portfolio.

A Walrasian economist would require a formal model for agents' willingness to hold money balances based on optimizing behavior. Such a model can be based on (1) theories treating money as a medium of exchange for transaction purposes, so that minimizing a derived cost function leads to optimizing behavior, and (2) theories treating money as a good producing utility, so that maximizing the utility function leads to optimizing behavior.

A Post Walrasian economist considers such models too specific to qualify as a benchmark for an empirical model based on nonexperimental time-series data. Too many untestable restrictions would have to be imposed from the outset, which would invalidate inference if not consistent with the information in the data. Instead, the idea is to start with a general description of the variation of the data from which we try to extract as much information as possible. To secure valid statistical inference, all underlying assumptions have to be properly tested.

To illustrate the empirical approach, we assume as a starting point that all three motives can affect agents' needs to hold money. Therefore, the initial assumption is that real money stock is a function of the level of real income, Y^r (assumed to determine the volume of transactions and precautionary money) and the cost of holding money $C = \{R_b - R_m, \pi - R_m\}$, where R_m is the yield on money holdings, R_b is the yield on bonds, and π is the inflation rate. The functional form of the money demand relation is assumed to be log linear signifying the importance of relative rather than absolute changes in a time-series context.

THE ECONOMIC MODEL AND THE VAR: A DICTIONARY

Discussions between economists and econometricians are often confused by the fact that the wording and the concepts used are often similar, or even identical, even though their economic and econometric meaning differs significantly. This section is, therefore, an attempt to bridge the language gap. We provide a basic dictionary for some of the most crucial concepts used in the formulation of economic hypotheses derived from the selected theory model, and the concepts used in the formulation of testable statistical hypotheses derived from a statistical model describing the data.

The Status of Variables

A theory model makes a distinction between the *endogenous* and *exogenous* variables, which explicitly enter the model, and the variables outside the model, which are, by assumption, given. Furthermore the endogenous are modeled, whereas the exogenous are given. An empirical model makes the distinction between variables in the model and variables outside the model. Since *all* variables entering the model are allowed to interact, the economic notion of endogenous and exogenous is not useful prior to the empirical analysis. But, since the selection of variables is strongly influenced by the theoretical model for the endogenous variables, the equations of the latter usually make more economic sense. The variables outside the model are not fixed; thus they are likely to influence the variables in the model through the stochastic error term and the lags of the included variables.

For example, in Romer's model for money demand it is assumed that interest rates and income are exogenous and thus given. In the empirical analysis, however, the two variables are included in the model and allowed to interact with the variables of interest (the endogenous variables), money, and prices. The *ceteris paribus* assumption of the economic model is taken care of by allowing lags of all variables in every equation. The notion of exogeneity is defined in terms of parameters and can be tested in view of the data. The remaining part of the economy, the economic environment, is assumed to vary freely.

The baseline model is the unrestricted VAR(k) for the p-dimensional vector process x_t

$$\mathbf{x}_t = \Pi_1 x_{t-1} + \cdots + \Pi_k x_{t-k} + \mu_0 + \varepsilon_t \tag{3}$$

or its equivalent equilibrium correction form

$$\Delta x_t = \Pi x_{t-1} + \Gamma_1 \Delta x_{t-1} + \cdots + \Gamma_{k-1} \Delta x_{t-k+1} + \mu_0 + \varepsilon_t \qquad (4)$$

where $\varepsilon_t \sim N_p(0, \Omega)$. As long as the parameters have been approximately constant over the sample period, and the residuals satisfy the assumptions made, the VAR model is just a convenient way of representing the covariances of the data.

The Notion of Shocks

Theoretical models often make an important distinction between *unanticipated* and *anticipated* shocks. In the VAR model, Δx_t is the empirical measure of a shock, whereas $E_{t-1}(\Delta x_t | \sigma_{t-1}) = \Pi x_{t-1} + \Gamma_1 \Delta x_{t-1} + \cdots + \Gamma_{k-1} \Delta x_{t-k+1} + \mu_0$ is a measure of its anticipated part and ε_t of its unanticipated part given σ_{t-1}, the information available in the process at time $t-1$. The anticipated part can be interpreted as agents' plans for the next period based on σ_{t-1}. As long as the unanticipated part, ε_t, is a white noise process (a testable assumption) the updating of the plans as new information becomes available will be consistent with rational behavior in the sense that agents do not make systematic forecast errors.

A shock in a theoretical model is generally called "structural" if it is a meaningful shock to a variable in a postulated economic structure, or model, keeping all other variables fixed. The estimated residuals have a different interpretation, as they capture partly the unanticipated effect of a change in a variable in the model and partly the unanticipated effect of changes of variables outside the model. For an estimated residual to qualify as a structural shock we assume that it describes a shock, the effect of which is (1) unanticipated (novelty), (2) unique (for example, a shock hitting money stock alone), and (3) invariant (no additional explanation by increasing the information set).

The novelty of a shock depends on the credibility of the expectations formation, that is, whether $\varepsilon_t = \Delta x_t - E_{t-1}\{\Delta x_t | \sigma_{t-1}\}$ is a correct measure of the unanticipated change in x_t. The uniqueness can be achieved *econometrically* by reformulating the VAR, so that the covariance matrix Ω becomes diagonal. For example, by postulating a causal ordering among the variables of the system, one can trivially achieve uncorrelated residuals. In general, the VAR residuals can be orthogonalized in many different ways and whether the orthogonalized residuals can be given an *economic* interpretation as unique structural shocks depends crucially on the plausibility of the identifying assumptions. Thus, different schools will claim structural explanations for differently derived estimates based on the same data.

Invariance requires that an estimated structural shock as a function of the VAR residuals $\hat{u}_t = f(\hat{\varepsilon}_t)$ should remain unchanged when increasing the information set. The invariance of the structural shock in the theory model relies on many simplifying assumptions including numerous *ceteris paribus* assumptions. In empirical models, the *ceteris paribus* assumption is taken account of by conditioning on the variables in the model. Since essentially all macroeconomic systems are stochastic and highly interdependent, the inclusion of additional *ceteris paribus* variables in the model is likely to change the VAR residuals and, hence, the estimated shocks.

Therefore, a structural interpretation is hard to defend, unless one can claim that the information set is complete, so that the errors in the model are not influenced by other unanticipated shocks from the economic environment.

As exemplified by Romer, theory models also make a distinction between *permanent* and *transitory* shock to a variable. The former is usually defined as a disturbance having a long-lasting effect on the variable and the latter as a disturbance with a short-lived effect. For example, a permanent increase v_t of the oil price is a permanent shock to the price level, whereas it is a transitory shock to inflation. This is because inflation increases in the period of the oil price shock by v_t, but goes back by $-v_t$ to its original level next period.

Thus, a transitory shock disappears in cumulation, whereas a permanent shock has a long-lasting effect on the level of the variable. This gives the rationale for defining a stochastic trend as the cumulation of shocks.

Persistence and the Notion of Stochastic and Deterministic Trends

Romer makes a distinction between shocks with either a temporary or a permanent effect on inflation, focusing on the latter as a potential cause of inflation in the economy. In time-series econometrics, the notion that inflation has been subject to permanent shocks is translated into the statement that inflation rate is modeled by an $I(1)$ variable

$$\pi_t = \pi_{t-1} + v_t = \sum\nolimits_{i=1}^{t} v_i + \pi_0, \qquad (5)$$

where $\pi_t \equiv \Delta p_t$ and v_t is a stationary disturbance, which can contain both permanent and transitory shocks. In the cumulation $\sum_{i=1}^{t} v_i$, only the effect of the permanent shocks remains. Thus, the difference between a stochastic and a deterministic linear trend is that the permanent increments of a stochastic trend change randomly, whereas those of a deterministic trend are constant over time.

An expression for price levels can be obtained by integrating the inflation rate:

$$p_t = \sum_{i=1}^{t} \Delta p_i + p_0 = \sum_{i=1}^{t} \pi_i + p_0 = \sum_{s=1}^{t} \sum_{i=1}^{s} v_i + \pi_0 t + p_0, \qquad (6)$$

and the notion of permanent shocks to inflation rate can be translated to the econometric statement that the DGP of prices contains a second order stochastic trend together with a first order linear trend. We note that the unit root is a *statistical approximation* of persistent behavior over the period of investigation. It should be stressed that it can rarely be given a direct interpretation as a *structural economic parameter*, that is, it is not a generic property of an economic model (Juselius, 1999).

As an illustration, the upper panel of Figure 16.2 shows a second order stochastic trend, $\ln P_t - b_1 t$, the middle panel shows the corresponding first order stochastic trend, $\Delta \ln P_t$, and the lower panel the first order stochastic trend in the log of real aggregate income, $\ln Y_t^r - b_2 t$.

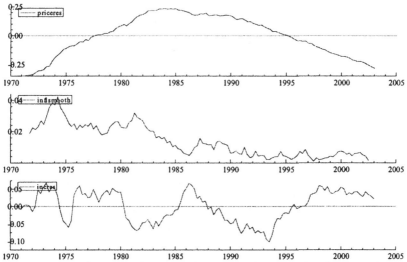

Figure 16.2. Stochastic trends in Danish prices, inflation, and real income, based on quarterly data 1973:1−2003:4.

The fact that macroeconomic variables typically have been (and continue to be) subject to permanent shocks explains why such data in levels are generally found to be strongly time dependent, whereas changes in variables, that is the shocks, are less so. From an empirical perspective it is, therefore, useful to distinguish between:

- stationary variables with a short time dependence, that is, with significant mean reversion, and
- (unit root) nonstationary variables with a long time dependence, that is, with insignificant mean reversion.

A further distinction is to classify the variable according to the degree of integration (persistence), for example into $I(-1)$, $I(0)$, $I(1)$, and $I(2)$ variables (Johansen, 1996). The co-integrated VAR model exploits this feature of the data as a means to classify variables with a similar persistency profile, that is variables which share a similar time path of persistent shocks.

The Notion of Equilibrium

The theoretical concept of a monetary equilibrium is defined as a point where money demand equals money supply. This definition is generally not associated with a specific point in time. In a VAR model an equilibrium point is a "resting position," that is a value of the process at which there are no adjustment forces at work. The empirical counterpart of the theoretical equilibrium (1), with the opportunity cost of holding money, $R = (R_b - R_m)$, is a co-integrating relation in the VAR model, that is:

$$\ln(M/P)_t - \ln(Y^r)_t - L(R_b - R_m)_t = v_t \qquad (7)$$

where v_t is a stationary equilibrium error. The econometric condition for this to be the case is either that

1. the liquidity ratio, $\ln(M/P)_t - \ln(Y^r)_t$ and the interest rate spread $(R_b - R_m)_t$ are both stationary, or that
2. the liquidity ratio, $\ln(M/P)_t - \ln(Y^r)_t$ and the interest rate spread $(R_b - R_m)_t$ are both nonstationary, but co-integrating.

In the first case, real money stock and real income have experienced the same cumulated permanent shocks (that is, they share the same stochastic trend). The same is true for the long-term bond rate and the short-term deposit rate. Thus, v_t is the sum of two stationary errors.

In the second case real money stock and real income have experienced different permanent shocks that have cumulated to a stochastic trend in the liquidity ratio, $\ln(M/P)_t - \ln(Y^r)_t$. If the interest rate spread $(R_b - R_m)_t$ has been subject to the same permanent shocks, then the stochastic trends cancel in the linear combination $\ln(M/P)_t - \ln(Y^r)_t - L(R_b - R_m)_t$, so that v_t becomes stationary.

The second case is illustrated in Figure 16.1 (lower panel) by the graph of the deviations from an estimated money demand relation based on Danish data with the opportunity cost of holding money being measured by $(R_b - R_m)_t$ (Juselius, 2005). The stationarity of v_t implies that whenever the system has been shocked, it will adjust back to equilibrium, but this adjustment need not be (and often is not) fast. In some cases, it is sluggish enough to make v_t look more like a nonstationary process.

The graphs in Figure 16.3 illustrate a situation where the stationary equilibrium error, v_t, is the sum of two nonstationary error processes (or possibly two stationary processes with a shift in the equilibrium mean). It also illustrates that the equilibrium point, $v_t = 0$, is essentially never observed. This is because when a shock has pushed the process away from its previous equilibrium position, the economic adjustment

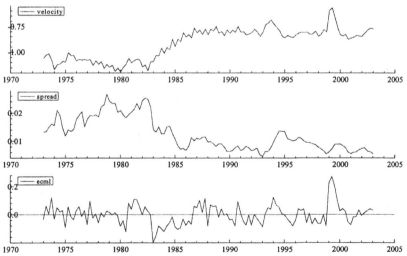

Figure 16.3. Money velocity (upper panel), the interest rate spread (midde panel), and money demand (lower panel) for Danish data.

forces begin to pull the process back towards its new position, but this adjustment is disturbed by new shocks and the system never comes to rest. Therefore, we will not be able to empirically observe an equilibrium position, except as a resting point towards which the process gravitates.

Interpretation of Coefficients

Empirical investigation of Eq. (7) based on co-integration analysis poses several additional problems. Although in a theoretical exercise it is straightforward to keep some of the variables fixed (the exogenous variables), in an empirical model none of the variables in Eq. (1), that is money, prices, income, or interest rates, can be assumed to be given. The stochasticity of all variables implies that the equilibrium adjustment can take place in either money, prices, income, or interest rates. Therefore, the magnitude of the long-run equilibrium error v_t is not necessarily due to a money supply shock at time t, but can originate from a long-run change in any of the other variables.

The interpretation of the coefficients in Eq. (7) is similar to the interpretation of usual regression coefficients, in the sense that the coefficient to $\ln Y_t^r$ is the long-run effect of $\ln Y^r$ on $\ln M^r$ under the assumption of long run *ceteris paribus* (see Johansen, 2005).

Causality

In Eq. (1) the money market equilibrium is an exact mathematical expression and it is straightforward to invert it to determine prices as is done in Eq. (2), provided one assumes causality from money to prices. The observations from a typical macroeconomic system are adequately described by a stochastic vector time series process. If the relation (2) is interpreted as a statement about a conditional expectation, and estimated by regression methods, then inversion is no longer guaranteed (for instance, see Hendry and Ericsson [1991]). The co-integrating relation (7) is a relation *between* variables and can be normalized on any variable without changing the relationship. The lagged co-integrating relations influence the current changes of the process through the adjustment coefficients to the disequilibrium errors. Thus, the causality in the reduced form VAR goes from lagged values to current values, not between current values.

Path Dependence

In a static theory model, the variables assume constant values. When dynamics are introduced, the variables follow trajectories set out by the dynamics of the model and the initial values. Thus, the development of a variable depends on which path it is on. In an empirical, or stochastic model, the trajectory of a variable is influenced both by the initial values and the dynamics, but furthermore by the stochastic shocks. Hence, the development over time changes at each time point as a function of the past and the new shock that hits the system. In this sense the variables show path dependence.

PULLING AND PUSHING FORCES
IN THE CO-INTEGRATED VAR

The purpose of this section is to illustrate that the co-integrated VAR model can provide a precise description of the pulling and pushing forces. For illustrative purposes we consider here the simple VAR model (4) with lag length $k = 1$, which we write in the form

$$\Delta x_t - \gamma = \alpha(\beta' x_{t-1} - \beta_0) + \varepsilon_t, \tag{8}$$

where $E\Delta x_t = \gamma$, $E\beta' x_t = \beta_0$, and $\beta'\gamma = 0$, and we define $\mu_0 = \gamma - \alpha\beta_0$. The long-run information in the data is summarized in the reduced rank restriction:

$$\Pi = \alpha\beta', \tag{9}$$

and α and β are $p \times r$, $r \leq p$.

Inversion of Eq. (8) yields the moving average representation or, as it is often called, the common trends representation:

$$x_t = C \sum_{i=1}^{t} \varepsilon_i + \gamma t + C^*(L)(\varepsilon_t + \mu_0), \tag{10}$$

where C is of reduced rank $p - r$:

$$C = \beta_\perp(\alpha'_\perp \beta_\perp)^{-1}\alpha'_\perp = \tilde{\beta}_\perp \alpha'_\perp, \tag{11}$$

where $\tilde{\beta}_\perp = \beta_\perp(\alpha'_\perp \beta_\perp)^{-1}$ and $\beta_\perp, \alpha_\perp$ are the orthogonal complements of β and α.

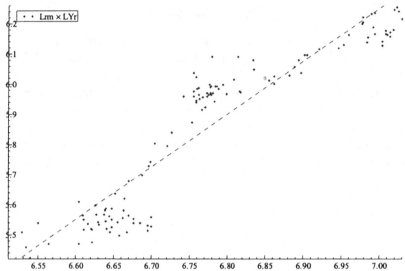

Figure 16.4. A cross plot of real aggregate income and real money stock (M3).

We now discuss how the two reduced rank conditions, (9) and (11), can be used to describe the forces pulling towards equilibrium versus the forces pushing the process along the attractor set defined by the relation $\beta'x = \beta_0$. We assume for illustrative purposes that the process is $x_t' = [m_t^r, y_t^r]$, where m_t^r is the log of real money stock and y_t^r is the log of real aggregate income. Figure 16.4 shows a cross plot of m_t^r against y_t^r. The straight line measures the attractor set $sp(\beta_\perp) = sp(1,1)$, and the distance from the dots to the line the disequilibrium error $\beta'x_t = m_t^r - y_t^r$.

The geometry of the co-integrated VAR model is illustrated in Figure 16.5. A constant liquidity ratio $m^r - y^r = \beta_0$ describes an equilibrium position between money stock and income. In the notation of Eq. (9) this implies that $\beta' = [1, -1]$, so that $\beta'x_t - \beta_0 = m_t^r - y_t^r - \beta_0 \neq 0$ measures a stationary disequilibrium error. The steady-state positions or attractor set $m_t^r - y_t^r - \beta_0 = 0$ describes a system at rest. If the errors were switched off starting from a point x_t, the trajectory of the process would be a straight line from x_t along the vector α until it hits the attractor set. The speed of the process is proportional to the length of the vector α and to the distance from the attractor set as measured by the disequilibrium error, $\beta'x_t - \beta_0$. At the (long-run) equilibrium point, x_∞, there is no economic adjustment force (incentive) to change the system to a new position.

When there are stochastic shocks to the system, the picture is almost the same. The process x_t is pulled towards the attractor set along the vector α

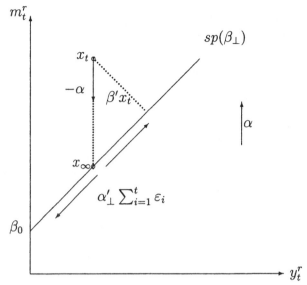

Figure 16.5. The process $x'_t = [y^r_t, m^r_t]$ is pushed along the attractor set by the common trends and pulled towards the attractor set by the adjustment coefficients.

and proportional to the disequilibrium error $m^r_t - y^r_t - \beta_0$ see Eq. (8), but is now disturbed by the random shocks ε_t. The process x_t never hits the attractor set, but fluctuates around it due to the shocks. The force with which it is being pulled along the attractor set is proportional to $\alpha'_\perp \sum_{i=1}^{t} \varepsilon_i$. The latter measures the cumulative effect of autonomous shocks hitting the system.

The pulling forces can be translated into the equilibrium correction model:

$$\begin{bmatrix} \Delta m^r_t \\ \Delta y^r_t \end{bmatrix} = \begin{bmatrix} \alpha_1 \\ \alpha_2 \end{bmatrix}(m^r_t - y^r_t - \beta_0) + \begin{bmatrix} \gamma_1 \\ \gamma_2 \end{bmatrix} + \begin{bmatrix} \varepsilon_{1,t} \\ \varepsilon_{2,t} \end{bmatrix}, \qquad (12a)$$

and the pushing forces into the corresponding common trends model:

$$\begin{bmatrix} m^r_t \\ y^r_t \end{bmatrix} = \begin{bmatrix} 1 \\ 1 \end{bmatrix}\alpha'_\perp \sum_{i=1}^{t} \varepsilon_i + \begin{bmatrix} \gamma_1 \\ \gamma_2 \end{bmatrix}t + C^*(L)\begin{bmatrix} \varepsilon_{1,t} + \mu_{01} \\ \varepsilon_{2,t} + \mu_{02} \end{bmatrix}, \qquad (12b)$$

with $\alpha'_\perp = \frac{1}{\alpha_1 - \alpha_2}[-\alpha_2, \alpha_1]$. Assume now that $\alpha' = [\alpha_1, 0]$, that is only money stock is equilibrium correcting when $m^r_t - y^r_t - \beta_0 \neq 0$. In this case $\alpha'_\perp = [0, 1]$, implying that the common stochastic trend driving this system originates from (real productivity) shocks to aggregate income. The cumulated sum of these shocks determines where on the attractor set (the 45° line) the system is located.

Note, however, that the interpretation of the equilibrium relation, $m_t^r = y_t^r + \beta_0$, is not that this relation will be satisfied in the limit as $t \to \infty$. An equilibrium position is something that exists at all time points as a resting point towards which the process is drawn after it has been pushed away.

The reliability of the empirical results, that is whether the structuring of the economic reality using the pushing and pulling forces of the co-integrated VAR model is empirically convincing, depends on how well the unrestricted baseline model describes the data. As long as a first order linear approximation of the underlying economic structure provides an adequate description of the empirical reality, the VAR model is essentially a convenient summary of the covariances of the data. Provided that further reductions (simplifications) of the model are based on valid statistical inference, the final parsimonious model would essentially reflect the information in the covariances of the data.

EMBEDDING ROMER'S MONEY DEMAND MODEL IN THE VAR

This section will illustrate how to address Romer's model of money demand and supply based on the time series vector $x_t' = \left[m, p, y^r, R_m, R_b \right]_t$, $t = 1, \dots, T$ where m is the log of M3 money stock, p the log of the implicit GNE price deflator, y^r the log of real GNE, R_m is the interest rate yield on M3, and R_b, the interest rate yield on ten-year bonds. All variables are stochastic and, thus, need to be statistically modeled, independently of whether they are considered endogenous or exogenous in the economic model.

The idea is now to translate the implications of the monetary inflation model into a set of testable hypotheses on the unrestricted VAR model. These will be formulated as restrictions on α and β, that is the pulling forces of the vector equilibrium correction model (8), and on $\tilde{\beta}_\perp$ and $\alpha_\perp$, that is the pushing forces of the common stochastic trends model (Eq. [10]).

The Pushing Forces

Based on an AD–AS system it seems natural to assume at least two *autonomous* empirical shocks $u_t^{nom} = \alpha'_{\perp,1}\varepsilon_t$ and $u_t^{real} = \alpha'_{\perp,2}\varepsilon_t$, where

u_t^{nom} describes a nominal shock and u_t^{real} a real shock, each of them measured as a linear combination of the VAR errors. The unrestricted common trends model with two autonomous shocks can be formulated as:

$$
\begin{bmatrix} m_t - p_t \\ y_t^r \\ \Delta p_t \\ R_{m,t} \\ R_{b,t} \end{bmatrix} = \underbrace{\begin{bmatrix} d_{11}\,d_{12} \\ d_{21}\,d_{22} \\ d_{31}\,d_{32} \\ d_{41}\,d_{42} \\ d_{51}\,d_{52} \end{bmatrix}}_{\tilde{\beta}_\perp} \underbrace{\begin{bmatrix} \sum u_i^{nom} \\ \sum u_i^{real} \end{bmatrix}}_{\alpha_\perp' \sum \varepsilon_i} + \begin{bmatrix} \gamma \\ \gamma \\ 0 \\ 0 \\ 0 \end{bmatrix} t + Z_t,
\tag{13}
$$

where Z_t consists of stationary components and the inflation and interest rates have been restricted a priori to have no deterministic trends.

The formulation (13) is just a convenient description of the information in the data. The only prior restrictions entering the model are the number of stochastic trends and the three exclusion restrictions on the deterministic trends. These low-level economic priors are testable and, thus, can act as a first sorting device between theory models that are consistent with the basic information in the data and those that are not. For example, many rational expectations models predict fewer stochastic trends than actually found in the data, suggesting that actual economic behavior is less informed than predicted by the RE assumption.

The next level of testable economic priors is associated with restrictions on the vectors determining the stochastic trends $\alpha_\perp$ and on their loading matrix $\tilde{\beta}_\perp$. Assuming that inflation is a pure monetary phenomenon, it is natural to call an unanticipated empirical shock to money stock a *nominal* shock, so that $\alpha_{\perp,1}' = [1, 0, 0, 0, 0]$ and, similarly, an unanticipated empirical shock to real aggregate income a real shock, so that $\alpha_{\perp,2}' = [0, 1, 0, 0, 0]$.

The prior restrictions on the loadings matrix should reflect the statement that "inflation is always and everywhere a monetary phenomenon." We will interpret this as a statement that a permanent increase in money stock in excess of real GNP will only result in an equivalent increase in prices, with no changes in real money stock and real aggregate income. Similarly, the stochastic trend in the inflation rate should only influence nominal but not real interest rates. Only permanent real (productivity) shocks would have a lasting impact on any of the real variables.

The data-generating process consistent with these priors can be formulated as a restricted version of Eq. (13):

$$
\begin{bmatrix} m_t - p_t \\ y_t^r \\ \Delta p_t \\ R_{m,t} \\ R_{b,t} \end{bmatrix} = \underbrace{\begin{bmatrix} 0 & d_{12} \\ 0 & d_{12} \\ d_{31} & 0 \\ d_{31} & 0 \\ d_{31} & 0 \end{bmatrix}}_{\tilde{\beta}_\perp} \underbrace{\begin{bmatrix} \sum u_i^{nom} \\ \sum u_i^{real} \end{bmatrix}}_{\alpha'_\perp \sum \varepsilon_i} + \begin{bmatrix} \gamma \\ \gamma \\ 0 \\ 0 \\ 0 \end{bmatrix} t + Z_t. \tag{14}
$$

It describes an economy where real aggregate income and real money stock have been subject to the same series of real shocks, $\sum u_i^{real}$, without any lasting impact from the nominal shocks, $\sum u_i^{nom}$. The nominal stochastic trend, $\sum u_i^{nom}$, is common for the inflation rate and the two interest rates, so that real interest rates and the interest rate spread are stationary variables.

The Pulling Forces

The specification of the pulling forces has to be consistent with the pushing forces as the moving average and the autoregressive representation are two sides of the same coin. Two autonomous shocks are consistent with three co-integration relations, $\beta_i' x_{t-1}$, $i = 1, 2, 3$, where β_i defines a stationary linear combination of the nonstationary variables. The unrestricted co-integrated VAR model can be formulated as:

$$
\begin{bmatrix} \Delta m_t^r \\ \Delta y_t^r \\ \Delta^2 p_t \\ \Delta R_{mt} \\ \Delta R_{b,t} \end{bmatrix} = \begin{bmatrix} a_{11} & a_{12} & a_{13} \\ a_{21} & a_{22} & a_{23} \\ a_{31} & a_{32} & a_{33} \\ a_{41} & a_{42} & a_{43} \\ a_{51} & a_{52} & a_{53} \end{bmatrix} \begin{bmatrix} \beta_1' x_{t-1} - \beta_{0,1} \\ \beta_2' x_{t-1} - \beta_{0,2} \\ \beta_3' x_{t-1} - \beta_{0,3} \end{bmatrix} + \begin{bmatrix} \gamma_1 \\ \gamma_2 \\ \gamma_3 \\ \gamma_4 \\ \gamma_5 \end{bmatrix} + \begin{bmatrix} \varepsilon_{1,t} \\ \varepsilon_{2,t} \\ \varepsilon_{3,t} \\ \varepsilon_{4,t} \\ \varepsilon_{5,t} \end{bmatrix} \tag{15}
$$

In Eq. (15) α and β are unrestricted and we need to impose some prior restrictions consistent with the representation (14). Given Eq. (14) $(m - p - y^r)$, $(R_b - R_m)$, and $(R_b - \Delta p)$ define stationary relations and can, therefore, be chosen as our economic priors for $\beta' x_{t-1}$. However, any linear combinations of them would also be stationary, so they are unique only in the sense of uniquely defining the co-integration space.

The following restrictions on α are consistent with the restrictions on $\alpha_{\perp}$ in Eq. (14):

$$\alpha'_{\perp} = \begin{bmatrix} 1 & 0 & 0 & 0 & 0 \\ 0 & 1 & 0 & 0 & 0 \end{bmatrix} \Leftrightarrow \alpha = \begin{bmatrix} 0 & 0 & 0 \\ 0 & 0 & 0 \\ * & * & * \\ * & * & * \\ * & * & * \end{bmatrix}$$

The assumption that inflation rate is positively related to money expansion in excess of money demand suggests that $a_{31} > 0$, $a_{32} > 0$. The sign of the coefficient a_{41} can be negative (lower interest rate when there is excess liquidity) or positive (if inflationary expectations, due to an increase in m, make the central bank increase its interest rate). The expectations hypothesis predicts that the long-term interest rate is determined by the sum of appropriately weighted interest rates of shorter maturity and the Fisher parity that the nominal bond rate should be related to the expected inflation rate. This leads to the hypothetical vector equilibrium correction model:

$$\begin{bmatrix} \Delta m^r_t \\ \Delta y^r_t \\ \Delta^2 p_t \\ \Delta R_m \\ \Delta R_{b,t} \end{bmatrix} = \begin{bmatrix} 0 & 0 & 0 \\ 0 & 0 & 0 \\ a_{31} & a_{32} & 0 \\ a_{41} & 0 & a_{43} \\ 0 & a_{52} & 0 \end{bmatrix} \begin{bmatrix} (m-p-y^r)_{t-1} - \beta_{0,1} \\ (R_b - R_m)_{t-1} - \beta_{0,2} \\ (R_m - \Delta p)_{t-1} - \beta_{0,1} \end{bmatrix}$$

$$+ \begin{bmatrix} \gamma_1 \\ \gamma_2 \\ \gamma_3 \\ \gamma_4 \\ \gamma_5 \end{bmatrix} + \begin{bmatrix} \varepsilon_{1,t} \\ \varepsilon_{2,t} \\ \varepsilon_{3,t} \\ \varepsilon_{4,t} \\ \varepsilon_{5,t} \end{bmatrix} \tag{16}$$

Thus, in order to explain monetary transmission mechanisms empirically (accounting for the fact that all variables are stochastic), it is not enough to formulate hypotheses about money demand and money supply. We also need to formulate empirically testable implications of the Fisher hypothesis and of the term structure of the interest rates.

The Role of Expectations

In a world where real growth rates are stationary variables (as usually found), the Fisher parity assumes that real interest rates are constant (or stationary with a constant mean) so that a nominal interest rate, R_t^m, of maturity m can be decomposed into a real interest rate, r_m, and the average expected inflation, $\frac{1}{m} \mathcal{E}_t \sum_{i=1}^m \Delta p_{t+i}$:

$$R_t^m = r^m + \frac{1}{m} \mathcal{E}_t(p_{t+m} - p_t) + \varepsilon_t = r^m + \frac{1}{m} \mathcal{E}_t \sum_{i=1}^m \Delta p_{t+i} + \varepsilon_t \quad (17)$$

where r^m denotes a constant real interest rate of maturity m. We note that a stationary real interest rate is logically consistent either with nominal interest rate and expected inflation rate both being nonstationary or, alternatively, both being stationary. Based on arbitrage arguments one would expect the yield of a financial asset to be unpredictable and, thus, nominal interest rates to approximately follow a random walk, that is to be nonstationary. In this case, a stationary real interest rate would be econometrically consistent with the expected inflation rate being a nonstationary variable.

Forecasting a nonstationary variable with a stationary forecast error is generally not feasible except possibly over very short periods. This is because many "extraordinary" future events are truly unpredictable and, thus, violate the probability formulation of the sample period (Clements and Hendry, 1999).

A further complication in the interpretation of the VAR is that the Fisher parity is defined in terms of the expected inflation rate, which is unobservable, whereas Eq. (14) is specified in terms of the actual inflation rate. Nevertheless, as long as the stochastic trend in the actual inflation rate is the same as in the expected inflation rate, the statistical inference regarding the long-run pulling and pushing forces is robust to this problem. For example, under the plausible assumption that agents (1) form expectations according to $E_t^e(\Delta p_{t+m}) = f(x_t)$ and (2) use forecasting models which have performed well historically, say $\Delta p_{t+1} = f(x_t) + v_t$, where v_t is stationary with mean zero, then Δp_t and $E_t(\Delta p_{t+m})$ would be co-integrating and we can substitute one for the other. Thus, under fairly weak assumptions on agents' expectations behavior, we can expect the *long-run VAR results* to be robust to the problem of unobservable inflationary expectations.

From a theoretical point of view the Fisher parity condition (17) should hold independently of whether m denotes a short or a long maturity.

When Fisher parity holds the interest rate spread would be related to the difference between expected average inflation rates over the short and the long maturity period, respectively:

$$R_t^l - R_t^s = r^l - r^s + \frac{1}{l}\mathcal{E}_t \sum_{i=1}^{l} \Delta p_{t+i} - \frac{1}{s}\mathcal{E}_t \sum_{i=1}^{s} \Delta p_{t+i}. \qquad (18)$$

Given that the Fisher parity holds, a stationary spread is achieved when the difference between the average expected inflation rates is a stationary variable.

To sum up: we have found that the hypothesis of inflation being a purely monetary phenomenon is econometrically consistent with stationary real interest rates, a stationary spread, and a stationary liquidity ratio. But we have also found that the logic of the reasoning may need to be modified to allow for persistent inflationary shocks and for "non-RE" expectations. Thus, both nonstationarity and expectations may potentially necessitate a reformulation of the theoretical priors.

DEDUCTIVE INFERENCE: EXTRACTING INFORMATION FROM THE DATA

The previous section illustrated how the data can be structured based on their integration properties and how this can be used to discriminate between the empirical logic of different economic hypotheses. We will provide an empirical example of pulling and pushing forces in a VAR analysis applied to Danish money demand data over the last three decades. To economize on space only the most important results will be reported and the interested reader is referred to the more detailed analyses in Juselius (2005).[1]

The baseline model is a five-dimensional VAR of real M3, real GNE, inflation rate, and a short- and a long-term interest rate. Furthermore, the VAR model includes a shift dummy $Ds83_t$ in the co-integration relations and a permanent intervention impulse dummy, $\Delta Ds83_t$, in the equations. This is to account for a significant shift in the equilibrium mean of the long-run money demand relation and in the spread between the two interest rates in 1983:1 as a result of deregulating the Danish capital markets.

---

[1] All analyses in this and subsequent sections have been performed using the software package CATS for RATS (Dennis et al., 2005).

Table 16.1. *Testing the stationarity of single relations when r = 3*

	m_t^r	y_t^r	Δp_t	R_{m_t}	R_{b_t}	$Ds83_t$	$\chi^2(v)$	p-value
Tests of liquidity ratio relations								
$\mathcal{H}_1$	1	−1	0	0	0	−0.34	1.5(2)	**0.47**
$\mathcal{H}_2$	0	1	−48.0	48.0	0	−0.70	8.8(1)	0.00
$\mathcal{H}_3$	0	1	−43.3	0	43.3	0.12	12.8(1)	0.00
$\mathcal{H}_4$	0	1	0	−163	−163	2.0	3.5(1)	0.06
$\mathcal{H}_5$	0	1	34.3	0	0	0.42	0.9(1)	**0.34**
Tests of inflation, real interest rates and the spread								
$\mathcal{H}_6$	0	0	1	0	0	0.021	9.0(1)	0.01
$\mathcal{H}_7$	0	0	1	−1	0	0.012	10.6(2)	0.00
$\mathcal{H}_8$	0	0	1	0	−1	−0.008	14.4(2)	0.00
$\mathcal{H}_9$	0	0	0	1	−1	−0.014	4.2(2)	**0.12**
Tests of combinations of interest rates and inflation rates								
$\mathcal{H}_{10}$	0	0	1	−0.45	0	0.016	4.9(1)	0.03
$\mathcal{H}_{11}$	0	0	1	0	−0.27	0.014	6.7(1)	0.01
$\mathcal{H}_{12}$	0	0	0	1	−0.82	−0.009	1.7(1)	**0.19**
Tests of homogeneity between inflation and the interest rates								
$\mathcal{H}_{13}$	0	0	0.10	1	−1	−0.016	4.4(1)	0.04
$\mathcal{H}_{14}$	0	0	−0.30	1	−0.70	−0.012	0.02(1)	**0.89**

Table 16.1 reports the co-integration results of testing the stationarity of a number of possible relations, among others the hypothetical relations in Eq. (16). The hypothesis $\mathcal{H}_1$ shows that the liquidity ratio can be considered stationary when allowing for an equilibrium mean shift at 1983:1. $\mathcal{H}_2$ and $\mathcal{H}_3$ test the stationarity of an *IS*-type relationship between real aggregate income and real (ex post) short-term and long-term interest rate, respectively. The stationarity of both is rejected, whereas a negative relation between the inflation rate and the real aggregate income, $\mathcal{H}_5$, can be accepted. It essentially reflects the steadily declining inflation rate and the steadily increasing real aggregate income over this period and should at most be interpreted as a "reduced form" relation. A more structural interpretation will be suggested in the next section.

$\mathcal{H}_6$ shows that inflation rate is nonstationary over this period, even if we allow for a mean shift at 1983. $\mathcal{H}_7$ and $\mathcal{H}_8$ show that real interest rates are found to be nonstationary, even if we allow the mean to be different before and after capital deregulation. $\mathcal{H}_9$ accepts the stationarity of the interest rate spread when allowing for a change in the mean (the risk premium)

Table 16.2. *An identified structure of long-run relations*

	m_t^r	y_t^r	Δp_t	$R_{m,t}$	$R_{b,t}$	$Ds83_t$
Test of overidentifying restr. $\chi^2(4) = 4.05\,[0.40]$						
$\hat{\beta}_1'$	1.00	−1.00	0.00	0.00	0.00	−0.34
						[−13.60]
$\hat{\beta}_2'$	0.00	0.00	−0.20	1.00	−0.80	−0.01
					[−15.65]	[−10.67]
$\hat{\beta}_3'$	0.00	0.03	1.00	0.00	0.00	0.01
		[3.67]				[5.46]

The adjustment coefficients

	$\hat{\alpha}_1$	$\hat{\alpha}_2$	$\hat{\alpha}_3$	Zero row in α $\chi^2_{0.95}(3)$ $=7.81$	Unit vector in α $\chi^2_{0.95}(2)$ $=5.99$
Δm_t^r	−0.21	3.38	0.24	17.56	3.81
	[−4.74]	[3.21]	[0.53]	[0.00]	[0.15]
Δy_t^r	0.06	−1.40	−0.44	6.84	10.32
	[2.27]	[−2.21]	[−1.59]	[0.08]	[0.01]
$\Delta^2 p_t$	−0.00	−0.29	−0.84	26.65	3.96
	[−0.11]	[−0.79]	[−5.33]	[0.00]	[0.14]
$\Delta R_{m,t}$	−0.00	−0.07	0.02	8.88	5.09
	[−0.28]	[−1.54]	[1.00]	[0.03]	[0.08]
$\Delta R_{b,t}$	0.00	0.13	0.05	4.64	6.88
	[0.69]	[2.04]	[1.87]	[0.20]	[0.03]

after deregulation. $\mathcal{H}_{10}$ and $\mathcal{H}_{11}$ test whether stationarity can be achieved by relaxing the unitary coefficient between nominal interest rates and inflation rates, but nonstationarity prevails. $\mathcal{H}_{13}$ is a test of Eq. (18), that is whether the stationarity of the spread is improved by including the inflation rate. No such evidence was found, but when testing the stationarity of a homogeneous relation between the inflation rate and the two interest rates in $\mathcal{H}_{16}$, stationarity was strongly supported.

Table 16.2 reports the joint estimation of the identified long-run structure $\{\mathcal{H}_1, \mathcal{H}_5, \text{ and } \mathcal{H}_{14}\}$ together with the estimated adjustment coefficients. The four overidentifying restrictions were accepted with a *p-value* of 0.40. All three relations have experienced a shift in the equilibrium mean at 1983:1, signifying the major impact of the deregulation of the Danish capital market. The second relation suggests that the short-term interest rate has been homogeneously related to the long-term bond rate (0.80) and the inflation rate (0.20).

The hypothesis that the cumulated residuals from a specific VAR equation measure a common driving trend can be specified as a zero row in α. This implies that the variable in question is weakly exogenous for the long-run parameters. The opposite hypothesis that the residuals of an equation have transitory but no permanent effects on the variables of the system can be specified as a unit vector in α. Both hypotheses are tested for each equation and the results reported in Table 16.2. We note that the bond rate can be assumed weakly exogenous with a *p-value* of 0.20, whereas real aggregate income is a borderline case with a *p-value* of 0.08. Thus, the estimated results suggest that cumulated empirical shocks to real aggregate income constitute one of the common stochastic trends consistent with the hypothetical scenario, whereas the second trend seems to be generated from cumulated empirical shocks to the long-term bond rate, rather than to money stock.

The unit vector hypothesis is accepted for real money stock with a *p-value* of 0.15, for inflation rate with *p-value* 0.14, and for the short-term interest rate with a *p-value* of 0.08. Thus, consistent with the weak exogeneity tests, these tests suggest that unanticipated empirical shocks to real money stock, inflation, and the short-term interest rate have only exhibited small, if any, permanent effects on the system. However, the residuals in the short-term and the long-term interest rate equations are simultaneously correlated (0.42) and, therefore, not uniquely defined. For example, a Cholesky decomposition of the residual covariance matrix might very well change the interpretation.

Whatever the case, the hypothetical scenario for the determination of money and inflation needs to be modified to account for the estimated α dynamics. We note that the first two adjustment coefficients in the money stock equation are highly significant and the combined effects can be shown to describe a long-run money demand relation toward which money stock has been equilibrium correcting:

$$\Delta m_t^r = \cdots - 0.21(m^r - y^r) + 3.38(R_m - 0.2\Delta p - 0.8R_b) + \cdots$$

$$= \cdots - 0.21(m^r - y^r + 3.2\Delta p - 16.1R_m + 12.9R_b)_{t-1} + \cdots$$

At the same time, the estimated α coefficients in the inflation equation show that inflation is not affected by excess money nor by the homogeneous interest rate relation. This suggests that money stock has been purely accommodating to money demand without any inflationary effects. Instead, the inflation rate is significantly error-correcting to the third co-integration relation, the implication of which will be discussed in the next section.

Even though the estimated co-integration results seemed to provide some support for our prior hypotheses, the picture changed quite significantly when the estimated dynamic adjustment mechanisms were taken into consideration. Thus, to exclusively focus on the co-integration implications of a theoretical model (as often done in the literature) is not sufficient for valid inference.

The empirical estimates of the corresponding moving average model (13) with $u_t^{real} = \alpha'_{\perp,1}\hat{\varepsilon}_t = \hat{\varepsilon}_{y,t}$, and $u_t^{nom} = \alpha'_{\perp,2}\hat{\varepsilon}_t = \hat{\varepsilon}_{Rb,t}{}^2$ are given by:

$$
\begin{bmatrix} m_t^r \\ y_t^r \\ \Delta p_t \\ R_{m,t} \\ R_{b,t} \end{bmatrix} = \underbrace{\begin{bmatrix} 0.70 & -11.84 \\ {\scriptstyle [3.75]} & {\scriptstyle [-5.07]} \\ 1.13 & -5.40 \\ {\scriptstyle [6.59]} & {\scriptstyle [-2.51]} \\ -0.04 & 0.08 \\ {\scriptstyle [-7.00]} & {\scriptstyle [1.27]} \\ 0.01 & 0.93 \\ {\scriptstyle [1.11]} & {\scriptstyle [5.51]} \\ 0.04 & 1.39 \\ {\scriptstyle [1.93]} & {\scriptstyle [5.31]} \end{bmatrix}}_{\tilde{\beta}_\perp} \underbrace{\begin{bmatrix} \sum_{i=1}^{t} \varepsilon_{y,i} \\ \sum_{i=1}^{t} \varepsilon_{Rb,i} \end{bmatrix}}_{\alpha'_\perp \sum \hat{\varepsilon}_i} + \begin{bmatrix} 0.026 \\ 0.029 \\ 0.000 \\ 0.000 \\ 0.000 \end{bmatrix} t + \cdots \quad (19)
$$

According to Eq. (14) the real stochastic trend should influence real money stock and real income with the same coefficients. The estimated coefficients are 0.70 to money stock and 1.13 to real income. Both are positive and not significantly different from the prior hypothesis in Eq. (14) of a unitary coefficient. However, the prior assumption that the nominal stochastic trend should not influence real money stock nor real aggregate income was clearly violated, in the sense that the second nominal trend (defined here as the cumulated empirical shocks to the long-term bond rate) has significantly affected both real money stock and real income negatively, but the former much more so.[3] Note, however, that the interpretation of the empirical results relying on Eq. (14) is no longer straightforward as one of the basic hypotheses, that the nominal stochastic trend derives from empirical shocks to excess money, was already rejected.

---

[2] Even though the joint weak exogeneity of the bond rate and real aggregate income was only borderline acceptable, the subsequent conclusions are robust to whether weak exogeneity is imposed or not.

[3] This suggests that money demand is more interest rate elastic than investment demand.

Finally, while the empirical shocks to real aggregate income are found to generate the second stochastic trend consistent with our prior, the way it affected the system variables is not.

INDUCTIVE INFERENCE: A EUROPEAN VIEW ON EMPIRICAL MACRO

Based on the first deductive part of the analysis we found that the empirical evidence did not fully support for the hypothetical structure, Eq. (16). By comparing the theoretical model with the corresponding empirical results we may get some understanding of why and where the theory model failed to be an adequate description of the empirical behavior.

We will first investigate why the stationarity of some of the prior hypotheses $\{\mathcal{H}_7, \mathcal{H}_8, \mathcal{H}_{10}, \mathcal{H}_{11}, \mathcal{H}_{13}\}$ in Table 16.1 was violated using the estimates in Eq. (19). We note that the inflation rate is significantly affected only by $\sum \varepsilon_y$ and the short-term interest rate only by $\sum \varepsilon_{Rb}$, whereas the bond rate is affected by both stochastic trends. Hence, co-integration between the inflation rate and either of the two interest rates is not possible. The fact that the inflation rate and the two interest rates share two common trends explains why the homogeneous interest rate–inflation rate relation, $\mathcal{H}_{14}$, was "more stationary" than the interest rate spread relation, $\mathcal{H}_9$. The "stationarity" of the latter was only achieved by suppressing the small but significant effect of $\sum \varepsilon_y$ on the bond rate. Thus, *the discrepancy between the Fisher parity and the empirical evidence is because the stochastic trend in inflation rate originates from different empirical shocks than the ones in interest rates.*

The discrepancy between the expectations hypothesis and the empirical evidence is because the bond rate, but not the short rate, has been affected by the empirical shocks to real aggregate income. Furthermore, the latter effect is similar to the effect on inflation rate but with opposite sign suggesting that the large public deficits (mostly to finance the large unemployment in this period) had a positive effect on the government bond rate and a negative effect on inflation rate.

We will now take a closer look at the common trends implications of the three co-integration relations reported in Table 16.2. The liquidity ratio is described by the common trends

$$m^r - y^r = (0.70 - 1.13) \sum \varepsilon_y - (11.8 - 5.4) \sum \varepsilon_{Rb}$$
$$= -0.43 \sum \varepsilon_y - 6.4 \sum \varepsilon_{Rb},$$

and the homogeneous inflation rate–interest rates relation by

$$R_m - 0.8R_b - 0.2\Delta p = -(0.032 - 0.008)\sum \varepsilon_y + (0.93 - 1.12)\sum \varepsilon_{Rb}$$
$$= -0.024\sum \varepsilon_y - 0.19\sum \varepsilon_{Rb}.$$

Combining the two gives:

$$m^r - y^r - 16.1(R_m - 0.8R_b - 0.2\Delta p) = 0.04\sum \varepsilon_y - 3.2\sum \varepsilon_{Rb}.$$

While the two stochastic trends almost cancel in the liquidity ratio, the results become much more stationary when combining the latter with the opportunity cost of holding money relative to holding bonds or real stock (the second co-integration relation).[4]

Finally, the co-integration implications underlying the less interpretable inflation–income relation can be inferred from:

$$\Delta p + 0.03y^r = -(0.04 - 0.04)\sum \varepsilon_y + (0.08 - 0.16)\sum \varepsilon_{Rb}$$
$$= 0.0\sum \varepsilon_y - 0.08\sum \varepsilon_{Rb}$$

From Eq. (19), we note that inflation rate has been significantly (and negatively) influenced by $\sum \varepsilon_y$ but positively by $\sum \varepsilon_{Rb}$, whereas the opposite is the case with real aggregate income explaining why these two variables are negatively related over this sample. While a negative effect of a bond rate shock on aggregate income is completely plausible, the negative effect of an income shock on inflation is less so. As the negative co-movement between inflation and real aggregate income is very pronounced and, therefore, statistically significant, it would be against the Popperian spirit to ignore this finding. It is an example of an important piece of information in the data signaling the need to dig deeper in order to understand more.

Altogether, the empirical analysis of our VAR model has found support for some prior hypotheses, but also detected a number of surprising results. First of all, the finding that the empirical shocks to excess money, inflation, and the short-term interest rate exclusively, had a transitory effect on each

---

[4] The two stochastic trends do not cancel completely because Eq. (19) was estimated under the two weak exogeneity restrictions, and the β coefficients were estimated without this restriction.

other and the other variables of the system strongly suggests that in the post-Bretton Woods period *the Danish inflation is not explained by monetary factors.* The question is whether this surprising result is related to the finding of a negative relation between inflation and real aggregate income.

This prompted us to investigate the possibility that in this period the Danish price inflation had its origin in wage inflation and/or imported inflation (Juselius, 2005). This study indicated that many of the surprising results in the monetary model can be explained by some institutional changes which strongly influenced macroeconomic mechanisms in this period. In particular, the creation of the European Community and more generally the deregulation of international capital markets seem to have been crucial in this respect. Two important explanations can be mentioned:

1. The increased global price competitiveness significantly weakened the labor unions and put a downward pressure on nominal wage claims.
2. The increased internationalization of the capital market moved the determination of the Danish bond rate away from the domestic to the international capital markets and, thus, made the Danish bond rate exogenously determined in the present model.

The increased price competitiveness seemed foremost to have resulted in an adjustment of labor productivity (increase in labor intensity combined with new technology) with a parallel increase in unemployment (firing part of the labor force, hiring fewer people, and outsourcing). Thus, the cumulated empirical shocks to real aggregate income are essentially measuring shocks to trend-adjusted productivity. Positive shocks to the latter have often been associated with improvements in labor intensity (producing the same output with less labor and working harder for the same pay). Evidence supporting this is, for example, that unemployment rate and trend-adjusted productivity have been positively co-integrated in this period.

The finding that $\sum \varepsilon_y$ loaded negatively into the inflation rate can be explained by the downward pressure on prices as a result of the high unemployment rates in this period. Similarly, the finding that $\sum \varepsilon_y$ loaded positively into the bond rate can be explained by the large increase in the supply of government bonds to finance huge unemployment compensation in this period.

The finding that the bond rate, rather than the short rate, was weakly exogenous[5] points to the importance of international capital markets as an increasingly important driving force in the domestic macroeconomy. Closely related is our finding of nonstationary Fisher parities, an (almost) nonstationary interest rate spread and in an extended study (Juselius, 2005) nonstationary real exchange rates and uncovered interest rates parities. As similar empirical results have been found in a variety of empirical studies based on other countries' data, it is a strong signal that we need to understand why the international parity conditions are so persistent and how this lack of fast adjustment or market clearing has influenced the mechanisms of our domestic economy.

As demonstrated above empirical puzzles detected in the VAR analyses often suggest how to proceed to make empirical evidence and theory fit together more closely. This includes modifying the theoretical model by extending the information set or changing the model altogether. In either case the analysis points forward, which is why we believe the co-integrated VAR methodology has the potential of being a progressive research paradigm.

CONCLUSIONS

The purpose of this chapter was to illustrate how to extract information from the data based on the co-integrated VAR model and its decomposition into pulling and pushing forces. Methodologically, the approach combines deduction and induction. The deductive part of the analysis is based on a theory model, the testable implications of which have been translated into a set of hypotheses on the parameters of the VAR model describing long-run relations, adjustment dynamics, driving trends, and their effects on the variables of the system. Since the theory model (by necessity) is based on numerous simplifying assumptions, the VAR analysis usually detects discrepancies between empirical and theoretical behavior. The inductive part of the analysis treats such discrepancies as a useful piece of information helping us to adjust our intuition of how the economic and the empirical model work together, sometimes leading to modifications of a too narrowly specified theoretical model, in other cases to the generation of new hypotheses.

---

[5] Even though the distinction between empirical shocks to the short-term and the long-term interest rate was not unambiguous, the weak exogeneity finding of the bond rate has been confirmed in other studies based on different sets of information and different temporal aggregation.

Thus, by embedding the theory model in a broader empirical framework, the analysis of the statistically based model often provides evidence of possible pitfalls in macroeconomic reasoning. It also generates a set of relevant "stylized facts," such as the number of autonomous shocks and how they affect the variables of the system. This is in contrast to the more conventional graphs, mean values, and correlation coefficients, of which the latter are inappropriate when data are nonstationary. Finally, it provides a check on how sensitive theory based conclusions are to the *ceteris paribus* assumption.

The empirical application of a model for monetary inflation demonstrated that many aspects of the theory model can be translated into a set of testable hypotheses, all of which should be accepted for the theory model to have full empirical validity. This is in contrast to many empirical investigations, where inference is based on test procedures that only make sense in isolation, but not in the full context of the empirical model.

Econometrically, the approach follows the principle of general-to-specific, starting essentially from the covariances of the selected data and then sequentially imposing more and more restrictions on the model, some of which might be consistent with the theoretical priors, others not. In the latter case the rich structure of pulling and pushing forces provides a wealth of information which should help to generate new hypotheses and guide the user to follow new paths of enquiry.

Thus, a careful analysis of the empirical results might at an early stage suggest how to modify either the empirical or the economic model. This is one way of translating the notion of a design of experiment and the link between theory and empirical evidence when the latter is based on data collected by passive observation suggested in Haavelmo (1944):

> In the second case we can only try to adjust our theories to reality as it appears before us. And what is the meaning of a design of experiment in this case. It is this: We try to choose a theory and a design of experiments to go with it, in such a way that the resulting data would be those which we get by passive observation of reality. And to the extent that we succeed in doing so, we become masters of reality — by passive agreement.

The alternative, which is to force the chosen economic model on the data, thereby squeezing an exuberant reality into "all-too-small-size clothes," is a frustrating experience that often makes the desperate researcher choose solutions that are not scientifically justified.

Macroeconomic data have often been found to be quite informative about hypothetical long-run relationships and the propagation mechanism driving them. Therefore, we are convinced that the policy usefulness of empirical macromodels can be vastly improved by properly accounting for the dynamic adjustment of feedback and interaction effects to long-run steady-states.

PART V

POLICY IMPLICATIONS

17

Economic Policy in the Presence of Coordination Problems

Russell W. Cooper[*]

This chapter considers the conduct of economic policy in the presence of strategic complementarities and multiple equilibria. As highlighted in Cooper and John (1988), the existence of strategic complementarities in the choices of individual agents is present in many interactions. The presence of complementarities can lead to inefficiencies and, in the extreme, coordination failures and thus a rationale for intervention. The actions of a government may influence the selection of an equilibrium and the level of economic activity as well. So it is natural to consider economic policy and multiplicity jointly.

But determining optimal government policy in the presence of multiple equilibria is quite difficult due to problems in identifying structural parameters and in designing optimal policy when there are multiple Nash equilibria for a given policy. Here we formalize these issues and problems. In the context of the example of bank runs, we argue that policy interventions may allow researchers to resolve an important identification problem and thus distinguish shocks to fundamentals from variations in confidence.

To many economists, strategic complementarities are present in many economic and social interactions.[1] On the social side, the languages we speak, our driving conventions, the bars, beaches and restaurants we choose to frequent, fashions, etc. are all driven by the presence of complementarities that lead us all, in effect, to "do what others are doing." In economics, the demand for fiat money, returns to effort and education, return to investment, the decision on bank deposits, the expectations we

*The research assistance of Shutao Cao is gratefully acknowledged as is support from the National Science Foundation.

[1] The next section briefly reviews these concepts.

hold, the tax rates we face, the prices we set, and the structure of markets have all been viewed from the perspective of strategic complementarities.[2]

All of these interactions seem to generate plausible environments where complementarities exist and multiple, Pareto-ranked equilibria become possible. Further, ample experimental evidence of coordination games suggests that in the presence of multiple equilibria, it is not the case that the Pareto-superior Nash equilibrium is naturally selected. Thus the potential for coordination failure, defined as the selection of the Pareto-inferior equilibrium, is certainly quite real. If so, there are clearly social gains to coordinating on the Pareto-superior equilibrium and to other interventions needed to internalize external effects.

To formalize these ideas, the next section of the chapter provides a brief review of coordination games. We then turn to the design of government policy in this environment with particular emphasis on estimation of structural parameters and identification problems.

COORDINATION GAMES: AN OVERVIEW

To fix the terminology, consider the following game in which there are two players and each can choose either a high or low level of effort.

	high effort	low effort
high effort	(2,2)	(x,y)
low effort	(y,x)	(1,1)

Coordination Game

Assume that $x \in (0, 1)$ and $y \in (1, 2)$. With these restrictions, this game exhibits strategic complementarity in that the gains from high effort, say by the row player, are increasing in the effort level of the column player: $2 - y > 0 > x - 1$. Further, there are two pure strategy Nash equilibria: one in which both agents choose high effort and a second in which both choose low effort. Further, these equilibria are Pareto-ranked. The outcome in which all agents select low effort is termed a *coordination failure*. While both agents realize that the outcome with low effort is socially undesirable, neither, acting alone, can do anything about it.

---

[2] Numerous examples along these lines with references are provided in Cooper (1999).

Though variations in the parameters (x, y) within the limits set above have no effect on the set of equilibria, there are some arguments that link (x, y) to the selection of an equilibrium. Carlsson and van Damme (1993) consider an incomplete information version of a coordination game in which the values of (x, y) influence which of the Nash equilibria of the game with complete information is the unique equilibrium of the game with incomplete information.[3]

A final comment on the number of players is in order. There is a more general version of the basic coordination game in which there are N players, where N can be very large. In one interpretation, all of the players are selecting low or high effort levels as in the game above. In that case, one can think of the columns as indicating the choice of $N-1$ players and the row showing the choices of a single player. The outcomes in which all players choose high effort and all choose low effort are clearly Nash equilibria of the game with N players.

An alternative setting is one in which there are many interlinked games between pairs or small numbers of players. These small groups can be linked by the presence of some players in multiple groups with payoffs that are additive across the groups. These players choose a single action which is their strategy for each of the games in which they are involved. Here there is again the possibility of coordination failure.

Not surprisingly, coordination games have been studied in experimental economics. This experimental evidence, summarized in Cooper (1999), indicates that play does ultimately evolve to one of the Nash equilibria. But the Nash equilibrium selected is not necessarily the Pareto-dominant Nash equilibrium. Instead, coordination failures appear.

ECONOMIC POLICY

This section considers government interventions in economies with multiple equilibria. What does the presence of multiple equilibria imply for economic policy? How can policy interventions be used to internalize the externalities inherent in coordination games?

Intuitively, there are two rationales for interventions in coordination games. First, there is the selection issue: the government can help to

---

[3] To be more precise, they consider a class of 2×2 coordination games and introduce incomplete information about payoffs. They argue that as the amount of noise about payoffs vanishes, the equilibrium outcome in the game of incomplete information is the risk dominant equilibrium of the game with complete information.

overcome coordination problems by taking actions which support play at the Pareto-superior Nash equilibrium. Second, government actions may help to internalize external effects and thus increase social welfare. This is easier said than done since the design of economic policy in an environment with multiple equilibria can be quite challenging.

To study these issues, we first introduce government policy into the coordination game. We then study the design of government policy.

Government Policy in a Coordination Game

We study a more general version of a coordination game and then add in government intervention.[4] Let the payoff of an individual agent be given by $\sigma(e, E; X, \Theta)$ where e is the agent's action, E is the common action of others, and X is common shock.[5] Let Θ represent the vector of parameters characterizing payoffs.

Given the actions of others and the realized value of X, denote the (assumed) unique optimal response of a player by $e = \phi(E; X, \Theta)$. The derivative $\partial e/\partial E = \phi_E(E; X, \theta)$ characterizes the response of a single agent to a change in the common action of the others. In this example, $\phi_E(E; X, \theta) > 0$ is the case of strategic complementarity.

The set of symmetric Nash equilibria is defined by

$$\xi(X, \Theta) = \{e|e = \phi(e; X, \Theta)\}.$$

This set may not be unique due to strategic complementarity.[6] To consider government policy in this model, we assume that the government can commit to an intervention denoted $\Pi(E, X)$. By assumption, there is no commitment problem here as the government moves before private agents.[7] Further, note that the government's action

---

[4] This section draws upon Chari, Kehoe, and Prescott (1989) and chapter 7 of Cooper (1999).

[5] For simplicity, all actions are scalars and payoffs are given only for the case of a common action by all others, denoted E. More generally, E would be a vector of actions of the other players.

[6] See Cooper and John (1988) for a discussion of the link between strategic complementarity and multiplicity. If there is strategic substitutability, $\phi_E(E; X, \theta) < 0$ then multiple symmetric Nash equilibria will not arise though there may be multiple asymmetric Nash equilibria.

[7] So, by assumption, we can focus on the interaction of the players through $\sigma(e, E; X, \Theta)$ rather than on a commitment problem of the government.

depends on E rather than e. Thus the government's behavior reflects the aggregate effort variable and not the choice of a single agent.[8]

Given the government policy, we can define the set of Nash equilibria as

$$\xi(X; \Theta, \Pi(\cdot)) = \{e | e = \phi(e; X, \Theta), \Pi(\cdot)\}.$$

Here the government's policy rule is indicated explicitly as part of the best response function of the private agent and in the set of equilibria.[9]

Note that the set of equilibria reflects two types of interactions. First, there are the interactions between private agents that were present in the initial game. Second, the form of the government policy introduces another dependence of e on E.[10]

The government intervention may take two forms. First, in equilibrium the government might be actively involved through taxation, subsidies, spending, etc. Second, the government intervention may be indirect through various forms of guarantees and promised actions. In this case, the government may be inactive in equilibrium though its policy may have real effects by influencing payoffs out of equilibrium.

Recall the bi-matrix game. Suppose that the government wishes to support the equilibrium in which all agents supply high effort. To do so, it might subsidize effort levels so as to increase the return to high effort. Of course, these subsidies would have to be financed by some form of taxation and this would be taken into account in the welfare analysis of the policy. This is a type of direct intervention in that, in equilibrium, the government would be taxing and subsidizing.

Alternatively, suppose that the government had a policy in which it offered a subsidy to a group of agents who chose high effort when other agents chose low effort. The policy could be structured so that in the event all agents chose high effort, the government had no obligation. If the subsidy was larger than $1-x$, then high effort is a dominant strategy for each agent. In this case, the low effort equilibrium is eliminated as high effort becomes a dominant strategy. Yet in the high effort equilibrium, the government is inactive.

---

[8] Here we are focusing on symmetric outcomes by private agents. More generally, the government rule depends in general on the fractions of agent's choosing different actions. The key is that an individual cannot influence the government's choices.

[9] Alternatively, the function $\Pi(E, X)$ could be implicit in $\phi(E; X, \Theta)$.

[10] This is the source of the idea that in some cases government policy can itself induce strategic complementarity.

This second type of government policy is a type of confidence building measure. These policies can have real effects in coordination games as these interventions influence payoffs that agents receive off of the equilibrium path. So in equilibrium the government appears to be doing nothing even though its policies matter.

Optimal Government Policy

We can now state the optimization problem faced by the government. Denote the payoff of the representative agent as $V(X; \Pi(\cdot), \Theta) = E_{e \in \xi(X; \Pi(\cdot), \Theta)} \sigma(e, e; X, \Pi(\cdot), \Theta))$. Here the expectation is over the set of equilibria induced by the policy.

The government sets $\Pi(\cdot)$ to max $V(X; \Pi(\cdot), \Theta)$. This optimization problem is not trivial for a number of reasons.

First, as with any government policy decision, knowing the underlying parameters of the economy is necessary. That is, what is Θ? The estimation of Θ is made more difficult by the presence of multiple equilibria.

Second, as is clear from the definition of $V(X; \Pi(\cdot), \Theta)$, for a given government policy, there may be multiple equilibria. In this case, the government is assumed to impose a distribution on the equilibrium outcomes given its policy. This may be viewed as a sunspot process that is imposed on the set $\xi(X; \Pi(\cdot), \Theta)$.[11]

Importantly, with this formulation the government may choose a policy that induces multiple equilibria. Whether it wishes to or not depends on the severity of the coordination problem and the costs of obtaining a unique equilibrium. Looking again at the bi-matrix coordination game: if the government can costlessly remove the low effort equilibrium, then clearly it will choose to do so. But if elimination of the low effort equilibrium is costly, thus reducing the payoffs in the remaining equilibrium, then the government may in fact allow the multiplicity to remain as long as the probability of the low effort equilibrium is sufficiently low.[12]

The following sections discuss these issues in turn. In the discussion that follows, we draw on specific examples in the literature on coordination games.[13]

---

[11] Part of the government policy may itself try to influence this selection process through cheap talk.

[12] More concretely, deposit insurance may eliminate bank runs but the adverse incentive effects on banks and depositors may outweigh the gains to eliminating strategic uncertainty.

[13] Some of this discussion draws heavily on Cooper (2002).

ESTIMATION OF Θ

In this section, we discuss the estimation of Θ when complementarities are present and can be strong enough to create multiple equilibria. We illustrate this by discussing two areas of applied research on complementarities, one related to social interactions and the second associated with technological complementarities.

The main message here is that structural parameters can be identified. In fact, it might even be that identification is helped along by the presence of nonlinearities which underlie the multiplicity of equilibria.

Social Interactions: the Reflection Problem

In many settings, we can imagine that the behavior of individuals depends on the actions of others. The nature and strength of those interactions are important for how we think about social outcomes and give advice on various forms of social policy.

For example, school performance by one student may well depend on the behavior of a reference group of other students, as well as observable variables (such as school characteristics, the characteristics of the reference group, individual income, parents' education). Or, the likelihood that an individual may engage in criminal activity could depend on the choices made by his friends (reference group) as well as other social and income variables characterizing the individual and the reference group.

In formalizing these types of interactions, Manski (1993) assumes that individual behavior is given by:

$$y = \alpha + \beta E(y|x) + z'\eta + \mu. \tag{1}$$

Here y is an individual outcome and $E(y|x)$ is the outcome for the reference group where x refers to the group of agents who influence the individual. This statement of the problem ignores the influence of exogenous aspects of a reference group on individual behavior. As discussed in Manski (1993) and Brock and Durlauf (2004b, d), inclusion of these interactions exacerbates the identification problem. The exogenous variables are represented by z and μ is a shock to the individual outcome. The issue here is identification of the interaction between the group and the individual. This interaction is parameterized by β. Can we identify this parameter?

To solve for the equilibrium of the interactions between the agents, one can compute $E(y \mid x)$ yielding

$$E(y \mid x) = \frac{\alpha}{1 - \beta} + E(z' \mid x) \frac{\eta}{1 - \beta}. \tag{2}$$

Using $E(\mu \mid x) = 0$. Substitution into Eq. (1) implies

$$y = \frac{\alpha}{1 - \beta} + E(z' \mid x) \frac{\beta \eta}{1 - \beta} + z' \eta + \mu. \tag{3}$$

From this regression, there are three parameters to estimate (α, β, η) and three reduced form coefficients are estimated. Thus we can identify β if the regressors, $(E(z' \mid x), z')$, are linearly independent. This means that there must be sufficient individual variation relative to the group.

This depends, in turn, on group formation. To gain information about interactions, there must be some variations in individuals within a reference group. Thus the formation of reference groups becomes an important element of the identification discussion.

Section 6 of Brock and Durlauf (2000) contains a lengthy discussion of this and related identification issues. As discussed there, it may be possible to identify interactions if there are other sources of exogenous variation. Further, the above formulation is linear yet many models of interactions rely on nonlinearities as a basis for the multiplicity of equilibria. Durlauf (2000) and Brock and Durlauf (2000) argue that these nonlinearities may actually help identification of model parameters.

Technological Complementarities

In macroeconomics, one of the more convenient specifications for interaction between agents is through the production technology.[14] This formulation can easily be placed inside of the standard stochastic growth model.

Here we start with a production function (in logs) for an individual production site augmented by the aggregate level of output.

$$y_t = \alpha_n n_t + \alpha_k k_t + \phi Y_t + a_t. \tag{4}$$

---

[14] See Bryant (1983), Baxter and King (1991), Benhabib and Farmer (1994), Cooper and Johri (1997) for examples.

Here Y_t is the output of the "reference group," y_t is the output of an individual producer, and (n_t, k_t) are the inputs of labor and capital. The parameter ϕ here is like the β in Eq. (1) as it parameterizes the interaction between a single producer and the aggregate economy. If $\phi > 0$, then the high levels of aggregate activity increase the productivity of an individual producer.

Assuming that the technology shocks (a_t) are common to the producers, it is natural to look at a symmetric equilibrium in which $y_t = Y_t$. Using this condition, Eq. (4) becomes

$$y_t = \frac{\alpha_n}{1 - \phi} n_t + \frac{\alpha_k}{1 - \phi} k_t + a_t. \qquad (5)$$

This expression is analogous to Eq. (3). But there are two important differences. First, in Eq. (5) there are only two reduced form coefficients to identify three parameters. Second, there is good reason to think that the regressors are correlated with the productivity shock, a_t.

As in Baxter and King (1991) and Cooper and Johri (1997), one way to overcome the identification problem is to impose constant returns to scale in the producers' own inputs, $\alpha_n + \alpha_k = 1$. With this restriction, all the structural parameters are identified.

As for the correlation of inputs with a_t, the usual approach is to find instruments that imply movement along the production surface for fixed technology. Instruments, such as monetary policy innovations as well as sectoral variations, have been used.

There seems to be some evidence of technological complementarities. For example, Cooper and Johri (1997) estimate contemporaneous and dynamic complementarities and find significant interactions of both forms.[15]

Alternatively, if the null model has sunspot driven fluctuations, then these variations are enough to identify the production function parameters. In this sense, the multiplicity may aid rather than impede identification if these sunspots can be used as instruments.[16]

---

[15] Dynamic complementarities link the productivity at a plant in period t with lagged aggregated economic activity. Cooper and Johri (1997) impose CRS and estimate the contemporaneous complementarity at 0.24 and the dynamic effect at 0.32.

[16] The reader though might object as this begs the question of identifying sunspots. On this point, there is a sense that distinguishing sunspots from real shocks may be difficult, as discussed in Kamihigashi (1996).

GOVERNMENT POLICY: SOURCE OR SOLUTION
TO MULTIPLICITY?

Suppose that we have identified Θ. The issue for the government is then to formulate an optimal policy given that for some choices of $\Pi(\cdot)$ there may be multiple equilibria. So the government is interested in choosing $\Pi(\cdot)$ to max $V(X; \Pi(\cdot), \Theta)$.

A Selection Process

Recall that the $V(\cdot)$ function includes an expectation over the equilibrium set. Where does this expectation come from?

One approach that has been used in the literature is to assume there is a process that assigns non-negative probabilities to each element of the equilibrium set. This assignment of probabilities might reflect the view, for example, that the selection of an equilibrium reflects the theme of Pareto-dominance. In that case, only the Pareto-dominant Nash equilibrium would have a positive probability associated with it. Or the assignment of probabilities might reflect the concept of risk dominance which, as discussed by Carlsson and van Damme (1993), has some attractive properties.

Once a selection principle has been established, then a sunspot variable with the required distribution can be used to represent the uncertainty over the equilibrium outcomes. So for each choice of $\Pi(\cdot)$, social welfare, represented by $V(X; \Pi(\cdot), \Theta)$ is well defined.

Creating or Destroying Multiplicity

The interaction between policy and multiplicity is complicated by the fact that the set of equilibria reflects $\Pi(\cdot)$ in a couple of ways. The government's policy may create multiple equilibria or destroy some of the equilibria.

First, as noted earlier, some economic policies actually create a basis for multiplicity. A well-known example arises from the Laffer curve in which a government seeks to raise a fixed amount of revenue.[17]

As a simple example, suppose the government has to raise per capita revenues of G from a tax on output τ. Private agents have access to a technology which allows them to produce consumption goods from

---

[17] Cooper (1999) discusses this example and provides references. More complex cases are studied in Schmitt-Grohé and Uribe (1997) and Guo and Harrison (2004).

labor time. The utility function is given by $U(c) - g(n)$ where $U(\cdot)$ is strictly increasing and strictly concave and $g(\cdot)$ is strictly increasing and strictly convex. In the presence of government taxation, the budget constraint of an agent is $c = An(1 - \tau)$ where A is a productivity parameter.[18] The first order condition for the agent is $A(1 - \tau)U'(A(1 - \tau)n) = g'(n)$ implying a decision rule of $n(\tau)$. Assuming that substitution effects dominate, $n(\tau)$ is a decreasing function.

The government's budget constraint is $G = A\tau N$ where N is the level of labor input by the representative agent. In equilibrium $n(\tau) = N$ so that the condition for equilibrium becomes

$$G = A\tau n(\tau). \tag{6}$$

This equation can have multiple solutions; that is, there may exist multiple values of τ which solve Eq. (6). For example, if $U(c) = c$ and $g(n) = n^2/2$ then $n(\tau) = A(1 - \tau)$ and Eq. (6) becomes $G = A^2\tau(1 - \tau)$. So one possible equilibrium has high tax rates and low economic activity and another has low tax rates and high economic activity. Absent a commitment by the government, there are multiple equilibria in this interaction between private agents. In a similar vein, some monetary policy rules have been shown to be the source of multiplicity as well.[19]

Second, the government could take actions to eliminate the multiplicity.[20] These interventions often take the form of government guarantees.

A leading example of this is deposit insurance. Absent incentive problems, deposit insurance provides a guaranteed return to agents and thus eliminates bank runs. The government can have huge effects by acting on agents' beliefs without being active in equilibrium. Of course, the government policy must be credible for it to have these effects.

Government Policy and Identification Revisited

A final view of government policy and multiplicity comes from the challenge in distinguishing models driven by fundamental shocks from those driven by expectations alone. An example is the study of the Great

---

[18] In this example, if $G = 0$ so that $\tau = 0$, there is no interaction between agents.

[19] On this important consideration, see Benhabib, Schmitt-Grohé, and Uribe (2001).

[20] It is not obvious this is always the best policy. At least in principle, the actions which eliminate the multiplicity may be so distortionary that private agents are better off dealing with strategic uncertainty.

Depression by Cooper and Corbae (2001) where sunspots determine the beliefs by private agents on the returns to intermediation and are the source of fluctuations in aggregate activity. However a competing model might generate similar fluctuations in activity from fundamental shocks to the intermediation process.

So are the fluctuations driven by expectations or fundamentals? This becomes an identification problem since there is a problem estimating the variance of the fundamental shock and the parameters determining the complementarity between agents and the sunspot process.[21]

One resolution of this identification problem might rest in examining the response of the economy to certain forms of government intervention. Consider the effects of deposit insurance. To a large degree, the deposit insurance eliminates the runs equilibrium, leaving the no-runs equilibrium intact. So, in equilibrium, there are no-runs and the government is inactive. Yet there was an effect through confidence of the government policy.

Contrast this with a model in which fluctuations are driven by fundamentals. In that case, it seems that the effects of the deposit insurance will be different since the fundamental shocks do not disappear when deposit insurance is introduced. Instead, the influence of these shocks reappear in other aspects of the economy.

To be sure, working this out requires a model of fundamentals and deposit insurance. The point of the discussion is simply to say that perhaps the response of the economy to some forms of government intervention may be quite revealing about the underlying sources of fluctuations.

CONCLUSION

This chapter studies government policy in a world of multiple equilibria. From the outset, it is quite natural to study government interventions in a setting with coordination failures since there are welfare gains from well-formulated policy.

Yet the existence of multiplicity produces additional problems for the design of optimal policy. These range from the difficulty of identifying parameters in the presence of complementarities to the selection of an equilibrium given government policy.

There is a positive side to the discussion here as well. For researchers studying models with complementarities, there is also the possibility that government policy interventions may actually help identification.

---

[21] Kamihigashi (1996) discusses this point in the context of the stochastic growth model.

18

Monetary Policy and the Limitations
of Economic Knowledge

Peter Howitt

I have always found it useful to think of a modern free-enterprise economy as a human anthill. Like an anthill, it organizes individuals' activities into patterns more complex than the individuals can fully comprehend, it performs collective tasks that the individuals are hardly aware of, and it can adapt to shocks whose consequences none of the individuals can predict. Of course we humans have more cognitive ability than ants, but the U.S. economy is correspondingly more complex than an anthill. The unsettled state of macroeconomics is testimony to the fact that even those of us who should know best do not really understand much about how the economy works. And yet it does seem to work, at least most of the time and reasonably well.

This is not to say that macroeconomists know nothing, or that macroeconomic wisdom is unattainable. As I will argue below, I think there is much to be learned by viewing the economy as an anthill, and much we have already learned from an emergent Post Walrasian literature that has adopted this viewpoint. This literature has taught us about aspects of economic policy that are not even visible from the viewpoint of rational-expectations-equilibrium analysis, an analysis that evades the issue of limited economic knowledge by assuming that everyone operates with a consistent and correct (at some level) set of economic beliefs. My purpose here is to point out some of the insights that this Post Walrasian perspective yields concerning one component of economic policy, namely monetary policy.

SOME BACKGROUND

The anthill metaphor raises two fundamental theoretical questions. The first concerns behavior in the face of radical uncertainty. How do people make choices in a world where the consequences of those choices will depend on the behavior of a system they do not fully understand, and which they know they do not fully understand? The other question is how a system that none of its participants understands can somehow or other make collective sense; that is, how can an economy like that of the United States be in a fairly coordinated state of affairs most of the time, usually within five or ten percent of a full-employment growth path, without chronic shortages or surpluses, when people are constantly acting at cross-purposes because of the mistakes that are inevitable under radical uncertainty, under what circumstances can the economy's regulatory mechanisms work best to keep the system well coordinated despite this confusion, and what is it that goes wrong when the mechanisms appear to break down as during the Great Depression of the 1930s?

Corresponding to these two broad theoretical questions are two related policy questions. How should policymakers themselves act when faced with the same kind of radical uncertainty as faced by the private actors in the system, and what kind of government policies are needed to allow the economy's regulatory mechanisms to keep the economy close to a fully coordinated state instead of permitting cumulative departures?

Such questions occupied a prominent place in pre-rational-expectations macroeconomics. Although in many dimensions Keynes and Friedman had opposing visions of the economic system, both of them put decision-making under deep uncertainty about economic relationships at the forefront of their analysis. To Keynes what mattered was the uncertainty faced by private decision-makers, especially by entrepreneurs and investors, which made aggregate investment depend more on "animal spirits" than on rational calculations. To Friedman what mattered was the uncertainty faced by policymakers, especially uncertainty concerning the long and variable lags in the effects of monetary policy, which he argued made discretionary policy likely to do more harm than good.

Moreover, both Keynes and Friedman argued that if the right kind of policies were not followed, the economic system's built-in stabilizing mechanisms would be unable to prevent departures from a coordinated full-employment state, although of course they differed in their definition of "the right kind of policies." For Keynes the right policies involved collective intervention to boost investment demand when animal spirits are low. He believed that if the economy were left to its own devices, the mechanisms which classical theory saw as stabilizing the system would actually destabilize it. In particular, wage- and price-flexibility might make departures from full employment cumulative, because of the dynamics of expectations, debt deflation and distributional effects. Although this instability argument was not picked up by mainstream Keynesianism, which for the most part focused on the more classical aspects of Keynes, specifically the stickiness of money wages, nevertheless it was prominent in the writings of influential interpreters of Keynes such as Tobin (1947, 1975), Patinkin (1948), Clower (1965) and Leijonhufvud (1968).

For Friedman the right policy was to keep the money supply growing at a constant rate. In his famous presidential address to the American Economic Association (Friedman, 1968) he argued that the attempt by a central bank to control something other than the money supply, or some other nominal variable that would be proportional to the money supply in a long-run equilibrium, would lead to a cumulative process of accelerating inflation or deflation. Controlling the money supply, on the other hand, would provide the system with a nominal anchor and allow the system's built-in stabilizers to do their job.

But the idea of the economy as an anthill whose ability to organize activities into stable patterns depends on macroeconomic policy was cast aside by the rational-expectations revolution that started with Lucas's seminal (1972) article. The rational-expectations paradigm, which was quickly embraced by macroeconomists of all stripes, Keynesians as well as monetarists, assumes that the economy is never out of a state of perfect coordination, that it always organizes activities into stable patterns in such quick order that the details of the stabilizing mechanism, and the uncertainty associated with those details, can safely be ignored. That is, in a rational-expectations equilibrium everyone's expectations about what will happen are consistent with the macroeconomic forces actually at work, and also consistent with everyone else's expectations, no matter what kinds of policies are pursued.

In contrast, the newly emergent Post Walrasian literature on macro policy takes seriously the radical uncertainty implied by our limited understanding of the economy, and analyzes the effects of policy even when the economy is far from a rational-expectations equilibrium. Some of this literature is directly addressed at how policymakers should take uncertainty into account.[1] But here my focus is on another branch of the literature, one that originated after the onset of the rational-expectations revolution when people began to think critically about the revolutionary new paradigm.

---

[1] For example, Sims (2002), Hansen and Sargent (2003a, b), and Brock, Durlauf, and West (2003).

In particular, Frydman and Phelps (1983) and Sargent (1993) made it clear that the assumption of rational-expectations makes sense only if people are capable of learning macroeconomic relationships from the experience of living in the economy, and the classical consistency theorems of statistical theory do not imply that these relationships are in fact learnable, because of the self-referential nature of macroeconomic learning. That is, statistical theory guarantees that under quite general conditions people should be capable of consistently estimating relationships from observing a long-enough series of data generated by those relationships. But in macroeconomics the relationships that we are trying to learn about are affected by our very attempts to learn about them, as when we change our expectations of inflation as a result of recent experience and this affects the actual rate of inflation by shifting the Phillips curve. Whether or not the attempt to learn about a system whose properties are affected by our very attempt to learn them will ever converge to a rational-expectations equilibrium is the subject of a now burgeoning literature, which was recently summarized by Evans and Honkapohja (2001). Much of this literature focuses on the question of equilibrium selection. But from my point of view the literature is important primarily because it also sheds light on the bigger question raised by the anthill metaphor, which is whether or not the economy is capable of converging to any kind of coordinated equilibrium at all.

Thinking about the economy in these terms yields a number of insights about how macropolicy works, and particularly about the role it plays in stabilizing or destabilizing the economy — making it closer to or further away from a full-employment rational-expectations equilibrium. I discuss below seven specific lessons that I think one can learn about monetary policy by taking this approach. I illustrate some of them in terms of very simple models, although I think they are all valid under much more general assumptions.

LESSONS FOR MONETARY POLICY

1. Interest-rate Rules

I begin with an argument that I presented about fifteen years ago (Howitt, 1992) concerning interest-rate rules. At the time, there was sizable literature on the subject of interest-rate smoothing as a strategy for conducting monetary policy, and it seemed to me that this literature was ignoring one of the most important lessons of Friedman's presidential address.

That lesson was his interpretation of Wicksell's cumulative process, according to which the attempt by a central bank to control interest rates too tightly would lead to accelerating inflation or deflation.

Friedman argued that at any given time there is a hypothetical ("natural") real rate of interest that would generate a full employment level of demand. If the central bank set nominal interest rates too low, given the expected rate of inflation, then the real interest rate would be below this hypothetical natural rate, and this would generate excess aggregate demand, which would cause inflation to rise faster than expected, because of an expectations-augmented Phillips curve. With inflation running faster than expected, people's expectations of inflation would at some point start to rise, and if the nominal rate of interest were kept fixed that would just fuel the fire even more by reducing the real rate of interest still further below its natural rate.

That idea made good sense to me but it seemed to have disappeared completely from the literature after the rational-expectations revolution.[2] I concluded that this was something that was invisible from the viewpoint of rational-expectations-equilibrium theory, that you cannot see the cumulative process if you assume the economy is always in a rational-expectations equilibrium, because the process involves the instability of the economy's equilibrating mechanism, the very mechanism that rational-expectations theory assumes can safely be ignored and prohibits you from analyzing.

The instability problem can be illustrated with the following model:

$$y_t = -\sigma \cdot \left(i_t - \pi_t^e - r^* \right), \tag{IS}$$

$$\pi_t = \pi_t^e + \phi \cdot y_t, \tag{PC}$$

where y_t is output, i_t is the nominal rate of interest, π_t and π_t^e are respectively the actual and expected rates of inflation, and r^* is the natural rate of interest. The first equation is the usual IS curve, in which the real rate of interest must equal the natural rate in order for output to equal its capacity (full-employment) value, here normalized to zero. The second equation is the expectations-augmented Phillips curve, expressed in terms of inflation and output rather than inflation and unemployment. (The coefficients σ and ϕ are both positive, as are all the coefficients in the equations below.)

[2] There was a literature about interest-rate rules and indeterminacy, but that was really a different issue.

Suppose that the central bank kept the nominal interest rate fixed, at some level i. Then the model would have a unique rational-expectations equilibrium in which the rate of inflation depends (positively) on the pegged rate of interest:

$$\pi_t = i - r^* = \pi^*.$$

Thus according to rational-expectations theory there would be no problem of accelerating or decelerating inflation. But suppose the economy departed from its rational-expectations equilibrium because people did not have enough knowledge to form rational expectations, then people would make forecast errors, and presumably they would try to learn from these errors. The problem is that under this particular policy regime the signals they would be receiving from their forecast errors would be misleading. Instead of leading the economy closer to the equilibrium these signals would lead it ever further away.

More precisely, from (IS) and (PC) the forecast error at any date t is:

$$\pi_t - \pi_t^e = \phi \cdot \sigma \cdot \left(\pi_t^e - \pi^* \right).$$

So when people are expecting more than the rational expectation π^*, as they are when the central bank pegs the interest rate too low,[3] they will find that the actual rate of inflation is more than they had expected, and any sensible learning rule will lead them to raise their expectation, taking it even further away from its unique equilibrium value π^*.

At the time I was first writing this, the state of the art in macrotheory was represented by Blanchard and Fisher's (1989) graduate textbook, where I finally found a contemporary reference (p. 577) to Wicksell's cumulative process. But that reference came with a warning that the idea was not to be taken seriously, because it was a relic of pre-rational-expectations thinking, dependent on a mechanical adaptive-expectations rule. Surely if people's expectations do not converge under adaptive expectations they will keep trying different ways of forming expectations until they finally do converge. And once they do the economy will be in a rational-expectations equilibrium in which inflation is constant, equal to π^*, rather than accelerating.

---

[3] That is, by the definition of π^*, the actual real interest rate $i - \pi_t^e$ is less than the natural rate r^* if and only if $\pi_t^e > \pi^*$.

That was the kind of thinking that even the best of us had been led into by the rational-expectations revolution. But it missed the essential point of Friedman's analysis. The problem is that when you are in the sort of world where every time you guess too high you get a signal that you are guessing too low, *any* rule that actually tries to learn from mistakes is bound to lead people astray, not just some fixed mechanical adaptive-expectations rule. The main purpose of my 1992 paper was to make just this point, only much more formally.

Moreover, as (PC) makes clear, when the economy generates higher and higher forecast errors it is also generating larger and larger departures of real output from its equilibrium value. In other words, the instability that is generated by a mistaken policy of trying to peg nominal interest rates is also preventing the economic system from converging to a full-employment equilibrium. This is the sort of problem that the anthill metaphor of Post Walrasian theory helps us to identify, and the sort of problem that rational-expectations theory assumes out of existence.

In that 1992 paper I also showed that the central bank can correct the Wicksellian instability problem by making the nominal rate of interest respond to the actual rate of inflation, provided that the response is greater than point-for-point. That provision has since come to be known as the "Taylor" principle. If followed it would at least make convergence to a rational-expectations equilibrium possible. Intuitively, following the "Taylor" principle would imply that once expectations caught up to the rise in actual inflation, the nominal rate of interest would rise by enough to ensure that the real rate of interest also rises. This would reduce the output gap, according to the (IS) relationship, and this in turn would make the actual inflation rate fall below the expected inflation rate, according to the expectations-augmented Phillips curve (PC).

In other words, if the "Taylor" principle is obeyed then when people forecast a rate of inflation that exceeds the unique rational-expectations value they will receive the correct signal that their forecast is indeed too high, because they will end up observing a rate of inflation lower than expected. This will help them to correct their expectational error, rather than compounding it as would happen with a fixed nominal rate of interest.

Thus an adaptive point of view allows one to see how Wicksell's cumulative process makes sense, how it threatens the economy's capacity for self-regulation, and what kind of policy it takes to avoid the problem. Moreover, Woodford (2003) shows that the analysis is much more general than my original analysis indicated, by proving that the "Taylor" principle is necessary for expectational stability in a broad class of New Keynesian models.

2. The Harrod Problem

Another problem for monetary policy arises when people's decisions are affected by their expectations of the growth rate of output, rather than or in addition to expectations of inflation. That complicates the problem of monetary policy and adds further requirements to the kind of interest-rate policy needed to stabilize the economy. I started thinking about this several years ago when I reread Harrod (1939) on the inherent instability of the warranted rate of growth.[4]

The issue Harrod raised lies at the heart of the coordination problem that Keynes was wrestling with. That is, when technological progress or capital accumulation creates a bigger capacity output, what guarantees that aggregate demand will rise by just the right amount to utilize the increased capacity? If demand does not rise by that much then the result will be excess capacity and unemployment. To avoid this, in the absence of an activist fiscal policy, it is necessary for investment demand to increase by just the right amount. But investment demand is driven by expectations of how fast the economy will be growing, and those expectations in turn depend on the economy's actual growth rate.

What Harrod argued, in the context of a simple multiplier-accelerator model, is that whenever investors' expected growth rate rises above the "warranted" growth rate — what we would now call simply the equilibrium growth rate — the familiar Keynesian multiplier raises the actual growth rate by more than the initial increase in the expected growth rate. So again we have the phenomenon of misleading signals; whenever investors are expecting more than the equilibrium rate, they will get a signal that they have forecast too little. In such a world the expectations needed for the economy to be in equilibrium are virtually unlearnable.

The multiplier-accelerator model that Harrod used is no longer on the frontier of macroeconomics. However, something very like his instability problem can be seen in a model that is on the frontier, one that also shows why Harrod's insight is important for monetary policy. Specifically, consider the following variant of the New-Keynesian model analyzed by Woodford (2003, Chapter. 4). It has a new IS curve with expectations

---

[4] My understanding of Harrod was helped greatly by reading Sen (1960) and Fazzari (1985).

of output on the right-hand-side as well as the level, an interest-rate rule and an expectations-augmented Phillips curve:

$$i_t = -\sigma \cdot \left(y_t - y_{t+1}^e\right) + \pi_{t+1}^e = \sigma \cdot g_{t+1}^e + \pi_{t+1}^e \tag{ISa}$$

$$i_t = \phi_\pi \pi_t + \phi_y g_t \tag{MP}$$

$$\pi_t = \pi_{t+1}^e + \phi \cdot \left(y_t - y_t^*\right) \tag{PCa}$$

In Woodford's analysis, the interest-rate rule (MP) reacts to the level of the output gap: $x_t = y_t - y_t^*$ instead of to the growth rate g_t of output, and the growth rate of capacity output is assumed to be a constant whose value is known by everyone. Under these assumptions he shows that if people form their expectations of x_t and π_t by taking sample averages, or by using ordinary least squares each period to estimate the parameters of the model, then there is a unique rational-expectations equilibrium, which is stable under these learning schemes, if and only if the monetary policy rule obeys the above-mentioned "Taylor" principle of my 1992 paper; that is if and only if the interest rate reacts more than point-for-point to inflation $(\phi_\pi > 1)$.[5]

However, things are different if the growth rate of capacity output is unknown and expectations are focused on the growth rate g_t rather than level x_t. For suppose that capacity output grows according to:

$$y_t^* = y_{t-1} + g_t^*, \quad g_t^* = \text{a serially uncorrelated random variable.} \tag{G}$$

Equation (G) allows for "hysteresis;" that is, a shortfall of output below capacity in period $t-1$ will lead to a reduction in capacity output in period t.[6] Then it can be shown, using the same methods as Woodford, that if people form their expectations of g_t and π_t by taking sample averages, or by using ordinary least squares each period to estimate the parameters of the model, then there is a unique rational-expectations equilibrium, which is stable under these learning schemes, if and only if the monetary policy rule obeys the two conditions:

$$\text{(a) } \phi_\pi > 1 \quad \text{and} \quad \text{(b) } \sigma < \phi \cdot \phi_\pi + \phi_y.$$

---

[5] In Woodford's analysis, the Phillips Curve (PCa) has a coefficient β slightly less than unity on expected inflation, which implies a slightly modified "Taylor" principle, but this small difference has no substantive implications for the issues at hand.

[6] Hysteresis could result from a number of different factors, including skill-loss by unemployed workers or reduced learning-by-doing.

Condition (a) is the "Taylor" principle, but it does not guarantee the additional condition (b). Under realistic values of the other parameters, (b) requires either a reaction coefficient to inflation that is much larger than unity or a significantly positive reaction coefficient to the growth rate.

Thus even this modern New-Keynesian analysis implies that the Harrod problem is potentially important, that growth-rate expectations are a potentially destabilizing force in an economic system, and that a monetary policy that ignores them by focusing simply on de-trended output or output gaps will give a misleading impression of what a central bank must do to make the economy self-regulating. In particular, the Harrod problem implies that macroeconomic stability requires an even more vigorous and activist monetary policy when people are uncertain about the growth of capacity output than when this uncertainty is not present. The problem is obviously important for monetary policy in the 1990s and early 2000s, where debates continue about the long-term growth implications of the "new economy." This is yet another effect that is not visible from a rational-expectations-equilibrium point of view, and yet another policy lesson that we can learn from viewing the economy as an adaptive mechanism characterized by imperfect economic understanding.

3. Keynes–Cagan–Tobin Instability

The difficulties raised in the two previous sections arise under a form of interest-rate targeting. But they do not imply that central banks should give up interest-rate targeting and go back to pure monetary targeting. For even if one could solve the velocity-instability problem that plagued attempts at monetary targeting in the 1970s and 1980s, there is no guarantee that a constant money-growth rule would allow the economy's automatic stabilizers to keep the system always near full employment as Friedman believed. For the possibility that Keynes raised, namely that relying on wage- and price-adjustment without any activist macropolicy might desta-bilize the economy rather than stabilize it, would not automatically be avoided by a Friedmanesque policy of a fixed rate of monetary expansion.

One of the destabilizing mechanisms that Keynes pointed out was that of inflation expectations. He argued that if the price level started falling in the face of excess capacity people might postpone purchases, waiting for prices to fall even further, thus exacerbating the problem of excess capacity rather than alleviating it. This is closely related to the problem that Cagan (1956) showed might destabilize inflation under a constant monetary growth rate. Cagan's analysis starts by noting that any rise in the expected rate of inflation will raise the opportunity cost of holding money, which will reduce the amount of purchasing power that people want to hold in the form of money. If there is no compensating reduction in the nominal supply of money then people's attempts to spend their excess money holdings will create inflationary pressure. Cagan showed that depending on the size of the interest-elasticity of the demand for money and the speed with which expectations adapt to forecast errors, the result could be to make the actual rate of inflation rise by even more than the expected rate of inflation, thus generating a cumulative process of accelerating inflation much like the process that Friedman later pointed out would arise under a fixed nominal rate of interest.

Cagan's analysis was conducted under the assumption of continuous full employment. However, an analysis similar to Tobin's (1975) shows that Cagan's results also hold in a simple Keynesian IS–LM system, in which the same stability condition that Cagan found is now a condition for the stability of full employment. This analysis makes it clear that inflation expectations can indeed impair an economy's capacity for self-regulation under a noninterventionist monetary policy, as Keynes had argued in his *General Theory* (1936, Chapter 19).

The key to this analysis is to recognize that the demand for money, which underlies the LM curve, depends on the nominal rate of interest, whereas the demand for real goods and services, which underlies the IS curve, depends on the real rate of interest. Because of this, the reduced-form level of output that is determined by the IS–LM system will depend positively on the expected rate of inflation. That is, for any given expected rate of inflation we can express both curves, IS and LM, as functions of the nominal rate of interest. But if the expected rate of inflation were to increase then any given nominal rate of interest would correspond to a lower real rate of interest, boosting aggregate demand and thus shifting the IS curve to the right.

Consider the following model:

$$y_t = a_m m_t + a_\pi \pi_t^e \qquad \text{(IS} - \text{--LM)}$$

$$\Delta m_t = \mu - \pi_t \qquad \text{(MPa)}$$

$$\pi_t = \pi_t^e + \phi \cdot y_t \qquad \text{(PC)}$$

$$\Delta \pi_t^e = \beta \cdot \left(\pi_t - \pi_t^e \right) \qquad \text{(AE)}$$

in which the reduced-form output from the IS and LM curves depends positively on the log m_t of the real money supply (which enters the LM curve) and also positively on the expected rate of inflation (which enters the IS curve as discussed above). Equation (MPa) states that the growth rate of the real money supply, which can be expressed as the change in m_t, is the difference between the constant growth rate μ of the nominal money stock and the rate of inflation. Equation (PC) is the familiar expectations-augmented Phillips curve and (AE) is the adaptive-expectations equation, which in modern terms is sometimes seen as a "constant-gain" learning algorithm[7] (Evans and Honkapohja, 2001, pp. 48 ff.).

It is straightforward to show that the conditions for stabilizing this model are identical to the Cagan stability conditions:

$$\beta \cdot a_\pi / a_m < 1,$$

the left-hand-side of which is precisely the speed of adaptation of expectations β times the semi-elasticity of demand for money with respect to the rate of interest.

Thus again Post Walrasian theory has resurrected what some had thought was a relic of pre-rational-expectations theory, namely the expectational instability problem that Keynes, Cagan, and Tobin analyzed, and has provided a new viewpoint from which we can see that this relic actually makes sense and that it raises policy issues which, although old, remain unresolved.

4. Uncertainty-Avoidance by the Private Sector

One of the ways in which people cope with radical uncertainty of macroeconomic forces is to avoid basing their decisions on expectations. Instead of attempting to anticipate the unforecastable they take a wait-and-see attitude, reacting only after the fact. Thus for example wage negotiations that do not respond to information that raises the likelihood of a future rise in inflation may cost workers something if that future inflation in fact materializes, but much of the cost can be recovered in the next round of negotiations by holding out for *ex post* increases to catch up

---

[7] A constant-gain algorithm makes sense in a world that exhibits structural shifts, because a decreasing-gain algorithm like least-squares learning with infinite memory would give almost no weight to recent observations and thus would fail to respond quickly to structural shifts.

with inflation. Indeed the work of Riddell and Smith (1982) provides strong evidence of such behavior in contractual wage data. Likewise firms may wait until costs have actually risen before marking up their prices rather than trying to anticipate unpredictable increases in their costs and in their rivals' prices.

This sort of behavior probably explains the evidence found by Fuhrer (1997) of backward-looking behavior in the Phillips curve. An extreme form of this backward-looking behavior would result in a Phillips curve like:

$$\pi_{t+1} = \pi_t + \phi \cdot \left(y_t - y_t^* \right) \qquad \text{(PCb)}$$

which differs from the more common expectations-augmented Phillips curves (PC) and (PCa) above in that the right-hand-side has the actual past rate of inflation instead of the expected future rate.

It turns out that this change has important implications for monetary policy. Indeed if the Phillips curve is given by the backward form (PC) instead of the forward form (PC) then the Cagan condition that guaranteed the stability of full employment in the system of the previous section is still necessary for this stability result, but it no longer provides a guarantee of stability. In effect, the backward Phillips curve (PC) together with (IS–LM) makes the second derivative of the price level (the change in the rate of inflation) depend negatively on the price-level itself. A linear model in which the second derivate of a variable depends negatively on its level would produce a pure sine wave, like a thermostat that raises the inflow of heat in proportion to the temperature. Such a system would lie exactly on the knife-edge between convergence and explosive divergence. In the economic system we are investigating, the destabilizing tendency imparted by having expected inflation in the IS curve can be enough to tip this system into explosive divergence.

So once again we see a reason why a nonactivist monetary policy might prevent an economy from being self-regulating, a reason that we have found by looking at the economy from an adaptive Post Walrasian perspective but which would be invisible from a rational-expectations viewpoint. In this case it would be invisible not because the system has a stable rational-expectations equilibrium. Indeed it can easily be shown that even if we replaced the adaptive-equations assumption (AE) by perfect foresight ($\pi_t^e = \pi_{t+1}$) the system would still be unstable. Rather it would be invisible because the system just does not make sense under rational-expectations; that is, the backward-looking Phillips curve (PC) depends on behavior that explicitly avoids reliance on expectations, rational or otherwise.

This instability result is a sort of dual to the analysis of Sargent (1999a), according to whom the U.S. inflation rate has been unstable because the Phillips curve is forward-looking, the Fed wrongly believes that it is backward-looking, and there is constant-gain learning by the Fed. In my model, inflation is unstable because the Phillips curve is backward-looking, the Fed acts as if it wrongly believes that it is forward-looking, and there is constant-gain learning by the public. Which model is closer to the truth is the subject of much ongoing empirical research on the nature of the Phillips curve,[8] none of which would make much sense from a strict rational-expectations-equilibrium point of view.

5. Learning-induced Volatility

Many of the fluctuations observed in the level of economic activity may be attributable not to fluctuations in fundamental driving variables, or even to fluctuations in extraneous sun spot variables, but rather to fluctuations in expectations that take place as part of the learning process. In this respect, there is an interesting recent paper by Orphanides and Williams (2003a). It takes a New Keynesian model with a hybrid forward/backward Phillips curve and supposes that people form expectations in accordance with a constant-gain learning algorithm. It compares the optimal policy for a policymaker trying to minimize a loss function involving inflation and output to what would be an optimal policy in a world where people had rational expectations and the central bank knew that they did.

What Orphanides and Williams argue is that monetary policy should be *less* activist in its response to fluctuations in output than in a rational-expectations world, and the reason again has to do with imperfect macroeconomic knowledge, specifically the difficulty of identifying shifts in the natural rate of unemployment. That is, when the central bank loosens its policy in response to a rise in the rate of unemployment, there is some chance that the rise in unemployment is actually a rise in the natural rate of unemployment, not a deviation above the natural rate. If so, then the policy reaction risks starting an inflationary process will be hard to bring under control. With people following a constant-gain learning algorithm it takes some time before inflation starts to take off, but then it also takes some time before inflation will come back down again once the mistake is

---

[8] For example, Galí and Gertler (1999), Rudd and Whelan (2003), and Mavroeidis (2004).

realized and policy is corrected. During the correction period the economy will have to undergo a recession, unlike what would happen under rational expectations.

This result of Orphanides and Williams offers an interesting alternative to Sargent's (1999a) explanation of the rise and fall of U.S. inflation. Specifically, it suggests that policy mistakes were made in the 1970s and 1980s by a Fed that persistently underestimated the natural rate of unemployment, and that once these mistakes were realized, the sluggishness of macroeconomic learning on the part of private agents implied that only by inducing a recession could the Fed bring inflation back down again.

An adaptive perspective makes that lesson quite clear, and suggests an extra degree of caution in the conduct of monetary policy over and above what would be implied by a rational-expectations perspective. Of course this lesson conflicts with those of the previous sections, which argued for a more interventionist policy, not less. But the lesson is worthwhile even if it is not right, because it shows us what to look for when carrying out the empirical analysis necessary to judge how interventionist policy should be. The role of theory is to point out possible effects and provide a framework in which to interpret empirical work aimed at quantifying the often conflicting effects suggested by theory. In this case only an adaptive theoretical framework is capable of performing those functions because the policy issues involved would simply not arise if the economy were always in a rational-expectations equilibrium.

6. Monetary Theory and Policy

Another benefit of viewing the economy as an anthill is that an adaptive approach makes it easier to understand the relationship between monetary theory and policy. We are part of the policy process, which is something that we do not always take into account. Indeed, monetary policy in industrialized countries has followed academic fashion pretty closely since World War II. In the 1950s and 1960s, when most academic macroeconomists were Keynesians, and believed that the quantity of money was not worth paying much attention to, that instead central banks should be looking closely at interest rates and various nonmonetary measures of liquidity, that is what central banks were doing. When monetarism rose in the academic literature, central banks started to experiment with monetary targeting. Then, as the profession started to lose faith in monetarism, central banks moved to exchange-rate targeting, and then to inflation targeting.

In many of these developments it was clear that economic theory played a leading role. Monetary theory was certainly one of the factors accounting for the apparent herding behavior of central banks, who always seemed to be doing the same thing at the same time.[9] That is, central banks learn from each other and also from academic economists. This social learning takes place in conferences, summit meetings, policy debates, and many other channels through which ideas about monetary theory and policy are constantly being exchanged.

Moreover, it is not just the policymakers that are learning from monetary theorists. Often the conduct of monetary policy is way ahead of the theory, and we academic economists often have more to learn from practitioners than they have from us. I came to realize this when I was a participant in monetary-policy debates in Canada in the early 1990s. The Bank of Canada was moving to inflation targeting at the same time as the country was phasing in a new goods and services tax. The new tax was clearly going to create a problem for the Bank by causing an upward blip in the price level. Even if the Bank could prevent this blip from turning into an inertial inflationary spiral, the immediate rise in inflation that would accompany the blip threatened to undermine the credibility of the new inflation-reduction policy.

The Bank dealt with this problem by estimating the first-round effect of the new tax on the price level, under the assumption that the path of wages would not be affected, and designing a policy to limit the price blip to that estimated amount. It announced that this was its intention, and that after the blip it would stabilize inflation and bring it down from about six percent to within a one to three percent band over the coming three years.

At that time I was very skeptical. Along with many other academic economists I thought it was foolish for the Bank to announce that it was going to control something like inflation, which it can only affect through a long and variable lag, with such a high degree of precision. To me the idea reeked of fine-tuning, and I thought the Bank was setting itself up for a fall. But I was wrong. In the end the Bank pulled it off just as planned. The price level rose by the amount predicted upon the introduction of the new tax,

[9] Another factor is the strategic complementarities involved in bureaucratic policy-formation. That is, it is easier for the officials of a central bank to defend its policies against criticism if they can show that the bank is just following state-of-the-art policy advice, like the other central banks around the world, than if the bank has set out on an independent course of its own.

and then inflation quickly came down to within the target range, where it has been almost continuously ever since.[10]

This is not the only recent example of a central bank succeeding in doing something that academic economists have declared to be foolish. Indeed it seems that the most successful central bankers in recent years have been those that have paid the least attention to academic economists. Alan Greenspan ignored mainstream academic advice when unemployment went below 4%. Economists kept telling him to watch out, that inflation was right around the corner if he continued to follow such an expansionary policy. He did it anyway, and we are still waiting for the predicted inflation almost a decade later.

The idea that theory might have more to learn from practice than vice versa would not surprise any student of Nathan Rosenberg, who has spent many years studying the relationship between science and technology. Rosenberg (1982) argued that since the Industrial Revolution, science has probably learned more from technology than technology has learned from science. The whole field of microbiology, for example, grew out of applied research conducted in the wine industry. That is, Pasteur was trying to solve problems arising in his family's wine business. So it is no surprise that the relationship between theory and policy is a reciprocal one that involves feedback in both directions.

Rosenberg points out that because of this two-way feedback it is wrong to think of technology as being "applied science." Technological knowledge is no more derivative from scientific knowledge than the other way round. Instead, technology and science produce different kinds of knowledge. Technological knowledge is the knowledge of what works, while scientific knowledge is the knowledge of why certain things work. I think the same relationship holds between society's stock of knowledge concerning the conduct of monetary policy and its knowledge concerning monetary theory. Monetary policy is not just applied monetary theory. Monetary policy shows what works, whereas monetary theory tries to explain why.

In short, one of the useful lessons we can learn once we take into account our limited understanding of macroeconomic forces is that we should be hesitant to criticize monetary policies on the grounds that they have no theoretical foundation. When theory and practice are at odds it is often the theory that is most in need of modification. A more hopeful lesson is that we do in fact have something to offer policymakers. This is again something we could not see from a rational-expectations point of view,

---

[10] For a detailed account of these events see Laidler and Robson (2004).

because if everyone (including policymakers) had rational expectations then there would be nothing we could tell central bankers about how the economy works that they did not already know.

7. Inflation Targeting

Finally, one of the things that we can learn from an adaptive approach is why the policy of inflation targeting followed by various central banks since 1990 has been such an apparent success. Inflation has come down since the 1980s throughout the world, not just in the United States. In many countries with a low degree of central-bank independence, like New Zealand, Canada, the United Kingdom, Sweden, and Australia, this reduction has been accomplished by an explicit inflation-targeting regime. Why is this? There is a rational-expectations answer, but in my view there is an even better Post Walrasian answer that invokes limited economic knowledge.

The rational-expectations answer is based on the Kydland–Prescott (1977) theory of time-inconsistency. According to this argument, inflation targeting is a way to constrain well-meaning but easily-tempted central bankers. It prevents them from trying to exploit the short-run Phillips curve that would be in place once people lowered their expectations of inflation. As long as a central bank is free to do this, so the argument goes, no attempt to reduce inflation will be credible. But under inflation targeting the central bank is constrained to keep inflation within a specific target range.

The Kydland–Prescott theory has never struck me as being a very persuasive explanation of inflation targeting, partly because central bankers are not the type that are easily tempted by temporary short-term gains to generate a long-term inflation problem. On the contrary they are typically much more averse to inflation and far-sighted in their thinking than most people. The Kydland–Prescott argument requires a particular kind of preference; the utility function of the governor of the central bank has to depend negatively on just two arguments, unemployment and inflation. I doubt that this is an accurate description of what motivates any central banker of record. Instead, I think the evidence favors the account that has been given by observers from Thornton (1802) and Bagehot (1873) through Milton Friedman,[11] namely that people entrusted with as much responsibility as a central banker are typically motivated by the hope

---

[11] Quoted by King (1997).

of being seen to have acquitted themselves admirably in fulfilling their duties, one of the most important of which is to preserve the value of the currency. This is not an objective that would be well-served by engineering an inflation in exchange for some fleeting short-term benefit.

Moreover, even if Kydland and Prescott were right about the utility function of central bankers, still not many of them would be tempted to undertake inflationary policies for a short-term improvement in the economy if left to their own devices. In the Kydland–Prescott theory they are tempted because an expansionary monetary policy is assumed to produce mostly benefits (falling unemployment) in the short run, whereas most of the inflation cost comes later. But in fact most countries where sudden expansionary policies are carried out suffer immediately from capital flight and from credibility problems. It is only later that they may possibly get the benefits, because the effects of monetary policy on the business cycle take several months to materialize. Because of this, the temptation they face, if anything, imparts a deflationary bias to monetary policy rather than the inflationary bias of the Kydland–Prescott analysis.

The explanation I prefer for the success of inflation targets starts by recognizing that it is not central bankers but their political masters that are tempted to follow inflationary policies, and the temptation comes from the obvious political advantage of avoiding a recession before an election and from the desire to secure low-cost debt-financing. It is important to realize that where inflation targeting is practiced it is not just the central bank that signs on to the policy; it is also the government. By doing so the government is making it very difficult for itself to coerce the central bank into pursuing inflationary policies for political reasons, especially in the more open and transparent environment that has accompanied inflation targeting. Thus it is no wonder that the central banks who have undertaken inflation targeting tend to be those who previously had the least amount of independence from their political masters. The new policy has provided them with a degree of de facto independence that allows them to pursue the long-run objective of low inflation free from short-term political pressure.

The second part of this explanation begins by noting that inflation is a target of monetary policy rather than an instrument. Because of this, inflation targeting has allowed central banks to maintain their credibility while experimenting and continuing to learn from experience. Recall what happened when the Bank of Canada attempted to follow a policy of targeting the growth rate of the money supply in the second half of the 1970s. After having committed itself to targeted reductions in M1 growth, the Bank soon learned that the demand for M1 was undergoing negative shocks which were nullifying the effects of these reductions on inflation. This put the Bank in the awkward situation of having to choose between allowing inflation to persist, thereby defeating the ultimate objective of the policy, or violating its commitment to the targets, thereby undermining its own credibility and reducing its ability to talk inflation down. Nor was the Bank of Canada the only central bank in the world that found itself in such a dilemma. As Goodhart (1984) pointed out, every country in the world that undertook a monetary targeting policy found that the demand for whatever M that they were targeting somehow suddenly started to decrease.

If these central banks had been committed to inflation targets rather than money-growth targets, the lessons that they learned in the 1970s when they tried reducing monetary growth could easily have been put to use without jeopardizing the long-run goal of inflation reduction. They could have started right away aiming for much lower monetary growth, or switched to controlling some other monetary aggregate, or they could even have abandoned the discredited policy in favor of some other approach to inflation control that placed less reliance on monetary aggregates. In the end that's what many of them did, but only after a lengthy and costly delay caused by the understandable wish to maintain their reputation for constancy.

Moreover, under the open and transparent framework of inflation targeting, central banks have been able to explain more clearly than ever what is going on when they change tactics. They can explain openly that what they are doing is just a tactical maneuver that in no way involves a change in the publicly announced policy of inflation control. In other words, they are free to benefit from new information that teaches them something about how the economy works, rather than having to hope that no such lessons will be forthcoming. This new environment has not only allowed monetary policy to be conducted more effectively, it has also helped the private sector in forming their forecasts.

This is one more example of how the anthill metaphor of Post Walrasian analysis helps us to understand why monetary policy works the way it does. Policy makers are involved in the adaptation process just like everyone else, and a policy that gives them clear goals and instrument-independence allows that adaptation to result in better policies rather than undermining credibility. Some may regard it as ironic that credibility, which rational-expectations theory did so much to bring to the forefront of monetary theory, could best be maintained by a policy that makes sense only from a perspective that denies the very premises of rational-expectations theory. But to see this as ironic would be to forget that central bankers have been concerned with maintaining their credibility since long before the notion of rational-expectations was conceived.

CONCLUSION

This chapter has discussed seven of the lessons to be learned from taking an adaptive view of monetary policy, one that sees the economy as a system in which the individual participants have limited understanding and are aware of those limitations. The lessons can be summed up broadly by the statement that whether or not an economic system is self-regulating, able to closely track a coordinated state of full employment in the face of continual external disturbances, depends very much on the conduct of monetary policy. One of our primary goals as monetary theorists should be to find out just what kinds of monetary policies best promote that kind of systemic stability.

This is an important question no matter what one's attitude is towards the efficacy of "the invisible hand." Believers in the free market often say that the best monetary policy is a nonactivist one that leaves the market free to do its job. Others often say that activism is required because left to its own a free market system is inherently unstable. Neither of these ideological positions is helpful, for both beg the question of what kind of policy is "activist" or "nonactivist." Friedman would argue that a non-activist policy is one that keeps the money supply growing at a predetermined constant rate. But central bankers in the 1950s thought that stabilizing nominal interest rates constituted a nonactivist policy because it avoided wild fluctuations in the instruments directly under their control. Both positions cannot be right.

To determine what kind of policy provides the best background and/or supplement to an economy's built-in regulatory mechanisms, we must go beyond ideology and develop objective models that are capable of being confronted with real-world data, models that take into account the possibility that the economy can be away from a fully coordinated state of full employment for more than an instant. The main virtue of the adaptive approach illustrated above is that it does take this possibility seriously. The approach has already begun to shed light on the human anthill, but the work is just beginning.

Bibliography

Achen, C. H. and Shively, W. P. (1995). *Cross-Level Inference*. Chicago: University of Chicago Press.

Adam, K. (2004). Learning to forecast and cyclical behavior of output and inflation. forthcoming. *Macroeconomic Dynamics*.

Adelman, I. and Adelman, F. L. (1959). The dynamic properties of the Klein-Goldberger model. *Econometrica*, **27**.

Aghion, P., Frydman, R., Stiglitz, J. and Woodford, M. (2003). *Knowledge, Information and Expectations in Modern Economics*. Princeton, NJ: Princeton University Press.

Aizer, A. and Currie, J. (2004). Networks or neighborhood? Correlations in the use of publicly-funded maternity care in California. *Journal of Public Economics*, **88**(12).

Akerlof, G. (2002). Behavioral macroeconomics and macroeconomic behavior. *The American Economic Review*, **92**.

Akerlof, G. and Kranton, R. (2000). Economics and identity. *Quarterly Journal of Economics*, **115**(3).

Akerlof, G. and Yellen, J. (1990). The fair-wage effort hypothesis and unemployment. *Quarterly Journal of Economics*, **105**.

Albin, P. S. (1998). *Barriers and Bounds to Rationality: Essays on Economic Complexity and Dynamics in Interactive Systems*. Princeton, NJ: Princeton University Press.

Albin, P. S. and Foley, D. (1992). Decentralized, dispersed exchange without an auctioneer: a simulation study. *Journal of Economic Behavior and Organization*, **18**.

Alchian, A. (1950). Uncertainty, evolution, and economic theory. *Journal of Political Economy*, **58**.

Aldous, D. (1985). Exchangeability and related topics. In *Lecture Notes in Mathematics*, No. 1117. Berlin: Springer-Verlag.

Allen, B. (1982). Some stochastic processes exhibiting externalities among adopters. *International Economic Review*, **23**(3).

Allen, T. M. and Carroll, C. D. (2001). Individual learning about consumption. *Macroeconomic Dynamics*, **5**(2).

Altuğ, S. (1989). Time-to-build and aggregate fluctuations: some new evidence. *International Economic Review*, **30**.

Ames, E. and Reiter, S. (1961). Distribution of correlation coefficients in economic time series. *Journal of the American Statistical Association*, **56**.

Andersen, L. C. and Jordan, J. L. (1968). Monetary and fiscal actions: a test of their relative importance in economic stabilization. *Federal Reserve Bank of St. Louis Review*, November.

Anderson, T. W. (1950). Estimation of the parameters of a single equation by the limited-information maximum-likelihood method. In *Statistical Inference in Dynamic Economic Models*, ed. K. C. Tjalling. Cowles Commission Monograph 10. New York, NY: John Wiley & Sons, Inc.

Anderson, T. W. and Rubin, H. (1949a). Estimation of the parameters of a single equation in a complete system of stochastic equations. *Annals of Mathematical Statistics*, **20**.

Anderson, T. W. and Rubin, H. (1949b). The asymptotic properties of estimates of the parameters of a single equation in a complete system of stochastic equations. *Annals of Mathematical Statistics*, **21**.

Anderson, R. M. and Sonnenschein, H. (1985). Rational expectations equilibrium with econometric models. *Review of Economic Studies*, **52**(3).

Anderson, P. W., Arrow, K. J. and Pines, D. (1988). *The Economy As an Evolving Complex System, Proceedings Volume V, Santa Fe Institute Studies in the Sciences of Complexity*. Reading, MA: Addison-Wesley.

Anderson, S. P., Goeree, J. K. and Holt, C. A. (1998). A theoretical analysis of altruism and decision error in public goods games. *Journal of Public Economics*, **70**.

Ando, A. and Modigliani, F. (1965). The relative stability of monetary velocity and the investment multiplier. *American Economic Review*, **55**, September.

Antoniak, C. (1969). *Mixture of Dirichlet Processes with Applications to Bayesian Nonparametric Problems*. Ph.D. dissertation, University of California, Los Angeles.

Aoki, M. (1995). Economic fluctuations with interactive agents: dynamic and stochastic externalities. *Japanese Economic Review*, **46**.

Aoki, M. (1996). *New Approaches to Macroeconomic Modeling: Evolutionary Stochastic Dynamics, Multiple Equilibria and Externalities as Field Effects*. New York: Cambridge University Press.

Aoki, M. (2002). *Modeling Aggregate Behaviour and Fluctuations in Economics: Stochastic Views of Interacting Agents*. New York: Cambridge University Press.

Aoki, M. and Yoshikawa, H. (2002). Demand saturation-creation and economic growth. *Journal of Behavioral Organization*, **48**.

Aoki, M. and Yoshikawa, H. (2003). Uncertainty, policy ineffectiveness and long stagnation of the macro economy. *Working Paper No. 316*, Center for Japan–U.S. Business and Economic Studies, Leonard N. Stern School of Business. New York University, NY.

Aoki, M. and Yoshikawa, H. (2005). *Effects of Demand Share Patterns on GDP, Okun's Law, Beveridge Curves and Sector Sizes*. Presentation at the 11th International Conference on Computing in Economics and Finance, Washington, DC, June.

Aoki, M. and Yoshikawa, H. (2006). *A Reconstruction of Macroeconomics: a Perspective from Statistical Physics and Combinatorial Stochastic Processes*. New York: Cambridge University Press.

Arifovic, J. (2000). Evolutionary algorithms in macroeconomic models. *Macroeconomic Dynamics*, **4**, 373–414.

Arifovic, J. and Gencay, R. (2000). Statistical properties of genetic learning in a model of exchange rate. *Journal of Economic Dynamics and Control*, **24**.

Arrow, K. J. (1987). Oral history I: an interview. In *Arrow and the Ascent of Modern Economic Theory*, ed. G. R. Feiwel. New York: New York University Press.

Arrow, K. J. and Hahn, F. H. (1971). *General Competitive Analysis*. San Francisco: Holden-Day.

Arthur, W. B. (1997). Asset pricing under endogenous expectations in an artificial stock market. In *The Economy as an Evolving Complex System II*, eds. W. B. Arthur, S. N. Durlauf, D. A. Lane and P. Taylor. Reading, MA: Addison-Wesley.

Arthur, W. B., Durlauf, S. N. and Lane, D. A., eds. (1997). *The Economy as an Evolving Complex System II*, Proceedings Volume XXVII, Santa Fe Institute Studies in the Sciences of Complexity. Reading, MA: Addison-Wesley.

Auerbach, R. (1982). Some modern varieties of monetarists. *Monetarism and the Federal Reserve's Conduct of Monetary Policy*, U.S. Congress Joint Economic Committee Report.

Auyang, S. M. (1998). *Foundations of Complex-System Theory in Economics, Evolutionary Biology and Statistical Physics*. Cambridge: Cambridge University Press.

Axelrod, R. (1984). *The Evolution of Co-operation*. New York: Basic Books.

Axelrod, R. (1997). *The Complexity of Cooperation: Agent-Based Models of Complexity and Cooperation*. Princeton, NJ: Princeton University Press.

Axelrod, R. (2006). Agent-based modeling as a bridge between disciplines. In *Handbook of Computational Economics*, Vol. 2: Agent-Based Computational Economics, Handbooks in Economic Series. Amsterdam: North-Holland.

Axelrod, R. and Tesfatsion, L. (2006). A guide for newcomers to agent-based modeling in the social sciences. In *Handbook of Computational Economics*, Vol. 2: Agent-Based Computational Economics, Hand Books in Economic Series. Amsterdam: North-Holland.

Axtell, R. L. (2000). Why agents? On the varied motivations for agent computing in the social sciences. In *Proceedings of the Workshop on Agent Simulation: Applications, Models and Tools*, eds. C. M. Macal and D. Sallach. Chicago, IL: Argonne National Laboratory.

Axtell, R. L. (2001). Zipf distribution of U.S. firm sizes. *Science*, **293**.

Axtell, R. L. (2002). Non-cooperative dynamics of multi-agent teams. In *Proceedings of the First International Joint Conference on Autonomous Agents and Multi-agent Systems*, Part 3, eds. C. Castelfranchi and W. L. Johnson. Bologna, Italy: ACM Press.

Axtell, R. L. (2003). Economics as distributed computation. In *Meeting the Challenge of Social Problems via Agent-Based Simulation*, eds. T. Terano, H. Deguchi and K. Takadama. Tokyo: Springer-Verlag.

Axtell, R. L. (2006). Mimeo. A methodology of agent computing in economics. Center on Social and Economic Dynamics.Washington, DC: The Brookings Institution.

Axtell, R. L. and Epstein, J. M. (1999). Coordination in transient social networks: an agent-based computational model of the timing of retirement. In *Behavioral Dimensions of Retirement Economics*, ed. H. J. Aaron. Washington, DC: The Brookings Institution Press.

Axtell, R. L., Epstein, J. M. and Young, H. P. (2001). The emergence of classes in a multi-agent bargaining model. In *Social Dynamics*, eds. S. N. Durlauf and H. P. Young. Cambridge, MA/Washington, DC: MIT Press/Brookings Institution Press.

Axtell, R. L., Epstein, J. M., Dean, J. S., Gumerman, G. J., Swedlund, A. C., Harburger, J., Chakravarty, S., Hammond, R., Parker, J. and Parke, M. T. (2002). Population growth and collapse in a multiagent model of the Kayenta Anasazi in Long House Valley. *Proceedings of the National Academy of Science USA*, **99**(suppl. 3).

Bagehot, W. (1873). *Lombard Street: a Description of the Money Market*. London: ed. Henry S. King (simultaneously with Scribner, Armstrong and Co., New York).

Baillie, R. T., Bollerslev, T. and Mikkelsen, H. O. (1996). Fractionally integrated generalized autoregressive conditional heteroskedasticity, *Journal of Econometrics*, **74**.

Barabasi, A.-L. (2002). *Linked: The New Science of Networks*. Boston: Perseus.

Barberis, N., Huang, M. and Santos, T. (2001). Prospect theory and asset prices. *Quarterly Journal of Economics*, **116**.

Barens, I. (1989). From the 'Banana Parable' to the principle of effective demand: some reflections on the origin, development and structure of Keynes' General Theory. In *Perspectives on the History of Economic Thought*, Vol. 2, ed. D. A. Walker. Aldershot, UK: Edward Elgar.

Barens, I. (1997). What went wrong with IS-LM/AS-AD analysis – and why? *Eastern Economic Journal*, **23**(1).

Barnett, W. A., Geweke, J. and Shell, K. (1989). *Economic Complexity: Chaos, Sunspots, Bubbles and Nonlinearity*. New York: Cambridge University Press.

Barr, A. and Serneels, P. (2004). Wages and Reciprocity in the Workplace. *Working Paper 2004–18*, Oxford University Center for the Study of African Economies, Oxford, UK.

Barreteau, O. (2003). Our companion modelling approach. *Journal of Artificial Societies and Social Simulation*, **6**(1). http://jasss.soc.surrey.ac.uk/6/2/1.html.

Barro, R. and Grossman, H. I. (1971). A general disequilibrium model of income and employment. *American Economic Review*, **61**(1).

Barro, R. and Grossman, H. I. (1976). *Money, Employment and Inflation*. Cambridge: Cambridge University Press.

Barro, R. and McCleary, R. (2003). Religion and economic growth across countries. *American Sociological Review*, **68**(5).

Basmann, R. L. (1962). Letter to the editor. *Econometrica*, **30**.

Basmann, R. L. (1974). *Exact Finite Sample distributions for some econometric estimators and test statistics: a survey and appraisal*. In Intriligator and Kendrick (1974).

Basmann, R. L. and Hwang, H.-S. (1990). A Monte Carlo study of structural estimator distributions after performance of likelihood ratio pre-tests. In *Contributions to Econometric Theory and Application: Essays in Honour of A.L. Nagar*. New York, NY: Springer-Verlag (1990).

Basmann, R. L., Battalio, R. C. and Kagel, J. H. (1976). An experimental test of a simple theory of aggregate per-capita demand functions. *Schweitz Zeitschrift für Volkswirtschaft und Statistik*. Heft2/1976.

Basmann, R. L., Molina, D. J. and Slottje, D. J. (1983). Budget constraint prices as preference changing parameters of generalized Fechner-Thurstone direct utility functions. *American Economic Review*, **73**.

Basu, N. and Pryor, R. J. (1997). Growing a Market Economy. *Sandia Report*. Albuquerque, NM: Sandia National Laboratories.

Batten, D. F. (2000). *Discovering Artificial Economics: How Agents Learn and Economies Evolve*. Boulder, Colorado: Westview Press.

Baumol, W. (1951). *Economic Dynamics*. London: Macmillan.

Baxter, M. and King, R. (1991). Production Externalities and Business Cycles, *Discussion Paper 53*, Federal Reserve Bank of Minneapolis.

Belew, R. K. and Mitchell, M., eds. (1996). *Adaptive Individuals in Evolving Populations: Models and Algorithms*, Proceedings Volume XXVI, Santa Fe Institute Studies in the Sciences of Complexity, Reading, MA: Addison-Wesley.

Bell, A. M. (1997). Bilateral trading on a network: convergence and optimality results. *Department of Economics Working Papers*, Vanderbilt University, Nashville, TN.

Bénabou, R. (1996). Equity and efficiency in human capital investment: The local connection. *Review of Economic Studies*, **63**(2).

Benartzi, S. and Thaler, R. (1996). Myopic loss aversion and the equity premium puzzle. *Quarterly Journal of Economics*, **110**.

Benhabib, J. and Farmer, R. (1994). Indeterminacy and increasing returns. *Journal of Economic Theory*, **63**.

Benhabib, J. and Farmer, R. E. A. (2000). The monetary transmission mechanism. *Review of Economic Dynamics*, **3**(3).

Benhabib, J. and Rustichini, A. (1994). Introduction: symposium on growth, fluctuations and sunspots: confronting the data. *Journal of Economic Theory*, **63**.

Benhabib, J., Schmitt-Grohé, S. and Uribe, M. (2001a). The perils of Taylor rules. *Journal of Economic Theory*, **96**.

Benhabib, J., Schmitt-Grohé, S. and Uribe, M. (2001b). Monetary policy and multiple equilibria. *American Economic Review*, **91**.

Bernanke, B. S. (2000). Japanese monetary policy: a case of self induced paralysis. In *Japan's Financial Crisis and Its Parallels to U.S. Experience*, eds. R. Mikitani and A. S. Posen. Washington, DC: Institute for International Economics.

Bernardo, J. and Smith, A. (1994). *Bayesian Theory*. New York: John Wiley.

Berndt, E. R. (1990). *The Practice of Econometrics: Classic and Contemporary*. Reading, MA: Addison-Wesley.

Bernstein, P. L. (1992). *Capital Ideas: the Improbable Origins of Modern Wall Street*. New York: Free Press.

Bertrand, M., Luttmer, E. and Mullainathan, S. (2000). Network effects and welfare cultures. *Quarterly Journal of Economics*, **115**(3).

Bewley, T. (1999). *Why Wages Don't Fall During a Recession*. Cambridge, MA: Harvard University Press.

Beyer, A. and Farmer, R. E. A. (2002). Natural rate doubts. *Working Paper Series, No. 121*, European Central Bank.

Beyer, A. and Farmer, R. E. A. (2003a). Identifying the monetary transmission mechanism using structural breaks. *European Central Bank Working Paper Series*, No. 275.

Beyer, A. and Farmer, R. E. A. (2003b). On the indeterminacy of determinacy and indeterminacy. *European Central Bank Working Paper Series*, No. 277.

Beyer, A. and Farmer, R. E. A. (2004). On the indeterminacy of New-Keynesian Economics. *European Central Bank Working Paper Series*, No. 323.

Binmore, K. G., Gale, J. and Samuelson, L. (1995). Learning to be imperfect: the ultimatum game. *Games and Economic Behavior*, **8**.

Bisin, A., Moro, A. and Topa, G. (2002). Mimeo. *The Empirical Content of Models with Multiple Equilibria*. New York University, New York.

Bisin, A., Horst, U. and Ozgur, O. (2004). Mimeo. *Rational Expectations Equilibria of Economies with Local Interactions*. New York University, New York.

Blanchard, O. (2000a). What do we know about macroeconomics that Fisher and Wicksell did not? *Quarterly Journal of Economics*, **115**(4), November.

Blanchard, O. (2000b). *Discussions of the Monetary Response − Bubbles, Liquidity Traps and Monetary Policy*, pp. 185−193.

Blanchard, O. and Fischer, S. (1989). *Lectures on Macroeconomics*. Cambridge, MA: MIT Press.

Blinder, A., et al. (1998). *Asking About Prices: a New Approach to Understanding Price Stickiness*. New York: Russell Sage.

Blount, S. (1995). When social outcomes aren't fair: the effect of causal attributions on preferences. *Organization Behavior and Human Decision Processes*, **63**.

Blume, L. (1993). The statistical mechanics of strategic interaction. *Games and Economic Behavior*, **5**(3).

Bodkin, R. G., Klein, L. R. and Marwah, K. (1991). *A History of Macroeconomic Model-Building*. Brookfield, VT: Edward Elgar Publishing Company.

Boivin, J. and Giannoni, M., Forthcoming. Has montetary policy become more effective? *Review of Economics and Statistics*.

Boozer, M. and Cacciola, S. (2001). Inside the black box of *project star*: estimation of peer effects using experimental data. *Discussion Paper No. 832*. Yale University Growth Center.

Bowles, S. and Gintis, H. (1993). The revenge of Homo economicus: contested exchange and the revival of political economy. *Journal of Economic Perspectives*, **7**(1).

Bowles, S. and Gintis, H. (1998). How communities govern: the structural basis of prosocial norms. In *Economics, Values and Organizations*, ed. L. Putterman and A. Ben-Ner. New York: Cambridge University Press.

Bowles, S. and Gintis, H. (2000a). Walrasian economics in retrospect. *Quarterly Journal of Economics*, **115**(4).

Branch, W. A. (2004). The theory of rationally heterogeneous expectations: evidence from survey data on inflation expectations. *Economic Journal*, **114**.

Branch, W. A. and Evans, G. W. (2004). Forthcoming. Intrinsic heterogeneity in expectation formation. *Journal of Economic Theory*.

Branch, W. A. and Evans, G. W. (2005). Mimeo. *Model Uncertainty and Endogenous Volatility*.

Branch, W. A. and McGough, B. (2005). Consistent expectations and misspecification in stochastic non-linear economies. *Journal of Economic Dynamics and Control*, **29**.

Brock, W. (1993). Pathways to randomness in the economy: emergent nonlinearity and chaos in economics and finance. *Estudios Economico*, **8**(3).

Brock, W. (2004). Mimeo. *Profiling Problems with Partially Identified Structure*. Department of Economics, University of Wisconsin, Madison, WI.

Brock, W. and Durlauf, S. (2000). Interactions based models. *NBER, Technical Working Paper No. 258*.

Brock, W. and Durlauf, S. (2001a). Discrete choice with social interactions. *Review of Economic Studies*, **68**(2).

Brock, W. and Durlauf, S. (2001b). Interactions-based models. In *Handbook of Econometrics*, Vol. 5, eds. J. Heckman and E. Leamer. Amsterdam: North-Holland.

Brock, W. and Durlauf, S. (2001c). Growth empirics and reality. *World Bank Economic Review*, **15**(2).

Brock, W. and Durlauf, S. (2004a). Elements of a theory of design: limits to optimal policy. *The Manchester School*, **72** (suppl. 2).

Brock, W. and Durlauf, S. (2004b). Mimeo. *Identification of Binary Choice Models with Social Interactions*. University of Wisconsin, Madison, WI.

Brock, W. and Durlauf, S. (2004c). Mimeo. *Local Robustness Analysis: Theory and Application*. Department of Economics, University of Wisconsin, Madison, WI.

Brock, W. and Durlauf, S. (2004d). Forthcoming. A multinomial choice model with social interactions. In *The Economy as an Evolving Complex System III*, eds. L. Blume and S. Durlauf. New York: Oxford University Press.

Brock, W. and Hommes, C. (1997). A rational route to randomness. *Econometrica*, **65**(5).

Brock, W. and Hommes, C. (1998). Heterogeneous beliefs and routes to chaos in a simple asset pricing model. *Journal of Economic Dynamics and Control*, **22**.

Brock, W., Hsieh, D. and LeBaron, B. (1991). *Nonlinear Dynamics, Chaos and Instability: Statistical Theory and Economic Evidence*. Cambridge, MA: MIT Press.

Brock, W., Durlauf, S. and West, K. (2003). Policy evaluation in uncertain economic environments (with discussion). *Brookings Papers on Economic Activity*, **1**.

Brock, W., Durlauf, S. and West, K. (2004). Mimeo. *Model Uncertainty and Policy Evaluation: Some Theory and Empirics*. Department of Economics, University of Wisconsin, Madison, WI.

Brooks-Gunn, J., Duncan, G., Klebanov, P. and Sealand, N. (1993). Do neighborhoods affect child and adolescent development? *American Journal of Sociology*, **99**(2).

Bryant, R. (1983). A simple rational expectations Keynes-type model. *Quarterly Journal of Economics*, **97**.

Bullard, J. and Duffy, J. (2001). Learning and excess volatility. *Macroeconomics Dynamics*, **5**(2).

Bullard, J. B. and Eusepi, S. (2005). Did the great inflation occur despite policymaker commitment to a Taylor rule? *Review of Economic Dynamics*, **8**(2).

Burke, M., Fournier, G. and Prasad, K. (2004). Mimeo. *Physician Social Networks and Geographical Variation in Medical Care*. Florida State University, Tallahassee, FL.

Cagan, P. (1956). The monetary dynamics of hyperinflation. In *Studies in the Quantity Theory of Money*, ed. M. Friedman. Chicago: University of Chicago Press.

Camerer, C. (2003). *Behavioral Game Theory: Experiments in Strategic Interaction*. Princeton, NJ: Princeton University Press.

Camerer, C. F. and Loewenstein, G. (2004). Behavioral economics: past, present and future. In *Advances in Behavioral Economics*, eds. C. F. Camerer, G. Loewenstein and M. Rabin. Princeton, NJ: Princeton University Press.

Campbell, J. Y. and Cochrane, J. H. (1999). By force of habit: {A} consumption-based explanation of aggregate stock market behavior. *Journal of Political Economy*, **107**.

Carlsson, H. and van Damme, E. (1993). Global games and economic selection. *Eca*, **61**.

Carpenter, J. (2002). The demand for punishment. *Working Paper 02-43*, Middlebury College, Middlebury, VT.

Carpenter, J. and Matthews, P. H. (2004). Social reciprocity. *Middlebury College Working Paper 02-29R*, Middlebury College, Middlebury, VT.

Carpenter, J. and Matthews, P. H. (2005). Norm enforcement: anger, indignation or reciprocity. *Middlebury College Working Paper 05-03*, Middlebury College, Middlebury, VT.

Carpenter, J. and Sakei, E. (2004). Do social preferences increase productivity? Field experimental evidence from fishermen in Toyoma Bay. *Middlebury College Working Paper 051-15*, Middlebury College, Middlebury, VT.

Carroll, C. D. (2002). Requiem for the representative agents? Aggregate implications of microeconomic consumption behavior. *American Economic Review*, **90**.

Carroll, C. D. (2003). Macroeconomic expectations of households and professional forecasters. *Quarterly Journal of Economics*, **118**.

Carter, M. and Castillo, M. (2004). Mimeo. *Identifying Social Effects with Economic Field Experiments*. Georgia Tech University.

Carter, R. A. L., Dutta, J. and Ullah, A., eds. (1990). *Contributions to Econometric Theory and Application: Essays in Honour of A. L. Nagar*. New York, NY: Springer-Verlag.

Cartwright, N. (1989). *Nature's Capacities and Their Measurement*. Oxford: Clarendon Press.

Cass, D. and Shell, K. (1983). Do sunspots matter. *Journal of Political Economy*, **91**(2), 295–329.

Cazavillan, G., Lloyd-Braga, T. and Pintus, P. (1998). Multiple steady-states and endogenous fluctuations with increasing returns to scale in production. *Journal of Economic Theory*, **80**(1), 60–107.

Chari, V. V. and Kehoe, P. (1999). Optimal fiscal and monetary policy. In *Handbook for Macroeconomics*, eds. J. Taylor and M. Woodford. Amsterdam: North-Holland.

Chari, V., Kehoe, P. and Prescott, E. (1989). Time consistency and policy. In *Modern Business Cycle Theory*, ed. R. Barro. Cambridge: Harvard University Press.

Chatterjee, S. and Ravikumar, B. (1999). Minimum consumption requirements: theoretical and quantitative implications for growth and distribution. *Macroeconomic Dynamics*, **3**(4).

Chernoff, H. (1954). Rational selection of decision functions. *Econometrica*, **22**(4).

Christ, C. (1951). A test of an econometric model for the United States, 1921–1947. In *NBER Conference on Business Cycles*. National Bureau of Economic Research, New York, NY. Also reprinted in Cowles Commission Papers, New Series No. 49 (1952).

Christ, C. (1960). Simultaneous equation estimation: any verdict yet? *Econometrica*, **28**(4).

Clarida, R., Gali, J. and Gertler, M. (2000). Monetary policy rules and macroeconomic stability: evidence and some theory. *Quarterly Journal of Economics*, **115**(1).

Clark, G. (1987). Why isn't the whole world developed? *Journal of Economic History*, **47**(1).

Clark, A. (1997). *Being There: Putting Brain, Body and World Together Again.* Cambridge, MA: MIT Press.

Clark, G. and van der Werf, Y. (1998). Work in progress? The industrious revolution. *Journal of Economic History*, **58**(3).

Clements, M. P. and Hendry, D. F. (1999). *Forecasting Non-stationary Economic Time Series.* Cambridge, MA: MIT Press.

Clower, R. (1965). The Keynesian counter-revolution: a theoretical appraisal. In *The Theory of Interest Rates*, eds. F. H. Hahn and P. R. Frank. London: Macmillan.

Clower, R. and Howitt, P. (1996). Taking markets seriously: groundwork for a post Walrasian macroeconomics. In *Beyond Microfoundations: Post Walrasian Macroeconomics*, ed. D. Colander. Cambridge, MA: Cambridge University Press.

Cochrane, J. H. (1998). What do the VARs mean? Measuring the output effects of monetary policy. *Journal of Monetary Economics*, **41**.

Cochrane, J. H. and Hansen, L. P. (1992). Asset pricing explorations for macro-economists. *NBER Macroeconomics Annual 1992*, **7**.

Coddington, A. (1976). Keynesian economics: The search for first principles. *Journal of Economic Literature*, **14**(4) December.

Cogley, T. and Sargent, T. (2004). Mimeo. *The Conquest of U.S. Inflation: Learning and Robustness to Model Uncertainty.* University of California at Davis.

Colander, D. (1984). Was Keynes a Lernerian? *Journal of Economic Literature*, **22**.

Colander, D. (1992). The new, the neo and the new neo: A review of new Keynesian economics, eds. N. G. Mankiw and D. Romer. *Methodus*, **3**.

Colander, D. (1994). The macrofoundations of microeconomics. *Eastern Economic Journal*, **21**.

Colander, D. (1995). The stories we tell: a reconsideration of AS/AD analysis. *Journal of Economic Perspectives*, **9**(3), Summer

Colander, D., ed. (1996). *Beyond Microfoundations: post Walrasian Macroeconomics.* Cambridge, MA: Cambridge University Press.

Colander, D. (1998). Beyond new Keynesian economics: Post Walrasian economics. In *New Keynesian Economics Post Keynesian Alternatives*, ed. R. Rotheim. Cheltenham, UK: Edward Elgar.

Colander, D. (2000). The death of neoclassical economics. *Journal of the History of Economic Thought*, **22**.

Colander, D. (2003a). Post-Walrasian macro policy and the economics of muddling through. *International Journal of Political Economy*, **33**(2). Also in *New Developments in Macroeconomic Policy*, ed. M. Setterfield. Armonk: Sharpe Publishing.

Colander, D. (2003b). Thinking outside the heterodox box: post Walrasian macro-economics and heterodoxy. *International Journal of Political Economy*, **33**(2). Also in *New Developments in Macroeconomic Policy*, ed. M. Setterfield. Armonk: Sharpe Publishing.

Colander, D. (2004). The strange persistence of the IS-LM model. *History of Political Economy*, **36**.

Colander, D. (2005). The Making of an Economist Redax. *Journal of Economic Perspectives*, **19**(1).

Colander, D. and Guthrie, R. (1980). Great expectations: what the dickens is rational expectations? *Journal of Post Keynesian Economics*, **3**(2), Winter.

Colander, D. and Landreth, H. (1996). *The Coming of Keynesianism to America.* Cheltenham, England: Edward Elgar.

Colander, D. and van Ess, H. (1996). Post Walrasian macroeconomic policy. In *Beyond Micro Foundations: Post Walrasian Macroeconomics*, ed. D. Colander. Cambridge: Cambridge University Press.

Colander, D., Holt, R. and Rosser, J. B. (2003). The Changing Face of Mainstream Economics. *Middlebury College Working Paper 03-27.* Middlebury College, Middlebury, VT.

Cole, H. and Ohanian, L. (2004). New deal policies and the persistence of the great depression. *Journal of Political Economy*, **112**(4).

Conley, T. and Topa, G. (2002). Socio-economic distance and spatial patterns in unemployment. *Journal of Applied Econometrics*, **17**(4).

Constantinides, G. M. (2002). Rational asset prices. *Journal of Finance*, **57**.

Constantinedes, G. M. and Duffie, D. (1996). Asset pricing with heterogeneous consumers. *Journal of Political Economy*, **104**.

Cook, C. and Tesfatsion, L. (2006). Agent-based computational laboratories for the experimental study of complex economic systems. *Working Paper*, Department of Economics, Iowa State University, Ames, IA, in progress.

Cooley, T. F. and LeRoy, S. F. (1985). A theoretical macroeconomics: a critique. *Journal of Monetary Economics*, **16**.

Cooper, R. (1999). *Coordination Games.* New York: Cambridge University Press.

Cooper, R. (2002). Estimation and identification of structural parameters in the presence of multiple equilibria. *Les Annales d'Economie et de Statistique*, **66**.

Cooper, R. and Corbae, D. (2001). Financial collapse and active monetary policy: a lesson from the Great Depression. *Federal Reserve Bank of Minneapolis: Staff report 289* (forthcoming, *Journal of Economic Theory*).

Cooper, R. and Ejarque, J. (1995). Financial intermediation and the Great Depression: a multiple equilibrium interpretation. *Carnegie-Rochester Series on Public Policy*, **43**.

Cooper, R. and John, A. (1988). Coordinating coordination failures in Keynesian models. *Quarterly Journal of Economics*, **103**.

Cooper, R. and John, A. (1997). Dynamic complementarities: a quantitative analysis. *Journal of Monetary Economics*, **40**.

Dagsvik, J. and Jovanovic, B. (1994). Was the Great Depression a low-level equilibrium? *European Economic Review*, **38**(9).

Darby, M. (1976). *Macroeconomics.* New York: McGraw-Hill.

Darley, V. (1994). Emergent phenomena and complexity. In *Artificial Life IV*, eds. R. A. Brooks and P. Maes. Cambridge, MA: MIT Press.

Darley, V., Outkin, A., Plate, T. and Gao, F. (2001). Learning, Evolution and Tick Size Effects in a Simulation of the NASDAQ Stock Market. *Proceedings of the 5th World Multi-Conference on Systemics, Cybernetics and Informatics (SCI 2001).* Orlando, FL: International Institute for Informatics and Systematics.

Davidson, P. (1978). *Money and the Real World.* 2nd edn. London: Macmillan.

Davidson, P. (1994). *Post Keynesian Macroeconomic Theory.* Aldershot: Edward Elgar.

Davidson, P. (1996). Did Keynes reverse the Marshallian speeds of adjustment? Using Harcourt's method to resolve theoretical controversies and gain insight into the real world. In *Capital Controversy, Post Keynesian Economics and the History of Economic Thought*, eds. P. Arestis, G. Palma and M. Sawyer. London: Routledge.

Davis, J. B. (2005). Complexity theory's network conception of the individual. *Marquette University Working Paper*, Marquette University, Milwaukee, WI.

Day, R. H. and Chen, P., eds. (1993). *Nonlinear Dynamics and Evolutionary Economics*. Oxford, UK: Oxford University Press..

De Vries, J. (1994). The industrial revolution and the industrious revolution. *Journal of Economic History*, **54**(2).

Del Negro, M. and Schorfheide, F. Forthcoming. Priors from general equilibrium models for VARs. *International Economic Review*.

Demiralp, S. and Hoover, K. D. (2004). Searching for the causal structure of a vector autoregression. *Oxford Bulletin of Economics and Statistics*, **65**.

Dennis, J., Johansen, S. and Juselius, K. (2005). *CATS for RATS: Manual to Cointegration Analysis of Time Series*. Illinois: Estima.

Derrida, B. (1994). From random walks to spin glasses. *Physica D*, **107**.

Diamond, P. (1982). Aggregate demand management in search equilibrium. *Journal of Political Economy*, **90**.

Diebold, F. (1998). The past, present and future of macroeconomic forecasting. *Journal of Economic Perspectives*, **12**, Spring.

Dierker, E. and Grodal, B. (1986). Non existence of Cournot-Walras equilibrium in a general equilibrium model with two oligopolists. In *Contributions to Mathematical Economics, in Honor of Gerard Debreu*, eds. W. Hildenbrand and A. Mas-Colell. Amsterdam: North-Holland.

Ding, Z., Granger, C. and Engle, R. F. (1993). A long memory property of stock market returns and a new model. *Journal of Empirical Finance*, **1**.

Doppelhofer, G., Miller, R. and Sala-i-Martin, X. (2000). Determinants of long-term growth: a Bayesian averaging of classical estimates (BACE) approach. *Working Paper 7750*, National Bureau of Economic Research, Cambridge, MA.

Draper, D. (1995). Assessment and propagation of model uncertainty. *Journal of the Royal Statistical Society* (series B), **57**.

Duesenberry, J. (1948). Income-consumption relations and their implications. In *Income, Employment and Public Policy*, ed. L. Metzler. New York: Norton Publishers.

Duffy, J. and Fisher, E. O'N. (2004). Sunspots in the laboratory. *SSRN Working Paper*.

Dufwenberg, M. and Kirchsteiger, G. (2004). *Forthcoming*. A theory of sequential reciprocity. *Games and Economic Behavior*.

Dupor, W. (1999). Aggregation and irrelevance in multi-sector models. *Journal of Monetary Economics*, **43**.

Durlauf, S. (1993). Nonergodic economic growth. *Review of Economic Studies*, **60**(2).

Durlauf, S. (1996). A theory of persistent income inequality. *Journal of Economic Growth*, **1**(1).

Durlauf, S. (2001). A framework for the study of individual behavior and social interactions. *Sociological Methodology*, **31**.

Durlauf, S. (2004). Neighborhood effects. In *Handbook of Regional and Urban Economics*, Vol. 4, eds. J. V. Henderson and J.-F. Thisse. Amsterdam: North-Holland.

Durlauf, S. N. and Young, H. P., eds. (2001). *Social Dynamics*. Cambridge, MA: MIT Press.

Durlauf, S., Johnson, P. and Temple, J. (2004). Growth econometrics. In *Handbook of Economic Growth*, eds. P. Aghion and S. Durlauf. Amsterdam: North-Holland.

Dyson, F. (2004). The world on a string. *New York Review of Books*, **51**(8), May.

Eckel, B. (2003). *Thinking in Java*, 3rd edn. NJ: Prentice Hall.

Ekeland, I., Heckman, J. and Nesheim, L. (2002). Identifying hedonic models. *American Economic Review*, **92**(2).

Ekeland, I., Heckman, J. and Nesheim, L. (2004). Identification and estimation of Hedonic models. *Journal of Political Economy*, **112**(suppl. 1).

Elster, J. (1998). Emotions and economic theory. *Journal of Economic Literature*, **36**.

Engle, R. F., Hendry, D. F. and Richard, J. F. (1983). Exogeneity. *Econometrica*, **55**(2).

Epstein, J. M. (2006). Remarks on the foundations of agent-based generative social science. In *Handbook of Computational Economics*, Vol. 2: Agent-Based Computational Economics Handbooks in Economic Series, Amsterdam: North-Holland.

Epstein, J. M. and Axtell, R. (1996). *Growing Artificial Societies: Social Science from the Bottom Up*. Washington, DC/Cambridge, MA: Brookings Institution Press/MIT Press.

Epstein, L. and Wang, T. (1994). Intertemporal asset pricing behavior under Knightian uncertainty. *Econometrica*, **62**.

Ericsson, N. and Irons, J. (1995). The Lucas critique in practice: theory without measurement. In *Macroeconometrics: Developments, Tensions and Prospects*, ed. K. D. Hoover. Boston: Kluwer.

Estrella, A. and Fuhrer, J. C. (1999). Are 'deep' parameters stable? The Lucas critique as an empirical hypothesis. *Working Paper no. 99-4*. Federal Reserve Bank of Boston.

Evans, G. W. and Honkapohja, S. (2001). *Learning and Expectations in Macroeconomics*. Princeton, NJ: Princeton University Press.

Evans, G. W. and Ramey, G. (2003). Adaptive expectations, underparameterization and the Lucas critique. *Journal of Monetary Economics*, **53**.

Evans, G. W., Oates, W. and Schwab, R. (1992). Measuring peer group effects: a study of teenage behavior. *Journal of Political Economy*, **100**(5).

Evans, G. W., Honkapohja, S. and Sargent, T. J. (1993). On the preservation of deterministic cycles when some agents perceive them to be random fluctuations. *Journal of Economic Dynamics and Control*, **17**.

Ewens, W. J. (1990). Population genetics theory—the past and future. In *Mathematical and Statistical Problems in Evolution*, ed. S. Lessard. Boston: Kluwer Academic Publishing.

Fagiolo, G., Dosi, G. and Gabriele, R. (2004). Towards an Evolutionary Interpretation of Aggregate Labor Market Regularities, *Sant'Anna School of Advanced Studies Working Paper*. Sant' Anna School of Advanced Studies.

Faith, J. (1998). Why gliders don't exist: anti-reductionism and emergence. In *Artificial Life VI*, eds. C. Adami, R. K. Belew, H. Kitano and C. E. Taylor. Cambridge, MA: MIT Press.

Falk, A. and Fehr, E. (2003). Why labor market experiments? *Journal of Labour Economics*, **1**(10).

Fang, H. and Loury, G. (2004). Mimeo. *Toward an Economic Theory of Cultural Identity*. Yale University.

Farmer, R. and Guo, J.-T. (1994). Real business cycles and the animal spirits hypothesis. *Journal of Economic Theory*, **63**(2).

Fazzari, S. M. (1985). Keynes, Harrod and the rational expectations revolution. *Journal of Post Keynesian Economics*, **8**, Fall.

Fehr, E. and Gächter, S. (2000). Cooperation and punishment in public goods experiments. *American Economic Review*, **90**.

Fehr, E. and Gächter, S. (2004). Third party punishment. *Evolution and Human Behavior*, **25**.

Fehr, E. and Tyran, J.-R. (2001). Does money illusion matter? *American Economic Review*, **91**.

Fehr, E., Kirchsteiger, G. and Riedl, A. (1996). Involuntary unemployment and non-compensating wage differentials in an experimental labor market. *Economic Journal*, **106**.

Fehr, E., Gächter, S. and Kirchsteiger, G. (1996). Reciprocal fairness and noncompensating wage differentials. *Journal of Institutional and Theoretical Economics*, **142**.

Fehr, E., Fischbacher, U. and Kosfeld, M. (2005). Neuroeconomic foundations of trust and social preferences. *IZA Working Paper No. 1641*.

Feigelman, M. V. and Ioffe, L. B. (1991). Hierarchical organization of memory. In *Models of Neural Networks*, eds. E. Domany, J. L. van Hemmen and S. Lessard. Berlin and New York: Springer-Verlag.

Feiwel, R. G. (1985). Quo vadis macroeconomics? Issues, tensions and challenges. In *Issues in Contemporary Macroeconomics and Distribution*, ed. G. R. Feiwel. State University of New York, Albany, pp. 1–100.

Felipe, J. and Fisher, F. M. (2003). Aggregation in production functions: what applied economists should know. *Metroeconomica*, **54**.

Fernandez, C., Ley, E. and Steel, M. (2001a). Benchmark priors for Bayesian model averaging. *Journal of Econometrics*, **100**(2).

Fernandez, C., Ley, E. and Steel, M. (2001b). Model uncertainty in cross-country growth regressions. *Journal of Applied Econometrics*, **16**(5).

Feynman, R. (1995). *Six Easy Pieces: Essentials of Physics Explained by its most Brilliant Teacher*. Reading, MA: Addison-Wesley.

Finch, J. H. and McMaster, R. (2004). On the paths of classical political economy and Walrasian economics through post Walrasian economics. *University of Aberdeen Economics Working Paper*. University of Aberdeen, Aberdeen, Scotland.

Fisher, M. F. (1983). *Disequilibrium Foundations of Equilibrium Economics*, Econometric Society Monographs No. 6. Cambridge, UK: Cambridge University Press.

Fisher, I. (1906). *The Nature of Capital and Income*. New York: Macmillan.

Fisher, I. (1907). *The Rate of Interest, Its Nature, Determination and Relation to Economic Phenomena*. New York: Macmillan.

Fisher, I. (1930). *The Theory of Interest as Determined by Impatience to Spend and Opportunity to Invest*. New York: Macmillan.

Flake, G. W. (1998). *The Computational Beauty of Nature: Computer Explorations of Fractals, Chaos, Complex Systems and Adaptation*. Cambridge, MA: MIT Press.

Föllmer, H., Horst, U. and Kirman, A. (2005). Equilibria in financial markets with heterogeneous agents: a new perspective. *Journal of Mathematical Economics*, **41**, 123–55.

Föllmer, H. (1974). Random economies with many interacting agents. *Journal of Mathematical Economics*, **1**(1), 51–62, March

Frank, R. (1987). If Homo economicus could choose his own utility function, would he want one with a conscience? *American Economic Review*, **77**.

Franklin, S. (1997a). Autonomous agents as embodied AI. *Cybernetics and Systems*, **28**.

Franklin, S. (1997b). *Artificial Minds*. Cambridge, MA: MIT Press.

Frederick, S., Loewenstein, G. and O'Donoghue, T. (2002). Intertemporal choice: a critical review. *Journal of Economic Literature*, **40**.

Friedman, M. (1948). A monetary and fiscal framework for economic stability. *American Economic Review*, **384**.

Friedman, M. (1949). The Marshallian demand curve. *Journal of Political Economy*, **57**.

Friedman, M. (1953a). The case for flexible exchange rates. In *Essays in Positive Economics*. Chicago, IL: University of Chicago Press.

Friedman, M. (1953b). The methodology of positive economics. In *Essays in Positive Economics*. Chicago, IL: Chicago University Press.

Friedman, M. (1955). Leon Walras and his economic system: a review article. *American Economic Review*, **45**.

Friedman, M. (1968). The role of monetary policy. *American Economic Review*, **58**, March, 1–17.

Friedman, M. (1970a). The counterrevolution in monetary theory, *Occasional Paper No 33*, Institute of Economic Affairs.

Friedman, M. (1970b). A theoretical framework for monetary analysis. *Journal of Political Economy*, **78**, March/April.

Friedman, M. (1971). A monetary theory of nominal income. *Journal of Political Economy*, **79**, March/April.

Friedman, M. (1972). Comments on the critics. *Journal of Political Economy*, **80**(5), September, October

Friedman, M. and Meiselman, D. (1963). The relative stability of monetary velocity and the investment multiplier in the United States, 1897–1958. In *Stabilization Policies*, Commission on Money and Credit. New York: Prentice Hall.

Friedman, M. and Schwartz, A. (1963). Money and business cycles. *Review of Economics and Statistics*. (suppl.), February.

Frisch, R. (1933). Editor's note. *Econometrica*, **1**.

Frisch, R. (1954). Linear expenditure functions: an expository article. *Econometrica*, **22**.

Frydman, R. and Phelps, E. S., eds. (1983). *Individual Forecasting and Aggregate Outcomes: Rational Expectations Examined*. New York: Cambridge University Press.

Fudenberg, D. and Levine, D. K. (1998). *The Theory of Learning in Games*. Cambridge, MA: MIT Press.

Fuhrer, J. C. (1997). The (un)importance of forward-looking behavior in price specifications. *Journal of Money, Credit and Banking*, **29**, August.

Fuhrer, J. C. and Rudebusch, G. D. (2003). Estimating the Euler equation for output. *Journal of Monetary Economics*, **51** (publication date 2004).

Gabaix, X. (2004). Mimeo. *The Granular Origins of Aggregate Fluctuations*. MIT, Cambridge, MA.

Gali, J. and Gertler, M. (1999). Inflation dynamics: a structural econometric analysis. *Journal of Monetary Economics*, **44**(2).

Gallant, A. R., Rossi, P. E. and Tauchen, G. (1992). Stock prices and volume. *The Review of Financial Studies*, **5**.

Gallant, A. R., Rossi, P. E. and Tauchen, G. (1993). Nonlinear dynamic structures. *Econometrica*, **61**.

Gartaganis, A. J. (1954). Autoregression in the United States economy 1870–1929. *Econometrica*, **22**.

Geanakoplos, J., Pearce, D. and Stacchettti, E. (1989). Psychological games and sequential rationality. *Games and Economic Behavior*, **1**.

Geanakoplos, J. (1996). The Hangman's Paradox and Newcomb's Paradox as psychological games. *Cowles Foundation Discussion Paper No. 1128*.

Giannoni, M. (2001). Mimeo. *Robust Optimal Monetary Policy in a Forward-Looking Model with Parameter and Shock Uncertainty*. Federal Reserve Bank of New York.

Giannoni, M. (2002). Does model uncertainty justify caution? Robust optimal monetary policy in a forward-looking model. *Macroeconomic Dynamics*, **6**.

Gibrat, R. (1931). *Les Inegalieies Economiques; Applications: Aux Inegalities des Richesses, a la Concentartion des Entreprises, Aux Populations des Villes, Aux Statistiques des Families, etc., d'une Loi Nouvelle, La Loi de l'Effet Proportionnel*. Paris: Librarie du Recueil Sirey.

Gigerenzer, G. and Selten R., eds. (2001). *Bounded Rationality: The Adaptive Toolbox*. Cambridge, MA: MIT Press.

Gilboa, I. and Schmeidler, D. (1989). Maximin expected utility with non-unique priors. *Journal of Mathematical Economics*, **18**.

Gillespie, R. P. (1951). *Integration*, London: Oliver and Boyd.

Gintis, H. (2000). *Game Theory Evolving*. Princeton, NJ: Princeton University Press.

Girshick, M. A. and Haavelmo, T. (1947). Statistical analysis of the demand for food: examples of simultaneous estimation of structural equations. *Econometrica*, **15**, 79–110. Reprinted in *Studies in Econometric Method*, Chapter V, eds. W. C. Hood and T. C. Koopmans. New York, NY: John Wiley & Sons (1953).

Glaeser, E., Sacerdote, B. and Scheinkman, J. (1996). Crime and social interactions. *Quarterly Journal of Economics*, **111**(2).

Glimcher, P. W. (2003). *Decisions, Uncertainty and the Brain: The Science of Neuroeconomics*. Cambridge, MA: MIT Press.

Gode, D. K. and Sunder, S. (1993). Allocative efficiency of markets with zero intelligence traders. *Journal of Political Economy*, **101**.

Gode, D. K. and Sunder, S. (2004). Double auction dynamics: structural effects of non-binding price controls. *Journal of Economic Dynamics and Control*, **28**.

Goeree, J. and Holt, C. (2001). Ten little treasures of game theory and ten intuitive contradictions. *American Economic Review*, **91**.

Goldberger, A. S. (1964). *Econometric Theory*. New York, NY: John Wiley & Sons.

Goodhart, C. A. E. (1984). *Monetary Theory and Practice: the U.K. Experience*. London: Macmillan.

Graham, B. (2005). Mimeo. *Identifying Social Interactions through Excess Variance Contrasts*. Cambridge, MA: Harvard University.

Graham, B. and Hahn, J. (2004). Mimeo. *Identification and Estimation of Linear-in-Means Model of Social Interactions*. Department of Economics, Harvard University.

Grandmont, J.-M. (1985). On endogenous competitive business cycles. *Econometrica*, **53**.

Grandmont, J.-M., Pintus, P. and DeVilder, R. (1998). Capital labor substitution and nonlinear endogenous business cycles. *Journal of Economic Theory*, **80**.

Green, E. (2005). A review of interest and prices: a foundation of monetary theory by Michael Woodford. *Journal of Economic Literature*, **43**(1) March.

Greenspan, A. (2004). Risk and uncertainty in monetary policy. *BIS Review*, **1**.

Guo, J. T. and Harrison, S. (2004). Balanced-budget rules and macroeconomic (in)stability. *Journal of Economic Theory*, http://faculty.ucr.edu/guojt/

Guzik, V. (2004). *Contextual Framing Effects in a Common Pool Resource Experiment*. Middlebury College Senior Honors Thesis. Middlebury College, Middlebury, VT.

Haavelmo, T. (1943). Statistical implications of a system of simultaneous equations. *Econometrica*, **11**.

Haavelmo, T. (1944). The Probability Approach in Econometrics. *Econometrica*, **12**.

Haavelmo, T. (1947). Methods of measuring the marginal propensity to consume. *Journal of the American Statistical Association*, **42**.

Haken, H. (1987). Synergetics: An Approach to Self Organization. In *Self-organzing systems: The emergence of order*, ed. F. E. Yates. Berlin: Plenum Press.

Hansen, L. and Jagannathan, R. (1991). Implications of security market data for models of dynamic economies. *Journal of Political Economy*, **99**.

Hansen, L. and Sargent, T. (1980). Formulating and estimating dynamic linear rational expectations models. *Journal of Economic Dynamics and Control*, **2**.

Hansen, L. and Sargent, T. (2001). Acknowledging misspecification in macro-economic theory. *Review of Economic Dynamics*, **4**.

Hanse, L. and Sargent, T. (2003a). Forthcoming. *Robust Control and Economic model Uncertainty*. Princeton, NJ: Princeton University Press. Also book manuscript, Hoover Institution, Stanford University, Stanford, CA.

Hansen, L. and Sargent, T. (2003b) Robust control of forward looking models. *Journal of Monetary Economics*, **50**, April.

Hansen, L. and Singleton, K. (1982). Generalized instrumental variables estimation of nonlinear rational expectations models. *Econometrica*, **50**.

Harrod, R. F. (1939). An essay in dynamic theory. *Economic Journal*, **49**, March.

Hart, O. (1995). *Firms, Contracts and Financial Structure*. Oxford: Oxford University Press.

Hartley, J. E., Hoover, K. D. and Salyer, K. D., eds. (1998). *Real Business Cycles: A Reader*. London: Routledge.

Hayek, F. A., von (1937). Economics and knowledge. *Economica*, **4**, new series.

Hayek, F. A., von (1945). The use of knowledge in society. *American Economic Review*, **35**(4).

Hayek, F. A., von (1964). Kinds of order in society. *New Individualist Review*, **3**(2).

Heckman, J. (1979). Sample selection bias as a specification error. *Econometrica*, **47**(1).

Hendry, D. F. (1995). *Dynamic Econometrics*. Oxford: Oxford University Press.

Hendry, D. F. and Ericsson, N. R. (1991). An econometric analysis of UK money demand. In *Monetary Trends in the United States and the United Kingdom*, eds. M. Friedman and A. J. Schwartz. *American Economic Review*, **81**, 8−38.

Hendry, D. F. and Krolzig, H. M. (1999). Improving on 'Data mining reconsidered' by K. D. Hoover and S. J. Perez. *Econometrics Journal*, **2**.

Hendry, D. F. and Krolzig, H. M. (2001). *Automatic Econometric Model Selection Using PcGets 1.0*. London: Timberlake Consultants.

Henrich, J., Boyd, R., Bowles, S., Camerer, C., Fehr, E., Gintis, H. and McElreath, R. (2001). Cooperation, reciprocity and punishment in fifteen small-scale societies. *American Economic Review*, **91**.

Hey, J. D. and di Cagno, D. (1998). Sequential markets: An experimental investigation of Clower's dual-decision hypothesis. *Experimental Economics*, **1**.

Hicks, J. (1936). Mr. Keynes's theory of employment. *Economic Journal*, **46**, June.

Hicks, J. (1937). Mr. Keynes and the classics: a suggested interpretation. *Econometrica*, **5**.

Hicks, J. (1939). *Value and Capital*. Oxford: Oxford University Press.

Hicks, J. (1965). *Capital and Growth*. Oxford: Oxford University Press.

Hicks, J. (1980). IS-LM: an explanation. *Journal of Post Keynesian Economics*, **3**(2).

Hicks, J. (1983). IS-LM: an explanation. In *Modern Macroeconomic Theory*, ed. J.-P. Fitoussi. Oxford: Basil Blackwell.

Hicks, J. (1989). *A Market Theory of Money*. Oxford: Clarendon Press.

Hirshleifer, J. (1958). On the theory of optimal investment decisions. *Journal of Political Economy*, **66**(4), August.

Hirshleifer, J. (1970). *Investment, Interest and Capital*. New York: Prentice-Hall.

Holland, J. H. (1995). *Hidden Order: How Adaptation Builds Complexity*. Reading, MA: Addison-Wesley.

Hommes, C. H. and Sorger, G. (1998). Consistent expectations equilibria. *Macroeconomic Dynamics*, **2**.

Hommes, C. H., Sorger, G. and Wagener, F. (2003). Mimeo. *Learning to Believe in Linearity in an Unknown Nonlinear Stochastic Economy*.

Hood, W. C. and Koopmans, T. C., eds. (1953). *Studies in Econometric Method*. Cowles Commission Monograph 14. New York: Wiley.

Hoover, K. D. (1988). *The New Classical Macroeconomics: A Skeptical Inquiry*. Cambridge, MA: Basil Blackwell.

Hoover, K. D. (1995). Facts and artifacts: calibration and the empirical assessment of real-business-cycle models. *Oxford Economic Papers*, **47**.

Hoover, K. D. (2001). *Causality in Macroeconomics*. Cambridge: Cambridge University Press.

Hoover, K. D. (2004). Lost causes. *Journal of the History of Economic Thought*, **26**.

Hoover, K. D. (2005). Forthcoming. Automatic Inference of the Contemporaneous Causal Order of a System of Equation. *Econometric Theory*, **21**(1).

Hoover, K. D. and Jorda, O. (2001). Measuring Systematic Monetary Policy. *Federal Reserve Bank of St. Louis Review*, **83**.

Hoover, K. D. and Perez, S. J. (1999). Data mining reconsidered: encompassing and the general-to-specific approach to specification search. *Econometrics Journal*, **2**.

Hoover, K. D. and Perez, S. J. (2004). Truth and robustness in cross-country growth regressions. *Oxford Bulletin of Economics and Statistics*, **66**(5).

Horst, U. and Scheinkman, J. (2004). Mimeo. *Equilibria in Systems of Social Interactions*. Princeton University, Princeton, NJ.

Horvath, M. (1998). Cyclicality and sectoral linkages: aggregate fluctuations from independent sectoral shocks. *Review of Economic Dynamics*, **1**.

Horvath, M. (2000). Sectoral shocks and aggregate fluctuations. *Journal of Monetary Economics*, **45**.

Houthakker, H. S. (1960). Additive preferences. *Econometrica*, **28**.

Howitt, P. (1990). *The Keynesian Recovery and Other Essays*. Ann Arbor, MI: The University of Michigan Press.

Howitt, P. (1992). Interest rate control and nonconvergence to rational expectations. *Journal of Political Economy*, **100**, August.

Howitt, P. (1996). Cash-in-advance: microfoundations in retreat. In *Inflation, Institutions, and Information*, eds. D. Vaz. and K. Velupillai. London: Macmillan.

Hurwicz, L. (1951). Some specification problems and applications to econometric models. *Econometrica*, **19**.

Ichimura, S. (1951). A critical note on the definition of related goods. *Review of Economic Studies*, **18**.

Ingber, L. (1982). Statistical mechanics of neocortical interactions. *Physica A*, **5**.

Ingram, B. F. (1995). Recent advances in solving and estimating dynamic macroeconomic models. In *Macroeconometrics: Developments, Tensions and Prospect*, ed. K. D. Hoover. Boston: Kluwer.

Ingram, B. and Whiteman, C. (1994). Supplanting the 'Minnesota' prior: forecasting macroeconomic time series using real business cycle priors. *Journal of Monetary Economics*, **34**(3), December.

Intriligator, M. D. and Kendrick, D. A. (1974). *Frontiers of Quantitative Economics*, Vol II, Amsterdam, NETH: North-Holland Publishing Company.

Ioannides, Y. (1990). Trading uncertainty and market form. *International Economic Review*, **31**(3).

Ioannides, Y. and Zabel, J. (2003a). Neighborhood effects and housing demand. *Journal of Applied Econometrics*, **18**.

Ioannides, Y. and Zabel, J. (2003b). Mimeo. *Interactions, Neighborhood Selection and Housing Demand*. Department of Economics, Tufts University, Medford, MA.

Ireland, P. (2001a). Technology shocks and the business cycle: an empirical investigation. *Journal of Economic Dynamics and Control*, **25**.

Ireland, P. (2001b). Money's role in the monetary business cycle. *Journal of Money, Credit and Banking*, **36**(6).

Ireland, P. (2004). A method for taking models to the data. *Journal of Economic Dynamics and Control*, **28**.

Irwin, E. and Bockstaed, N. (2002). Interacting agents, spatial externalities and the evolution of residential land use patterns. *Journal of Economic Geography*, **2**.

Janssen, M. A. and Ostrom, E. (2006). Governing social-ecological systems. In *Hand Book of Computational Economics*, Vol. 2: Agent-Based Computational Economics Handbooks in Economic Series. Amsterdam: North-Holland.

Jennings, N. R. (2000). On agent-based software engineering. *Artificial Intelligence*, **17**.

Johansen, S. (1996). *Likelihood Based Inference in Cointegrated VAR Models*. Oxford: Oxford University Press.

Johansen, S. (2005). The interpretation of cointegrating coefficients in the cointegrated VAR model, *Oxford Bulletin of Economics and Statistics*, **67**, 93–104.

Johnson, A. (2001). *Emergence: The Connected Lives of Ants, Brains, Cities and Software*. New York: Scribner.

Jonson, P. (1996). On the economics of Say and Keynes' interpretation of Say's Law. *Eastern Economic Journal*, **21**, Spring.

Jordan, J. S. (1982). The competitive allocation process is informationally efficient uniquely. *Journal of Economic Theory*, **28**.

Jovanovic, B. (1987). Micro shocks and aggregate risk. *Quarterly Journal of Economics*, **102**.

Judd, K. (1997). Computational economics and economic theory: substitutes or complements? *Journal of Economic Dynamics and Control*, **21**(6).

Judd, K. (1998). *Numerical Methods in Economics*. Cambridge, MA: MIT Press.

Judd, K. (2006). Computationally intensive analyses in economics. In *Handbook of Computational Economics*, Vol. 2: Agent-Based Computational Economics Handbooks in Economic Series. Amsterdam: North-Holland.

Juselius, K. (1999). Models and relations in economics and econometrics. *Journal of Economic Methodology*, **6**.

Juselius, K. (2005). *The Cointegrated VAR Model: Methodology and Applications*, Oxford University Press.

Kahneman, D. and Tversky, A. (1979). Prospect theory: an analysis of decisions under risk. *Econometrica*, **47**.

Kahneman, D., Knetsch, J. L. and Thaler, R. H. (1990). Experimental tests of the endowment effect and the Coase theorem. *Journal of Political Economy*, **86**.

Kalai, E. and Lerner, E. (1993). Rational learning leads to Nash equilibrium. *Econometrica*, **61**(5).

Kamihigashi, T. (1996). Real business cycles and sunspot fluctuations are observationally equivalent, *Journal of Monetary Economics*, **37**.

Kapetanios, G., Pagan A. and Scott A. (2005). Making a match: combining theory and evidence in policy oriented macro economic modeling. *Australian National University Working Paper CAMA*.

Katzner, D. (1989). *The Walrasian Vision of the Microeconomy: an Elementary Exposition of the Structure of Modern General Equilibrium Theory*. Ann Arbor, MI: University of Michigan Press.

Kelly, M. (1997). The dynamics of Smithian growth. *Quarterly Journal of Economics*, **112**(3).

Keynes, J. M. (1921). *A Treatise on Probability*. London: Macmillan.

Keynes, J. M. (1926). *The End of Laissez Faire*. London: Hogarth.

Keynes, J. M. (1930). *A Treatise on Money*. 2 Vols. (Vol. 1: The Pure Theory of Money; Vol. 2: The Applied Theory of Money). London: Macmillan and Co. Limited.

Keynes, J. M. (1936). *The General Theory of Employment, Interest and Money*. New York: Harcourt, Brace (Reprinted in 1965).

Keynes, J. M. (1939). Professor Tinbergen's method. *Economic Journal*, **49**.

King, M. (1997). Changes in UK monetary policy: rules and discretion in practice. *Journal of Monetary Economics*, **39**, June.

Kingman, J. F. C. (1978). The representation of partition structure. *Journal of London Mathematics Society*, **18**.

Kingman, J. F. C. and K. Schalten, eds. (1978). Random partitions in population genetics. *Proceedings of the Royal Society, Series A.* London.

Kirman, A. P. (1983a). Mistaken beliefs and resultant equilibria. In *Individual Forecasting and Collective Outcomes*, eds. R. Frydman and E. Phelps. Cambridge University Press.

Kirman, A. P. (1983b). Communication in markets: a suggested approach. *Economic Letters*, **12**(2).

Kirman, A. P. (1991). Epidemics of opinion and speculative bubbles in financial markets. In *Money and Financial Markets*, Chapter 17, ed. M. Taylor. London: Macmillan.

Kirman, A. P. (1992). Whom or what does the representative agent represent? *Journal of Economic Perspectives*, **6**(2).

Kirman, A. P. (1993). Ants, rationality and recruitment. *Quarterly Journal of Economics*, **108**.

Kirman, A. P. (1997). The economy as an interactive system. In *The Economy as an Evolving Complex System II*, eds. W. B. Arthur, S. N. Durlauf and D. A. Lane. Proceedings Volume XXVII, Santa Fe Institute Studies in the Sciences of Complexity. Reading, MA: Addison-Wesley.

Kirman, A. P. and Teyssiere, G. (1998). *Microeconomic Models for Long-Memory in the Volatility of Financial Time Series*, Technical report, EHESS, Universite d'Aix-Marseille III, Marseille, France.

Klein, L. R. (1950). *Economic Fluctuations in the United States, 1921–1941.* Cowles Commission Monograph 11. New York, NY: John Wiley & Sons.

Klein, L. R. (1960). Single equation vs equation system methods of estimation in econometrics. *Econometrica*, **28**(4).

Klein, L. R. and Rubin, H. (1947). A constant-utility cost of living index. *Review of Economic Studies*, **15**.

Klemperer, P. (2002a). What really matters in auction design. *Journal of Economic Perspectives*, **16**.

Klemperer, P. (2002b). *Using and abusing economic theory*. Alfred Marshall Lecture to the European Economic Association, December. http://www.paulklemperer.org/

Knack, S. and Keefer, P. (1997). Does social capital have an economic payoff? A cross-country investigation. *Quarterly Journal of Economics*, **112**(4).

Kocherlakota, N. (1996). The equity premium: it's still a puzzle. *Journal of Economic Literature*, **34**.

Koesrindartoto, D. and Tesfatsion, L. (2004). Testing the economic reliability of FERC's wholesale power market platform: an agent-based computational economics approach. In *Energy, Environment and Economics in a New Era*, Proceedings of the 24th USAEE/IAEE North American Conference, Washington DC, July.

Koopmans, T. C. (1949). Identification problems in economic model construction. *Econometrica*, **17**. Reprinted in Hood and Koopmans (1953).

Koopmans, T. C., ed. (1950). *Statistical Inference in Dynamic Economic Models.* Cowles Commission Monograph 10. New York: Wiley.

Koopmans, T. C. and Hood, W. C. (1953). The estimation of simultaneous linear relationships. *Studies in Econometric Method.* Cowles Commission Monograph 14. New York: Wiley.

Koopmans, T. C. and Reiersøl, O. (1950). The identification of structural characteristics. *Annals of Mathematical Statistics*, **21**.

Krauth, B. (2003). Mimeo. *Peer Effects and Selection Effects on Youth Smoking in California*. Simon Fraser University, Burnaby, BC, Canada.

Krauth, B. (2004). Mimeo. *Simulation-Based Estimation of Peer Effects*. Simon Fraser University, Burnaby, BC, Canada.

Krugman, P. (1996). *The Self-Organizing Economy*. Cambridge, UK: Blackwell Publishers.

Krugman, P. (1998). It's back: Japan's slump and the return of the liquidity trap. *Brookings Papers on Economic Activity*, (2).

Krusell, P. and Smith, A. (1998). Income and wealth heterogeneity in the macroeconomy. *Journal of Political Economy*, **106**(5).

Kuhn, T. (1962). *The Structure of Scientific Revolutions*. Chicago: University of Chicago Press.

Kurz, M. (1997). *Endogenous Economic Fluctuations: Studies in the Theory of Rational Beliefs*. New York: Springer-Verlag.

Kwakernaak, H. and Sivan, R. (1972). *Linear Optimal Control Systems*. New York: John Wiley and Sons.

Kydland, F. E. and Prescott, E. C. (1977). Rules rather than discretion: the inconsistency of optimal plans. *Journal of Political Economy*, **85**, June.

Kydland, F. E. and Prescott, E. C. (1982). Time to build and aggregate fluctuations. *Econometrica*, **50**.

Laidler, D. E. W. (1999). Fabricating the Keynesian revolution: studies of the inter-war literature on money, the cycle and unemployment. *Historical Perspectives on Modern Economics*. New York and Cambridge: Cambridge University Press.

Laidler, D. E. W. and Robson, W. B. P. (2004). *Two Percent Target: Canadian Monetary Policy Since 1991*. Toronto, Canada: C. D. Howe Institute.

Landes, D. (1998). *The Wealth and Poverty of Nations*. New York: W. W. Norton.

Lange, O. (1940). Complementarity and interrelations of shifts in demand. *Review of Economic Studies*, **8**.

Leamer, E. (1978). *Specification Searches*. New York: John Wiley and Sons.

Leamer, E. E. (1985). Vector autoregressions for causal inference. In *Understanding Monetary Regime*, eds. K. Brunner and A. H. Meltzer. Carnegie-Rochester Conference Series on Public Policy, Vol. 22, Spring. Amsterdam: North-Holland.

LeBaron, B. (2001a). A builder's guide to agent-based financial markets. *Quantitative Finance*, **1**.

LeBaron, B. (2001b). Evolution and time horizons in an agent-based stock market. *Macroeconomic Dynamics*, **5**.

LeBaron, B. (2001c). Empirical regularities from interacting long and short memory investors in an agent based stock market. *IEEE Transactions on Evolutionary Computation*, **5**.

LeBaron, B. (2001d). Stochastic volatility as a simple generator of apparent financial power laws and long memory. *Quantitative Finance*, **1**.

LeBaron, B. (2002a). *Calibrating an Agent-Based Financial Market*, Technical report. Waltham, MA: Brandeis University.

LeBaron, B. (2002b). Short-memory traders and their impact on group learning in financial markets. *Proceedings of the National Academy of Science: Colloquium*, **99**(suppl. 3).

Ledyard, J. O. (1995). Public goods: a survey of experimental research. In *The Handbook of Experimental Economics*, eds. J. H. Kagel and A. Roth. Princeton, NJ: Princeton University Press.

Leeper, E. M. (1991). Equilibria under 'active' and 'passive' monetary and fiscal policies. *Journal of Monetary Economics*, **27**(1).

Leijonhufud, A. (1967). Keynes and the Keynesians: a suggested interpretation. *American Economic Review*, **57**(2).

Leijonhufvud, A. (1968). *On Keynesian Economics and the Economics of Keynes: a Study in Monetary Theory*. New York: Oxford University Press.

Leijonhufvud, A. (1981a). The Wicksell Connection. In *Information and Coordination: Essays in Macroeconomic Theory*, ed. A. Leijonhufvud. Oxford: Oxford University Press.

Leijonhufvud, A. (1981b). *Information and Coordination: Essays in Macroeconomic Theory*. New York: Oxford University Press.

Leijonhufvud, A. (1993). Towards a not-too-rational macroeconomics. *Southern Economic Journal*, **59**. (Reprinted in Leijonhufvud, A., *Beyond Microfoundations: Post Walrasian Macroeconomics*, ed. D. Colander. Cambridge, MA: Cambridge University Press, pp. 39–55.)

Leijonhufvud, A. (1996). Towards a not-too-rational macroeconomics. In *Beyond Microfoundations: Post Walrasian Macroeconomics*, ed. D. Colander. Cambridge, MA: Cambridge University Press, pp. 39–55.

Leijonhufvud, A. (1997). The Wicksellian heritage. *Economic Notes*, **26**(1).

Leijonhufvud, A. (1999). Mr. Keynes and the moderns. In *The Impact of Keynes on Economics in the 20th Century*, eds. L. Pasinetti and B. Schefold. Cheltenham, UK: Edward Elgar. (Previously published in *The European Journal of the History of Economic Thought*, **5**(1), Spring (1998).)

Leijonhufvud, A. (2004a). The long swings in economic understanding. In *Macroeconomic Theory and Economic Policy: Essays in Honor of Jean-Paul Fitoussi*, ed. K. Velupillai. London: Routledge.

Leijonhufvud, A. (2004b). The metamorphosis of neoclassical economics. In *Evolution of the Market Process: Austrian and Swedish Economics*, eds. M. Bellet, S. Gloria-Palermo and A. Zouache. London: Routledge.

Leland, W. E., Taqqu, M. S., Willinger. W. and Wilson, D. V. (1994). On the self-similar nature of Ethernet traffic. *IEEE/ACM Transactions on Networking*, **2**.

Leombruni, R. and Richiardi, M., eds. (2004). *Industry and Labor Dynamics: the Agent-Based Computational Economics Approach*, Proceedings of the WILD@ACE 2003 Conference. Singapore: World Scientific Press.

Lerner, A. (1940). Some Swedish Stepping Stones. *Canadian Journal of Economics*, **6**.

Levin, A. and Williams, J. (2003). Robust monetary policy with competing reference models. *Journal of Monetary Economics*, **50**.

Levy, M., Levy, H. and Solomon, S. (2000). *Microscopic Simulation of Financial Markets*. New York, NY: Academic Press.

Liesenfeld, R. (2001). A generalized bivariate mixture model for stock price volatility and trading volume. *Journal of Econometrics*, **104**.

Lindbeck, A., Nyberg, S. and Weibull, J. (1999). Social norms and economic incentives in the welfare state. *Quarterly Journal of Economics*, **114**.

Liu, T.-C. (1960). Underidentification, structural estimation and forecasting. *Econometrica*, **28**.

Ljungqvist, L. and Sargent, T. J. (2000). *Recursive Macroeconomic Theory*. Cambridge, MA: MIT Press.

Logato, I. and Velasco, C. (2000). Long memory in stock-market trading volume. *Journal of Business and Economic Statistics*, **18**.

Long, J. and Plosser, C. (1983). Real business cycles. *Journal of Political Economy*, **91**.

Loury, G. (1977). A dynamic theory of racial income differences. In *Women, Minorities and Employment Discrimination*, eds. P. Wallace and A. Lamond. Lexington, MA: Lexington Books.

Lubik, T. A. and Schorfheide, F. (2003). Testing for indeterminacy: an application to U.S. monetary policy. *American Economic Review*, **94**(1).

Lucas, R. E., Jr. (1972). Expectations and the neutrality of money. *Journal of Economic Theory*, **4**, April.

Lucas, R. E., Jr. (1976). Econometric policy evaluation: a critique. In *The Phillips Curve and Labor Markets*, eds. K. Brunner and A. H. Meltzer. Carnegie-Rochester Conference Series on Public Policy, Vol. 5(11), Spring. Amsterdam: North-Holland.

Lucas, R. E., Jr. (1977). Understanding business cycles. In *Studies in Business Cycle Theory*, ed. R. E. Lucas Jr. ed. Oxford: Blackwell.

Lucas, R. E., Jr. (1980). Methods and problems in business cycle theory, *Journal of Money, Credit and Banking*, **12**, November.

Lucas, R. E., Jr. (1987). *Models of Business Cycles*. Oxford: Blackwell.

Lucas, R. E., Jr, and Sargent, T. J. (1981). Introduction. In *Rational Expectations and Econometric Practice*, Vol. 1, eds. R. E. Lucas, Jr. and T. J. Sargent. Minneapolis, MN: University of Minnesota Press.

Lux, T. (1998). The socioeconomic dynamics of speculative markets: interacting agents, chaos and the fat tails of return distributions. *Journal of Economic Behavior and Organization*, **33**.

Lux, T. and Marchesi, M. (1999). Scaling and criticality in a stochastic multi-agent model of a financial market. *Nature*, **397**.

Malinvaud, E. (1977). *The Theory of Unemployment Reconsidered*. Oxford: Basil Blackwell.

Mankiw, G. (1985). Small menu costs and large business cycles: a macroeconomic model of monopoly. *Quarterly Journal of Economics*, **100**.

Mankiw, G. (1986). The equity premium and the concentration of aggregate shocks. *Journal of Financial Economics*, **17**.

Mankiw, G. (1991). *The Reincarnation of Keynesian Economics*. Paper presented at the September 1991 meeting of The European Economic Association in Cambridge, UK.

Mankiw, G. and Romer, D. (1990). *New Keynesian Economics*. Cambridge, MA: MIT Press.

Manski, C. (1993). Identification of endogenous social effects: the reflection problem. *Review of Economic Studies*, **60**(3).

Manski, C. (2000). Economic analysis of social interactions. *Journal of Economic Perspectives*, **14**(3).

Manski, C. (2003). *Partial Identification of Probability Distributions*. New York: Springer-Verlag.

Manski, C. (2004). Statistical treatment rules for heterogeneous population. *Econometrica*, **72**(4).

Manski, C. and McFadden, D. (1981). *Structural Analysis of Discrete Data with Econometric Applications*. Cambridge, MA: MIT Press.

Mantegna, R. N. and Stanley H. E. (1999). *An Introduction to Econophysics: Correlations and Complexity in Finance*. Cambridge, UK: Cambridge University Press.

Marcellino, M. and Salmon, M. (2002). Robust decision theory and the Lucas critique. *Macroeconomic Dynamics*, **6**(1).

Marcet, A. and Sargent, T. J. (1989). Convergence of least-squares learning in environments with hidden state variables and private information. *Journal of Political Economy*, **97**.

Marschak, J. (1950). Statistical inference in economics, an introduction. In *Statistical Inference in Dynamic Economic Models*, ed. T. C. Koopmans. New York: John Wiley and Sons.

Marschak, J. (1953). Economic measurements for policy and predictions. In *Studies in Econometric Method*, eds. W. C. Hood and T. C. Koopmans. Cowles Foundations Monograph no. 14. New York: Wiley.

Marshall, A. (1890). *Principles of Economics*, 8th edn. (1920). London: Macmillan.

Marshall, A. 1885 (1925). The present position of economics. In *Memorials of Alfred Marshall*, ed. A. C. Pigou. London: Macmillan.

Mas-Colell, A. (1982). The Cournot foundations of Walrasian equilibrium theory: an exposition of recent theory. In *Advances in Economic Theory*, ed. W. Hildenbrand. Cambridge University Press, Cambridge.

Mavroeidis, S. (2004). Weak identification of forward-looking models in monetary economics. *Oxford Bulletin of Economics and Statistics*, **66**, September.

McMillan, J. (2002). *Reinventing the Bazaar: A Natural History of Markets*. New York, NY: W.W. Norton & Co.

Mehra, R. and Prescott, E. C. (1988). The equity risk premium: a solution? *Journal of Monetary Economics*, **22**.

Mehrling, P. (1997). *The Money Interest and the Public Interest: American Monetary Thought, 1920–1970*. Cambridge, MA: Harvard University Press.

Mehrling, P. (1999). The vision of Hyman P. Minsky. *Journal of Economic Behavior and Organization*, **39**(2), June

Mehrling, P. (2001). Love and death: the wealth of Irving Fisher. In *Research in the History of Economic Thought and Methodology*, eds. W. J. Samuels and J. E. Biddle. Amsterdam: Elsevier Science.

Mehrling, P. (2005). *Fischer Black and the Revolutionary Idea of Finance*. Hoboken, NJ: John Wiley and Sons.

Mehrling, P. (2006). Forthcoming. Mr. Woodford and the challenge of finance. *Journal of the History of Economic Thought*.

Meltzer, A. (1988). *Keynes's Monetary Theory: A Different Interpretation*. Cambridge: Cambridge University Press.

Meyer, C. and Davis, S. (2003). *It's Alive: The Coming Convergence of Information, Biology and Business*. Crown Business.

Minsky, H. (1975). *John Maynard Keynes*. New York: Columbia University Press.

Mirowski, P. (2004). Markets come to bits: evolution, computation and the future of economic science. *Working Paper*, Department of Economics and Policy Studies, University of Notre Dame, South Bend, IN.

Mises, L. von (1966). *Human Action*. 3rd edn. Chicago: Regnery.

Mizon, G. E. (1995). Progressive modelling of economic time series: the LSE methodology. In *Macroeconometrics: Developments, Tensions and Prospects*, ed. K. D. Hoover. Boston: Kluwer.

Modigliani, F. (1944). Liquidity preference and the theory of interest and money. *Econometrica*, **12**, January.

Modigliani, F. (1963). The monetary mechanism and its interaction with real phenomena. *Review of Economics and Statistics*, **38**(1), February

Montgomery, J. (1990). Mimeo. *Social Networks and Persistent Inequality in the Labor Market*. Department of Economics, Northwestern University, Evanston, IL.

Morgan, M. S. (1990). *The History of Econometric Ideas*. Cambridge: Cambridge University Press.

Mullainathan, S. and Thaler, R. H. (2000). *Behavioral Economics*, Technical Report 7948, National Bureau of Economic Research.

Muth, J. F. (1961). Rational expectations and the theory of price movements. *Econometrica*, **29**.

Nagel, K. and Paczusik, M. (1995). Emergent traffic jams. *Physical Review E*, **5**.

Nakajima, R. (2003). Mimeo. *Measuring Peer Effects in Youth Smoking Behavior*. University of Osaka, Osaka, Japan.

Negishi, T. (1961). Monopolistic competition and general equilibrium. *Review of Economic Studies*, **29**, 196–201.

Negishi, T. (1962). The stability of a competitive economy: a survey article. *Econometrica*, **30**, 635–91.

Nelson, R. (1995). Recent evolutionary theorizing about economic change. *Journal of Economic Literature*, **33**.

Nelson, R. and Winter, S. (1982). *An Evolutionary Theory of Economic Change*. Cambridge, MA: Harvard University Press.

Nesheim, L. (2002). Equilibrium sorting of heterogeneous consumers across locations: theory and implications. *Working Paper No. CWP08/02*, Centre for Microdata Methods and Practice.

Newman, M. E. J., Watts, D. J. and Strogatz, S. H. (2002). Random graph models of social networks. *Proc Natl Acad Sci USA*, **99** (suppl. 1).

Novshek, W. and Sonnenschein, H. (1978). Cournot and Walras equilibrium. *Journal of Economic Theory*, **19**.

Okun, A. M. (1983). *Economics for Policymaking: Selected Essays of Arthur M. Okun*, ed. J. A. Pechman. Cambridge, MA: MIT Press.

Onatski, A. and Stock, J. (2002). Robust monetary policy under model uncertainty in a small model of the U.S. economy. *Macroeconomic Dynamics*, **6**.

Onatski, A. and Williams, N. (2003). Modeling model uncertainty. *Journal of the European Economic Association*, **1**.

Oomes, N. (2003). Local network trades and spatially persistent unemployment. *Journal of Economic Dynamics and Control*, **27**, 11–12.

Orcutt, G. H. and Irwin, J. O. (1948). A study of the autoregressive nature of the time series used for Tinbergen's model of the economic system of the United States, 1919–1932. *Journal of the Royal Statistical Society, Series B*, **10**.

Orphanides, A. and Williams, J. C. (2003a). Imperfect knowledge, inflation expectations and monetary policy. In *Inflation Targeting*, eds. B. S. Bernanke and M. Woodford. Chicago: University of Chicago Press.

Orphanides, A. and Williams, J. C. (2003b). Unpublished. *The Decline of Activist Stabilization Policy: Natural Rate Misperceptions, Learning and Expectations*.

Patinkin, D. (1948). Price flexibility and full employment. *American Economic Review*, **38**, September.

Patinkin, D. (1956). *Money, Interest and Prices: An Integration of Monetary and Value Theory*. New York: Harper and Row.

Pearl, J. (2000). *Causality: Models, Reasoning and Inference*. Cambridge: Cambridge University Press.

Peirce, C. S. (1934–58). *Collected Papers of Charles Sanders Peirce*, Vol. 5, eds. C. Hartshorne and P. Weiss. Cambridge, MA: Belknap Press.

Penrose, R. (1989). *The Emperor's New Mind*. Oxford University Press, Oxford, UK.

Phelps, E. S. (1967). Phillips curves, expectations of unemployment and optimal unemployment over time. *Economica*, **34**, August.

Phelps, E. S. (1968). Money wage dynamics and labor market equilibrium. *Journal of Political Economy* **76** (4 Part 2) August. (Reprinted in somewhat revised form in (1970) *Microeconomic Foundations of Employment and Inflation Theory*, eds. E. S. Phelps, et al. New York: Norton.)

Phelps, E. S., ed. (1971). *Microeconomic Foundations of Employment and Inflation Theory*. New York: Norton.

Phillips, A. W. (1958). The relation between unemployment and the rate of change of money wage rates in the United Kingdom, 1861–1957. *Economica*, **25**.

Pingle, M. and Tesfatsion, L. (1991). Overlapping generations, intermediation and the First Welfare Theorem. *Journal of Economic Behavior and Organization*, **15**.

Pingle, M. and Tesfatsion, L. (1998a). Active intermediation in overlapping generations economies with production and unsecured debt. *Macroeconomic Dynamics*, **2**.

Pingle, M. and Tesfatsion, L. (1998b). Active intermediation in a monetary overlapping generations economy. *Journal of Economic Dynamics and Control*, **22**.

Pitman, J. (2002). Lecture Notes. *Combinatorial Stochastic Processes*. St. Flour Summer Institute, St. Flour, France.

Prescott, E. C. (1986). Theory ahead of business cycle measurement. *Federal Reserve Bank of Minneapolis Quarterly Review*, **10**.

Prescott, E. C. (1996). The computational experiment: an econometric tool. *Journal of Economic Perspectives*, **10**(1).

Rabin, M. (1993). Incorporating fairness into game theory and economics. *American Economic Review*, **83**.

Raftery, A., Madigan, D. and Hoeting, J. (1997). Bayesian model averaging for linear regression models. *Journal of the American Statistical Association*, **92**.

Ramal, R. and Toulouse, G. (1986). Ultrametricity for physicists. *Rev. Mod. Phys.*, **58**.

Riddell, C. and Smith, P. (1982). Expected inflation and wage changes in Canada. *Canadian Journal of Economics*, **15**, August.

Rivkin, S. (2001). Tiebout sorting, aggregation and the estimation of peer group effects. *Economics of Education Review*, **20**.

Robertson, D. (1915). *A Study of Industrial Fluctuation*. London: PS King.

Robertson, D. (1926). *Banking Policy and the Price Level*. London: Macmillan.

Robertson, J. and Tallman, E. (1999). Vector autoregressions: forecasting and reality. Federal Reserve Bank of Atlanta. *Economic Review*, **84**, First Quarter.

Rogoff, K. (2002). Stop deflation first for the revival of the Japanese economy. *Nikkei Newspaper*, October 7.

Romer, D. (1996). *Advanced Macroeconomics*. New York: McGraw Hill.

Rosenberg, N. (1982). How exogenous is science? In *Inside the Black Box: Technology and Economics*, ed. N. Rosenberg. New York: Cambridge University Press.

Roth, A. E. (2002). The economist as engineer: game theory, experimentation and computation as tools for design economics. *Econometrica*, **70**.

Rubenstein, M. (2001). Rational markets: Yes or no? The affirmative case. *Financial Analyst Journal*, **17**.

Rubinstein, A. (1998). *Modeling Bounded Rationality*. Cambridge, MA: MIT Press.

Rubinstein, A. and Wolinsky, A. (1990). Decentralized trading, strategic behavior and the Walrasian outcome. *Review of Economic Studies*, **57**.

Rudd, J. B. and Whelan, K. (2003). Unpublished. *Can Rational Expectations Sticky-Price Models Explain Inflation Dynamics?*

Saari, D. and Simon, C. P. (1978). Effective price mechanisms. *Econometrica*, **46**.

Sacerdote, B. (2001). Peer effects with random assignment: results for Dartmouth roomates. *Quarterly Journal of Economics*, **116**.

Samuelson, L. (2005). Foundations of human sociality: a review essay. *Journal of Economic Literature*.

Samuelson, P. (1947). *Foundations of Economic Analysis*. Cambridge: Harvard University Press.

Samuelson, P. (1948). *Economics*. New York: McGraw Hill.

Sargent, T. (1971). A note on the accelerationist controversy. *Journal of Money, Credit and Banking*, **3**.

Sargent, T. (1976). A classical macroeconomic model for the United States. *Journal of Political Economy*, **84**(2).

Sargent, T. (1993). Bounded rationality in macroeconomics, *The Arne Ryde Memorial Lectures*. Oxford, UK: Clarendon Press.

Sargent, T. (1999a). *The Conquest of American Inflation*. Princeton, NJ: Princeton University Press.

Sargent, T. (1999b). Comment. In *Monetary Policy Rules*, ed. J. Taylor. Chicago: University of Chicago Press.

Sargent, T. and Wallace, N. (1975). Rational expectations, the optimal monetary instrument and the optimal money supply rule. *Journal of Political Economy*, **83**, April.

Sargent, T. and Wallace, N. (1976). Rational expectations and the theory of economic policy. *Journal of Monetary Economics*, **84**, 3.

Say, J. B. (1821). *Letters to Malthus on Political Economy and Stagnation of Commerce*. Source: Rod Hay's Archive for the History of Economic Thought, McMaster University, Canada

Schelling, T. C. (1978). *Micromotives and Macrobehavior*. New York: W.W. Norton & Company.

Schmitt-Grohé, S. and Uribe, M. (1997). Balanced-budget rules, distortionary taxes and aggregate instability. *Journal of Political Economy*, **105**.

Schmitt-Grohé, S. and Uribe M. (2005). Optimal fiscal and monetary policy in a medium-scale macroeconomic model. *NBER Macroeconomics Annual 2005*.

Schorfheide, F. (2000). Loss function evaluations of DSGE models. *Journal of Applied Economics*, **15**.

Scitovsky, T. (1945). Consequences of the habit of judging quality by price. *Review of Economic Studies*, **13**.

Sen, A., ed. (1960). Introduction. In *Growth Economics*. Harmondsworth, UK: Penguin, pp. 9–40.

Shackle, G. L. S. (1974). *Keynesian Kaleidics*. Edinburgh: Edinburgh University Press.

Shafir, E., Diamond, P. and Tversky, A. (1998). Money illusion. *Quarterly Journal of Economics*, **112**.

Shapiro, C. and Stiglitz, J. (1984). Equilibrium unemployment as a worker discipline device. *American Economic Review*, **74**.

Shiller, R. (1981). Do stock prices move too much to be justified by subsequent changes in dividends? *American Economic Review*, **71**.

Shiller, R. (2000). *Irrational Exuberance*. Princeton, NJ: Princeton University Press.

Shiller, R. (2003). From efficient market theory to behavioral finance. *Journal of Economic Perspectives*, **17**.

Shubik, M. (1991). *A Game-Theoretic Approach to Political Economy, Fourth Printing*. Cambridge, MA: MIT Press.

Simon, H. A. (1953) Causal ordering and identifiability. In *Models of Man*. New York: Wiley.

Simon, H. A. (1982). *The Sciences of the Artificial*, 2nd edn. Cambridge, MA: MIT Press.

Simon, H. A. (1996). *The Sciences of the Artificial*. Cambridge, MA: MIT Press.

Simon, H. A. (1997). *Models of Bounded Rationality*. Cambridge, MA: MIT Press.

Simon, H. A. and Bonini, C. (1958). The size distribution of business firms. *American Economic Review*, **48**(4).

Sims, C. A. (1980). Macroeconomics and reality. *Econometrica*, **48**.

Sims, C. A. (1982). Policy analysis with econometric models. *Brookings Papers on Economic Activity*.

Sims, C. A. (1986). Are forecasting models usable for policy analysis? *Federal Reserve Bank of Minneapolis Quarterly Review*, **10**(1), Winter.

Sims, C. A. (1999). The role of interest rate policy in the generation and propagation of business cycles: what has changed since the '30s? In *Beyond Shocks: What Causes Business Cycles*, eds. J. C. Fuhrer and S. Schuhrs. Federal Reserve Bank of Boston Conference Series, No. 42.

Sims, C. A. (2002). The role of models and probabilities in the monetary policy process. *Brooking Papers on Economic Activity*, **2**.

Sirakaya, S. (2003). Mimeo. *Recidivism and Social Interactions*. Department of Economics, University of Washington, Seattle, WA.

Smith, A. (1778) 1976. *An Inquiry into the Nature and Causes of the Wealth of Nations*. New York: Oxford University Press.

Söderlind, P. (1999). Solution and estimation of RE macro models with optimal policy. *European Economic Review*, **43**.

Solomon, S. and Levy, M. (1996). *Spontaneous Scaling Emergence in Generic Stochastic Systems*. arXiv:adap-org/9609002v1 11 Sep 96.

Solow, R. and Samuelson, P. (1960). Analytical aspects of anti-inflation policy. *American Economic Review*, **50**(2).

Spanos, A. (1995). On theory testing in econometrics: modeling with nonexperimental data. *Journal of Econometrics*, **676**.

Spirtes, P., Glymour, C. and Scheines, R. (2000). *Causation, Prediction and Search*. 2nd edn. Cambridge, MA: MIT Press.

Steindl, J. (1965). *Random Processes and the Growth of Firms*. New York: Hafner Publishing Company.

Stigler, S. M. (1986). *The History of Statistics: Measurement of Uncertainty Before 1900*. Cambridge, MA: Belknap Press.

Stiglitz, J. E. (1993). Post Walrasian and post Marxian economics. *Journal of Economic Perspectives*, **7**(1).

Summers, L. H. (1992). The scientific illusion in empirical macroeconomics. *Scandinavian Journal of Economics*, **93**(2).

Svensson, L. E. O. (2001). The zero bound in an open economy: a foolproof way of escaping from a liquidity trap. *Monetary and Economic Studies*, **19**.

Swanson, N. R. and Granger, C. W. J. (1997). Impulse response functions based on a causal approach to residual orthogonalization in vector autoregressions. *Journal of the American Statistical Association*, **92**.

Takayama, A. (1985). *Mathematical Economics*, 2nd edn. Cambridge University Press, Cambridge, UK.

Tarshis, L. (1947). *Elements of Economics*. Boston: Houghton Mifflin.

Taylor, J. B. (1979). Staggered wage setting in a macro model. *American Economic Review*, **69**.

Taylor, J. B. (1980). Aggregate dynamics and staggered contract. *Journal of Political Economy*, **88**(1).

Taylor, J. B. (1999). *Monetary Policy Rules*. Chicago: University of Chicago Press.

Taylor, P. D. and Jonker, L. (1978). Evolutionarily stable strategies and game dynamics. *Mathematical Bioscience*, **40**.

Taylor, J. B. and Woodford, M. (1999). *Handbook for Macroeconomics*. Amsterdam: North-Holland.

Teller, P. Forthcoming. Twilight of the Perfect Model Model. *Erkenntis*.

Tesfatsion, L. (2002). Agent-based computational economics: growing economies from the bottom up. *Artificial Life*, **8**.

Tesfatsion, L. (2006). *Agent-Based Computational Economics: A Constructive Approach to Economic Theory*, Chapter 1 in Tesfatsion and Judd (2006), op. cit.

Tesfatsion, L. and Judd, K. L., eds. (2006). *Handbook of Computational Economics*, Vol. 2: Agent-Based Computational Economics, Handbooks in Economics Series. Elsevier. Amsterdam: North-Holland.

Tesfatsion, L. (Guest, ed.) (2001a). Special issue on agent-based computational economics. *Journal of Economic Dynamics and Control*, **25**(3–4).

Tesfatsion, L. (Guest, ed.) (2001b). Special issue on agent-based computational economics, *Computational Economics*, **18**(1).

Tesfatsion, L. (Guest, ed.) (2001c). Special issue on the agent-based modeling of evolutionary economic systems, *IEEE Transactions on Evolutionary Computation*, **5**(5), 437–560.

Tetlow, R. and von zur Muehlen, P. (2001). Robust monetary policy with misspecified models: does model uncertainty always call for attenuated policy? *Journal of Economic Dynamics and Control*, **25**(6–7).

Thaler, R. (1991). *Quasi Rational Economics*. New York: Russell Sage Foundation.

Thaler, R. (1993). *Advances in Behavioral Finance*. New York, NY: Russell Sage Foundation.

Thornton, H., 1962 (1802). *An Enquiry into the Nature and Effects of the Paper Credit of Great Britain*. Fairfield, NJ: Augustus M. Kelley.

Tinbergen, J. (1939). *Statistical Testing of Business-Cycle Theories*. 2 Vols. Geneva: League of Nations.

Tintner, G. (1952a). Complementarity and shifts in demand. *Metroeconomica*, **4**.

Tintner, G. (1952b). *Econometrics*. New York, NY: John Wiley & Sons.

Tirole, J. (2003). *The Theory of Industrial Organization*. Cambridge, MA: MIT Press.

Tobin, J. (1947). Money wage rates; and Employment. In *The New Economics*, ed. S. E. Harris. New York: Albert A. Knopf.

Tobin, J. (1963). Commercial Banks as Creators of Money. In *Banking and Monetary Studies: in Commemoration of the Centennial of the National Banking System*, ed. D. Carson. Homewood, IL: Irwin.

Tobin, J. (1969). A general equilibrium approach to monetary theory. *Journal of Money, Credit and Banking*, **1**(1).

Tobin, J. (1974). Friedman's Theoretical Framework. In *Milton Friedman's Monetary Framework: A Debate with his Critics*, ed. R. J. Gordon. Chicago: University of Chicago Press.

Tobin, J. (1975). Keynesian models of recession and depression. *American Economic Review Papers and Proceedings*, **65**, May.

Tobin, J. and Dolbear, F. T. (1963). Comments on the relevance of psychology to economic theory and research. In *Psychology: A Study of a Science*, Vol. 6, ed. S. Koch. New York: McGraw-Hill.

Topa, G. (2001). Social interactions, local spillovers and unemployment. *Review of Economic Studies*, **68**(2).

Tversky, A. and Kahneman, D. (1986). Rational choice and the framing of decisions. In *Rational Choice: the Contrast between Economics and Psychology*, eds. R. M. Hogarth and M. W. Reder. Chicago: University of Chicago Press.

Tversky, A. and Kahneman D. (1991). Loss aversion in riskless choice: a reference-dependent model. *Quarterly Journal of Economics*, **106**.

Veblen, T. (1898). Why is economics not an evolutionary science? *Quarterly Journal of Economics*, **12**.

Voth, H.-J. (1998). Time and work in eighteenth century London. *Journal of Economic History*, **58**(1).

Vriend, N. J. (2002). Was Hayek an ace? *Southern Economic Journal*, **68**(4).

Wald, A. (1950). *Statistical Decision Functions*. New York: John Wiley.

Walker, D. A. (1983). *William Jaffe's Essays on Walras*. Cambridge and New York: Cambridge University Press.

Walker, D. A. (2005). *Walras' Market Model*. Cambridge and New York: Cambridge University Press.

Walras, L. (1874). *Elements of Pure Economics*. Lausanne: L. Borbax.

Watson, M. W. (1994). Vector autoregressions and cointegration. In *Handbook of Econometrics*, Vol. 2, eds. R. F. Engle and D. L. McFadden. Amsterdam, New York, Oxford, and Tokyo: North-Holland.

Watts, D. (1999). *Small Worlds: the Dynamics of Networks between Order and Randomness*. Princeton, NJ: Princeton University Press.

Weatherford, J. (1997). *The History of Money*. New York: Three Rivers Press.

Weibull, J. W. (2004). Testing game theory. *Boston University Economics Department Working Paper*.

Weinberg, B., Reagan, P. and Yankow, J. (2004). Do neighborhoods affect hours worked? Evidence from longitudinal data. *Journal of Labor Economics*.

Weiss, G., ed. (1999). *Multiagent Systems: a Modern Approach to Distributed Artificial Intelligence*. Cambridge, MA: MIT Press.

Weitzman, M. (2004). Mimeo. *The Bayesian Family of Equity Non-Puzzles*. Department of Economics, Harvard University.

West, K. (1996). Asymptotic inference about predictive ability. *Econometrica*, **64**.

White, H. (1994). *Estimation, Inference and Specification Analysis*, Cambridge: Cambridge University Press.

Wicksell, K. (1898). *Geldzins und Güterpreise*. Jena: Gustav Fisher. Trans. Richard Kahn as *Interest and* Prices. London: Macmillan (1936).

Wicksell, K. (1935). *Lectures on Political Economy*. London : Routledge and Kegan Paul. (Orig. pub. 1901 in Swedish.)

Wilhite, A. (2001). Bilateral trade and 'Small-World' networks. *Computational Economics*, **18**(1).

Williams, N. (2003). Mimeo. *Adaptive Learning and Business Cycles*.

Witt, U. (1993). *Evolutionary Economics*. Cheltenham, UK: Edward Elgar Publishers.

Wolcott, S. and Clark, G. (1999). Why nations fail?: managerial decisions and performance in Indian cotton textiles, 1890–1938. *Journal of Economic History*, **59**(2).

Woodford, M. (1990). Learning to believe in sunspots. *Econometrica*, **58**, 272–307.

Woodford, M. (1999). *Revolution and Evolution in Twentieth-Century Macroeconomics*. Paper prepared for the conference on Frontiers of the Mind in the Twenty-First Century, Library of Congress, Washington, DC, June.

Woodford, M. (2003). *Interest and Prices: Foundations of a Theory of Monetary Policy*. Princeton, NJ: Princeton University Press.

Woodford, M. and Farmer, R. (1997). Self-fulfilling prophecies and the business cycle. *Macroeconomic Dynamics*, **1**(4).

Wu, B.-F. and Jonckheere, E. (1992). A simplified approach to Bode's theorem for continuous and discrete time systems. *IEEE Transactions on Automatic Control*, **37**(100).

Yeager, L. (1973). The Keynesian diversion. *Western Economic Journal*, **11**, June.

Yeager, L. (1986). The significance of monetary disequilibrium. *Cato Journal*, **6**, Fall.

Young, W. (1987). *Interpreting the IS/LM Enigma*. Boulder, CO: Westview Press.

Young, H. P. (1993). An evolutionary model of bargaining. *Journal of Economic Theory*, **59**(1).

Young, H. P. (1996). The economics of convention. *Journal of Economic Perspectives*, **10**, Spring.

Young, H. P. (1998). *Individual Strategy and Social Structure: An Evolutionary Theory of Institutions*. Princeton, NJ: Princeton University Press.

Young, H. P. (1999). *Diffusion in Social Networks. Center on Social and Economic Dynamics Working Paper*. Washington, DC: Brookings Institution.

Young, H. P. and Burke, M. (2001). Competition and custom in economic contracts: a case study of Illinois agriculture. *American Economic Review*, **91**(3).

Young, H. P. and Burke, M. (2003). Mimeo. *On the Distributional Effects of Contractual Norms: the Case of Cropshare Contracts*. Department of Economics, Johns Hopkins University, Baltimore, MD.

Zabell, S. L. (1992). Predicting the unpredictable. *Synthese*, **90**.

Index

Printed in the United States
By Bookmasters